CURTAIN CALLS

Noel Coward

CURTAIN CALLS

DOUBLEDAY, DORAN AND COMPANY, INC.

New York

1940

CONTENTS

TONIGHT AT 8:30

LADIES AND GENTLEMEN

THE IDEA of presenting three short plays in an evening instead of one long one is far from original. In fact, if one looks back over the years, one finds that the "triple bill" formula has been used, with varying degrees of success, since the earliest days of the theatre. Latterly, however, that is during the last quarter of a century, it has fallen from favour. Occasionally still a curtain-raiser appears in the Provinces but wearing a sadly hang-dog expression, because it knows only too well, poor thing, that it would not be there at all were the main attraction of the evening long enough.

Its spirit is further humiliated by the fact that the leading actors treat it with the utmost disdain, seldom leaving their star dressing-rooms to glance at it, let alone play it. Therefore it has to get along as well as it can in the hands of small-part actors and understudies who, although frequently far more talented and charming than their principals, have neither the name, authority nor experience to triumph over rustling programmes, banging seats and a general atmosphere of bored impatience.

A short play, having a great advantage over a long one in that it can sustain a mood without technical creaking or over-padding, deserves a better fate, and if, by careful writing, acting and producing I can do a little towards reinstating it in its rightful pride, I shall have achieved one of my more sentimental ambitions.

From our point of view behind the footlights the experiment

will obviously be interesting. The monotony of repetition will be reduced considerably, and it is to be hoped that the stimulus Miss Lawrence, the Company and I will undoubtedly derive from playing several roles during a week instead of only one, will communicate itself to the audience, thereby ensuring that a good time be had by all.

All of the plays included in the programmes have been written especially. There has been no unworthy scuffling in cupboards and bureau drawers in search of forgotten manuscripts, and no hurried refurbishing of old, discarded ideas.

The primary object of the scheme is to provide a full and varied evening's entertainment for theatregoers who, we hope, will try their best to overcome any latent prejudices they may have against short plays and, at least, do us the honour of coming to judge for themselves.

CONTENTS

I

II

III

WE WERE DANCING

A Comedy in Two Scenes

CHARACTERS

LOUISE CHARTERIS
HUBERT CHARTERIS
KARL SANDYS
CLARA BETHEL
GEORGE DAVIES
EVA BLAKE
MAJOR BLAKE
IPPAGA
Two or three unnamed members of the Country Club.

SCENE I. *Verandah of the Country Club at Samolo. Evening.*
SCENE II. *The same. Early morning.*

Time: The Present.

SCENE I

The Scene is the verandah of the Country Club at Samolo. On the right is a room in which dances are held every Saturday night. For these occasions a dance-band flies up from Pendarla by the new Imperial Inter-State Airways. The band arrives in the afternoon, plays all night and departs early on Sunday for Abbachi where it repeats the same procedure for the inhabitants there, returning wearily on Mondays to the Grand Hotel, Pendarla where, during the week, it plays for the Tourists.

When the curtain rises the verandah is deserted. A full moon is shining over the sea and, far away, above the chatter and music of the dance-room, there can occasionally be heard the wailing of native music rising up from the crowded streets by the harbour.

IPPAGA, a Samolan boy, crosses the verandah from right to left carrying a tray of drinks. He is yellowish brown in colour and, like most Samolans, comparatively tall. He wears a scarlet fez, a green, purple and mustard-coloured sarong, black patent-leather shoes, silver ear-rings and three wooden bracelets.

As he goes off on the left the dance-music stops and there is the sound of applause.

GEORGE DAVIES and EVA BLAKE come out of the dance-room. GEORGE DAVIES is a hearty, nondescript young man dressed in the usual white mess-jacket, black evening trousers and cummerbund.

EVA, equally nondescript, is wearing a pink taffeta bunchy little dress, pink ribbon in her hair and pink shoes and stockings which do not quite match. She carries a diamanté evening bag and a blue chiffon handkerchief round her wrist. She also wears a necklace of seed pearls and a pendant.

[5]

WE WERE DANCING

The dance music starts again. EVA *looks furtively over her shoulder.*

GEORGE *enters first and walks up to balcony and calls:*
GEORGE: Eva! Eva!
EVA: It's all right, they're playing an encore.
GEORGE: Come on, then.
EVA: Where's the car?
GEORGE: I parked it at the end of the garden, where the road turns off. My boy's looking after it.
EVA: He won't say anything, will he?
GEORGE: Of course not. He's been with me for years.
EVA: Oh, George!
GEORGE [*impatiently*]: It's all right—come on——
EVA: Where are we going?
GEORGE: Mahica beach, nobody ever comes near it.
EVA: Oh, George!
GEORGE [*taking her hand*]: Come on——
They go off right.
The band is playing a waltz and the stage is empty for a moment.

LOUISE CHARTERIS *and* KARL SANDYS *come dancing in from the left. They are both in the thirties, soignée and well-dressed, and they dance together as though they had never been apart.*

They waltz three times round the stage finishing in the centre with a prolonged kiss. The music ends, there is the sound of applause. TWO WOMEN *and a* MAN *come in. They stop short on observing* LOUISE *and* KARL, *they whisper together for a moment and then go back into the dance-room.*

LOUISE *and* KARL *remain clasped in each other's arms oblivious of everything. The music starts again.*

HUBERT CHARTERIS *and* CLARA BETHEL *come out of the dance-room.* CLARA *is a nice-looking, grey-haired woman in the forties.* HUBERT *her brother, is about the same age. He has dignity and reserve and looks intelligently British.*

[6]

They both stand for a moment looking at KARL *and* LOUISE *who, still entranced with their kiss, have not even noticed them.*

HUBERT [*quietly*]: Louise.

LOUISE [*jumping*]: Oh!

CLARA [*reproachfully*]: Louise, really!

LOUISE *and* KARL *step a little away from each other.*

LOUISE [*with a social manner*]: This is my husband. [*She hesitates and turns to* KARL.] I'm afraid I didn't catch your name?

KARL: Karl. Karl Sandys. [*To* HUBERT *and* CLARA.] How do you do?

HUBERT [*with perfect control*]: The car's here, I think we'd better go if you're ready.

LOUISE: I'm not ready.

CLARA [*going towards her*]: Come along, Louise.

LOUISE: I can't go, really I can't.

HUBERT: This is most embarrassing, please don't make it worse.

LOUISE: I'm sorry, Hubert. I do see that it's all very difficult.

KARL: I fear I was partly to blame.

HUBERT [*ignoring him*]: Please come home now, Louise.

LOUISE [*gently*]: No, Hubert.

HUBERT: I'm afraid I must insist.

LOUISE: We have fallen in love.

KARL: Deeply in love.

HUBERT: I would prefer not to discuss the matter with you, sir.

LOUISE: That's silly, Hubert.

HUBERT [*sternly*]: Please come away.

LOUISE: I've told you, I can't.

KARL: Have a drink?

HUBERT [*irritably*]: Good God!

LOUISE: That is a good idea, Hubert, let's all have a drink.

KARL: We might also sit down.

CLARA: Listen, Louise, you can't behave like this, it's too idiotic.

[7]

LOUISE: It's true, can't you see? It's true.

CLARA: What's true? Don't be so foolish.

KARL: We're in love, that's what's true, really it is, Mrs.—Mrs.——

LOUISE: Bethel. This is my husband's sister, Mrs. Bethel.

KARL: How do you do?

CLARA: I appeal to you, Mr.—Mr.——

KARL: Sandys.

CLARA: Mr. Sandys—please go away. Go away at once.

KARL: That's quite impossible.

HUBERT: I detest scenes and I am finding this very unpleasant. I don't know who you are or where you come from, but if you have any sense of behaviour at all you must see that this situation is intolerable. Will you kindly leave the club immediately and never speak to my wife again in any circumstances whatever?

LOUISE: It's more important than that, Hubert, really it is.

KARL: It's the most important thing that has ever happened to me in my whole life, Mr.—Mr.——

LOUISE: Charteris.

KARL: Mr. Charteris.

HUBERT: Once more, Louise, for the last time, will you come home?

LOUISE: No—I can't.

HUBERT: Very well. Come, Clara.

He turns to go away. LOUISE *catches his arm.*

LOUISE: You can't go, either. I know you hate scenes and that you're trying to be as dignified as possible, and that I'm apparently behaving very badly, but it's true, this thing that's happened, I mean—we have fallen in love——

HUBERT: Please let go of my arm, Louise, and don't be ridiculous.

LOUISE: Look at me—look closely—I've been your wife for thirteen years. You're wise and intelligent and you know me well—look at me!

[8]

CLARA [*anxiously*]: Please go, Mr. Sandys.

KARL [*shaking his head*]: No.

HUBERT [*to* LOUISE]: I'm looking at you.

LOUISE [*emotionally*]: Well—don't you see?

HUBERT *looks quickly at* CLARA *then at* KARL *and then back to* LOUISE *again.*

HUBERT: Yes—I see.

CLARA: Hubert.

MAJOR BLAKE *comes in from the dance-room. He is a red-faced, elderly man.*

MAJOR BLAKE: I say, have you seen Eva?

HUBERT: What?

MAJOR BLAKE: I can't find Eva.

CLARA: I think she went home.

MAJOR BLAKE: She can't have, the car's there.

CLARA: She told me she was driving back with the Baileys.

MAJOR BLAKE: Oh, did she, did she really?

CLARA: She told practically everybody in the club that she was driving back with the Baileys, I'm surprised she didn't mention it to you.

MAJOR BLAKE: Oh, she's all right then—thanks—thanks awfully.

CLARA [*after a pause*]: You'll be able to pick her up on the way home.

MAJOR BLAKE: It's hardly on the way, it means going all round by the Woo Ching road.

HUBERT: Why not telephone her?

MAJOR BLAKE: They won't have got there yet, it's an hour's drive.

CLARA: Why not wait until they have got there?

MAJOR BLAKE: Yes, I suppose I'd better. Anybody feel like a Stengah?

HUBERT: No, thanks.

MAJOR BLAKE [*to* KARL]: Do you, sir?

KARL: No, thank you.

MAJOR BLAKE: All right—I shall go back to the bar——

KARL: Bar.

MAJOR BLAKE: Thanks very much.

He goes out to R.

KARL: Who is Eva?

CLARA: His wife.

KARL: And who are the Baileys?

CLARA [*with irritation*]: Does it matter?

KARL: I don't know.

LOUISE: They live in that large reddish-looking house at the top of the hill.

KARL: I've never been to the top of the hill.

CLARA: Good night, Mr. Sandys.

KARL: Good night.

CLARA [*with almost overdone ordinariness*]: Come along, Louise.

LOUISE: Don't be silly, Clara.

CLARA: I'm not being silly. I'm acutely uncomfortable. You're behaving abominably and putting Hubert in an insufferable position. For heaven's sake pull yourself together and be reasonable. You talk a lot of nonsense about being in love. How could you possibly be in love all in a minute like that——?

KARL: We are.

CLARA: Please be quiet and let me speak.

LOUISE: Hubert, do make Clara shut up.

CLARA: You must be insane.

HUBERT: Shut up, Clara.

CLARA: And you must be insane, too, I'm ashamed of you, Hubert.

LOUISE: It's no use railing and roaring, Clara. Hubert's much wiser than you. He's keeping calm and trying to understand and I'm deeply grateful to him——

CLARA: Grateful indeed!

LOUISE: Yes, if he behaved as you seem to think he ought to behave, it would only make everything far worse. I suppose you want him to knock Mr.—— [*To* KARL.] What is your first name?

KARL: Karl.

LOUISE: —Karl in the jaw?

CLARA: I don't want anything of the sort. I want him to treat the situation as it should be treated, as nothing but a joke, a stupid joke, in extremely bad taste.

LOUISE: It's more than that, Clara, and you know it is, that's why you're scared.

CLARA: I'm not in the least scared.

HUBERT: You'd better allow me to deal with this, Clara, in my own way.

CLARA: There is such a thing as being too wise, too understanding.

LOUISE: You're usually pretty intelligent yourself, Clara. I can't think what's happened to you. This thing is here—now— between Karl and me. It's no use pretending it isn't, or trying to flip it away as a joke, nor is it any use taking up a belligerent attitude over it. God knows I'm confused enough myself— utterly bewildered, but I do know that it's real, too real to be dissipated by conventional gestures——

CLARA: What is real? What are you talking about?

KARL: Love, Mrs. Bethel, we've fallen in love.

CLARA: Rubbish!

LOUISE: It's not rubbish! It's not nonsense. Be quiet!

HUBERT [*to* LOUISE]: What do you want me to do?

LOUISE [*looking at* KARL]: I don't know.

KARL: May I ask you a question?

HUBERT [*stiffly*]: What is it?

KARL: Are you in love with Louise?

CLARA: Well really!

HUBERT: I am devoted to Louise. We have been married for many years.

KARL: I said are you in love with her?

HUBERT: I love her.

[*11*]

LOUISE: Don't go on evading, Hubert, you know perfectly well what he means.

HUBERT: Of course I know what he means. [*To* KARL.] I'll answer you truly. I am not in love with Louise in the way that you imagine yourself to be in love with her——

KARL: I worship her.

HUBERT: You know nothing about her.

KARL: I know that suddenly, when we were dancing, an enchantment swept over me. An enchantment that I have never known before and shall never know again. It's obvious that you should think I'm mad and that she's mad too, our behaviour looks idiotic, cheap, anything you like, but it's true, this magic that happened, it's so true that everything else, all the ordinary ways of behaviour look shabby and unreal beside it—my heart's thumping, I'm trembling like a fool, even now when I'm trying so hard, so desperately hard to be calm and explain to you reasonably, I daren't look at her, if I did, my eyes would brim over with these silly tears and I should cry like a child——

LOUISE [*making a movement towards him*]: Oh, my darling——

KARL: Don't, don't speak—let him speak, let him say what's to be done.

KARL *leaves the three of them and goes up to the verandah rail and looks out at the sea.*

CLARA: You didn't even know his name.

LOUISE: Oh, Clara! What the hell does that matter?

CLARA [*walking about*]: This is really too fantastic—it's beyond belief—it's——

LOUISE [*gently*]: Listen. I know you feel dreadfully upset for Hubert and for me too, but it's no use huffing and puffing and getting yourself into a state. Here it is this thing that's happened—it's terribly real—as large as life—larger than life, and we'd all better look at it clearly and as sensibly as we can.

HUBERT: You go home, Clara, you can send the car back for me.

CLARA: I shall do no such thing.

LOUISE [*hurriedly—to* HUBERT]: We'd better go away—he and I—as soon as possible.

HUBERT: Where to?

LOUISE: I don't know—anywhere——

HUBERT: For God's sake be reasonable. How can you? How can I let you?

LOUISE: How much do you mind—really?

HUBERT: That obviously has nothing to do with it.

LOUISE: I want to know.

HUBERT: I want to know, too. I can't possibly tell. You've made this up, this magic that he talked about, you've conjured it out of the air and now it's smeared over everything—over me, too—none of it seems real but it has to be treated as if it were. You ask me how much I mind—you want that as well, don't you, in addition to your new love?

LOUISE: Want what? What do you mean?

HUBERT [*almost losing control*]: You want me to mind—don't you—don't you?

LOUISE: Oh, Hubert—please don't look like that——

HUBERT: You want everything—everything in the world, you always have.

LOUISE: You're pitying yourself. How beastly of you to be so weak, how contemptible of you!

CLARA: Louise!

LOUISE: I've been faithful to you all these years, we stopped being in love with each other ages ago—we became a habit—a well-ordered, useful, social habit. Have you been as faithful to me as I have to you?

KARL: That's nothing to do with us—what's the use of arguing?

He joins the group again.

LOUISE: Answer me. Have you?

HUBERT: No.

CLARA: Hubert!

[*13*]

LOUISE: Fair's fair.

CLARA: Hubert! Louise!

LOUISE: Do stop saying Hubert and Louise, Clara, it's maddening.

KARL: What is all this? Can't you keep to the point both of you? What does it matter whether he's been faithful to you or not, or you to him either? You're not in love with each other any more, that's clear enough, and even if you were this forked lightning that has struck Louise and me would shatter it—scorch it out of existence——

CLARA: Forked lightning indeed!

KARL: Earthquake then, tidal wave, cataclysm!

HUBERT: I've never not loved you, Louise.

LOUISE [*irritably*]: I know that perfectly well. I'm deeply attached to you, too. I hated it when you had your tiresome little affairs on the side——

HUBERT: With your heart?

LOUISE: Of course not. Don't be so damned sentimental. You haven't come near my heart for years.

CLARA: If Hubert doesn't strike you in a minute, I will.

IPPAGA *comes out of the dance-room with an empty tray.*

KARL: Boy, bring four whisky-and-sodas.

IPPAGA: Yes, sir.

LOUISE: They're called Stengahs here.

KARL: Four Stengahs then.

CLARA: I'd rather have lemonade.

KARL: You seem bent on complicating everything. [*To* IPPAGA.] Four Stengahs.

IPPAGA: Yes, sir.

He goes off.

LOUISE: Karl, where were we?

HUBERT: Nowhere—nowhere at all. [*He turns away.*]

KARL [*to* HUBERT]: Listen, Charteris—I know you won't believe me, or even care, but I really am dreadfully sorry, about

[*14*]

all this—not about falling in love, that's beyond being sorry about, but that it should happen to be your wife——

HUBERT: Who are you, where do you come from?

KARL: My name is Karl Sandys. I come from Hampshire. My father is Admiral Sandys——

LOUISE: Dear darling, I wouldn't mind if he were only a bosun's mate.

KARL: I know you wouldn't, sweetheart, but I must explain to your husband——

CLARA: How you can have the impertinence to be flippant, Louise, at a moment like this——

LOUISE: There's never been a moment like this, never before in the history of the world—I'm delirious.

HUBERT [to KARL]: Please go on.

KARL: I was in the Navy myself but I was axed in 1924.

LOUISE: What's axed?

KARL: Kicked out.

LOUISE: Oh dear, whatever for?

HUBERT: Never mind that, I understand, go on.

KARL: I'm now in the shipping business. I represent the I.M.C.L.

LOUISE: What in God's name is the I.M.C.L.?

HUBERT: Imperial Malayan China Line.

KARL: Passenger and Freight.

HUBERT: I know.

KARL: I've come from Singapore, I've been interviewing our agents in Pendarla——

HUBERT: Littlejohn Thurston and Company?

KARL: Littlejohn Thurston and Company.

LOUISE [to CLARA]: Littlejohn Thurston and Company.

KARL: I flew up here in the morning 'plane because I wanted to see a little of the country before I sail on Wednesday.

LOUISE: Wednesday!

HUBERT: Are you married?

KARL: I was, but we were divorced in 1927.

[*15*]

LOUISE: Oh, Karl. Did you love her?

KARL: Of course I did.

LOUISE: The moment's changed—I'm not delirious any more —I can't think of you ever having loved anybody else——

HUBERT: Have you any money?

KARL: Not very much—enough.

LOUISE: What was her name?

KARL: Ayleen.

LOUISE: You mean Eileen.

KARL: I do not, I mean Ayleen—A-y-l-e-e-n.

LOUISE: Very affected.

KARL: It's you I love, more than anyone in the world, past or future——

LOUISE: Oh, Karl!

HUBERT [*sharply*]: Please—just a moment—both of you.

KARL: I'm sorry. That was inconsiderate.

HUBERT: I'm trying to be as detached as possible. It isn't easy.

LOUISE: I know it isn't, it's beastly for you, I do see that.

CLARA: You're all being so charming to each other it's positively nauseating.

LOUISE: My dear Clara, just because your late husband was vaguely connected with the Indian Army, there is no reason for you to be so set on blood-letting——

CLARA: I'm not—I should like to say——

LOUISE: You're no better than a Tricoteuse.

KARL: What's a Tricoteuse?

LOUISE: One of those horrid old things in the French Revolution with knitting-needles.

HUBERT: All this is beside the point.

LOUISE: Clara's been beside the point for years.

KARL: Dearest, I want you so.

LOUISE: Oh, Karl!

CLARA: This is disgusting——

HUBERT: You'd much better go home, Clara——

CLARA: I've told you before I shall do no such thing, I'm

apparently the only one present with the remotest grip on sanity. I shall stay as long as you do, Hubert.

KARL: Dear Mrs. Bethel.

CLARA: I beg your pardon?

KARL: I said, "Dear Mrs. Bethel," because I admire your integrity enormously and I do hope when all this has blown over that we shall be close friends.

CLARA: I think you're an insufferable cad, Mr. Sandys.

LOUISE: Blown over! Oh, Karl.

KARL: Darling, I didn't mean that part of it.

HUBERT: I have something to say to you, Louise. Will everybody please be quiet for a moment?

CLARA: Hubert, I honestly think——

LOUISE: That's exactly what you don't do.

HUBERT: This man, whom you so abruptly love, is sailing on Wednesday.

KARL: On the *Euripedes.*

LOUISE: But the *Euripedes* goes to Australia, I know because the MacVities are going on it.

KARL: That can't be helped, I have to interview our agents in Sydney——

LOUISE: We'll have to go on another boat, I can't travel in sin with the MacVities.

HUBERT: Do you really mean to go with him?

LOUISE: Yes, Hubert.

CLARA: You're stark staring mad all of you; Hubert, for God's sake——

HUBERT: Excuse me—— [*Gently.*] Louise, how true is this to you?

LOUISE: Oh, Hubert, don't be too kind.

HUBERT: Will it be worth it?

LOUISE: Oh yes, yes, of course it will—it must!

HUBERT: What has happened exactly—how do you know so surely, so soon?

[*17*]

WE WERE DANCING

SONG: "WE WERE DANCING"

Verse 1

If you can
Imagine my embarrassment when you politely asked me to
  explain
Man to man
I cannot help but feel conventional apologies are all in vain.
You must see
We've stepped into a dream that's set us free
Don't think we planned it
Please understand it.

Refrain

We were dancing
And the gods must have found it entrancing
For they smiled
On a moment undefiled
By the care and woe
That mortals know.
We were dancing
And the music and lights were enhancing
Our desire
When the World caught on fire
He and I were dancing.

Verse 2

Love lay in wait for us
Twisted our fate for us
No one warned us
Reason scorned us
Time stood still

[*18*]

In that first strange thrill.
Destiny knew of us
Guided the two of us
How could we
Refuse to see
That wrong seemed right
On this lyrical enchanted night
Logic supplies no laws for it
Only one cause for it.

Repeat Refrain

We were dancing . . . etc.

LOUISE: We were dancing—somebody introduced us, I can't remember who, we never heard each other's names—it was a waltz—and in the middle of it we looked at each other—he said just now that it was forked lightning, an earthquake, a tidal wave, cataclysm, but it was more than all those things—much more—my heart stopped, and with it the world stopped too—there was no more land or sea or sky, there wasn't even any more music—I saw in his eyes a strange infinity—only just him and me together for ever and ever—and—ever——

She faints. KARL *catches her in his arms.*

IPPAGA *enters with a tray of drinks.*

IPPAGA: Stengahs, sir.

KARL: Bring them here, quick.

KARL *lowers* LOUISE *gently into a chair and kneels beside her with his arm under her head.* HUBERT *kneels on the other side of her.* CLARA *kneels in front of her and endeavours to make her swallow a little whisky. After a moment her eyelids flutter and she moves her head.*

The dance music which has been playing intermittently throughout the scene comes to an end, there is the sound of applause, then it strikes up the National Anthem.

[*19*]

LOUISE [*weakly*]: Good God! God Save the King!

She staggers to her feet supported by KARL. *The others rise also and they all stand to attention as the lights fade on the scene.*

SCENE II

When the lights come up on the scene, CLARA, HUBERT, LOUISE *and* KARL *are all sitting in attitudes of extreme weariness. There is a table near them on which are the remains of bacon and eggs and sandwiches.* IPPAGA *is lying on the floor on the right, fast asleep. Dawn is breaking and the stage gets lighter and lighter as the scene progresses.* LOUISE, *in a state of drooping exhaustion, is arranging her face in the mirror from her handbag which* HUBERT *is holding up for her.*

LOUISE [*petulantly*]: —But surely you could interview your agents in Sydney another time——

KARL: I can't see why I should alter the whole course of my career just because of the MacVities.

LOUISE: It isn't only the MacVities, it's Australia.

KARL: What's the matter with Australia?

LOUISE: I don't know, that's what's worrying me.

HUBERT: Haven't you got any agents anywhere else?

KARL: There's Havermeyer, Turner and Price in Johannesburg but I've seen them.

LOUISE: You could see them again, couldn't you? It's not much to ask.

KARL: If I start giving in to you now, darling, we shall never have a moment's peace together.

CLARA: Well I wish you'd make up your minds where you're going and when, it's very early and I'm tired.

LOUISE: You've been wonderfully patient, both of you—I'm tired too.

HUBERT: Would you like another sandwich, dear? There are three left.

LOUISE [*patting his hand*]: No thank you, Hubert, they're filthy.

KARL: I'd like to say too how grateful I am to you, you've been understanding and direct and absolutely first-rate over the whole business.

HUBERT: I'm terribly fond of Louise, I always have been.

CLARA: Fortunately Hubert's leave is almost due so we shan't have to face too much unpleasantness in the Colony.

HUBERT: What time does your 'plane leave?

KARL [*glancing at his watch*]: Seven-thirty—it's now a quarter to six.

LOUISE: I'll come by the night train and join you in Pendarla in the morning.

HUBERT: I shall miss you dreadfully, Louise.

LOUISE: I shall miss you, too.

KARL: I'm not sure that I shan't miss you, too.

LOUISE: Oh, dear, I do wish it didn't have to be Australia.

KARL: Now then, Louise!

CLARA: Some parts of Australia can be lovely.

LOUISE: Yes, but will they?

CLARA: And there's always New Zealand.

KARL: I haven't any agents in New Zealand.

LOUISE: I shall have to write to mother and explain. I'm afraid it will be dreadfully muddling for her.

HUBERT: Serve her right.

LOUISE: Hubert! It's not like you to be unchivalrous about mother.

HUBERT: Now that you're leaving me the situation has changed.

LOUISE: Yes. You're quite right. I do see that.

HUBERT: Without wishing to wound you, Louise, I should like to take this opportunity of saying that she lacks charm to a remarkable degree.

[*21*]

LOUISE: It's funny, isn't it, when you think how attractive father was.

KARL: This seems an ideal moment for you to give us a detailed description of where you lived as a girl.

LOUISE: I do hope you're not going to turn out to be testy.

CLARA: Never mind, come along, Hubert, we can't stay here any longer, the Fenwicks will be arriving to play golf in a minute.

HUBERT [*to* LOUISE]: Do you want to come now or stay until his 'plane goes?

LOUISE: I'll stay for just a little while, send the car back.

HUBERT [*to* KARL]: Would you care to come to the house and have a bath?

KARL: No, thanks, I can have one here.

HUBERT: Then I shan't be seeing you again.

KARL: Not unless you come and see us off on the boat.

HUBERT: I shan't be able to on Wednesday, I have to go up-country.

KARL: Well, good-bye, then.

HUBERT: Good-bye.

They shake hands.

Try to make her happy, won't you?

KARL: I'll do my best.

HUBERT: Clara——

CLARA [*to* KARL]: Good-bye.

KARL: Good-bye.

CLARA: I wish my husband were alive.

KARL: Why?

CLARA: Because he'd horsewhip you and, Tricoteuse or no Tricoteuse, I should enjoy it keenly.

KARL: Thank you very much.

CLARA *and* HUBERT *go off.*

LOUISE *gets up and goes to the verandah rail, she leans on it and looks out at the sea.*

LOUISE: I feel as if I'd been run over.

[22]

KARL [*joining her*]: Dearest.

LOUISE: Don't.

KARL: Don't what?

LOUISE: Don't call me dearest, just for a minute.

KARL: I love you so.

LOUISE: We ought to be able to see Sumatra really at this time of the morning.

KARL: I don't want to see Sumatra.

LOUISE: I think I will have another sandwich after all.

KARL: All right.

They come down from the rail and pensively take a sandwich each.

LOUISE: Are you happy?

KARL: Wildly happy. Are you?

LOUISE: Dear Karl!

KARL: What's the matter?

LOUISE: You're doing splendidly.

KARL: Don't talk like that, my sweet, it's unkind.

LOUISE: Ayleen would be proud of you.

KARL: That was worse than unkind.

LOUISE: Where is it, our moment? What's happened to the magic?

KARL [*sadly*]: I see.

LOUISE: I wonder if you do really?

KARL: Dance with me a minute.

LOUISE: Very well.

She hasn't quite finished her sandwich so she holds it in her left hand while they waltz solemnly round the stage.

KARL: Of course the music makes a great difference.

LOUISE: There isn't always music.

KARL: And moonlight.

LOUISE: Moonlight doesn't last.

They go on dancing. The sound of a native pipe is heard a long way off in the distance.

KARL: There's music for us.

[23]

LOUISE: It's the wrong sort.

KARL: I wish you'd finish your sandwich.

LOUISE: I have.

KARL: Kiss me.

LOUISE: My dear——

They kiss.

You see!

KARL: The joke is on us.

LOUISE: It was a nice joke, while it lasted.

KARL: We've never even been lovers.

LOUISE: I don't want to now, do you?

KARL: Not much.

LOUISE: We missed our chance——

KARL: Don't talk like that, it sounds so depressing—— [*They turn away from each other.*]

LOUISE: What's the name of your agents in Sydney?

KARL: Eldrich, Lincoln and Barret.

LOUISE: Give them my love.

She pats his face very gently and sweetly and goes quickly away. He makes a movement as if to follow her, then pauses and lights a cigarette. He hums for a moment the tune to which they were dancing and then goes up to the rail where he stands leaning against a post looking out into the morning.

GEORGE DAVIES *and* EVA BLAKE *come quietly, almost furtively on from the right; they talk in whispers.*

EVA: It's awfully light.

GEORGE: There's nobody about.

EVA: Oh, George, you're so wonderful!

GEORGE: Shhh!

They kiss swiftly.

I suppose it's all right about the Baileys?

EVA: Yes, Marion promised—she'll never say a word.

GEORGE: I won't take you right up to the house, I'll just drop you off at the end of the garden——

EVA: Oh, George, you think of everything——

KARL: Excuse me, is your name Eva?

EVA: Yes.

KARL: I congratulate you!

EVA *and* GEORGE *go off.*

KARL *comes down and kicks* IPPAGA *gently.*

Wake up—wake up, it's morning——

IPPAGA *stretches himself as the curtain falls.*

THE ASTONISHED HEART

A Play in Six Scenes

CHARACTERS

CHRISTIAN FABER
BARBARA, his wife
LEONORA VAIL
TIM VERNEY
SUSAN BIRCH
SIR REGINALD FRENCH
ERNEST

The action of the entire play takes place in the drawing-room of the Fabers' flat in London.

SCENE I. *Late afternoon. November 1935.*
SCENE II. *Late afternoon. November 1934.*
SCENE III. *Midnight. January 1935.*
SCENE IV. *Dawn. April 1935.*
SCENE V. *Evening. November 1935.*
SCENE VI. *Late afternoon. November 1935.*

SCENE I

The action of the entire play takes place in the drawing-room of the Fabers' flat in London. The flat is on the top floor of one of the newly erected apartment buildings in the region of Hyde Park. The furniture is comfortable and good without conceding too much to prevailing fashion. On the left double doors lead to the hall, dining-room and BARBARA's *bedroom and bathroom, etc. On the right other double doors lead to* CHRISTIAN's *part of the flat, his bedroom, consulting-room and office.*

When the curtain rises it is late afternoon in November 1935. The lights are on but the curtains have not been drawn and BARBARA *is standing looking out of the window into the foggy dusk. She is a tranquil, intelligent woman of about thirty-six or seven. Her back is to the room and she is drumming her fingers on the window pane.* SUSAN BIRCH *is seated on the sofa with her hands clasped on her lap. Her age is somewhere between thirty and forty and she is plainly and efficiently dressed as befits a secretary. She is sitting very still although occasionally she bites her lip nervously.* TIM VERNEY, *a nice-looking man in the early thirties, is standing in front of the fireplace on the right smoking a cigarette. There is an air of strain in the room as though any one of them might cry out at any moment. The silence is broken by* BARBARA.

BARBARA: It looks terribly dreary out, but it's like that any-how, at this time of year, isn't it?

TIM: Yes.

BARBARA: The traffic seems slower than usual—— I expect that's my imagination.

TIM: Don't you think you'd better come away from the window now?

BARBARA: Yes, I suppose I had.

She comes slowly down and sits on the sofa next to SUSAN. Don't worry, Tim, about the window I mean, it's something we've got to get used to like everything else—part of the whole thing.

TIM: Yes, I know.

BARBARA [*to* SUSAN]: She answered the telephone herself, didn't she?

SUSAN [*with an effort*]: Yes.

BARBARA: She ought to be here by now.

SUSAN [*looking at her wrist-watch*]: Yes—yes she ought.

BARBARA: I suppose Ernest would be shocked if we had a cocktail, wouldn't he?

TIM: That doesn't matter.

BARBARA [*almost irritably*]: I know it doesn't matter, Tim, I was only thinking how funny it is that whether Ernest should be shocked or not shocked, should come into my mind at all—will you ring for him?

TIM: All right. [*He rings the bell by the fireplace.*]

BARBARA [*impulsively patting* SUSAN's *hand*]: I expect you think I'm talking too much.

SUSAN [*trying to smile*]: No, I don't, dear.

BARBARA: Talking's useful, it makes a little noise but not too much, just enough to distract the attention——

SUSAN: I know. [*She gets up.*]

BARBARA: What is it?

SUSAN: I thought perhaps I'd better go into the office.

BARBARA: No, don't, sit down again, stay with us.

SUSAN: Very well. [*She sits down again.*]

ERNEST, *the butler, enters.*

ERNEST: You rang, madame?

BARBARA: Make a cocktail will you, Ernest, a Dry Martini I think, don't you, Tim?

[32]

TIM [*absently*]: Yes, a Dry Martini.

ERNEST: Very good, madame.

BARBARA: When Mrs. Vail arrives—I'm—I'm expecting her——
[*Her voice breaks slightly.*]

ERNEST: Yes, madame.

He goes out.

BARBARA: That was silly of me, wasn't it?—Unnecessary—he
knew perfectly well we were expecting her——

TIM: She's probably held up in the traffic.

BARBARA: Yes, it's bad at this time of day—I'd like a cigarette,
Susan, there's a box just by you.

SUSAN *silently hands her the box and she takes a cigarette
and lights it.*

TIM: Poor woman.

BARBARA: Leonora? Yes—it's awful for her.

SUSAN [*bitterly*]: She'll get over it.

BARBARA: So shall we I expect—in time.

SUSAN: It doesn't matter to her, not really, not like it matters
to us—she'll cry a lot and be beautifully heartbroken——

BARBARA: Don't be unkind.

SUSAN [*violently*]: I hate her.

BARBARA [*turning away*]: Oh, don't, Susan—what's the use of
that——

SUSAN: I don't care whether it's any use or not—I hate her,
more than I've ever hated anyone in my whole life——

BARBARA: You might just as well hate a piece of notepaper,
because someone's written something cruel on it.

SIR REGINALD FRENCH *comes through the double doors on the
right. He is an authoritative, elderly surgeon.*

SIR REGINALD: She hasn't arrived yet?

TIM: She's on her way.

SIR REGINALD: Good. [*He turns to go again.*]

BARBARA: There isn't much time is there?

SIR REGINALD [*gently*]: No, I'm afraid not.

BARBARA: Is he—conscious?

[33]

SIR REGINALD: Only for a brief moment, every now and then.

BARBARA: It's then that he asks for her? In those brief moments?

SIR REGINALD: Yes.

BARBARA: I'll send her straight in when she comes.

SIR REGINALD: Do, my dear.

He goes out.

SUSAN: Oh God! [*She breaks down and cries softly.*]

BARBARA [*putting her arm round her*]: Don't, dear.

TIM: Shut up, Susan.

SUSAN: I can't help it—it would have been much better if only you'd let me go into the office when I wanted to.

BARBARA: I'd rather you cried here with us than all by yourself in there.

SUSAN [*dabbing her eyes*]: I'm all right now.

BARBARA: Don't make too much of an effort, Susan, it's a dreadful strain—I'd cry if I could—tears are fine, a little relief—they let the grief out for a minute or two—I envy them——

ERNEST *enters with a tray on which is a cocktail shaker and four glasses.*

Here are the cocktails. Put them on the small table, Ernest—Tim, you pour them out—thank you, Ernest.

ERNEST *puts down the tray and goes out.* TIM *gives the shaker a couple of extra shakes and pours out a cocktail for each of them. They take them in silence.*

TIM [*drinking*]: He's certainly made it dry enough.

BARBARA [*sipping hers and smiling faintly*]: Strong enough too—oh, dear——

There is the sound of the front door bell. They all jump slightly.

TIM: Here she is—at last——

BARBARA [*suddenly*]: How extraordinary—d'you see what I mean? It's the same, exactly the same as a year ago—you were there, Tim, just where you are now, with a cocktail glass in your hand—you were there, Susan, only you had your glasses on and a packet of papers in your lap—don't you remember—the first time she ever came into this room——?

ERNEST *opens the door and announces:* MRS. VAIL *as the lights fade.*

SCENE II

When the lights come up on the scene BARBARA, TIM, SUSAN *and* ERNEST *are all in the same positions as the preceding scene.* SUSAN *is wearing glasses and has a packet of papers in her lap, her jumper is blue instead of grey.* BARBARA *is wearing a tea gown.* TIM *is in the same suit but wearing a different tie.*

ERNEST [*announcing*]: Mrs. Vail.

LEONORA VAIL *enters. She is a lovely creature of about thirty, exquisitely dressed and with great charm of manner.*

BARBARA [*greeting her*]: My dear—after all these years——

LEONORA: Isn't it lovely?

They kiss affectionately.

BARBARA: Bring some fresh cocktails, Ernest.

ERNEST: Yes, madame.

He goes out.

BARBARA [*introducing her*]: This is Susan Birch, Chris's right hand and this is Tim Verney, Chris's left hand—or perhaps it's the other way round—settle it among yourselves—Leonora Vail—Ames that was——

LEONORA: Leonora Ames, terrible at games! Do you remember?

BARBARA: Of course I do.

They both laugh.

LEONORA [*shaking hands with* SUSAN]: How do you do?

SUSAN: How do you do?

LEONORA [*shaking hands with* TIM]: I think Barbara wrote that beastly little rhyme herself.

[35]

TIM [*smiling*]: Was it true?

LEONORA: Absolutely.

BARBARA: I can't possibly say you haven't changed a bit, you've changed more thoroughly than anyone I've ever seen——

LEONORA: Having our hair up makes a great difference.

BARBARA: Your voice has changed too, but I recognised it on the telephone.

LEONORA: I'd have known yours anywhere.

TIM: Have a cocktail, it's mostly water now—perhaps you'd rather wait for a fresh one.

LEONORA: That'll do beautifully to start with.

He pours out a cocktail and she holds it up towards BARBARA. The nastiest girl in the school.

BARBARA [*laughing*]: But the best King Lear.

LEONORA [*also laughing*]: Oh, of course—I'd forgotten that.

BARBARA: I foresee a flood of reminiscence.

TIM: So do I—come along, Susan, we'd better go.

BARBARA: No, don't go—you can bear it, Tim, you'll probably discover a lot of useful little psychological echoes from my childhood——

SUSAN [*rising*]: I must go anyhow—all these have to be dealt with. [*She indicates the papers in her hand.*]

TIM: Is there a patient in there now?

SUSAN [*glancing at her watch*]: Yes, but her time's nearly up.

LEONORA [*to* BARBARA]: Does he work all day long, your husband?

BARBARA: Yes, most of the night as well sometimes.

LEONORA: What's he like?

BARBARA: Horrible.

LEONORA: I sympathise, mine was an absolute darling, so much so that I divorced him after eighteen months——

SUSAN: Good-bye, Mrs. Vail.

LEONORA: Good-bye.

TIM: We shall probably meet again very soon.

LEONORA: I hope so.

[*36*]

BARBARA: Tell Chris to come in for a second if he can when he's got rid of his patient.

TIM: All right.

He and SUSAN *go out.*

LEONORA: What a nice man.

BARBARA: Tim's a dear, he's extremely brilliant, too, Chris thinks the world of him.

LEONORA: He must be wonderful.

BARBARA: Who, Chris?

LEONORA: Yes, a little frightening though I should think.

BARBARA [*smiling*]: Oh no, he's not in the least frightening— he gets a bit abstracted every now and then—when he's working too hard.

LEONORA: Dear Barbara, how nice this is—how long ago is it?——

BARBARA: Seventeen—no eighteen years—I'm thirty-five now, I left long before you did——

LEONORA: I remember missing you dreadfully.

BARBARA: It was after the war when you went to America?

LEONORA: Yes, just after. Father left Brazil in 1918 and at the beginning of 1919 we went to Washington.

BARBARA: When were you married?

LEONORA: Oh, a long while after, several years.

BARBARA: Was he really such a—a darling?

LEONORA: Oh, it was all horrid. He was much older than me, very rich—fortunately—that's all there was to it really.

BARBARA: And you never wanted to marry again?

LEONORA: I wanted to once, but it wasn't possible, everything went wrong——

[ERNEST *comes in with fresh cocktails.*]

BARBARA: I'm so sorry.

LEONORA: I minded horribly at the time but I travelled a bit and got over it, it's a long while ago anyhow.

BARBARA: How long have you been in England?

LEONORA: Only two weeks—I've got a darling little house, only rented of course, I moved in on Monday—when will you come and dine?

BARBARA: Whenever you like.

LEONORA: And your husband, Chris?

BARBARA: I'm sure he'd love to but it all depends, you can never count on him——

LEONORA: I'm longing to see him.

ERNEST *having deposited the cocktail shaker on the tray, goes out, taking with him the empty one.*

BARBARA: He'll probably come in soon for a moment.

LEONORA: Is it never more than a moment?

BARBARA: Oh, yes—not quite as bad as that—but being married to eminence requires a little forbearance, especially if the eminence is dear to you.

LEONORA: No holidays?

BARBARA: Yes—last year we got a full month—we went to Italy, Como first and then down to Venice, it was lovely. He got a bit restive during the last week, but I persuaded him to stay the course.

LEONORA: I should be jealous I think.

BARBARA: Jealous?

LEONORA: But you're better balanced than I am—less emotional—you always were——

BARBARA: It would be tiresome to go on being emotional after twelve years of marriage. [*She gives her a cocktail.*]

LEONORA: I don't really want another.

BARBARA: Come on—one more—I will too.

LEONORA: All right.

BARBARA: Old times. [*She drinks.*]

LEONORA: Old times. [*She drinks.*] What does he do exactly?

BARBARA: Chris?

LEONORA: Yes.

BARBARA [*gently*]: He's only one of the most celebrated psychiatrists in the world, dear.

LEONORA [*laughing*]: I know that—be patient with me—psy-

[*38*]

chiatrist is only a word to me—it's nothing to do with bone setting, is it?

BARBARA [*laughing too*]: No, nothing whatever—you're thinking of osteopathy——

LEONORA: No, I'm not, it's something like psychiatrist—another word.

BARBARA: Chiropractor.

LEONORA: That's it.

BARBARA: You'd better not mention that to Chris, he doesn't approve of chiropractors at all——

LEONORA: What's a psychiatrist then?

BARBARA: Someone who cures diseases of the mind——

LEONORA: Oh, repressions and inhibitions and all that sort of thing.

BARBARA: Yes, all that sort of thing.

LEONORA: How exciting.

BARBARA: Yes, more interesting than exciting.

LEONORA: You have a superior look in your eye, Barbara, and I resent it deeply.

BARBARA: I'm sorry, dear.

LEONORA: I know I'm idiotic really, but it's most tactless of you to remind me of it. How does he start his treatments? Just a series of embarrassing questions?

BARBARA: Frightfully embarrassing.

LEONORA: I've read about it in books. You have to remember sinister little episodes of your childhood—falling in love with the cook—or being frightened by a goat—then you have to determine the cook or sublimate the goat or something, and you go away completely cured and sleep like a top.

BARBARA: I see that your ignorance was only an affectation, you have the whole thing in a nutshell.

LEONORA: It must be fascinating work, unearthing everybody's rattling little skeletons and fitting them together like Meccano. What about himself?

BARBARA: How do you mean?

LEONORA: Does he know all about himself right from the beginning? Is everything cut and dried and accounted for?

BARBARA: I expect so.

LEONORA: And you? Has he a chart of you hanging up over his desk?

BARBARA: He doesn't need a chart of me, Leonora.

LEONORA: Something in your manner tells me that I've gone too far—oh dear—I didn't mean to—don't be cross.

BARBARA [*smiling*]: I'm not in the least cross.

LEONORA: I suppose he'd know all about me in a minute, wouldn't he? The very first second he clapped eyes on me.

BARBARA: Certainly.

LEONORA: How terrifying.

BARBARA: Don't pretend, Leonora, I'm perfectly sure you're not terrified of anyone.

LEONORA: Do his patients fall in love with him?

BARBARA: Practically always.

LEONORA: Don't you hate that?

BARBARA: You are funny, Leonora.

LEONORA: Am I? Nicely funny or nastily funny?

BARBARA: Charmingly funny.

LEONORA: Oh dear, I can't wait to see him, do tell someone to hurry him up, I shall have to go in a minute. He hasn't got a moustache, has he?

BARBARA: No.

LEONORA: Beard?

BARBARA: No beard.

LEONORA: Tall or short?

BARBARA: Short.

LEONORA: Fat?

BARBARA: Not exactly fat, let's say a little podgy.

LEONORA: Oh, Barbara!

BARBARA: He has very little chance of getting exercise you see, still he does his best with those things in the bathroom——

LEONORA [*horrified*]: What things?

[*40*]

BARBARA: You know, they're attached to the wall and you gasp and strain and they snap back again—he has a rowing machine too.

LEONORA: I know, I've seen them in gymnasiums on ships.

BARBARA: He finds it very effective.

LEONORA: You're lying, aren't you?

BARBARA: Yes, Leonora.

LEONORA: I suppose he's eight feet high and absolutely bewitching.

BARBARA: If you care for long black moustaches, yes.

LEONORA: I've made up my mind to fall in love with him on sight.

BARBARA: He's quite used to that.

LEONORA: You're positively smug about him, Barbara—tell me seriously—do you really adore him?

BARBARA: I love him very much.

LEONORA: How marvellous. And does he love you?

BARBARA: Really, Leonora!

LEONORA: I know I'm behaving badly, but it seems so funny——

BARBARA: What seems so funny?

LEONORA: I know what I mean, but it's awfully difficult to explain.

BARBARA [*drily*]: Don't try.

LEONORA: Darling, I think I'd like just another little sip if there's any more in the shaker——

BARBARA: It's practically full——

BARBARA *refills her glass.* CHRISTIAN FABER *comes into the room. He is about forty years old, tall and thin. He moves quickly and decisively as though there was never quite enough time for all he had to do.*

LEONORA: At last!

CHRIS [*surprised*]: What?

BARBARA: This is Mrs. Vail, Chris, one of my oldest friends, we were at school together——

CHRIS [*absently*]: Oh—how do you do. [*He shakes hands.*]

BARBARA: Cocktail?

CHRIS: No, I've got some more work to do.

LEONORA: I think it only fair that you should know that until Barbara disillusioned me I thought that you were a chiropractor.

CHRIS [*smiling perfunctorily*]: Did you really? [*To* BARBARA.] Listen, dear, we are dining with Mary to-night, aren't we?

BARBARA: Yes.

CHRIS: Well, you go without me and tell her I'll come in for coffee——

BARBARA [*laughing*]: She knows that already, darling, she told me on the telephone this morning.

CHRIS [*with a smile*]: Mary is one of the most sensible women I know.

LEONORA [*with slightly forced impudence*]: I also thought you had a long moustache!

CHRIS [*not quite understanding*]: What——?

BARBARA [*quickly*]: Moustache, dear, Leonora thought you had a moustache.

CHRIS [*with a completely empty smile*]: Oh, no—I haven't a moustache.

He bows politely and goes out.

LEONORA: I'd rather he was a chiropractor.

BARBARA: Never mind.

LEONORA: He didn't even see me, I do think it's a shame.

BARBARA: He saw you all right.

LEONORA: You're being superior again, how odious of you.

BARBARA: When do you want us to come and dine?

LEONORA: I shan't even ask him, I like the other young man much better, Tim whatever his name was, bring him instead—next Wednesday?

BARBARA [*going to her book on the desk*]: Wait a minute.

LEONORA: Do you want to go to a play or just sit and talk?

BARBARA: I don't mind a bit, whichever you like—but I'd rather make it Thursday.

LEONORA: All right—Thursday—we'll decide whether to go out or not later.

BARBARA: That'll be lovely.

LEONORA: I really must go now——

BARBARA: You're sure you wouldn't like to stay and have your bones set or anything?

LEONORA: No, I've given up the whole idea.

BARBARA: What whole idea?

LEONORA: About falling madly in love with your husband and him falling madly in love with me and then me having a lovely "old friends together" scene with you and everyone behaving beautifully and making sacrifices all round——

BARBARA: You were always romantic, even at school, do you remember Monsieur Brachet?

LEONORA: I adored him, didn't I? But still he was rather sweet.

BARBARA: His eyes were very close together.

LEONORA: Practically two in one, darling, but charm—that's what counts, darling——

BARBARA: What's your telephone number?

LEONORA: You're not going to put me off, are you?

BARBARA: Don't be so silly, of course not.

LEONORA: Kensington 3382.

BARBARA [*scribbling it down*]: Kensington 3382.

LEONORA: I'll expect you on Thursday—about eight?

BARBARA: Do you really want me to ask Tim?

LEONORA: Of course, he's an angel, and bring your old chiropodist too if he'll come——

BARBARA [*laughingly, as they go out*]: I'll try to persuade him——

Their voices are heard talking and laughing in the hall. TIM *comes in and goes over to the desk, he rummages about on it.* BARBARA *returns.*

BARBARA: Oh, Tim, you made me jump. What are you doing?

TIM: Is there a Bible in the house?

[*43*]

BARBARA: I suppose there must be somewhere. Whatever do you want it for?

TIM: Chris wants a quotation to use in his lecture on Friday——

BARBARA: Does he know a special one——?

TIM: Vaguely—something in Deuteronomy——

ERNEST *enters.*

BARBARA: Have you got a Bible, Ernest?

ERNEST: I think the cook has one, madame.

BARBARA: Ask her if she'll lend it to me for a minute, will you?

ERNEST: Very good, madame.

He goes out.

BARBARA: Isn't she lovely?

TIM: Who? The cook?

BARBARA: No, don't be so silly, Leonora.

TIM: Very smooth and shiny.

BARBARA: Didn't you like her?

TIM: Yes, I suppose so, I only saw her for a moment.

BARBARA: She loved you at first sight, she wants you to dine with her on Thursday.

TIM: Good God!

BARBARA: It's all right, I shall be there to protect you.

TIM: I hate dinner parties.

BARBARA: You mustn't be disagreeable.

ERNEST *re-enters with a Bible.*

Ah, thank you, Ernest.

ERNEST: Have you finished with the cocktail things, madame?

BARBARA: Yes, thank you.

ERNEST *takes the cocktail tray away as* SUSAN *enters.*

SUSAN: Did you find one?

TIM: Yes, it's the cook's.

SUSAN: It's Moses, Deuteronomy twenty something—— It starts with "The Lord shall smite thee—"

They look through the Bible together.

SUSAN [*to* BARBARA]: It's for his paper on the Development of Psychopathology starting with Hippocrates——

TIM: This must be it—— [*He reads.*] "The Lord shall smite thee with madness, and blindness, and astonishment of the heart."

SUSAN: Yes, that's it.

She takes the Bible and goes off as the lights fade.

SCENE III

When the lights come up on the scene, CHRIS *and* LEONORA *are discovered standing by the fireplace, his arms are round her and he is kissing her. She is wearing a diaphanous evening gown, he, a dinner jacket. About two months have passed since the preceding scene. The time is after midnight. There is a tray of sandwiches and drinks on the small table by the sofa. She detaches herself from his arms and moves away.*

LEONORA [*in a strained voice*]: I must go.

CHRIS [*quietly*]: Must you?

LEONORA: Of course.

CHRIS: Isn't that rather inconsistent?

LEONORA: Yes—I suppose it is.

CHRIS: What's the matter?

LEONORA: I didn't mean it to be like this——

CHRIS: Don't go away from me yet.

LEONORA: I must.

CHRIS: Do you want to?

LEONORA [*softly*]: No.

CHRIS: Come back to my arms, it's cold over here by the fire.

LEONORA [*with her face turned away from him*]: I lied just now when I said I didn't mean it to be like this.

CHRIS: Does it matter?

LEONORA: Yes—it matters dreadfully——

CHRIS [*moving towards her*]: My dear——

LEONORA [*with panic in her voice*]: Please stay there.

CHRIS [*stopping*]: Very well.

LEONORA [*with a rush*]: I did mean it to be like this but—but not quite like this—I mean—it was all a trick—I planned it—the first day I came, you remember, when you snubbed me—I teased you about it at dinner to-night—I made up my mind then to make you fall in love with me—now I wish I hadn't—I feel cheap—I feel frightened—I wish with all my heart I hadn't.

CHRIS [*with a smile*]: I think it was rather a gay trick. Don't be upset. There's nothing to be upset about. Let's sit down quietly and have a drink.

He comes over to the sofa and pours out a drink.

Will you have one?

LEONORA: No, thank you.

CHRIS [*sitting*]: Do come and sit down.

LEONORA: Now you're treating me like a patient.

CHRIS: Only because you're behaving like one.

LEONORA: I see. [*She laughs suddenly.*]

CHRIS: That's better.

LEONORA: Give me a cigarette. [*She sits down next to him.*]

CHRIS: Here. [*He lights one for her.*] You're a lovely creature.

LEONORA: I'm all right outside, but I'm not very pleased with myself inside at the moment.

CHRIS: Pangs of conscience are tiresome, Leonora, they're also exceedingly bad for you.

LEONORA: I'm feeling better now.

CHRIS: I gather that the trick is on again.

LEONORA [*sharply*]: That was unkind.

CHRIS: You're very touchy.

LEONORA: What about Barbara?

CHRIS: She's very well, thank you—I had a letter from her this morning.

LEONORA: Are you in love with her?

CHRIS: What on earth did you say that for?

LEONORA: Are you in love with her?

CHRIS: You're behaving like a patient again.

LEONORA: Are you?

CHRIS: Barbara has nothing to do with this.

LEONORA: You're certainly not in love with me.

CHRIS: You have lovely eyes, but there's a little sadness in them, a little disappointment, I could tell your fortune by your eyes—shall I?

LEONORA: I'd rather you didn't.

CHRIS: And your nose——

LEONORA: I'd rather you didn't mention my nose at all.

CHRIS: It's the most unwise nose I've ever seen.

LEONORA: Do stop.

CHRIS: Then there's your mouth——

LEONORA: I must go——

CHRIS: You'd be astounded if you knew how desperately I want to kiss your mouth—again——

LEONORA: Please, Chris——

CHRIS: You're so foolish, up on your romantic high horse— how often have you ridden it wildly until it went lame and you had to walk home?

LEONORA: Often enough to teach me never to do it again.

CHRIS: That's what made the sadness in your eyes—you should never have left school, it was a grave mistake.

LEONORA: You win.

CHRIS: Do I?

LEONORA: I knew you would—quite early in the evening I knew.

CHRIS: Has it been a happy evening—for you?

LEONORA: No, not really—rather strained.

CHRIS: Were you really angry—that first time we met?

LEONORA: Yes—I think I was.

CHRIS: I didn't mean to be rude.

LEONORA: You certainly did.

CHRIS: Yes, now I come to think of it, I did.

LEONORA: Why?

CHRIS: You irritated me, you were so conscious of how absolutely beautiful you looked.

LEONORA: I never thought that.

CHRIS: Your manner demanded attention insistently, like a child banging its spoon on the table, making a clamour—yelling for more——

LEONORA: How horrid that sounds.

CHRIS: Quite natural though, I expect you've always been spoilt.

LEONORA: No, I haven't.

CHRIS: Have you had many lovers?

LEONORA [*looking down*]: No—not many.

CHRIS: And the few—whoever they were—did you love them?

LEONORA: Please don't be quite so—clinical.

CHRIS [*impulsively*]: Forgive me—I wanted to know.

LEONORA: I loved somebody once—very much—never so much before—and never so much since.

CHRIS: I see.

LEONORA: I know you think my conscience is tiresome and, considering how obviously I threw myself at you, a trifle ill-timed, but it's there all the same and it's making me uneasy—— Please listen, I'm being really honest now—if you and I had an—an affair—how much would it hurt Barbara?

CHRIS: I don't know. If she knew, I expect it would upset her a good deal, but it would upset her just as much, if not more, if she thought we wanted to and were denying ourselves on her account. Barbara's that sort of person.

LEONORA: You have been married twelve years.

CHRIS: How naïve you are.

LEONORA: Do you love her? You never answered me before.

CHRIS: Yes, I love her deeply and truly and for ever.

LEONORA: I see.

CHRIS: I don't suppose you do, but it doesn't matter.

LEONORA: It matters a lot.

CHRIS: What do you want? Truth or lies—reality or pretence?

LEONORA: How clever of you to know, without looking, what you have in your safe.

CHRIS: Don't be unkind to me, Leonora.

LEONORA: It's you who are unkind to me.

CHRIS: Why? In what way?

LEONORA: It's my own fault of course——

CHRIS: Entirely.

LEONORA: If you feel that it would make our—our flirtation any more satisfactory, I have some X-ray plates of my teeth.

CHRIS: Stop being quarrelsome, Leonora.

LEONORA: I can't help it, you make me angry—horribly angry —I want to hit out at you.

CHRIS: Any other impulse at this particular stage of the proceedings would be abnormal.

LEONORA: You're so superbly sure of yourself, aren't you?

CHRIS [*seriously*]: No, the basis of everything I've ever learned is not being sure—not being sure of anyone or anything in the world—myself least of all—— [*He turns away.*]

LEONORA: Hand me my bag, it's just behind you.

CHRIS: What for?

LEONORA: I want to powder my—unwise nose.

CHRIS [*handing it to her*]: Here.

LEONORA: Thank you.

She opens her bag and scrutinizes herself in the glass inside it. She puts on some lipstick and powders her nose. CHRIS *watches her.*

CHRIS: There's a bit of fluff on the left.

LEONORA: I can see it.

CHRIS: You mustn't be ungracious.

LEONORA: I want to go home now. [*She rises.*]

CHRIS [*also rising*]: I'll take you—there's always a taxi on the rank.

LEONORA: Please don't, I'd really rather you didn't.

[49]

CHRIS: You must be mad as a hatter.

LEONORA: Why—what do you mean?

CHRIS: To imagine—— Oh, what's the use——

He suddenly crushes her in his arms and kisses her violently.

LEONORA: Don't—please, Chris—don't—— [*She struggles.*]

CHRIS [*pressing her to him*]: Don't be unkind—I want you dreadfully—you must know that—don't leave me—not just yet —it wasn't all a trick—it may have started as a trick, but it isn't that now, is it? Is it?

LEONORA [*breaking away from him, breathlessly*]: Yes—yes it is.

CHRIS: Liar. [*He takes her hand.*] Look at me.

LEONORA [*near tears*]: No. [*She turns away.*]

CHRIS: Please.

He turns her slowly and looks into her eyes.

LEONORA [*in a whisper*]: Well—what's my fortune?

CHRIS: You're going to love me a little.

LEONORA [*shaking her head*]: That's not enough.

CHRIS: Oh, yes—yes—more than enough.

LEONORA: Are you sure?

CHRIS: Oh, my dear—my dear——

She slips into his arms again as the lights fade on the scene.

SCENE IV

It is now April, three months having passed since the preceding scene. The time is about five or six a.m.

There is a greyness in the room because dawn is not far away.

BARBARA *is sitting in a chair by the fire smoking a cigarette. She is wearing a dressing-gown, and there is an ash-tray by her side, almost filled with cigarette ends. She shivers slightly, then gets up and pours herself a brandy and soda; she returns to her chair and then her attention is caught by the sound of the front door opening softly. She closes her eyes for an instant and bites her lip as though she were trying to gather courage.*

[50]

CHRIS *comes quietly in from the left; he is wearing a light overcoat and hat. His face is tired and strained.*

BARBARA [*in as ordinary a voice as she can manage*]: Hallo, darling!

CHRIS [*startled*]: Barbara!

BARBARA: I'm sorry if I made you jump.

CHRIS: What on earth——?

BARBARA: I couldn't sleep.

CHRIS [*switching on the lights*]: Oh, I see——

BARBARA: Not all the lights, Chris.

CHRIS: All right. [*He switches on the desk light and turns the others off again.*]

BARBARA: Would you like a drink?

CHRIS: No—no, thanks.

BARBARA: I'm having one—it's—it's a bit chilly.

CHRIS [*in a flat voice*]: I'm awfully sorry, darling.

BARBARA: There isn't anything to be sorry for—I mean this isn't a scene—really it isn't, only I do want to talk to you. I've wanted to for a long while.

CHRIS: I know.

BARBARA: It's probably a bad moment, but—but during the day it's difficult—there never seems to be any time——

CHRIS: I meant it when I said I was sorry—I am—desperately sorry.

BARBARA: Of course you are. Don't be silly—I know that—it's all beastly—I'm sorry, too, I'm sorry for you and me and—I'm even sorry for Leonora—— [*She gives a little laugh.*]

CHRIS [*noticing the ash-tray*]: Have you smoked all those to-night?

BARBARA: Yes—it looks awfully unattractive, doesn't it—like after a party—— [*She empties the ash-tray into the fireplace.*]

CHRIS [*looking away from her*]: You know about me loving you all the same, don't you—more than anybody in the world?

BARBARA: Yes, of course I do, but I'd rather you didn't go on

[51]

about it just at the moment. I want so very much not to be emotional.

CHRIS: Are you very unhappy?

BARBARA: Not any more than you, I don't suppose. That's the worst of the whole business, nobody's having a good time. How is Leonora?

CHRIS: She's all right, I've just left her.

BARBARA: I didn't imagine you'd been to a Masonic dinner, darling.

CHRIS [*smiling wryly*]: No, I didn't think you did.

BARBARA: I hate her quite normally with all my feminine instincts; sometimes I get almost violent, all by myself—it's funny, isn't it, after so many years?—I've got over wishing to strangle her, though, now; I just wish she'd never been born.

CHRIS: I think I do, too.

BARBARA: I don't see how we can go on like this quite, do you? It really is too uncomfortable—that's why I sat up for you. I'm dreadfully worried, the personal, loving you part of the affair I could manage, I think—painful as it is—but it's everything else, too—we're all in a state, Tim and Susan—I think even Ernest's getting a bit agitated—— [*She laughs again nervously.*] You're working under such tremendous pressure, and you're so terribly strained and tired—we're all frightened that you'll crack up or something.

CHRIS: Don't worry, I shan't crack up.

BARBARA: Do you want to marry her?

CHRIS: No—it isn't anything to do with marriage.

BARBARA: Does she want you to marry her?

CHRIS: No, I don't think so—no, I'm sure she doesn't.

BARBARA: I can't see why that should make me feel a bit better, but it does.

CHRIS: Oh, Baba—— [*He breaks off miserably.*]

BARBARA [*brightly*]: And I'll trouble you not to call me Baba just now, darling—as a psychologist you really ought to know better.

CHRIS [*trying to smile at her*]: All right.

BARBARA: I have a plan, you know, otherwise I wouldn't have pounced like this, but before I tell you what it is, I want to know a little more.

CHRIS: Very well, fire away.

BARBARA: First of all, how clearly do you see the situation in your more detached moments, I mean?

CHRIS: Quite clearly, but the detached moments are getting rarer, I'm afraid.

BARBARA: Can you be detached now?

CHRIS: I'm trying with all my might.

BARBARA: Don't worry about me, please don't! I can tread water indefinitely—it would be different if I were still in love with you, but I'm not, any more than you are with me; that was all settled years ago. We are tremendously necessary to each other, though, and I hope to God we always shall be, and I want to know—I want to know—— [*Her voice breaks.*]

CHRIS: How long?

BARBARA [*with control*]: Yes.

CHRIS: I'm submerged now—I can't tell.

BARBARA: Very well then, you must go away.

CHRIS: Go away! How can I?

BARBARA: You must.

CHRIS: I've thought of it. I wanted to but it's quite impossible, also even if I could, even if there wasn't work or anything to prevent me, it wouldn't be any use—running away never is any use.

BARBARA: I didn't mean you to go away alone, it's too late for that now. I meant you to go away with her—take two months, three months if necessary—go to the most lovely, beautiful place you can think of—relax utterly—give yourself up to loving her without any sense of strain or responsibility—don't think about work or me or any of the things that are standing in the way——

CHRIS: I can't, Baba, you know I can't.

BARBARA: I don't know anything of the sort. It's clear, cold sense. I'm not being noble and self-sacrificing and thinking only of your happiness. I'm thinking of my own happiness too, and, more important still, of your job—you can't deal wisely and successfully with twisted nerve-strained people if you're twisted and nerve-strained yourself. You must see that. It isn't your passion for Leonora alone that's undermining you, it's the fight you're putting up, you're being torn in half——

CHRIS: Darling, you're making me so dreadfully ashamed.

BARBARA: That's idiotic, unreasonable and idiotic. You said just now that you were submerged—that's true, you are; you've crushed down your emotions for years, and now you're paying for it. It's nothing to be ashamed of, with your sort of temperament it was inevitable—it had to happen, I've been waiting for it.

CHRIS: Baba!

BARBARA: Let me go on. I'm not submerged, I'm seeing the whole thing clearly—unless you put a stop to this agonising battle between your emotions and your intelligence, you'll break completely.

CHRIS [*tortured*]: How can I put a stop to it? It's there—it's there all the time—every moment of the day and night—it started so easily, so gaily—little more than a joke; there were no danger signals whatever. I felt just a few conscience pangs over you, but not seriously, the whole thing was so apart from us and all we mean to each other—my intelligence lied to me— my intelligence insisted that it was nothing, just a little emotional flutter that would probably loosen me up and do me a power of good; then suddenly I felt myself being swept away and I started to struggle, but the tide was stronger than I knew; now I'm far from the land, darling—far from my life and you and safety—I'm struggling still, but the water's terribly deep and I'm frightened—I'm frightened. [*He comes close to her and puts his head down on her shoulder.*]

BARBARA [*gently*]: I know—I really do know——

[54]

CHRIS: It isn't Leonora, it's nothing to do with Leonora any more; it's the thing itself—her face and her body and her charm make a frame, but the picture's in me, before my eyes constantly, and I can't get it out——

BARBARA: Stop struggling.

CHRIS: I can't! If I stop struggling I shall be lost for ever. If I didn't know all the processes it would be easier, but I do—I watch myself all the time—when I'm talking to patients—in case I make a slip; it's as much as I can do sometimes to prevent myself from suddenly shrieking in their faces—'Why are you here? What do you come to me for? How can I help you when there's a little brooch between us—a little brooch with emeralds and sapphires that someone gave to Leonora years ago—long before I ever knew her—how can I ease your poor mind when a handsome young man is burnt to death in a plane —here in the room—he was the one she really loved, you know, the only one she ever really loved——'

BARBARA: Oh, my dear—oh, my poor dear!

CHRIS [*with a great effort at control*]: Tim and Susan are fine —their behaviour's almost too good. There's no reproach in their eyes, just a concentrated determination to bolster me up as much as they can. Nurse Hoskins is not so good—she ushers in the patients warily now—I think she listens outside the door, too, in case of accidents. Then there's Leonora herself—she's having a hell of a time. The ecstasy's still there—just for a few flaming moments—but in between there are bad hours. You see, I'm finding out things all the time—things about her and things about myself. We're seldom alone together—the ghosts of the people she loved before, or thought she loved, come and join us—they make me sick with jealousy, Baba—me of all people. We can laugh about that one day, can't we? I ask her questions, you see, because I can't stop myself—and out of her answers the scenes build themselves—and it's those dead moments that torture me. Can you imagine the foolishness of that? Things that happened years ago long before I even knew she existed—

then I lose control and say dreadful cruel things to her. I dis-
tort her memories for her, smear them with mockery, dissect
them in front of her until they're spoilt and broken into little
pieces. Then she cries, not false crying, but real tears for something that's lost . . . and all the time my brain's raising its eyebrows at me and sneering, and then the only thing left is to be
sorry—humbly bitterly sorry—and swear never again to be unkind—never, never, never again—until the next time——

*He leaves her and goes over to the window. She watches him
and then takes a cigarette and lights it.*

BARBARA [*quietly*]: It's only the strain that makes all that,
darling. I wish I could make you see. If only I could get it into
your head that there is no reason in the world why you
shouldn't love Leonora as much as you want to—for as long as
it lasts—you'd be able to give yourself up to it and be happy—
you'd probably have quarrels—one always does—but they'd be
normal ones, not these dreadful twisted agonies. You must do
as I say—it's your only chance. Let Tim take over everything
for three months; he can manage all right with Susan. Wipe
me from your mind entirely; I shall go away somewhere myself.
Laura's in Paris, I can go and stay with her, and Mary's taken
the Birrels' house in Kent for six months. It's absolutely lovely
and I shall be so much happier than I am now, if only I know
you're being sensible and giving yourself space.

CHRIS: Space?

BARBARA: Room to enjoy the best parts of it, without that
horrid feeling of hours passing—without the consciousness that
there's work to be done the next day and people to see and
decisions to make.

CHRIS: It sounds easy, but it wouldn't be.

BARBARA: After a week or so it would, really—I know I'm right
—anyhow it's worth trying.

CHRIS: It is running away all the same——

BARBARA: What on earth does that matter? It's being wise that
matters. Take the car—don't stop too long in one place, forget

[*56*]

everything but just what you're doing at the moment. You really must try it, darling—you see, I've had time to think and you haven't had any time at all.

CHRIS: You don't hate her, do you?

BARBARA [*suddenly angry*]: Good God! what does it matter if I do!

CHRIS: I'm sorry.

BARBARA: I'm fighting for you. Leonora's only on the fringe of the business. It's you and me that make my world and the work you've got to do, and the happiness we've had and can have again. My jealousy is not for the desire you have for her, nor for the hours of illusion you buy from her. I'm jealous of the time in between—the waste—those bad hours you told me about just now. I sense futility in all that, and it's that futility that's nagging at you and humiliating you so. Stop trying to balance yourself—come off your tight-rope, it's better to climb down than fall down, isn't it?

CHRIS: It's bitter, isn't it, to be made to put on rompers again at my age?

BARBARA: Whether you intended it or not, that remark was definitely funny.

CHRIS: I miss not being able to laugh.

BARBARA: That'll all come back.

CHRIS: Just at this moment—this now—this immediate moment I'm all right, you know—I expect it's because you're so strong.

BARBARA: Well, make the most of it.

CHRIS: You needn't tell me it won't last, I know that.

BARBARA: Hang on to it anyhow as long as you can, even when you're submerged again, try to remember it.

CHRIS: Have you ever loved anyone else, since me?

BARBARA: No, I've never happened to want to.

CHRIS: Would you have, if you had wanted to, I mean?

BARBARA [*lightly*]: I expect so.

CHRIS: I wonder how much I should mind.

[57]

BARBARA: Do stop whirling about among fictions, there are enough facts to occupy us, God knows. Go away—offer yourself up—get on with it.

CHRIS: It all seems so unreal!

BARBARA: It's real enough to make us damned uncomfortable!

CHRIS [*turning*]: I don't believe I really love her at all.

BARBARA: This is no moment to go into a technical argument about that, my sweet. Love is a very comprehensive term, you're certainly obsessed, by her, or by yourself through her, and that's quite enough. Oh, dear, it's more than enough—— [*She gives a little laugh.*] Please, Chris——

CHRIS: All right.

BARBARA [*cheerfully*]: Well, that's settled—we'll lash Tim into a frenzy of responsibility to-morrow—I mean to-day—you'd better try to get some sleep now.

CHRIS: Yes—I'll try.

BARBARA: Good morning, darling—— [*She puts her arms round him, kisses him lightly and goes quickly out of the room.*]

CHRIS [*as the door closes on her*]: Thank you, Baba.

He leans against the window with his head in his arms as the lights fade.

SCENE V

Seven months have passed since the preceding scene. It is midnight on the night before the first scene of the play. When the lights go up on the scene LEONORA *is lying face downwards on the sofa, sobbing.* CHRIS *is leaning on the mantelpiece gazing into the fire.*

CHRIS: For the love of God stop crying. [*She continues to sob.*] I'm sorry—I've said I was sorry——

LEONORA: I can't bear any more.

CHRIS [*coming over to her*]: Darling, please——

[58]

LEONORA: Don't—don't come near me.

CHRIS: You must forgive me—you must!

LEONORA [*slowly sitting up*]: It isn't forgiving—it's that I can't bear any more. I mean it this time—I really can't!

CHRIS [*bitterly*]: I should like to know what you propose to do then.

LEONORA: I'm going—I'm going away for good.

CHRIS: I see.

LEONORA [*rising*]: I'm going now——

CHRIS [*holding her arms*]: No, you're not.

LEONORA: Please, Chris——

CHRIS: You can't possibly go.

LEONORA: You're hurting me.

CHRIS [*coldly*]: Why do you struggle then?

LEONORA: Don't be such a fool, what's the use of behaving like this?

CHRIS: I was under the impression that you loved me——

LEONORA: Let go of my arms.

CHRIS: More than anyone or anything in the world. How long ago was that you said that to me—how long ago—answer me . . . [*He shakes her.*]

LEONORA [*crying again*]: Oh, for God's sake, Chris——

CHRIS: You love me so much that you have to lie to me—you love me so much that you play small shabby little tricks on me —you twist me and torture me until I'm driven beyond endur- ance—then you sob and cry and say I'm cruel.

LEONORA [*almost screaming*]: Let me go!

CHRIS: Stay still——

LEONORA [*frantically*]: You're mad—don't look at me like that —you're mad——

CHRIS [*grimly*]: Answer me one question, my darling—my dear darling——

LEONORA: Let me go—let me go!

CHRIS: Why did you say you hadn't been out to dine with him when you had?

[59]

LEONORA: Because I knew you'd make a dreadful scene about it.

CHRIS: Why didn't you stay the night with him then—you wanted to, didn't you? What held you back? Your love for me! Or was it fear——?

LEONORA [*wrenching herself free from him*]: Oh, what's the use—what's the use——

CHRIS [*brokenly*]: Do you think I like this situation? You not loving me any more, and me wanting you so——

LEONORA [*turning*]: Why do you say that—you've worked it all up in your imagination. None of it's true—none of it's real.

CHRIS: Don't lie any more.

LEONORA: I'm not—I'm not.

CHRIS: How do I know? You've lied before—I've caught you out, trivial enough they were, I grant you, but they were lies all the same—little lies or big lies—what's the difference? Perhaps you forget that charming little episode in Cairo——

LEONORA: Oh, God!

CHRIS: All right—all right. I know I'm dragging things up from the past—why shouldn't I? After all, the past held portents enough—sign-posts pointing to the present—this present now—this dreary misery.

LEONORA [*with a great effort to be calm*]: Listen, Chris, I want to go away for a little. I must—I've told you—I really can't bear any more.

CHRIS: You can't bear any more! What about me?

LEONORA: It's not my fault that you imagine things and torture yourself.

CHRIS: Tell me one thing—without lying or evading—tell me one thing honestly——

LEONORA [*wearily*]: What is it?

CHRIS: Do you still—love me?

LEONORA: Oh, Chris! [*She turns away hopelessly.*]

CHRIS: Do you?

LEONORA [*tonelessly*]: Yes.

[60]

CHRIS: As much as you did in the beginning?

LEONORA: Differently, Chris, things have changed—a year has gone by since the beginning.

CHRIS: That's an evasion.

LEONORA: It's the truth—nothing stays the same.

CHRIS: You wanted me in the beginning, didn't you? Whenever I came near you—whenever I touched you—it was more important than anything in the world, wasn't it?

LEONORA: Yes—it was.

CHRIS: And now it isn't any more?

LEONORA: Chris—what's the use of——

CHRIS: Answer me!

LEONORA [*quivering*]: What do you want me to say—I'll answer—I'll say whatever you want.

CHRIS: I want the truth.

LEONORA: There isn't any truth anywhere—you've smashed everything into bits——

CHRIS: Do you love me as much as you did in the beginning?

LEONORA [*violently*]: No—no—no!

CHRIS: At last!

LEONORA: That's what you wanted, isn't it?—the truth—that's the truth!

CHRIS: Then you have been lying—for weeks—for months probably——

LEONORA: Yes, I have—I have.

CHRIS: When did it die, this poor shabby love of yours?

LEONORA [*wildly*]: A long while ago—you strangled it yourself with your insane jealousies and cruelties. You never trusted me —never for a minute—you've spoiled hours that could have been perfect by making scenes out of nothing. You've humiliated me and shamed me—you've dug up things that were once dear to me and made them look cheap and horrible. I can't even go back into my own memory now without finding you there jeering on every threshold—walking with me through the

[*61*]

empty rooms—making them tawdry—shutting them off from me for ever. I hate you for that bitterly.

CHRIS: Sentiment for the dead at the expense of the living—very interesting—quite magnificent!

LEONORA: The dead at least have the sense to be quiet.

CHRIS: Long live the dead!

LEONORA [*with bitterness*]: You are one of them now.

There is a dreadful silence for a moment. They stand quite still looking at each other.

CHRIS [*quietly*]: Did you mean that?

LEONORA [*hesitantly*]: Yes—I think I did.

CHRIS: Oh—please—please don't mean that!

LEONORA: Let me go away now.

CHRIS: Couldn't you wait another minute?

LEONORA: It isn't any use—you know it isn't.

CHRIS: Very well.

LEONORA: Good-bye, Chris.

CHRIS: I love you, my darling.

LEONORA: No, it's not love, it hasn't anything to do with love.

CHRIS: I know it's over now—I really do—I won't make any more scenes.

LEONORA: Good-bye.

She goes to him slowly and kisses him—he crushes her in his arms.

CHRIS [*hoarsely*]: Is it quite dead—quite dead?

LEONORA [*struggling*]: Don't, Chris—please!

CHRIS: All passion spent—everything tidied up and put back in the box.

LEONORA: Let me go.

CHRIS: The last time I shall kiss you—the last time I shall feel you in my arms—the very last time of all——

LEONORA [*trying to twist away from him*]: Chris——

CHRIS: Stay still!

LEONORA: Let me go!

CHRIS: God damn you, stay still!

He kisses her again violently and throws her away from him. She staggers and falls.

How does it feel to be so desirable—to be wanteᴅ so much—tell me, please—I want to know—I want to know what your heart's doing now, your loving female heart! How enviable to be able to walk away into the future, free of love, free of longing, a new life before you and the dead behind you—not quite the dead, though, let's say the dying—the dying aren't as sensibly quiet as the dead—they can't help crying a little—you must walk swiftly out of earshot and don't—don't, I implore you, look back, it would make too dreary a picture for your neat, sentimental memory book. There's little charm in dying—it's only clinically interesting—the process of defeat, but your viewpoint is far from clinical, my sweet—you're a sane, thrilling animal without complications, and the fact that my life has been broken on your loveliness isn't your fault. I don't believe it's even mine—it's an act of God, darling, like fire and wind and pestilence. You're in on a grand tragedy, the best tragedy of all, and the best joke, the triumphant, inevitable defeat of mind by matter! Just for a minute I'm seeing it all clearly, myself and you and the world around us—but it's only a last flare, like a Verey light shooting through the sky, it'll splutter out in a second leaving everything darker than before, for me too dark to bear. You see, I had a life to live and work to do and people to love, and now I haven't any more. They're eager to help, those people I loved and who love me. I can see them still, gentle and wise and understanding, trying to get to me, straining to clutch my hand, but it's too late—they can't reach me . . . Get up and go—it doesn't matter any more to me whether you're here or in the moon. Get up and go——

LEONORA *rises to her feet. She is trembling.* CHRIS *goes over to the window and stands there with his back to her.*

She takes her bag from the table, and goes quietly out of the room, closing the door behind her.

CHRIS *turns at the sound of the door closing and stands tense*

[63]

and quivering waiting for the front door to slam. When it does he starts to walk about the room. He goes to the table and pours out a tumbler of neat whisky. He drinks it down in one gulp and chokes a little. He pours himself another and drinks it, then he sits down for a moment, waiting for it to have some effect. Suddenly he stands up, then the tension of his muscles relaxes and with infinite weariness he goes to the window, opens it wide, climbs on to the sill and drops.

The lights fade on the scene.

SCENE VI

This scene is the continuation of Scene I.

BARBARA, TIM *and* SUSAN *are in the same places and* ERNEST *is standing by the door.*

ERNEST [*announcing*]: Mrs. Vail.

LEONORA *comes in. Her eyes are red from crying. She is obviously trying with all her will to control herself.*

BARBARA: Leonora—— [*She takes her hand.*] I'm so glad you came——

LEONORA: Is he—is he——?

BARBARA: He asked for you.

TIM [*brusquely*]: You'd better go in—at once.

BARBARA: Here, drink this—— [*She hands her her cocktail.*] It's important that you don't break down.

LEONORA: I'll be all right.

BARBARA: Please drink it.

LEONORA: Very well. [*She gulps it down.*]

BARBARA: Tim, will you please take her——

TIM: Come this way, will you?

TIM *goes to the doors on the right and holds one open for* LEONORA. *She says 'Thank you' huskily as she goes through.* TIM *follows her and returns in a moment.*

[64]

BARBARA: It wasn't so foggy.

SUSAN: What?

BARBARA: Last year, I mean, when she came for the first time —it wasn't so foggy.

SUSAN: No—I remember—it wasn't.

BARBARA *wanders about the room.*

BARBARA: I wish—I do wish this moment hadn't had to happen too.

TIM [*gently*]: Do sit down, my dear.

BARBARA: No—I'm all right—I like wandering——

TIM [*at cocktail shaker*]: Do you want some more, Susan?

SUSAN: No, thank you.

BARBARA [*with a tremulous smile*]: It's too much of a good thing—it really is—— [*She breaks off and turns her head away.*]

TIM *and* SUSAN *look at her miserably. She recovers herself quickly and comes back to the sofa again.*

I have a dreadful feeling that I'm making it all much horrider for you——

TIM: Don't be so foolish!

BARBARA: I know what I mean, though—I'm behaving well, almost consciously well; that's always much more agonising for other people.

SUSAN: No, it isn't—it's ever so much better.

BARBARA [*blowing her nose*]: I'm not at all sure. If I broke down, collapsed completely, there'd be something to do— something for us all to do—smelling salts and brandy and all that.

TIM: Burnt feathers.

BARBARA: Yes, burnt feathers. [*She gives a polite little laugh.*]

SUSAN [*looking at the door*]: I wonder——

TIM [*quickly*]: Don't wonder anything—it's better not.

BARBARA: You mustn't snap at Susan, Tim, it's beastly of you.

TIM: Sorry, Susan, I didn't mean to snap.

SUSAN [*trying to smile at him*]: I didn't even hear——

BARBARA [*suddenly*]: I wish she'd come out now—I wish to God she'd come out now.

TIM: She will—in a minute——

They wait in silence. Presently LEONORA *comes quietly back into the room. She goes to* BARBARA.

BARBARA: Is it all over? Is he——?

LEONORA: Yes.

BARBARA: Oh—oh, dear—— [*She sinks back again on to the sofa.*]

LEONORA: He didn't know me, he thought I was you, he said—'Baba—I'm not submerged any more'—and then he said 'Baba' again—and then—then he died.

LEONORA *goes out of the room very quickly as the Curtain falls.*

"RED PEPPERS"
An Interlude with Music

CHARACTERS

GEORGE PEPPER
LILY PEPPER
BERT BENTLEY
MR. EDWARDS
MABEL GRACE
ALF

The action of the play takes place on the stage, a dressing-room, and the stage again of the Palace of Varieties in one of the smaller English provincial towns.

The time is Saturday night, present day.

"RED PEPPERS"

An Interlude with Music

The interlude occurs in the Palace Theatre of Varieties in one of the smaller English provincial towns on a Saturday night.

GEORGE *and* LILY PEPPER *are a singing and dancing comedy act. They are both somewhere in the thirties. They have been married for many years and in the Profession since they were children. Their act consists of a 'Man-About Town' Dude number for which they wear smooth red wigs, tails, silk hats and canes, and a 'Sailor' number for which they wear curly red wigs, sailor clothes with exaggerated bell-bottomed trousers and carry telescopes.*

They are first discovered performing 'in one' before a back-cloth on which is painted an ordinary street scene.

"HAS ANYBODY SEEN OUR SHIP?"
(Sailor Number)

VERSE I

What shall we do with the drunken sailor?
So the saying goes.
We're not tight but we're none too bright
Great Scott! I don't suppose!
We've lost our way
And we've lost our pay,
And to make the thing complete,
We've been and gone and lost the bloomin' fleet!

[*71*]

Has anybody seen our ship?
The H.M.S. Peculiar.
We've been on shore
For a month or more,
And when we see the Captain we shall get 'what for.'
Heave ho, me hearties,
Sing Glory Halleluiah,
A lady bold as she could be
Pinched our whistles at 'The Golden Key.'
Now we're in between the devil and the deep blue sea
Has anybody seen our ship?

Ad lib. from orchestra.

GEORGE [*singing*]: La la la la—la la la la——
LILY: Here, what are you singing about?
GEORGE: What am I singing about?
LILY: Yes, what are you singing about?
GEORGE: What's the matter with my singing?
LILY: What isn't the matter with it!
GEORGE: Don't you think I could ever do anything with my voice?
LILY: Well, it might be useful in case of fire!
GEORGE: Oi! Skip it.
LILY: Who was that lady I saw you walking down the street with the other morning?
GEORGE: That wasn't a lady, that was my wife!
LILY: Keep it clean. Keep it fresh. Keep it fragrant!
GEORGE: Was that your dog I saw you with in the High Street?
LILY: Yes, that was my dog.
GEORGE: What's his name?
LILY: Fruit Salts.
GEORGE: Fruit Salts?

LILY: Yes, Fruit Salts.

GEORGE: Why?

LILY: Ask him—Eno's.

GEORGE: Keep it clean. Keep it fresh. Keep it fragrant!

BOTH: La la la la—la la la la.

GEORGE: Why did you leave school?

LILY: Appendicitis.

GEORGE: Appendicitis?

LILY: Yes, appendicitis.

GEORGE: What do you mean, appendicitis?

LILY: Couldn't spell it!

GEORGE: I heard you had adenoids.

LILY: Adenoids?

GEORGE: Yes, adenoids.

LILY: Don't speak of it.

GEORGE: Why not?

LILY: Adenoids me!

GEORGE: Oi! Skip it! Skip it!

BOTH: La la la la—la la la la.

GEORGE: I saw a very strange thing the other day.

LILY: What was it?

GEORGE: Twelve men standing under one umbrella and they didn't get wet.

LILY: How's that?

GEORGE: It wasn't raining! (Wait for it—wait for it.)

LILY: Do you know what a skeleton is?

GEORGE: Do I know what a skeleton is?

LILY: Do you know what a skeleton is?

GEORGE: Yes.

LILY: Well, what is it?

GEORGE: A lot of bones with the people scraped off!

LILY: Keep it clean. Keep it fresh. Keep it fragrant.

GEORGE: Why is twelve midnight like the roof of a house?

LILY: Why is twelve midnight like the roof of a house?

GEORGE: Yes, why is twelve midnight like the roof of a house?

LILY: S'late!

BOTH: La la la la—la la la la.

LILY: Where did you go last night?

GEORGE: The cemetery.

LILY: Anyone dead?

GEORGE: All of 'em!

LILY: Are we going fishing?

GEORGE: Yes, we're going fishing.

LILY: We're not taking the dog with us, are we?

GEORGE: Of course we're taking the dog with us.

LILY: Why?

GEORGE: He's got the worms!

REFRAIN 2

Has anybody seen our ship?
The H.M.S. Disgusting,
We've three guns aft
And another one fore
And they've promised us a funnel for the next world war.
Heave ho, me hearties,
The quarter-deck needs dusting.
We had a binge last Christmas year,
Nice plum puddings and a round of beer,
But the captain pulled his cracker and we cried 'Oh dear!
Has anybody seen our ship?'

REFRAIN 3

Has anybody seen our ship?
The H.M.S. Suggestive
She sailed away
Across the bay,
And we haven't had a smell of her since New Year's Day.
Heave ho, me hearties,
We're getting rather restive,

We pooled our money, spent the lot,
The world forgetting by the world forgot.
Now we haven't got a penny for the you know what!
Has anybody seen our ship?

VERSE 2 [if necessary]

What's to be done with the girls on shore
Who lead our Tars astray?
What's to be done with the drinks galore
That make them pass away?
We got wet ears
From our first five beers—
After that we lost control,
And now we find we're up the blinking pole!

Their exit consists of a neat walk off together, one behind the other, with their telescopes under their arms. Unfortunately, in course of this snappy finale, LILY, *who is behind* GEORGE, *drops her telescope and hurriedly retrieves it thereby ruining the whole effect.* GEORGE *shoots her a look of fury and mutters something to her out of the corner of his mouth. The curtain falls and they take a call before it breathless and smiling, but with a certain quality of foreboding behind their smiles.*

The curtain rises on the interior of their dressing-room. It is a fairly squalid room, for although they are comparatively well-known in the provinces, they have never, to date, achieved the dignity of the star dressing-room or the pride of topping the bill. The room is three sides of a square. There is a wooden shelf all the way round with, above it, mirrors and lights at set intervals.

Down-stage on the right there is a door leading to the passage. Down-stage on the left there is a lavatory basin with a screen round it. In the centre is a wooden hanging arrangement for clothes.

[75]

GEORGE's *dressing place is on the right and* LILY's *is on the left. As the curtain rises on the scene they both enter in silence but wearing expressions of set rage. They are still breathless and extremely hot.* GEORGE *goes to his dressing place and* LILY *goes to hers. They both take off their wigs and fling them down, then, still in silence, they proceed to rip off their sailor clothes. These are made with zippers in order to facilitate their quick change.* LILY *is wearing a brassière and silk knickers, and* GEORGE *a vest and drawers. They both have black shoes with taps on them and black socks and sock suspenders.*

GEORGE: Now then.

LILY: Now then what?

GEORGE [*contemptuously*]: Now then what!

LILY: I don't know what you're talking about.

GEORGE: Oh, you don't, don't you?

LILY: No I don't, so shut up.

GEORGE: I suppose you don't know you mucked up the whole exit!

LILY: It wasn't my fault.

GEORGE: Whose fault was it then, Mussolini's?

LILY [*with sarcasm*]: Funny, hey?

GEORGE [*witheringly*]: I suppose you didn't drop your prop, did you? And having dropped it, you didn't have to go back for it, leaving me to prance off all by meself—who d'you think you are, Rebla?

LILY: The exit was too quick.

GEORGE: It was the same as it's always been.

LILY: It was too quick, I tell you, it's been too quick the whole week, the whole number's too quick——

GEORGE: Bert Bentley takes that number at the same tempo as he's always done.

LILY: You and your Bert Bentley, just because he stands you a Welsh rarebit at the Queen's you think he's God Almighty.

GEORGE: Bert Bentley's the best conductor in the North of England and don't you make any mistake about it.

LILY: Best conductor my foot! I suppose he thinks it's funny to see us leaping up and down the stage like a couple of grey-hounds.

GEORGE: If you're a greyhound I'm Fred Astaire.

LILY: Oh, you're Fred Astaire all right, with a bit of Pavlova thrown in—you're wonderful, you are—there's nothing you can't do, except behave like a gentleman.

GEORGE: Oh, so you expect me to behave like a gentleman, do you? That's a good one, coming from you.

LILY: Oh, shut up, you make me tired.

GEORGE: I make *you* tired! I suppose it was me that mucked up the exit—I suppose it was me that dropped me bloody tele-scope!

LILY [*heated*]: Now look here, George Pepper——

GEORGE: Stop George Peppering me—why can't you admit it when you're in the wrong?—You mucked up the exit—nobody else did—you did!

LILY: Well, what if I did? It was an accident, wasn't it? I didn't do it on purpose.

GEORGE: It doesn't matter how you did it or why you did it, you did it.

LILY [*screaming*]: All right, I did it!

GEORGE [*triumphantly*]: Well, don't do it again.

There is a knock on the door.

LILY: Who is it?

ALF [*outside*]: Me, Alf.

LILY: All right, come in.

ALF, *the callboy, enters. He is laden with the* PEPPERS' *dis-carded evening suits, silk hats and canes. He plumps them down.*

ALF: There!

GEORGE: Thanks. [*He gets some money out of his coat pocket.*]

Here, tell Fred to pop out and get me twenty Players' and a large Guinness.

LILY: Why can't you wait and have it with your steak?

GEORGE: You mind yours and I'll mind mine.

ALF: You'll have to wait until Mabel Grace is finished.

LILY: She's been finished for years as far as I'm concerned.

GEORGE: What's the matter with Mabel Grace?

LILY: Ask the public, dear, just ask the public.

ALF [*about to leave*]: Same as usual, I suppose, between the houses?

GEORGE: Yes, and tell 'em not to forget the salt, like they did last night.

ALF: Righto.

ALF *goes out.*

LILY *starts to pack various things into a large hamper which has emblazoned on it in large black letters: "The Red Peppers."*

GEORGE: What did you want to say that about Mabel Grace for in front of him?

LILY [*grandly*]: It happens to be my opinion.

GEORGE: Well, in future you'd better keep your opinions to yourself in front of strangers.

LILY [*mumbling*]: If you're so fond of Mabel Grace I wonder you don't go and ask her for her autograph—she'd drop dead if you did—I bet nobody's asked her for one since Trelawney of the Wells.

GEORGE: Mabel Grace is an artist and don't you forget it—she may be a bit long in the tooth now but she's a bigger star than you'll ever be, so there!

LILY: You make me sick, sucking up to the topliners.

GEORGE: Who sucks up to the topliners?

LILY: You do—look at Irene Baker!

GEORGE: What's the matter with Irene Baker?

LILY: When last heard from she was falling down drunk at the Empire, Hartlepool.

GEORGE: That's a dirty lie, Irene never touches a drop till after the show and well you know it.

LILY [*contemptuously*]: Irene! It was Miss Baker this and Miss Baker that, the last time you saw her.

GEORGE: That's all you know.

LILY: Trying to make me think you got off with her, eh? What a chance!

GEORGE: Oh, shut up nagging!

LILY [*muttering*]: Irene——!

GEORGE: If a day ever dawns when you can time your laughs like Irene Baker does, I'll give you a nice red apple!

LILY: Time my laughs! That's funny. Fat lot of laughs I get when you write the gags.

GEORGE [*grandly*]: If you're dissatisfied with your material you know what you can do with it.

LILY: I know what I'd like to do with it.

GEORGE: You can't even do a straight walk off without balling it up.

LILY: Oh, we're back at that again, are we?

GEORGE: Yes we are, so there!

LILY [*coming over to him*]: Now look here, just you listen to me for a minute. . . .

GEORGE: I've been listening to you for fifteen years, one more minute won't hurt.

LILY: I've had about enough of this. I'm sick of you and the whole act. It's lousy, anyway.

GEORGE: The act was good enough for my Mum and Dad and it's good enough for you.

LILY [*with heavy sarcasm*]: Times have changed a bit since your Mum and Dad's day, you know. There's electric light now and telephones and a little invention called Moving Pictures. Nobody wants to see the "Red Peppers" for three bob when they can see Garbo for ninepence!

GEORGE: That's just where you're wrong, see! We're flesh and blood we are—the public would rather see flesh and blood any day than a cheesy photograph. Put Garbo on on a Saturday night in Devonport, and see what would happen to her!

LILY: Yes, look what happened to us!

GEORGE: That wasn't Devonport, it was Southsea.

LILY: Well, wherever it was, the Fleet was in.

GEORGE: If you think the act's so lousy it's a pity you don't rewrite some of it.

LILY: Ever tried going into St. Paul's and offering to rewrite the Bible?

GEORGE: Very funny! Oh, very funny indeed! You're wasted in the Show Business, you ought to write for *Comic Cuts* you ought.

LILY: At that I could think up better gags than you do—"That wasn't a lady, that was my wife!"—"D'you mind if I smoke?" "I don't care if you burn!"—hoary old chestnuts—they were has-beens when your grandmother fell off the high wire.

GEORGE: What's my grandmother got to do with it?

LILY: She didn't fall soon enough, that's all.

GEORGE [*furiously*]: You shut your mouth and stop hurling insults at my family. What were you when I married you, I should like to know! One of the six Moonlight Maids—dainty songs and dances, and no bookings!

LILY [*hotly*]: When we did get bookings we got number one towns which is more than your Mum and Dad ever did!

GEORGE: Who wants the number one towns, anyway? You can't get a public all the year round like my Mum and Dad by doing a parasol dance twice a year at the Hippodrome Manchester!

LILY: The Moonlight Maids was just as good an act as the "Red Peppers" any day, and a bloody sight more refined at that!

GEORGE: You've said it. That's just what it was—refined. It was so refined it simpered itself out of the bill——

LILY: A bit of refinement wouldn't do you any harm——

GEORGE: Perhaps you'd like to change the act to "Musical

Moments" with me playing a flute and you sitting under a standard lamp with a 'cello?

There is a knock at the door.

LILY: Who is it?

BERT [*outside*]: Me—Bert Bentley.

GEORGE: Come in, old man.

LILY [*under her breath*]: Old man——

BERT BENTLEY *enters. He is the musical director, a flashy little man wearing a tail suit and a white waistcoat that is none too clean.*

BERT [*cheerfully*]: Well, well, well, how's tricks?

GEORGE: Mustn't grumble.

BERT: Anybody got a Gold Flake?

GEORGE: Here's a Player's, that do?

BERT [*taking one*]: It's your last?

GEORGE: I've sent Fred out for some more.

BERT: Okay—thanks.

GEORGE: Sketch on?

BERT: Yes, the old cow's tearing herself to shreds.

GEORGE: It's a pretty strong situation she's got in that sketch —I watched it from the side first house on Wednesday——

BERT: She nearly got the bird second house.

LILY: Too refined, I expect. For this date.

BERT: Well, they're liable to get a bit restless, you know, when she stabs herself—she takes such a hell of a time about it— that's legits all over—we had Robert Haversham here a couple of months ago—what a make-up—stuck together with stamp paper he was—Robert Haversham the famous tragedian and company! You should have seen the company: a couple of old tats got up as Elizabethan pages with him doing a death scene in the middle of them—he died all right.

GEORGE: Did he buy it?

BERT: He bought it—three and eightpence in coppers and a bottle of Kola.

LILY: Poor old man, what a shame!

[*81*]

BERT: Well, what did he want to do it for? That sort of stuff's no good. They're all alike—a few seasons in the West End and they think they're set.

LILY: Lot of hooligans birding the poor old man.

BERT [*with slight asperity*]: This is as good a date as you can get, you know!

LILY: I've played better.

GEORGE: Oh, dry up, Lil, for heaven's sake! [*To* BERT.] Sorry I can't offer you a drink, old man, Fred hasn't brought it yet.

BERT: That's all right, George—I'll have one with you in between the houses. By the way, don't you think that exit of yours is dragging a bit?

LILY [*explosively*]: Dragging?

GEORGE: Lil thinks it was a bit too quick.

BERT: Whatever you say, it's all the same to me.

GEORGE: Maybe you could pep it up a little.

LILY: Maybe it would be better if we did the whole act on skates!

GEORGE [*conciliatorily*]: Bert's quite right, you know, Lil.

LILY: I don't know any such thing.

BERT: All right, all right, all right—there's no need to get nasty.

GEORGE: Oh, don't take any notice of her, she don't know what she's talking about.

LILY [*with overpowering sweetness*]: My husband's quite right, Mr. Bentley, my husband is always quite right. You don't have to pay any attention to me, I don't count—I'm only a feed.

GEORGE: Oh, dry up.

LILY [*continuing*]: But I should just like to say one thing, Mr. Bentley, if you'll forgive me for stepping out of my place for a minute, and that is, that if you take that exit any quicker at the second house, I shall not drop my telescope—— Oh no—I shall sock you in the chops with it!

BERT: Who the hell d'you think you are, talking to me like that!

GEORGE: You ought to be ashamed of yourself!

LILY: You and your orchestra—orchestra! More like a hurdy-gurdy and flat at that!

BERT: What's wrong with my orchestra?

LILY: Nothing, apart from the instruments and the men what play 'em.

BERT: My orchestra's played for the best artists in the business——

LILY: Yes, but not until they were too old to care.

BERT: I didn't come up here to be insulted by a cheap little comedy act.

GEORGE [*incensed*]: What's that! What's that? What's that?

BERT: You heard. You're damned lucky to get this date at all!

GEORGE: Lucky! My God, it's a fill-in—that's all—a fill-in!

BERT: I suppose Nervo and Knox use it as a fill-in, and Lily Morris and Flanagan and Allen?

LILY: They probably have friends living near.

BERT [*making a movement to go*]: Before you start saucing me just take a look at your place on the bill—that's all—just take a look at it.

GEORGE: We're in the second half, anyway.

BERT: Only because the acrobats can't make their change.

LILY: It's in our contract—after the interval's in our contract.

BERT: Well, make the most of it while you've got it.

GEORGE: Get the hell out of here, you twopenny-halfpenny little squirt—lucky for you we've got another show to play.

BERT: Not so damned lucky—I've got to look at it.

LILY: Well, it'll be the first time—maybe we'll get the tempos right for a change!

BERT: You set your tempos Monday morning and they haven't been changed since.

LILY: That's your story, but don't forget you were sober on Monday morning.

BERT: Are you insinuating that I drink during the show?

LILY: Insinuating! That's a laugh. I'm not insinuating, I'm stating a fact. I can smell it a mile off.

BERT: What a lady! And what an artist, too—I don't suppose!

GEORGE: Don't you talk in that tone to my wife.

LILY: Send for the manager, George. Send for Mr. Edwards.

BERT: I'm the one that's going to send for Mr. Edwards——

GEORGE: Get out of here before I crack you one——

ALF *knocks at the door.*

LILY: Come in.

ALF *pushes open the door with his foot and comes in carrying a tray on which are two plates of steak and chips with other plates over them to keep them hot, a bottle of A.1. sauce and three bottles of Guinness.*

ALF: You're wanted, Mr. Bentley, the sketch is nearly over.

BERT [*grimly to the* PEPPERS]: I'll be seeing you later.

He goes out, slamming the door after him.

GEORGE [*after him*]: Lousy son of a——Lounge Lizard.

LILY [*to* ALF]: Here, put it down on the hamper.

ALF [*doing so*]: I've got the Player's in me pocket.

LILY [*feeling for them*]: All right.

GEORGE: Come back later for the tray.

ALF: Righto.

He goes out.

GEORGE: Mr. Edwards—I'll have something to say to Mr. Edwards.

LILY: Lucky to play this date, are we? We'll see about that.

GEORGE: You were right, old girl.

LILY: What about—him?

GEORGE: Yes—dirty little rat.

LILY [*dragging up two chairs to the hamper*]: Well, we all make mistakes sometimes—open the Guinness, there's a dear——

GEORGE: He's a little man, that's his trouble, never trust a man with short legs—brains too near their bottoms.

LILY: Come and sit down.

GEORGE [*opening a bottle of Guinness*]: 'Alf a mo'——

LILY: That exit was too quick, you know!

GEORGE: All right—all right——

They both sit down and begin to eat.

They've forgotten the salt again——

LILY: No, here it is in a bit of paper——

GEORGE: Well, thank God for that anyway——

The lights fade on the scene.

When the lights come up on the scene, GEORGE *and* LILY *are sitting at the dressing places freshening their make-ups. They both have a glass of Guinness within reach, and they are both wearing the rather frowsy dressing-gowns that they had put on during the preceding scene. The tray, with the remains of their dinner on it, is on the floor beside the hamper.*

GEORGE *gets up, opens the door and listens.*

LILY: What's on?

GEORGE: The Five Farthings.

LILY: That's the end of the first half—we'd better get a move on——

GEORGE [*returning to his place*]: Fancy putting an act like that on at the end of the first half—you'd think they'd know better, wouldn't you?

LILY: I wouldn't think they'd know better about anything in this hole.

GEORGE: It's a badly run house and it always has been.

He proceeds to put on his dress shirt, collar and tie, which are all in one with a zipper up the back. LILY *is doing the same on her side of the room. They stuff wads of Kleenex paper in between their collars and their necks to prevent the make-up soiling their ties.*

There is a knock at the door.

LILY: Who is it?

MR. EDWARDS [*outside*]: Mr. Edwards.

LILY [*pulling on her trousers*]: Just a minute——

[85]

GEORGE [*under his breath*]: Go easy—Bert Bentley's been at him.

LILY: I'll have something to say about that.

GEORGE: You leave it to me—I'll do the talking.

LILY: That'll be nice—— Come in!

MR. EDWARDS *enters. He is the house manager and very resplendent. He is smoking a large cigar.*

GEORGE [*rising and offering him a chair*]: Good evening, Mr. Edwards.

MR. EDWARDS [*disdaining it*]: Good evening.

LILY [*amiably*]: How's the house?

MR. EDWARDS: Same as usual—full.

GEORGE: That's fine, isn't it?

MR. EDWARDS [*grimly*]: I watched your act to-night, first house.

GEORGE [*gaily*]: There you are, Lil, what did I tell you—I had a sort of hunch you was out there—I said to my wife—what's the betting Mr. Edwards is out front?—you know—you have a sort of feeling——

LILY: Went well, didn't it?

MR. EDWARDS: I've seen things go better.

GEORGE: We follow Betley Delavine, you know—a ballad singer—they always take a bit of warming up after a ballad singer.

LILY: I'd defy Billy Bennett to get away with it in our place on the bill—I'd defy him—see?

MR. EDWARDS: There isn't anything wrong with your place on the bill.

GEORGE: Well, I'd be willing to make a little bet with you—put the Five Farthings on before us and change Betley Delavine to the end of the first half and see what happens!

LILY: You'd send them out to the bars and they'd stay there.

MR. EDWARDS: I did not come here to discuss the running of my theatre.

GEORGE: Oh—sorry, I'm sure.

MR. EDWARDS: That exit of yours killed the whole act.

GEORGE: A little mishap that's all—anybody might drop a telescope——

LILY: Even a sailor.

MR. EDWARDS: It looked terrible.

GEORGE: The tempo was all wrong, Mr. Edwards.

MR. EDWARDS: Sounded all right to me.

GEORGE: Maybe it did, but we know our own numbers, you know.

MR. EDWARDS: It didn't look like it from the front.

GEORGE: We've never had any trouble before—that exit's stopped the show in every town we've played.

LILY: A musical director can make or mar an act, you know—make or mar it.

MR. EDWARDS: Mr. Bentley is one of the finest musical directors in the business.

LILY: Then he's wasted here, that's all I can say.

GEORGE [warningly]: Lily!

LILY: Well, if he's so wonderful, why isn't he at the Albert Hall—doing *Hiawatha*——

MR. EDWARDS: I understand you had words with Mr. Bentley.

GEORGE: We did, and we will again if he starts any of his funny business.

MR. EDWARDS: I understand that you accused him of drinking during the show.

LILY: Getting quite bright, aren't you?

GEORGE: Shut up, Lil, leave this to me.

MR. EDWARDS: Did you or did you not?

GEORGE: Look here, who d'you think you are—coming talking to us like this?

MR. EDWARDS: Did you or did you not accuse Mr. Bentley of drinking during the show?

LILY [heatedly]: Yes, we did, because he does, so there!

MR. EDWARDS: That's serious, you know—it's slander!

LILY: I don't care if it's arson, it's true!

MR. EDWARDS: Now look here, Mrs. Pepper, I think it only fair to warn you——

LILY: And I think it's only fair to warn you that unless you get a better staff in this theatre and a better orchestra and a better musical director, you'll find yourself a cinema inside six months!

MR. EDWARDS: You won't gain anything by losing your temper.

GEORGE: And you won't gain anything by coming round backstage and throwing your weight about—your place is in the front of the house—my theatre this and my theatre that—it's no more your theatre than what it is ours—you're on a salary same as us, and I'll bet it's a damn sight less, too, and don't you forget it——

MR. EDWARDS [*losing his temper*]: I'm not going to stand any more of this——

LILY: Oh, go and play with yourself and shut up——

MR. EDWARDS: I'll guarantee one thing, anyhow, you'll never play this date again as long as I'm in charge——

GEORGE: In charge of what, the Fire Brigade!

LILY: Play this date—anybody'd think it was the Palladium to hear you talk——

GEORGE: You'd better be careful, Mr. Edwards—you don't want a scandal like this to get around the profession——

MR. EDWARDS: What are you talking about?

GEORGE: I'm talking about the way this house is run.

MR. EDWARDS [*working up*]: You mind your own business.

LILY: More than one act's been mucked up here, you know, by that orchestra of yours—it's beginning to get a name——

MR. EDWARDS: Oh, it is, is it?

GEORGE: They're all over the shop—no discipline.

LILY: What can you expect with a drunk in charge of it!

MR. EDWARDS [*raising his voice*]: Look here—you stop talking like that or it'll be the worse for you.

GEORGE: His tempos are wrong and he hasn't got any authority over his men——

LILY: This date's only a fill-in for us, you know——

GEORGE: You ask our agents.

MR. EDWARDS: I shall report this conversation.

LILY: Do—report it to the Lord Mayor—if you're sober enough to remember the lyrics.

GEORGE: Shut up, Lil.

MR. EDWARDS: I will not stay here and argue——

GEORGE: You're dead right, you won't——

MR. EDWARDS: You were a flop last time you played here and you've been a flop this time and that's enough for me——

LILY [*screaming*]: Flop! What d'you mean flop! We're a bigger draw than anybody on the bill——

There is a knock on the door.

GEORGE [*loudly*]: Come in——

MISS MABEL GRACE *enters. She is a faded ex-West End actress wearing a towel round her head to keep her hair in place, and an elaborate dressing-gown.*

MABEL GRACE [*acidly*]: Good evening—I'm sorry to intrude—but you're making such a dreadful noise I'm quite unable to rest——

MR. EDWARDS: I'm very sorry, Miss Grace——

MABEL GRACE: I find it hard enough to play a big emotional scene twice a night in any case——

LILY: Oh, that's an emotional scene, is it? I wondered what it was——

MABEL GRACE: I am not accustomed to being spoken to in that tone, Mrs. Whatever your name is——

LILY: Pepper's the name—Pepper—PEPPER—same as what you put in your soup.

MABEL GRACE [*coldly*]: Very interesting.

MR. EDWARDS: I apologise, Miss Grace.

MABEL GRACE [*grandly*]: Thank you, Mr. Edwards.

GEORGE [*in an affected voice*]: What you must think of us, Miss Grace—so common—we're mortified, we are really—and you fresh from His Majesty's.

LILY: Fairly fresh.

MABEL GRACE: Mr. Edwards, I'm really not used to dressing-room brawls—I'll leave it to you to see that there is no further noise——

LILY: Except for the raspberries at the end of your sketch—even Mr. God Almighty Edwards can't control those——

MABEL GRACE: You're almost as vulgar off the stage as you are on, I congratulate you.

LILY [*very loudly*]: Vulgar, are we! I'd like to ask you something. If you're so bloody West End why the hell did you leave it?

GEORGE: There'll be an answer to that in next Sunday's edition.

LILY: Thank you, George.

MR. EDWARDS: Look here, you two, I've had about enough of this——

GEORGE: You've had about enough, have you? What about us? *The conversation becomes simultaneous.*

LILY: You and your cigar and your shirt-front and your Woolworth studs! Alfred Butt with knobs on——

GEORGE: You get out of here, you fat fool, before I throw you out!——

MABEL GRACE: Thank you for your courtesy, Mr. Edwards——

MR. EDWARDS: I'll see you don't play this date any more or any other date either——

GEORGE: Oh, put it where the monkey put the nuts——

LILY: —Play this date again—thank you for the rabbit—I'd sooner play Ryde Pier in November——

In the middle of the pandemonium ALF *puts his head round the door.*

ALF [*yelling*]: Red Peppers—three minutes——

GEORGE: Good God! We're off——

LILY [*wildly*]: Get out, all of you—get out——

GEORGE *takes* MR. EDWARDS *by the shoulders, and shoves him out of the room.* MABEL GRACE, *laughing affectedly, follows him.* LILY *and* GEORGE *put on their wigs, powder their make-ups.*

*tweak their ties into place, grab their hats and canes—then,
muttering curses under their breaths, they collect their sailor
clothes and sailor wigs and telescopes and rush out of the room
as the lights fade.*

*The lights come up on the curtain as the orchestra is playing
their introduction music. The curtain rises on the street scene
again. They make their entrance for the "dude" number, "Men
About Town."*

ROUTINE

"MEN ABOUT TOWN" (Dude Number)

VERSE

We're two chaps who
Find it thrilling
To do the killing
We're always willing
To give the girls a treat.
Just a drink at the Ritz
Call it double or quits
Then we feel the world is at our feet.
Top hats white spats
Look divine on us,
There's a shine on us
Get a line on us
When we come your way.
Gad! Eleven o'clock!
Let's pop into the Troc:
Ere we start the business of the day.

REFRAIN I

As we stroll down Picc—Piccadilly
In the bright morning air,

[91]

All the girls turn and stare
We're so nonchalant and frightfully debonair.
When we chat to Rose, Maud or Lily
You should see the way their boy friends frown,
For they know without a doubt
That their luck's right out,
Up against a couple of men about town.

As we stroll down Picc—Piccadilly
All the girls say "Who's here?
Put your hat straight, my dear,
For it's Marmaduke and Percy Vere de Vere."
As we doff hats, each pretty filly
Gives a wink at us and then looks down
For they long with all their might
For a red-hot night
When they see a couple of men about town.

They proceed to execute a complicated tap dance, during which BERT BENTLEY *vengefully takes the music faster and faster. They try vainly to keep up with it, finally* GEORGE *slips and falls, whereupon* LILY *loses her temper and flings her hat at* BERT BENTLEY.

LILY [*screaming*]: You great drunken fool!

THE CURTAIN FALLS AMID DISCORD.

TONIGHT AT 8.30
II

HANDS ACROSS THE SEA
A Light Comedy in One Scene

CHARACTERS

LADY MAUREEN GILPIN (Piggie)
COMMANDER PETER GILPIN, R.N., her husband
THE HON. CLARE WEDDERBURN
LIEUT. COMMANDER ALASTAIR CORBETT, R.N.
MAJOR GOSLING (Bogey)
MR. WADHURST
MRS. WADHURST
MR. BURNHAM
WALTERS

*The action of the play takes place in the drawing-room
of the Gilpins' flat in London.*
Time: Present Day.

The Scene is the drawing-room of the GILPINS' *flat in London.
The room is nicely furnished and rather untidy. There is a
portable gramophone on one small table and a tray of cocktail
things on another; apart from these, the furnishings can be
left to the discretion of the producer.*
When the Curtain rises the telephone is ringing. WALTERS, *a
neat parlourmaid, enters and answers it. The time is about
six p.m.*

WALTERS [*at telephone*]: Hallo—yes—no, her ladyship's not back yet—she said she'd be in at five, so she ought to be here at any minute now—what name, please?—Rawlingson—Mr. and Mrs. Rawlingson—— [*She scribbles on the pad.*] Yes—I'll tell her——

She hangs up the receiver and goes out. There is the sound of voices in the hall and LADY MAUREEN GILPIN *enters, followed at a more leisurely pace by her husband,* PETER GILPIN. MAUREEN, *nicknamed* PIGGIE *by her intimates, is a smart, attractive woman in the thirties.* PETER *is tall and sunburned and reeks of the Navy.*

PIGGIE [*as she comes in*]: —and you can send the car back for me at eleven-thirty—it's quite simple, darling, I wish you wouldn't be so awfully complicated about everything——

PETER: What happens if my damned dinner goes on longer than that and I get stuck?

PIGGIE: You just get stuck, darling, and then you get unstuck and get a taxi——

PETER [*grumbling*]: I shall be in uniform, clinking with medals——

PIGGIE: If you take my advice you'll faint dead away at eleven o'clock and then you can come home in the car and change and have time for everything——

PETER: I can't faint dead away under the nose of the C.-in-C.

PIGGIE: You can feel a little poorly, can't you—anybody has the right to feel a little poorly—— [*She sees the telephone pad.*] My God!

PETER: What is it?

PIGGIE: The Rawlingsons.

PETER: Who the hell are they?

PIGGIE: I'd forgotten all about them—I must get Maud at once—— [*She sits at the telephone and dials a number.*]

PETER: Who are the Rawlingsons?

PIGGIE: Maud and I stayed with them in Samolo, I told you about it, that time when we had to make a forced landing—they practically saved our lives—— [*At telephone.*] Hullo—Maud—darling, the Rawlingsons are on us—what—the RAW-LINGSONS—yes—I asked them to-day and forgot all about it—you must come at once—but, darling, you *must*—Oh, dear—no, no, that was the Frobishers, these are the ones we stayed with—mother and father and daughter—you must remember—pretty girl with bad legs—— No—they didn't have a son—we swore we'd give them a lovely time when they came home on leave—I know they didn't have a son, that was those other people in Penang—— Oh, all right—you'll have to do something about them, though—let me ask them to lunch with you to-morrow—all right—one-thirty—I'll tell them—— [*She hangs up.*]—she can't come——

PETER: You might have warned me that a lot of Colonial strangers were coming trumpeting into the house——

PIGGIE: I tell you I'd forgotten——

PETER: That world trip was a grave mistake——

PIGGIE: Who can I get that's celebrated—to give them a thrill?

PETER: Why do they have to have a thrill?

PIGGIE: I'll get Clare, anyway—— [*She dials another number.*]

PETER: She'll frighten them to death.

PIGGIE: Couldn't you change early and come in your uniform? That would be better than nothing——

PETER: Perhaps they'd like to watch me having my bath!

PIGGIE [*at telephone*]: I want to speak to Mrs. Wedderburn, please—yes—— [*To* PETER.] I do wish you'd be a little help-ful—— [*At telephone.*] Clare?—this is Piggie—I want you to come round at once and help me with the Rawlingsons—no, I know you haven't, but that doesn't matter—— Mother, father and daughter—very sweet—they were divine to us in the East—

I'm repaying hospitality—Maud's having them to lunch to-morrow and Peter's going to take them round the dockyard——

PETER: I'm not going to do any such thing——

PIGGIE: Shut up, I just thought of that and it's a *very* good idea—— [*At telephone.*] All right, darling—as soon as you can—— [*She hangs up*]—I must go and change——

PETER: You know perfectly well I haven't time to take mothers and fathers and daughters with bad legs round the dockyard——

PIGGIE: It wouldn't take a minute, they took us all over their rubber plantation.

PETER: It probably served you right.

PIGGIE: You're so disobliging, darling, you really should try to conquer it—it's something to do with being English, I think —as a race I'm ashamed of us—no sense of hospitality—the least we can do when people are kind to us in far-off places is to be a little gracious in return.

PETER: They weren't kind to me in far-off places.

PIGGIE: You know there's a certain grudging, sullen streak in your character—I've been very worried about it lately—it's spreading like a forest fire——

PETER: Why don't you have them down for the week-end?

PIGGIE: Don't be so idiotic, how can I possibly? There's no room to start with and even if there were they'd be utterly wretched——

PETER: I don't see why.

PIGGIE: They wouldn't know anybody—they probably wouldn't have the right clothes—they'd keep on huddling about in uneasy little groups——

PETER: The amount of uneasy little groups that three people can huddle about in is negligible.

ALASTAIR CORBETT *saunters into the room. He is good-looking and also distinctly Naval in tone.*

ALLY: Hallo, chaps.

PIGGIE: Ally, darling—how lovely—we're in trouble—Peter'll tell you all about it——

[*101*]

The telephone rings and she goes to it. The following conversations occur simultaneously.

ALLY: What trouble?

PETER: More of Piggie's beach friends.

ALLY: Let's have a drink.

PETER: Cocktail?

ALLY: No, a long one, whisky and soda.

PETER [*going to drink table*]: All right.

ALLY: What beach friends?

PETER: People Maud and Piggie picked up in the East.

PIGGIE [*at 'phone*]: Hullo!—Yes—Robert, dear—how lovely! [*To others.*] It's Robert.

ALLY: Piggie ought to stay at home more.

PIGGIE [*on 'phone*]: Where are you?

PETER: That's what I say!

PIGGIE [*on 'phone*]: Oh, what a shame!—No—Peter's going to sea on Thursday—I'm going down on Saturday.

ALLY: Rubber, I expect—everybody in the East's rubber.

PIGGIE [*on 'phone*]: No—nobody particular—just Clare and Bogey and I think Pops; but he thinks he's got an ulcer or something and might not be able to come.

PETER: We thought you might be a real friend and take them over the dockyard.

ALLY: What on earth for?

PETER: Give them a thrill.

PIGGIE [*on 'phone*]: All right—I'll expect you—no, I don't think it can be a very big one—he looks as bright as a button.

ALLY: Why don't you take them over the dockyard?

PETER: I shall be at sea, Thursday onwards—exercises!

PIGGIE [*on 'phone*]: No, darling, what is the use of having her—she only depresses you—oh—all right! [*Hangs up.*] Oh, dear——

PETER: It's quite easy for you—you can give them lunch on board.

ALLY: We're in dry dock.

PETER: They won't mind. [*To* PIGGIE.] What is it?

PIGGIE: Robert—plunged in gloom—he's got to do a course at Greenwich—he ran into a tram in Devonport—and he's had a row with Molly—he wants me to have her for the week-end so that they can make it up all over everybody. Have you told Ally about the Rawlingsons?

PETER: Yes, he's taking them over the dockyard, lunching them on board and then he's going to show them a submarine——

PIGGIE: Marvellous! You're an angel, Ally—I must take off these clothes, I'm going mad——

She goes out of the room at a run.

There is the sound of the front-door bell.

PETER: Let's go into my room—I can show you the plans——

ALLY: Already? They've been pretty quick with them.

PETER: I made a few alterations—there wasn't enough deck space—she ought to be ready by October, I shall have her sent straight out to Malta——

ALLY: Come on, we shall be caught——

They go off on the left as WALTERS *ushers in* MR. *and* MRS. WADHURST *on the right.*

The WADHURSTS *are pleasant, middle-aged people, their manner is a trifle timorous.*

WALTERS: Her ladyship is changing, I'll tell her you are here.

MRS. WADHURST: Thank you.

MR. WADHURST: Thank you very much.

WALTERS *goes out.*

The WADHURSTS *look round the room.*

MRS. WADHURST: It's a very nice flat.

MR. WADHURST: Yes—yes, it is.

MRS. WADHURST [*scrutinising a photograph*]: That must be him.

MR. WADHURST: Who?

MRS. WADHURST: The Commander.

MR. WADHURST: Yes—I expect it is.

MRS. WADHURST: Sailors always have such nice open faces, don't they?

MR. WADHURST: Yes, I suppose so.

MRS. WADHURST: Clean-cut and look you straight in the eye— I like men who look you straight in the eye.

MR. WADHURST: Yes, it's very nice.

MRS. WADHURST [*at another photograph*]: This must be her sister—I recognise her from the *Tatler*—look—she was Lady Hurstley, you know, then she was Lady Macfadden and I don't know who she is now.

MR. WADHURST: Neither do I.

MRS. WADHURST: What a dear little boy—such a sturdy little fellow—look at the way he's holding his engine.

MR. WADHURST: Is that his engine?

MRS. WADHURST: He has rather a look of Donald Hotchkiss, don't you think?

MR. WADHURST: Yes, dear.

MRS. WADHURST: I must say they have very nice things—oh, dear, how lovely to be well off—I must write to the Brostows by the next mail and tell them all about it.

MR. WADHURST: Yes, you must.

MRS. WADHURST: Don't you think we'd better sit down?

MR. WADHURST: Why not?

MRS. WADHURST: You sit in that chair and I'll sit on the sofa. *She sits on the sofa. He sits on the chair.*

MR. WADHURST: Yes, dear.

MRS. WADHURST: I wish you wouldn't look quite so uncomfortable, Fred, there's nothing to be uncomfortable about.

MR. WADHURST: She does expect us, doesn't she?

MRS. WADHURST: Of course, I talked to her myself on the telephone last Wednesday, she was perfectly charming and said that we were to come without fail and that it would be divine.

MR. WADHURST: I still feel we should have telephoned again just to remind her. People are always awfully busy in London.

MRS. WADHURST: I do hope Lady Dalborough will be here, too—I should like to see her again—she was so nice.

MR. WADHURST: She was the other one, wasn't she?

MRS. WADHURST [*irritably*]: What do you mean, the other one?

MR. WADHURST: I mean not this one.

MRS. WADHURST: She's the niece of the Duke of Frensham, her mother was Lady Merrit, she was a great traveller too—I believe she went right across the Sahara dressed as an Arab. In those days that was a very dangerous thing to do.

MR. WADHURST: I shouldn't think it was any too safe now.

WALTERS *enters and ushers in* MR. BURNHAM, *a nondescript young man carrying a longish roll of cardboard.*

WALTERS: I'll tell the Commander you're here.

MR. BURNHAM: Thanks—thanks very much.

WALTERS *goes out.*

MRS. WADHURST [*after a slightly awkward silence*]: How do you do?

MR. BURNHAM: How do you do?

MRS. WADHURST [*with poise*]: This is my husband.

MR. BURNHAM: How do you do?

MR. WADHURST: How do you do?

They shake hands.

MRS. WADHURST [*vivaciously*]: Isn't this a charming room—so—so lived in.

MR. BURNHAM: Yes.

MR. WADHURST: Are you in the Navy, too?

MR. BURNHAM: No.

MRS. WADHURST [*persevering*]: It's so nice to be home again—we come from Malaya, you know.

MR. BURNHAM: Oh—Malaya.

MRS. WADHURST: Yes, Lady Maureen and Lady Dalborough visited us there—my husband has a rubber plantation up-country—there's been a terrible slump, of course, but we're trying to keep our heads above water—aren't we, Fred?

MR. WADHURST: Yes, dear, we certainly are.

MRS. WADHURST: Have you ever been to the East?

MR. BURNHAM: No.

MRS. WADHURST: It's very interesting really, although the climate's rather trying until you get used to it, and of course the one thing we do miss is the theatre——

MR. BURNHAM: Yes—of course.

MRS. WADHURST: There's nothing my husband and I enjoy so much as a good play, is there, Fred?

MR. WADHURST: Nothing.

MRS. WADHURST: And all we get is films, and they're generally pretty old by the time they come out to us—— [*She laughs gaily.*]

MR. WADHURST: Do you go to the theatre much?

MR. BURNHAM: No.

There is silence which is broken by the telephone ringing. Everybody jumps.

MRS. WADHURST: Oh, dear—do you think we ought to answer it?

MR. WADHURST: I don't know.

The telephone continues to ring. CLARE WEDDERBURN *comes in. She is middle-aged, well-dressed and rather gruff. She is followed by* "BOGEY" GOSLING, *a Major in the Marines, a good-looking man in the thirties.*

CLARE: Hallo—where's the old girl?

MRS. WADHURST [*nervously*]: I—er, I'm afraid I——

CLARE [*going to the telephone*]: Mix a cocktail, Bogey— I'm a stretcher case—— [*At telephone.*] Hallo—no, it's me— Clare—— God knows, dear—shall I tell her to call you back?— all right—no, it was bloody, darling—a gloomy dinner at the Embassy, then the worst play I've ever sat through and then the Café de Paris and that awful man who does things with a duck—I've already seen him six times, darling—oh, you know, he pinches its behind and it quacks Land of Hope and Glory— I don't know whether it hurts it or not—I minded at first but I'm past caring now, after all, it's not like performing dogs, I

mind about performing dogs terribly—all right—good-bye——
[*She hangs up and turns to* MRS. WADHURST.] Ducks are pretty
bloody anyway, don't you think?

MRS. WADHURST: I don't know very much about them.

CLARE: The man swears it's genuine talent, but I think it's
the little nip that does it.

MRS. WADHURST: It sounds rather cruel.

CLARE: It's a gloomy form of entertainment anyhow, particularly as I've always hated Land of Hope and Glory——

BOGEY: Cocktail?

CLARE [*taking off her hat*]: Thank God!

BOGEY *hands round cocktails, the* WADHURSTS *and* MR. BURNHAM
accept them and sip them in silence.

BOGEY: I suppose Piggie's in the bath.

CLARE: Go and rout her out.

BOGEY: Wait till I've had a drink.

CLARE [*to* MRS. WADHURST]: Is Peter home or is he still darting
about the Solent?

MRS. WADHURST: I'm afraid I couldn't say—you see——

BOGEY: I saw him last night with Janet——

CLARE: Hasn't she had her baby yet?

BOGEY: She hadn't last night.

CLARE: That damned baby's been hanging over us all for
months——

The telephone rings—CLARE *answers it.*

[*At telephone.*] Hallo—yes—hallo, darling—no, it's Clare—yes,
he's here—— No, I really couldn't face it—yes, if I were likely
to go to India I'd come, but I'm not likely to go to India—— I
think Rajahs bumble up a house-party so terribly—yes, I know
he's different, but the other one's awful—Angela had an agonising time with him—all the dining-room chairs had to be
changed because they were leather and his religion prevented
him sitting on them—all the dogs had to be kept out of the
house because they were unclean, which God knows was true
of the Bedlington, but the other ones were clean as whistles—

and then to round everything off he took Laura Merstham in his car and made passes at her all the way to Newmarket—all right, darling—here he is—— [*To* BOGEY] It's Nina, she wants to talk to you——

She hands the telephone to BOGEY, *who reaches for it and lifts the wire so that it just misses* MRS. WADHURST's *hat. It isn't quite long enough so he has to bend down to speak with his face practically touching her.*

BOGEY [*at telephone*]: Hallo, Nin—— I can't on Wednesday, I've got a Guest Night—it's a hell of a long way, it'd take hours——

PIGGIE *comes in with a rush.*

PIGGIE: I am so sorry——

CLARE: Shhh!

BOGEY: Shut up, I can't hear——

PIGGIE [*in a shrill whisper*]: Who is it?

CLARE: Nina.

BOGEY [*at telephone*]: Well, you can tell George to leave it for me—and I can pick it up.

PIGGIE: How lovely to see you again!

BOGEY [*at telephone*]: No, I shan't be leaving till about ten, so if he leaves it by nine-thirty I'll get it all right——

PIGGIE: My husband will be here in a minute—he has to go to sea on Thursday, but he's arranged for you to be taken over the dockyard at Portsmouth——

BOGEY [*at telephone*]: Give the old boy a crack on the jaw.

PIGGIE: It's the most thrilling thing in the world. You see how the torpedoes are made—millions of little wheels inside, all clicking away like mad—and they cost thousands of pounds each——

BOGEY [*at telephone*]: No, I saw her last night—not yet, but at any moment now—I should think—— All right—— Call me at Chatham—if I can get away I shall have to bring Mickey, too——

PIGGIE: How much do torpedoes cost each, Clare?

CLARE: God knows, darling—something fantastic—ask Bogey——

PIGGIE: Bogey——

BOGEY: What?

PIGGIE: How much do torpedoes cost each?

BOGEY: What?—[*at telephone*]—wait a minute, Piggie's yelling at me——

PIGGIE: Torpedoes—— [*She makes a descriptive gesture.*]

BOGEY: Oh, thousands and thousands—terribly expensive things—ask Peter—— [*At telephone.*]—If I do bring him you'll have to be frightfully nice to him, he's been on the verge of suicide for weeks——

PIGGIE: Don't let her go, I must talk to her——

BOGEY [*at telephone*]: Hold on a minute, Piggie wants to talk to you—all right—I'll let you know—here she is——

PIGGIE *leans over the sofa and takes the telephone from* BOGEY, *who steps over the wire and stumbles over* MRS. WADHURST.

BOGEY: I'm most awfully sorry——

MRS. WADHURST: Not at all——

PIGGIE [*to* MRS. WADHURST]: It's so lovely you being in England—— [*At telephone.*] Darling—what was the meaning of that sinister little invitation you sent me?

BOGEY: You know what Mickey is.

PIGGIE [*at telephone*]: No, dear, I really can't—I always get so agitated——

CLARE: Why does he go on like that? It's so tiresome.

PIGGIE [*at telephone*]: I'll come if Clare will—— [*To* CLARE.] Are you going to Nina's Indian ding-dong?

CLARE: Not without an anæsthetic.

PIGGIE [*at telephone*]: She's moaning a bit, but I'll persuade her—what happens after dinner?—the man with the duck from the Café de Paris—— [*To the room in general.*] She's got that sweet duck from the Café de Paris——

CLARE: Give me another cocktail, Bogey, I want to get so drunk that I just can't hear any more——

PIGGIE [*at telephone*]: But, darling, do you think it's quite *wise*—I mean Maharajahs are terribly touchy and there's probably something in their religion about ducks being mortal sin or something—you know how difficult they are about cows and pigs—just a minute— [*To the* WADHURSTS.] You can tell us, of course——

MR. WADHURST: I beg your pardon?

PIGGIE: Do Indians mind ducks?

MR. WADHURST: I—I don't think so——

BOGEY: Do you come from India?

MRS. WADHURST: No, Malaya.

PIGGIE: It's the same sort of thing, though, isn't it?—if they don't mind them in Malaya it's unlikely that they'd mind them in India—— [*At telephone.*] It'll probably be all right, but you'd better get Douglas Byng as a standby.

CLARE: There might be something in their religion about Douglas Byng.

PIGGIE: Shh! [*At telephone.*] Everyone's making such a noise! The room's full of the most frightful people. Darling, it definitely *is* Waterloo Station—— No, I'm almost sure he can't—he's going to sea on Thursday—don't be silly, dear, you can't be in the Navy without going to sea *sometimes*——

PETER *enters, followed by* ALLY.

[*At telephone.*] Here he is now, you can ask him yourself—— [*To* PETER.] Peter, it's Nina, she wants to talk to you—— [*To the* WADHURSTS.] This is my husband and Commander Corbett—he's been longing to meet you and thank you for being so sweet to us—I told him all about your heavenly house and the plantation——

MRS. WADHURST [*bridling—to* ALLY]: It was most delightful, I assure you, to have Lady Maureen with us——

PIGGIE: Not him, him—that's the wrong one——

MRS. WADHURST: Oh, I'm sorry——

PETER [*shaking hands with* MRS. WADHURST]: It was so kind of you—my wife has talked of nothing else——

[*110*]

PIGGIE [*grabbing him*]: Here—Nina's yelling like a banshee——

PETER: Excuse me. [*He takes the telephone.*] Hallo, Nin—what for?—— No, I can't, but Piggie probably can—— [*To* PIGGIE.] Can you go to Nina's party for the Rajahs?

PIGGIE: We've been through all that——

PETER: All right—I didn't know——[*At telephone.*] No, I shall be at sea for about three days—it isn't tiresome at all, I like it——

PIGGIE [*to* MRS. WADHURST]: How's your daughter?

MRS. WADHURST [*surprised*]: She's a little better, thank you.

PIGGIE: Oh, has she been ill? I'm so sorry.

MR. WADHURST [*gently*]: She's been ill for five years.

PIGGIE [*puzzled*]: How dreadful for you—are you happy with that cocktail, or would you rather have tea?

MRS. WADHURST: This is delicious, thank you.

PETER [*at telephone*]: I honestly can't do anything about that, Nina, you might be able to find out from the Admiral—well, if his mother was mad too that is an extenuating circumstance—he'll probably be sent home—— [*To* CLARE.] Did you know that Freda Bathurst had once been in an asylum?

CLARE: No, but it explains a lot.

PIGGIE: Why?

PETER: Her son went mad in Hong Kong.

CLARE: What did he do?

PETER: I don't know, but Nina's in a state about it.

PIGGIE: I don't see what it's got to do with Nina——

PETER: He's a relation of some sort—— [*At telephone.*] What did he do, Nina?—— Oh—— Oh, I see—— Oh—well, he'll certainly be sent home and a good job too, we can't have that sort of thing in the Service—— If I were you I'd keep well out of it—all right—— Good-bye. [*He hangs up.*]

PIGGIE: What was it?

PETER: I couldn't possibly tell you.

PIGGIE: Poor boy, I expect the climate had something to do

[*111*]

with it—the climate's awful in Hong Kong—look at poor old
Wally Smythe——

ALLY [*to the* WADHURSTS]: Did you ever know Wally Smythe?

MRS. WADHURST: No, I'm afraid not.

CLARE: You didn't miss much.

PIGGIE: I adored Wally, he was a darling.

CLARE: He kept on having fights all the time—I do hate
people hitting people—— [*To* MRS. WADHURST.] Don't you?

MRS. WADHURST: Yes.

There is suddenly complete silence—PIGGIE *breaks it with
an effort.*

PIGGIE [*vivaciously to the* WADHURSTS]: Maud was so frightfully sorry that she couldn't come to-day—she's pining to see
you again and she asked me to ask you if you'd lunch there to-
morrow?

MRS. WADHURST: How very kind of her.

PIGGIE: She's got a divine little house hidden away in a mews,
it's frightfully difficult to find—— [*The telephone rings.*] I've
got millions of questions I want to ask you, what happened to
that darling old native who did a dance with a sword?——
[*At telephone.*] Hallo— [*Continuing to everyone in general.*]
It was the most exciting thing I've ever seen, all the villagers sat
round in torchlight and they beat—— [*At telephone.*] Hallo—
yes, speaking—— [*Continuing*] beat drums and the—— [*At
telephone*] hallo—darling, I'd no idea you were back—— [*to
everybody*] and the old man tore himself to shreds in the middle, it was marvellous—— [*At telephone.*] I can't believe it,
where are you speaking from?—— My dear, your *not!*—— [*To
everybody.*] It's Boodie, she got back last night and she's staying with Norman——

CLARE: Is Phyllis there?

PIGGIE [*at telephone*]: Is Phyllis there?—— She's away?——
[*To* CLARE.] She's away.

PETER [*to* MR. WADHURST]: That's the best joke I ever heard.

CLARE: It's made my entire season that's all, it's just made it.

PIGGIE [*at telephone*]: You'd better come and dine to-night—I'm on a diet, so there's only spinach, but we can talk—— Yes, she's here—absolutely worn out—we all are—— Oh yes, it was pretty grim, it started all right and everything was going beautifully when Vera arrived, unasked, my dear, and more determined than Hitler—of course there was the most awful scene—Alice flounced upstairs with tears cascading down her face and locked herself in the cook's bedroom—— Clare tried to save the situation by dragging Lady Borrowdale on to the terrace——

CLARE [*sibilantly*]: That was *afterwards!*——

PIGGIE [*at telephone*]: Anyhow hell broke loose—you can imagine—Janet was there, of course, and we were all worried about her—no, it hasn't arrived yet, but the odds are mounting—— [*To everybody.*] She hasn't had it yet, has she, Peter?

PETER: If she has it was born in the gramophone department at Harrods—I left her there at four-thirty——.

PIGGIE [*at telephone*]: No, it's still what's known as on the way—I'll expect you about eight-thirty—I've got to do my feet and then I'm going to relax—all right—yes, she's here—— [*To* CLARE.] Here, Clare, she wants to talk to you——

CLARE *in order to reach the telephone comfortably has to kneel on the sofa.*

CLARE: Excuse me.

MRS. WADHURST: I'm so sorry.

CLARE [*at telephone*]: Darling—I'm dead with surprise——

PIGGIE [*to* MRS. WADHURST]: Now you must tell me some more——

MRS. WADHURST: Well, really, I don't——

CLARE: Shhh!—I can't hear a word—— [*At telephone.*] He what?—When?—— He must be raving——

PIGGIE [*in a harsh whisper*]: Have you still got that sweet dog?

MRS. WADHURST [*also whispering*]: Yes, we've still got Rudolph.

PIGGIE [*to everybody*]: Rudolph's an angel, I can never tell you how divine he was—he used to come in every morning with my breakfast tray and jump on to the bed——

MRS. WADHURST [*horrified*]: Oh, you never told me that, how very naughty of him—he's very seldom allowed in the house at all——

PIGGIE [*puzzled*]: But—but——

MR. WADHURST: Perhaps you're thinking of some other dog, Lady Maureen—Rudolph is a Great Dane——

PIGGIE [*bewildered*]: Oh, yes, of course, how idiotic of me——

CLARE [*at telephone*]: —Well, all I can say is she ought to be deported—you can't go about making scenes like that, it's so lacking in everything—all right, darling—call me in the morning—I've got a hairdresser in the afternoon, why don't you make an appointment at the same time?—lovely—— Good-bye. [*She hangs up.*]

PIGGIE: Do sit down, Clare, and stop climbing about over everybody. [*To* MRS. WADHURST.] You must forgive me—this is a mad-house—it's always like this—I can't think why——

CLARE [*in a whisper to* PETER, *having noticed* MR. BURNHAM]: Why's that man got a roll of music, is he going to sing?

PETER [*also in a whisper*]: I don't know—he ought by rights to be a lovely girl of sixteen——

MRS. WADHURST: Have you been in London for the whole season?

PIGGIE: Yes, it's been absolutely frightful, but my husband is getting leave soon, so we shall be able to pop off somewhere——

ALLY [*to* MR. WADHURST]: I suppose you've never run across a chap in Burma called Beckwith?

MR. WADHURST: No, I've never been to Burma.

ALLY: He's in rubber too, I believe—or tea—he's very amusing.

MRS. WADHURST [*to* PIGGIE]: We did hope you'd come and lunch with us one day—but I expect you're terribly busy——

PIGGIE: My dear, I'd worship it—— [*The telephone rings.*] Oh really, this telephone never stops for one minute—— [*At*

telephone.] Hallo—yes, speaking—— Who?—Mrs. Rawlingson—— Oh, yes, yes, yes—— [*She hands the telephone to* MRS.
WADHURST.] Here—it's for you——

MRS. WADHURST [*astonished*]: For me? How very curious——

PIGGIE: Give me a cocktail, Bogey—I haven't had one at all
yet and I'm exhausted——

MRS. WADHURST [*at telephone*]: Hallo—what—who?—I'm
afraid I don't quite understand——

BOGEY [*giving* PIGGIE *a cocktail*]: Here you are—it's a bit
weak——

MRS. WADHURST [*still floundering*]: —I think there must be
some mistake—just a moment—— [*To* PIGGIE.] It's for you,
Lady Maureen—a Mrs. Rawlingson——

PIGGIE [*laughing*]: Now isn't that the most extraordinary co-
incidence—— [*She takes the telephone.*] —Hallo—yes—speaking—— [*She listens and her face changes.*]—Oh yes, of course,
how stupid of me—— [*She looks hurriedly at the* WADHURSTS,
then at PETER.] I'm so awfully sorry, I only just came in——
Oh, what a shame—no, no, no, it doesn't matter a bit——
No—indeed you must call me up the first moment he gets over
it—— Yes—I expect it was—yes—— Good-bye.

She slowly hangs up the receiver, looking at the WADHURSTS *in
complete bewilderment. She makes a sign to* PETER *over* MRS.
WADHURST'S *shoulder, but he only shakes his head.*

PIGGIE [*brightly, but with intense meaning*]: That was Mrs.
Rawlingson.

PETER: Good God!

PIGGIE [*with purpose, sitting next to* MRS. WADHURST]: Did you
ever meet the Rawlingsons out East?

MRS. WADHURST: No—I don't know them.

PIGGIE: Maud and I stayed with them too, you know.

MRS. WADHURST: Where?

PIGGIE: It was in Malaya somewhere, I think—I do get so
muddled.

MRS. WADHURST: I think we should have heard of them if they lived in Malaya.

PETER *meanwhile has gone to the piano and started to strum idly—he begins to hum lightly at the same time.*

PETER [*humming to a waltz refrain, slightly indistinctly, but clearly enough for* PIGGIE *to hear*]: If these are not them who are they? Who are they? Who are they?

PIGGIE *rises and saunters over to the piano.*

PIGGIE: Play the other bit, dear, out of the second act—— [*She hums*]—you know—"I haven't the faintest idea—— Oh no—I haven't the faintest idea."

PETER [*changing tempo*]: "Under the light of the moon, dear —you'd better find out pretty soon, dear."

CLARE: What on earth's that out of?

PIGGIE: Don't be *silly,* Clare—all I ask is that you shouldn't be *silly!*

CLARE [*understanding*]: Oh yes—I see.

There is silence except for PETER'S *playing—everyone looks covertly at the* WADHURSTS. PIGGIE *goes over to* MR. WADHURST.

PIGGIE [*with determination*]: What ship did you come home in?

MR. WADHURST: The *Naldera.*

ALLY: P & O?

MRS. WADHURST: Yes.

PIGGIE: I suppose you got on at Singapore?

MR. WADHURST: No, Penang.

PIGGIE [*the light breaking*]: Penang! Of course, Penang.

MRS. WADHURST: Yes, we have some friends there, so we went by train from Singapore and stayed with them for a couple of days before catching the boat.

PIGGIE [*sunk again*]: Oh yes—yes, I see.

PETER [*at piano, humming to march time*]: "When you hear those drums rat-a-plan—rat-a-plan—find out the name of the place if you can—la la la la la la la la——"

PIGGIE [*persevering*]: How far is your house from the sea? Maud and I were arguing about it for hours the other day——

MR. WADHURST: It's right on the sea.

PIGGIE: That's exactly what I said, but you know Maud's so vague—she never remembers a thing——

CLARE: I suppose it's hell hot all the year round where you are?

MRS. WADHURST: Yes, the climate is a little trying, but one gets used to it.

BOGEY: Are you far from Kuala Lumpur?

MRS. WADHURST: Yes, a long way.

BOGEY: Oh, I knew some people in Kuala Lumpur once.

MR. WADHURST: What were their names?

BOGEY: Damn it, I've forgotten—something like Harrison——

PIGGIE [*helpfully*]: Morrison?

ALLY: Williamson?

PETER: Lightfoot?

BOGEY: No, it's gone——

PIGGIE [*irritably*]: Never mind—it couldn't matter less really, could it?

MRS. WADHURST [*rising*]: I'm afraid we must really go now, Lady Maureen——

PIGGIE: Oh no—please——

MRS. WADHURST: We have to dress because we're dining and going to the theatre—that's the one thing we do miss dreadfully in Pendarla—the theatre——

CLARE: We miss it a good deal here, too.

PIGGIE [*remembering everything*]: Pendarla—oh dear, what a long way away it seems—dear Mrs. Wadhurst—[*She shoots a triumphant glance at* PETER]—it's been so lovely having this little peep at you—you and Mr. Wadhurst must come and dine quietly one night and we'll go to another theatre——

MRS. WADHURST: That would be delightful—Fred——

MR. WADHURST: Good-bye.

[*117*]

PIGGIE: Peter—come and say good-bye to Mr. and Mrs. Wadhurst.

PETER [*coming over and shaking hands*]: Good-bye—I can never tell you how grateful I am to you for having been so kind and hospitable to my wife——

MRS. WADHURST: Next time, I hope you'll come and call on us too.

PETER: I should love to.

MRS. WADHURST: Good-bye.

CLARE: Good-bye——

Everybody says good-bye and shakes hands, PETER *opens the door for the* WADHURSTS *and they go out on a wave of popularity. He goes out into the hall with them closing the door after him.* PIGGIE *collapses on to the sofa.*

PIGGIE [*hysterically*]: Oh, my God, that was the most awful half an hour I've ever spent——

CLARE: I thought it all went down like a dinner.

PIGGIE: I remember it all now, we stayed one night with them on our way from Siam—a man in Bangkok had wired to them or something——

ALLY: That was a nice bit you did about the old native dancing with a sword——

PIGGIE: Oh dear, they must have thought I was drunk.

PETER *re-enters.*

PETER: Next time you travel, my darling, I suggest you keep a diary.

PIGGIE: Wasn't it frightful—poor angels—I must ring up Maud—— [*She dials a number.*] I think they had a heavenly time though, don't you—I mean they couldn't have noticed a thing——

PETER: Oh no, the whole affair was managed with the utmost subtlety—I congratulate you——

PIGGIE: Don't be sour—Peter—— [*At telephone.*] Hallo—Maud?—darling, it's not the Rawlingsons at all, it's the Wadhursts—— [*To everybody.*] Good heavens, I never gave them

[*118*]

Maud's address. [*At telephone.*] I forgot to give them your address—how can you be so unkind, Maud, you ought to be ashamed of yourself—they're absolute pets, both of them——

PETER: Come on, Ally, I've got to dress——

ALLY: All right——

CLARE: Shall I see you on Sunday?

ALLY: Yes—I'll be over——

PIGGIE [*at telephone*]: —they had a lovely time and everybody was divine to them——

CLARE: Come on, Bogey, we must go, too——

PIGGIE: Wait a minute, don't leave me—I've got to do my feet—— [*At telephone*]—no, I was talking to Clare—— My dear, I know, she rang me up too—she's staying with Norman —Phyllis will be as sour as a quince——

PETER *and* ALLY *go off talking.*

CLARE: Darling, I really *must* go——

PIGGIE [*at telephone*]: —all right—I'll try to get hold of them in the morning and put them off—I do think it's horrid of you though, after all, they were frightfully sweet to us—I've done all I can—well, there's no need to get into a rage, I'm the one to get into a rage—yes, you are, I can hear you—your teeth are chattering like dice in a box—— Oh, all right! [*She hangs up.*] Maud's impossible——

CLARE: Listen, Piggie——

PIGGIE: Wait just one minute, I've got to get the things to do my feet——

She rushes out of the room.

CLARE: I really don't see why we should all wait about—— [*She suddenly sees* MR. BURNHAM.] Oh—hallo.

MR. BURNHAM [*nervously*]: Hallo.

CLARE: I thought you'd left with your mother and father.

MR. BURNHAM: They weren't my mother and father—I'm from Freeman's. I've brought the designs for the Commander's speed boat—Mr. Driscoll couldn't come——

CLARE: Well, you'd better wait—he'll be back soon——

MR. BURNHAM: I'm afraid I can't wait much longer—I have to get back to the shop——

CLARE: You should have piped up before——

BOGEY: Listen, Clare, we must push off——

CLARE: All right.

MR. BURNHAM *retires again into the shadows as* PIGGIE *returns with several bottles, a towel and a pair of scissors. She sits on the sofa and takes her shoes and stockings off.*

PIGGIE: —The trouble with Maud is, she's too insular——

CLARE: Are you driving down on Saturday?

PIGGIE: Yes—I promised to stop off at Godalming and have a cutlet with Freda on the way—do you want to come?

CLARE: You know perfectly well I hate Freda's guts.

PIGGIE [*beginning on her feet*]: All right, darling—I'll expect you in the afternoon——

*The telephone rings—*PIGGIE *reaches for it with one hand and goes on painting her toe nails with the other—at telephone:* Hallo—yes. Oh, David, I'm *so* sorry—I completely forgot——

CLARE *and* BOGEY *hiss good-bye at her, she waves to them, and they go out.*

I couldn't help it, I had to be sweet to some people that Maud and I stayed with in Malaya—— Oh! David darling, don't be so soured-up—yes, of course I do, don't be so silly—— No, I'm quite alone doing my feet—well, I can't help that, I happen to *like* them red—well, after all they are my feet, I suppose I can paint them blue if I want to——

MR. BURNHAM *begins to tiptoe out of the room, he leaves his roll of designs on the table.* PIGGIE *catches sight of him just as he is gingerly opening the door.*

[*To* MR. BURNHAM.] Oh, good-bye—it's been absolutely lovely, you're the sweetest family I've ever met in my life——

CURTAIN

FUMED OAK
A Comedy in Two Scenes

CHARACTERS

HENRY GOW
DORIS, his wife
ELSIE, his daughter
MRS. ROCKETT, his mother-in-law

SCENE I. *Morning.*
SCENE II. *Evening.*

The action of the play passes in the sitting-room of the Gows' house in South London.

The time is the present day.

SCENE I

The Gows' sitting-room is indistinguishable from several thousand other suburban sitting-rooms. The dominant note is refinement. There are French windows at the back opening on to a narrow lane of garden. These are veiled discreetly by lace curtains set off by a pelmet and side pieces of rather faded blue casement cloth. There is a tiled fireplace on the right; an upright piano between it and the window; a fumed oak sideboard on the left and, below it, a door leading to the hall, the stairs of the front door. There is a fumed oak dining-room suite consisting of a table, and six chairs; a sofa; an armchair in front of the fire; a radio, and a plentiful sprinkling over the entire room of ornaments and framed photographs.

When the curtain rises it is about eight-thirty on a spring morning. Rain is trickling down the windows and breakfast is laid on the table.

MRS. ROCKETT is seated in the armchair by the fire; on a small table next to her is a cup of tea, and a work-basket. She is a fattish, grey-looking woman dressed in a blouse and skirt and a pepper and salt jumper of artificial silk. Her pince-nez snap in and out of a little clip on her bosom and her feet are bad which necessitates the wearing of large quilted slippers in the house.

DORIS, aged about thirty-five, is seated at the table reading a newspaper propped up against the cruet. She is thin and anæmic and whatever traces of past prettiness she might have had are obscured by the pursed-up, rather sour gentility of her expression. She wears a nondescript coat-frock, a slave bangle and a necklace of amber glass beads. ELSIE, her daughter aged about fourteen, is sitting opposite to her, cutting her toast into strips in order to dip them into her boiled egg. She is a straight-haired ordinary-looking girl dressed in a navy blue school dress with a glacé red leather waist belt.

There is a complete silence broken only by the occasional rattle of a spoon in a cup or a sniffle from ELSIE *who has a slight head cold.*

HENRY GOW *comes into the room. He is tall and spare, neatly dressed in a blue serge suit. He wears rimless glasses and his hair is going grey at the sides and thin on the top. He sits down at the table without a word.* DORIS *automatically rises and goes out, returning in a moment with a plate of haddock which she places in front of him and resumes her place.* HENRY *pours himself out some tea.* DORIS, *without looking at him, being immersed in the paper, passes him the milk and sugar.*

The silence continues until ELSIE *breaks it.*

ELSIE: Mum?

DORIS: What?

ELSIE: When can I put my hair up?

DORIS [*snappily*]: When you're old enough.

ELSIE: Gladys Pierce is the same age as me and she's got hers up.

DORIS: Never you mind about Gladys Pierce, get on with your breakfast.

ELSIE: I don't see why I can't have it cut. That would be better than nothing.

This remark is ignored.

Maisie Blake had hers cut last week and it looks lovely.

DORIS: Never you mind about Maisie Blake neither. She's common.

ELSIE: Miss Pritchard doesn't think so. Miss Pritchard likes Maisie Blake a lot, she said it looked ever so nice.

DORIS [*irritably*]: What?

ELSIE: Her hair.

DORIS: Get on with your breakfast. You'll be late.

ELSIE [*petulantly*]: Oh, Mum——

DORIS: And stop sniffling. Sniffle sniffle sniffle! **Haven't you** got a handkerchief?

ELSIE: Yes, but it's a clean one.

DORIS: Never mind, use it.

MRS. ROCKETT: The child can't help having a cold.

DORIS: She can blow her nose, can't she, even if she has got a cold?

ELSIE [*conversationally*]: Dodie Watson's got a terrible cold, she's had it for weeks. It went to her chest and then it went back to her head again.

MRS. ROCKETT: That's the worst of schools, you're always catching something.

ELSIE: Miss Pritchard's awful mean to Dodie Watson, she said she'd had enough of it.

DORIS: Enough of what?

ELSIE: Her cold.

There is silence again which is presently shattered by the wailing of a baby in the house next door.

MRS. ROCKETT: There's that child again. It kept me awake all night.

DORIS: I'm very sorry, I'm sure.

MRS. ROCKETT [*fiddling in her work basket*]: I wasn't blaming you.

DORIS: The night before last it was the hot-water pipes.

MRS. ROCKETT: You ought to have them seen to.

DORIS: You know as well as I do you can't stop them making that noise every now and then.

MRS. ROCKETT [*threading a needle*]: I'm sure I don't know why you don't get a plumber in.

DORIS [*grandly*]: Because I do not consider it necessary.

MRS. ROCKETT: You would if you slept in my room—gurgle gurgle gurgle all night long—it's all very fine for you, you're at the end of the passage.

DORIS [*with meaning*]: You don't have to sleep there.

MRS. ROCKETT: What do you mean by that?

DORIS: You know perfectly well what I mean.

MRS. ROCKETT [*with spirit*]: Listen to me, Doris Gow. I've got a perfect right to complain if I want to and well you know it. It isn't as if I was staying here for nothing.

DORIS: I really don't know what's the matter with you lately, Mother, you do nothing but grumble.

MRS. ROCKETT: Me, grumble! I like that, I'm sure. That's rich, that is.

DORIS: Well, you do. It gives me a headache.

MRS. ROCKETT: You ought to do something about those headaches of yours. They seem to pop on and off at the least thing.

DORIS: And I wish you wouldn't keep passing remarks about not staying here for nothing.

MRS. ROCKETT: Well, it's true, I don't.

DORIS: Anyone would think we was taking advantage of you.

MRS. ROCKETT: Well, they wouldn't be far wrong.

DORIS: Mother, how can you! You're not paying a penny more than you can afford.

MRS. ROCKETT: I never said I was. It isn't the money, it's the lack of consideration.

DORIS: Pity you don't go and live with Nora for a change.

MRS. ROCKETT: Nora hasn't got a spare room.

DORIS: Phyllis has, a lovely one, looking out over the railway. I'm sure her hot-water pipes wouldn't annoy you, there isn't hot water in them.

MRS. ROCKETT: Of course, if I'm not wanted here, I can always go to a boarding-house or a private hotel.

DORIS: Catch you!

MRS. ROCKETT: I'm not the sort to outstay my welcome any-where——

DORIS: Oh, for heaven's sake don't start that again——

MRS. ROCKETT [*addressing the air*]: It seems as though some of us had got out of bed the wrong side this morning.

ELSIE: Mum, can I have some more toast?

DORIS: No.

ELSIE: I could make it myself over the kitchen fire.

DORIS: No, I tell you. Can't you understand plain English? You've had quite enough and you'll be late for school.

MRS. ROCKETT: Never mind, Elsie, here's twopence, you can buy yourself a sponge-cake at Barret's.

ELSIE [*taking the twopence*]: Thanks, Grandma.

DORIS: You'll do no such thing, Elsie. I'm not going to have a child of mine stuffing herself with cake in the middle of the High Street.

MRS. ROCKETT [*sweetly*]: Eat it in the shop, dear.

DORIS: Go on, you'll be late.

ELSIE: Oh, Mum, it's only ten to.

DORIS: Do as I tell you.

ELSIE: Oh, all right.

She goes sullenly out of the room and can be heard scampering noisily up the stairs.

MRS. ROCKETT [*irritatingly*]: Poor little soul.

DORIS: I'll trouble you not to spoil Elsie, Mother.

MRS. ROCKETT: Spoil her! I like that. Better than half starving her.

DORIS [*hotly*]: Are you insinuating——

MRS. ROCKETT: I'm not insinuating anything. Elsie's getting a big girl, she only had one bit of toast for her breakfast and she used that for her egg, I saw her.

DORIS: It's none of your business and in future I'd be much obliged if you'd keep your twopences to yourself.

MRS. ROCKETT [*hurt*]: Very well, of course if I'm to be abused every time I try to bring a little happiness into the child's life——

DORIS: Anyone would think I ill-treated her the way you talk.

MRS. ROCKETT: You certainly nag her enough.

DORIS: I don't do any such thing and I wish you'd be quiet.

She flounces up from the table and goes over to the window, where she stands drumming her fingers on the pane. HENRY *quietly appropriates the newspaper she has flung down.*

[*129*]

MRS. ROCKETT [*unctuously*]: There's no need to lose your temper.

DORIS: I am not losing my temper.

MRS. ROCKETT: If I'd known when you were Elsie's age what you were going to turn out like I'd have given you what for, I can tell you.

DORIS: Pity you didn't, I'm sure.

MRS. ROCKETT: One thing, I never stinted any of my children.

DORIS: I wish you'd leave me to bring up my own child in my own way.

MRS. ROCKETT: That cold's been hanging over her for weeks and a fat lot you care——

DORIS: I've dosed her for it, haven't I? The whole house stinks of Vapex. What more can I do?

MRS. ROCKETT: She ought to have had Doctor Bristow last Saturday when it was so bad. He'd have cleared it up in no time.

DORIS: You and your Doctor Bristow.

MRS. ROCKETT: Nice thing if it turned to bronchitis. Mrs. Henderson's Muriel got bronchitis, all through neglecting a cold; the poor child couldn't breathe, they had to have two kettles going night and day——

DORIS: I suppose your precious Doctor Bristow told you that.

MRS. ROCKETT: Yes, he did, and what's more he saved the girl's life, you ask Mrs. Henderson.

DORIS: Catch me ask Mrs. Henderson anything, not likely, stuck up thing——

MRS. ROCKETT: Mrs. Henderson's a very nice lady-like woman, just because she's quiet and a bit reserved you say she's stuck up——

DORIS: Who does she think she is anyway, Lady Mountbatten?

MRS. ROCKETT: Really, Doris, you make me tired sometimes, you do really.

DORIS: If you're so fond of Mrs. Henderson it's a pity you don't see more of her. I notice you don't go there often.

MRS. ROCKETT [*with dignity*]: I go when I am invited.

DORIS [*triumphantly*]: Exactly.

MRS. ROCKETT: She's not the kind of woman that likes people dropping in and out all the time. We can't all be Amy Fawcetts.

DORIS: What's the matter with Amy Fawcett?

ELSIE *comes into the room wearing a mackintosh and a tam-o'-shanter. She stamps over to the piano and begins to search untidily through the pile of music on it.*

MRS. ROCKETT: Well, she's common for one thing, she dyes her hair for another, and she's a bit too free and easy all round for my taste.

DORIS: She doesn't put on airs, anyway.

MRS. ROCKETT: I should think not, after the sort of life she's led.

DORIS: How do you know what sort of a life she's led?

MRS. ROCKETT: Everybody knows, you only have to look at her; I'm a woman of the world, I am, you can't pull the wool over my eyes——

DORIS: Don't untidy everything like that, what are you looking for?

ELSIE: 'The Pixie's Parade,' I had it last night.

DORIS: If it's the one with the blue cover it's at the bottom.

ELSIE: It isn't—oh dear, Miss Pritchard will be mad at me if I can't find it.

MRS. ROCKETT: Perhaps you put it in your satchel, dear, here, let me look—— [*She opens* ELSIE's *satchel, which is hanging over the back of a chair and fumbles in it.*] Is this it?

ELSIE: Oh yes, thanks, Grandma.

DORIS: Go along now, for heaven's sake, you'll be late.

ELSIE: Oh, all right, Mum. Good-bye, Mum, good-bye, Grandma, good-bye, Dad.

HENRY: Good-bye.

MRS. ROCKETT: Good-bye, dear, give Grandma a kiss.

ELSIE *does so*

DORIS: Don't dawdle on the way home.

ELSIE: Oh, all right, Mum.

She goes out. The slam of the front door shakes the house.

DORIS [*irritably*]: There now.

MRS. ROCKETT [*with studied politeness*]: If you are going down to the shops this morning, would it be troubling you too much to get me a reel of white cotton?

DORIS: I thought you were coming with me.

MRS. ROCKETT: I really don't feel up to it.

DORIS: I'll put it on my list.

She takes a piece of paper out of the sideboard drawer and scribbles on it.

MRS. ROCKETT: If it's out of your way, please don't trouble, it'll do another time.

DORIS: Henry, it's past nine.

HENRY [*without looking up*]: I know.

DORIS: You'll be late.

HENRY: Never mind.

DORIS: That's a nice way to talk, I must say.

MRS. ROCKETT: I'm sure if my Robert had ever lazed about like that in the mornings, I'd have thought the world had come to an end.

DORIS: Henry'll do it once too often, mark my words.

MRS. ROCKETT [*biting off her thread*]: Well, that corner's finished.

DORIS [*to* HENRY]: You'll have to move now, I've got to clear.

HENRY [*rising—absently*]: All right.

MRS. ROCKETT: Where's Ethel?

DORIS: Doing the bedroom.

She takes a tray which is leaning against the wall by the sideboard and proceeds to stack the breakfast things on to it.

HENRY *quietly goes out of the room.*

DORIS: Look at that wicked waste. [*Throws more scraps in fire.*]

MRS. ROCKETT: What's the matter with him?

DORIS: Don't ask me, I'm sure I couldn't tell you.

MRS. ROCKETT: He came in very late last night, I heard him go into the bathroom. [*There is a pause.*] That cistern makes a terrible noise.

DORIS: Does it indeed!

MRS. ROCKETT: Yes, it does.

DORIS [*slamming the teapot on to the tray*]: Very sorry, I'm sure.

MRS. ROCKETT: Where'd he been?

DORIS: How do I know?

MRS. ROCKETT: Didn't you ask him?

DORIS: I wouldn't demean myself.

MRS. ROCKETT: Been drinking?

DORIS: No.

MRS. ROCKETT: Sounded very like it to me, all that banging about.

DORIS: You know Henry never touches a drop.

MRS. ROCKETT: I know he says he doesn't.

DORIS: Oh, do shut up, Mother, we're not all like father.

MRS. ROCKETT: You watch your tongue, Doris Gow, don't let me hear you saying anything against the memory of your poor father.

DORIS: I wasn't.

MRS. ROCKETT [*belligerently*]: Oh yes, you were, you were insinuating again.

DORIS [*hoisting up the tray*]: Father drank and you know it —everybody knew it.

MRS. ROCKETT: You're a wicked woman.

DORIS: It's true.

MRS. ROCKETT: Your father was a gentleman, which is more than your husband will ever be, with all his night-classes and his book reading—night-classes indeed!

DORIS: Who's insinuating now?

MRS. ROCKETT [*angrily*]: I am, and I'm not afraid to say so.

DORIS: What of it?

[*133*]

MRS. ROCKETT [*with heavy sarcasm*]: I suppose he was at a night-class last night?

DORIS [*loudly*]: Mind your own business.

HENRY *comes in wearing his mackintosh and a bowler hat.*

HENRY: What's up?

DORIS: Where were you last night?

HENRY: Why?

DORIS: Mother wants to know and so do I.

HENRY: I was kept late at the shop and I had a bit of dinner in town.

DORIS: Who with?

HENRY: Charlie Henderson.

He picks up the paper off the table and goes out. After a moment the front door slams.

The baby next door bursts into fresh wails.

MRS. ROCKETT: There goes that child again. It's my belief it's hungry.

DORIS: Wonder you don't go and give it twopence to buy sponge-cake.

She pulls the door open with her foot and goes out with the tray as the lights fade on the scene.

SCENE II

It is about seven-thirty in the evening. ELSIE *is sitting at the piano practising with the loud pedal firmly down all the time.*

MRS. ROCKETT *is sitting in her chair by the fire, but she is dressed in her street things and wearing a black hat with a veil.*

DORIS, *also in street clothes, is clearing some paper patterns and pieces of material from the table.*

There is a cloth across the end of the table on which is set a loaf, a plate of cold ham, a saucer with two tomatoes in it, a bottle of A.1 sauce and a teapot, teacup, sugar basin and milk jug.

HENRY *comes in, taking off his mackintosh. He gives one look round the room and goes out into the hall again to hang up his things.* ELSIE *stops playing and comes over to* DORIS.

ELSIE: Can we go now?

DORIS: In a minute.

ELSIE: We'll miss the Mickey.

DORIS: Put on your hat and don't worry.

ELSIE [*grabbing her hat from the sideboard*]: Oh, all right.

HENRY *re-enters.*

DORIS: Your supper's all ready, the kettle's on the gas stove when you want it. We've had ours.

HENRY: Oh!

DORIS: And you needn't look injured either.

HENRY: Very well.

DORIS: If you managed to get home a bit earlier it'd save a lot of trouble all round.

HENRY [*amiably*]: Sorry, dear.

DORIS: It's all very fine to be sorry, you've been getting later and later these last few weeks, they can't keep you overtime every night.

HENRY: All right, dear, I'll tell them.

DORIS: Here, Elsie, put these away in the cupboard.

She hands her a pile of material and pieces of paper. ELSIE *obediently takes them and puts them in the left-hand cupboard of the sideboard.*

HENRY [*sitting at the table*]: Cold ham, what a surprise!

DORIS [*looking at him sharply*]: What's the matter with it?

HENRY: I don't know, yet.

DORIS: It's perfectly fresh, if that's what you mean?

HENRY: Why are you all so dressed up?

ELSIE: We're going to the pictures.

HENRY: Oh, I see.

DORIS: You can put everything on the tray when you've finished and leave it in the kitchen for Ethel.

[*135*]

HENRY: Good old Ethel.

DORIS [*surprised*]: What?

HENRY: I said good old Ethel.

DORIS: Well, it sounded very silly, I'm sure.

MRS. ROCKETT [*scrutinising him*]: What's the matter with you?

HENRY: Nothing, why?

MRS. ROCKETT: You look funny.

HENRY: I feel funny.

MRS. ROCKETT: Have you been drinking?

HENRY: Yes.

DORIS: Henry!

MRS. ROCKETT: I knew it.

HENRY: I had a whisky and soda in town and another one at the Plough.

DORIS [*astounded*]: What for?

HENRY: Because I felt like it.

DORIS: You ought to be ashamed of yourself.

HENRY: I'm going to have another one too, a bit later on.

DORIS: You'll do no such thing.

HENRY: That hat looks awful.

DORIS [*furiously*]: Don't you speak to me like that.

HENRY: Why not?

DORIS [*slightly nonplussed*]: Because I won't have it, so there.

HENRY: It's a common little hat and it looks awful.

DORIS [*with an admirable effort at control*]: Now listen to me, Henry Gow, the next time I catch you drinking and coming home here and insulting me, I'll——

HENRY [*interrupting her gently*]: What will you do, Dorrie?

DORIS [*hotly*]: I'll give you a piece of my mind, that's what I'll do.

HENRY: It'll have to be a very little piece, Dorrie, you can't afford much! [*He laughs delighted at his own joke.*]

DORIS: I'd be very much obliged if you'd kindly tell me what this means?

HENRY: I'm celebrating.

[*136*]

DORIS: What do you mean, celebrating? What are you talking about?

HENRY: To-night's our anniversary.

DORIS: Don't talk so soft, our anniversary's not until November.

HENRY: I don't mean that one. To-night's the anniversary of the first time I had an affair with you and you got in the family way.

DORIS [*shrieking*]: Henry!

HENRY [*delighted with his carefully calculated effect*]: Hurray!

DORIS [*beside herself*]: How dare you say such a dreadful thing, in front of the child, too.

HENRY [*in romantic tones*]: Three years and a bit after that wonderful night our child was born! [*Lapsing into his normal voice.*] Considering all the time you took forming yourself, Elsie, I'm surprised you're not a nicer little girl than you are.

DORIS: Go upstairs, Elsie.

HENRY: Stay here, Elsie.

DORIS: Do as I tell you.

ELSIE: But, Mum——

DORIS: Mother, take her for God's sake! There's going to be a row.

HENRY [*firmly*]: Leave her alone and sit down.

MRS. ROCKETT *hesitates*.
Sit down, I tell you.

MRS. ROCKETT [*subsiding into a chair*]: Well, I never, I——

HENRY [*happily*]: See? It works like a charm.

DORIS: A fine exhibition you're making of yourself, I must say.

HENRY: Not bad, is it? As a matter of fact I'm rather pleased with it myself.

DORIS: Go to bed!

HENRY: Stop ordering me about. What right have you got to nag at me and boss me? No right at all. I'm the one that pays the rent and works for you and keeps you. What do you give me in return, I'd like to know! Nothing! I sit through breakfast while you and mother wrangle. You're too busy being snappy and bad-tempered even to say good morning. I come home tired after working all day and ten to one there isn't even a hot dinner for me; here, see this ham? This is what I think of it! [*He throws it at her feet.*] And the tomatoes and the A.1 bloody sauce! [*He throws them too.*]

DORIS [*screaming*]: Henry! All over the carpet.

HENRY [*throwing the butter-dish face downwards on the floor*]: And that's what I think of the carpet, now then!

DORIS: That I should live to see this! That I should live to see the man I married make such a beast of himself!

HENRY: Stop working yourself up into a state, you'll need all your control when you've heard what I'm going to say to you.

DORIS: Look here——

HENRY: Sit down. We'll all sit down, I'm afraid you'll have to miss the pictures for once.

DORIS: Elsie, you come with me.

MRS. ROCKETT: Yes, go on, Ducks.

She makes a movement towards the door, but HENRY *is too quick for her. He locks the door and slips the key into his pocket.*

HENRY: I've been dreaming of this moment for many years, and believe me it's not going to be spoilt for me by you running away.

DORIS [*on the verge of tears*]: Let me out of this room.

HENRY: You'll stay where you are until I've had my say.

DORIS [*bursting into tears and sinking down at the table*]: Oh! Oh! Oh!——

ELSIE [*starting to cry too*]: Mum—oh, Mum——

HENRY: Here you, shut up, go and get the port out of the sideboard and give some to your mother—go on, do as I tell you.

ELSIE, *terrified and hypnotised into submission, goes to the sideboard cupboard and brings out a bottle of invalid port and some glasses, snivelling as she does so.* DORIS *continues to sob.* That's right.

MRS. ROCKETT [*quietly*]: You drunken brute, you!

HENRY [*cheerfully*]: Worse than that, Mother, far worse. Just you wait and see.

MRS. ROCKETT [*ignoring him*]: Take some port, Dorrie, it'll do you good.

DORIS: I don't want any—it'd choke me——

HENRY [*pouring some out*]: Come on—here——

DORIS: Keep away from me.

HENRY: Drink it and stop snivelling.

DORIS: I'll never forgive you for this, never, never, never as long as I live! [*She gulps down some port.*]

HENRY [*noting her gesture*]: That's better.

MRS. ROCKETT: Pay no attention, Dorrie, he's drunk.

HENRY: I'm not drunk. I've only had two whiskies and sodas, just to give me enough guts to take the first plunge. You'd never believe how scared I was, thinking it over in cold blood. I'm not scared any more though, it's much easier than I thought it was going to be. My only regret is that I didn't come to the boil a long time ago, and tell you to your face, Dorrie, what I think of you, what I've been thinking of you for years, and this horrid little kid, and that old bitch of a mother of yours.

MRS. ROCKETT [*shrilly*]: Henry Gow!

HENRY: You heard me, old bitch was what I said, and old bitch was what I meant.

MRS. ROCKETT: Let me out of this room, I'm not going to stay here and be insulted—I'm not——

HENRY: You're going to stay here just as long as I want you to.

MRS. ROCKETT: Oh, am I? We'll see about that——

With astonishing quickness she darts over to the window and manages to drag one open. HENRY *grabs her by the arm.*

HENRY: No, you don't.

MRS. ROCKETT: Let go of me.

DORIS: Oh, Mother, don't let the neighbours know all your business.

HENRY: Not on your life!

MRS. ROCKETT [*suddenly screaming powerfully*]: Help! Help! Police! Help! Mrs. Harrison—help!——

HENRY *drags her away from the window, turns her round and gives her a light slap on the face, she staggers against the piano, meanwhile he shuts the window again, locks it and pockets the key.*

DORIS [*looking at him in horror*]: Oh, God! Oh, my God!

ELSIE [*bursting into tears again*]: Oh, Mum, Mum, he hit Grandma! Oh, Mum——

She runs to DORIS *who puts her arm round her protectively.*

MRS. ROCKETT [*gasping*]: Oh—my heart! I think I'm going to faint—oh—my heart——

HENRY: Don't worry, I'll bring you round if you faint——

MRS. ROCKETT: Oh—oh—oh, dear——

MRS. ROCKETT *slides on to the floor, perceptibly breaking her fall by clinging on to the piano stool.*

DORIS *jumps up from the table.*

DORIS: Mother!

HENRY: Stay where you are.

HENRY *goes to the sideboard and pours out a glass of water.* DORIS, *disobeying him, runs over to her mother.* ELSIE *wails.*

HENRY: Stand out of the way, Doris, we don't all want to get wet.

He approaches with the glass of water. MRS. ROCKETT *sits up weakly.*

MRS. ROCKETT [*in a far-away voice*]: Where am I?

HENRY: Number Seventeen Cranworth Road, Clapham.

MRS. ROCKETT: Oh—oh, dear!

HENRY: Look here, Mother, I don't want there to be any mis-understanding about this. I liked slapping you just now, see? It was lovely, and if you don't behave yourself and keep quiet I shall slap you again. Go and sit in your chair and remember if you feel faint the water's all ready for you.

He helps her up and escorts her to her chair by the fire. She collapses into it and looks at him balefully.

Now then. Sit down, Dorrie, you look silly standing about.

DORIS [*with a great effort at control*]: Henry——

HENRY [*slowly, but very firmly*]: Sit down! And keep Elsie quiet or I'll fetch her one, too.

DORIS [*with dignity*]: Come here, Elsie. Shut up, will you!

She sits at the table, with ELSIE.

HENRY: That's right.

He walks round the room slowly and in silence, looking at them with an expression of the greatest satisfaction on his face. Finally he goes over to the fireplace; MRS. ROCKETT *jumps slightly as he approaches her, but he smiles at her reassuringly and lights a cigarette. Meanwhile* DORIS, *recovering from her fear, is beginning to simmer with rage, she remains still, however, watching.*

Now then. I'm going to start, quite quietly, explaining a few things to you.

DORIS: Enjoying yourself, aren't you?

HENRY: You've said it.

DORIS [*gaining courage*]: You'll grin on the other side of your face before I've done with you.

HENRY [*politely*]: Very likely, Dorrie, very likely indeed!

DORIS: And don't you Dorrie me, either! Coming home here drunk, hitting poor mother and frightening Elsie out of her wits.

HENRY: Maybe it'll do her good, do 'em both good, a little excitement in the home. God knows, it's dull enough as a rule.

DORIS [*with biting sarcasm*]: Very clever, oh, very clever, I'm sure.

HENRY: Fifteen, no sixteen years ago to-night, Dorrie, you and me had a little rough and tumble in your Aunt Daisy's house in Stansfield Road, do you remember?

DORIS: Henry——

HENRY [*ignoring her*]: We had the house to ourselves, it being a Sunday, your Aunt had popped over to the Golden Calf with

Mr. Simmonds, the lodger, which, as the writers say, was her wont——

MRS. ROCKETT: This is disgusting, I won't listen to another word.

HENRY [*rounding on her*]: You will! Shut up!

DORIS: Pay no attention, Mother, he's gone mad.

HENRY: Let me see now, where was I? Oh yes, Stansfield Road. You had been after me for a long while, Dorrie, I didn't know it then, but I realised it soon after. You had to have a husband, what with Nora married and Phyllis engaged, both of them younger than you, you had to have a husband, and quick, so you fixed on me. You were pretty enough and I fell for it hook, line and sinker; then, a couple of months later you'd told me you'd clicked, you cried a hell of a lot, I remember, said the disgrace would kill your mother if she ever found out. I didn't know then that it'd take a sight more than that to kill that leathery old mare——

MRS. ROCKETT [*bursting into tears*]: I won't stand it, I won't! I won't!

HENRY [*rising above her sobs*]: I expect you were in on the whole business, in a refined way of course, you knew what was going on all right, you knew that Dorrie was no more in the family way than I was, but we got married; you both saw to that, and I chucked up all the plans I had for getting on, perhaps being a steward in a ship and seeing a bit of the world. Oh yes, all that had to go and we settled down in rooms and I went into Ferguson's Hosiery.

DORIS: I've given you the best years of my life and don't you forget it.

HENRY: You've never given me the best of anything, not even yourself. You didn't even have Elsie willingly.

DORIS [*wildly*]: It's not true—stop up your ears, Elsie, don't listen to him, he's wicked—he's wicked——

HENRY [*grimly*]: It's true all right, and you know it as well as I do.

[*142*]

DORIS [*shrilly*]: It was only right that you married me. It was only fair! You took advantage of me, didn't you? You took away my innocence. It was only right that you paid for it.

HENRY: Come off it, Dorrie, don't talk so silly. I was the innocent one, not you. I found out you'd cheated me a long, long time ago, and when I found out, realised it for certain, I started cheating you. Prepare yourself, Dorrie, my girl, you're going to be really upset this time. I've been saving! Every week for over ten years I've been earning a little bit more than you thought I was. I've managed, by hook and by crook, to put by five hundred and seventy-two pounds—d'you hear me?—five hundred and seventy-two pounds!

MRS. ROCKETT [*jumping to her feet*]: Henry! You never have —it's not true——

DORIS [*also jumping up*]: You couldn't have—you'd have given it away—I should have found out——

HENRY: I thought that'd rouse you, but don't get excited, don't get worked up. I haven't got it on me, it's in the bank. And it's not for you, it's for me—all but fifty pounds of it, that much is for you, just fifty pounds, the last you'll ever get from me——

DORIS: Henry! You couldn't be so cruel! You couldn't be so mean!

HENRY: I've done what I think's fair and what I think's fair is damn sight more than you deserve. I've transferred the freehold of this house into your name, so you'll always have a roof over your head—you can take in lodgers at a pinch, though God help the poor bastards if you do!

DORIS: Five hundred and seventy-two pounds! You've got all that and you're going to leave me to starve!

HENRY: Cut out the drama, Dorrie, and have a look at your mother's savings bank book—I bet you'll find she's got enough to keep you in comfort till the day you die. She soaked her old man plenty, I'm sure—before he took to soaking himself!

MRS. ROCKETT: It's a lie!

HENRY: Now listen to me, Mother Machree—you've 'ad one

sock in the jaw this evening and you're not just asking for another, you're sitting up and begging for it.

MRS. ROCKETT: I'll have you up for assault. I'll have the police on you, my fine fellow!

HENRY: They'll have to be pretty nippy—my boat sails first thing in the morning.

DORIS [*horrified*]: Boat!

HENRY: I'm going away. I've got my ticket here in my pocket, and my passport. My passport photo's a fair scream, I wish I could show it to you, but I don't want you to see the nice new name I've got.

DORIS: You can't do it, I can have you stopped by law. It's desertion.

HENRY: That's right, Dorrie, you've said it. Desertion's just exactly what it is.

DORIS [*breathlessly*]: Where are you going, you've got to tell me. Where are you going?

HENRY: Wouldn't you like to know? Maybe Africa, maybe China, maybe Australia. There are lots of places in the world you know nothing about, Dorrie. You've often laughed at me for reading books, but I've found out a hell of a lot from books. There are islands in the South Seas for instance with cocoa palms and turtles and sunshine all the year round—you can live there for practically nothing, then there's Australia or New Zealand, with a little bit of capital I might start in a small way sheep-farming. Think of it; miles and miles of open country stretching as far as the eye can see—good food and fresh air— that might be very nice, that might suit me beautifully. Then there's South America. There are coffee plantations, there, and sugar plantations, and banana plantations. If I go to South America I'll send you a whole crate. 'Ave a banana, Dorrie! 'Ave a banana!

DORIS: Henry, listen to me, you can't do this dreadful thing, you can't! If you don't love me any more, think of Elsie.

HENRY [*still in his dream*]: Then there's the sea, not the sea we know at Worthing with the tide going in and out regular and the band playing on the pier. The real sea's what I mean. The sea that Joseph Conrad wrote about, and Rudyard Kipling and lots of other people, too, a sea with whacking great waves and water spouts and typhoons and flying-fish and phosphorus making the foam look as if it was lit up. Those people knew a thing or two I can tell you. They knew what life could be like if you give it a chance. They knew there was a bit more to it than refinement and fumed oak and lace curtains and getting old and miserable with nothing to show for it. I'm a middle-aged man, but my health's not too bad taken all round. There's still time for me to see a little bit of real life before I conk out. I'm still fit enough to do a job of work—real work, mind you—not bowing and scraping and wearing myself out showing fussy old cows the way to the lace and the china ware and the bargain basement.

DORIS [*hysterically*]: God will punish you, you just see if He doesn't, you just see——

HENRY: God's been punishing me for fifteen years, it's high time He laid off me now. He's been punishing me good and proper for being damn fool enough to let you get your claws into me in the first place——

DORIS [*changing tactics*]: Henry, have pity, please don't be so cruel, please—please——

HENRY: And don't start weeping and wailing either, that won't cut any ice with me, I know what you're like, I know you through and through. You're frightened now, scared out of your wits, but give you half a chance and you'd be worse than ever you were. You're a bad lot, Dorrie, not what the world would call a bad lot, but what I call a bad lot. Mean and cold and respectable. Good-bye, Dorrie——

DORIS [*flinging her arms round him and bursting into tears*]: Listen to me, Henry, you've got to listen—you must. You can't leave us to starve, you can't throw us on to the streets—if I've been a bad wife to you, I'm sorry—I'll try to be better, really

[*145*]

FUMED OAK

I will, I swear to God I will—— You can't do this, if you won't forgive me, think of Elsie, think of poor little Elsie——

HENRY: Poor little Elsie, my eye! I think Elsie's awful. I always have ever since she was little. She's never done anything but whine and snivel and try to get something for nothing——

ELSIE [*wailing*]: Oh, Mum, did you hear what he said? Oh, Dad, oh dear——

MRS. ROCKETT [*comforting her*]: There, there, dear, don't listen to him——

HENRY: Elsie can go to work in a year or so, in the meantime Dorrie, you can go to work yourself, you're quite a young woman still and strong as an ox.—Here's your fifty pounds——

He takes an envelope out of his pocket and throws it on to the table. Then he goes towards the door. DORIS *rushes after him and hangs on to his arm.*

DORIS: Henry, Henry, you shan't go, you shan't——

HENRY [*struggling with her*]: Leave hold of me.

DORIS: Mother, mother—help—help me, don't let him go——

HENRY *frees himself from her and, taking her by the shoulders, forces her back into a chair, then he unlocks the door and opens it.*

HENRY: I'm taking my last look at you, Dorrie. I shall never see you again as long as I live——

DORIS: Mother! Oh God!—oh, my God!——

She buries her head in her arms and starts to sob loudly. ELSIE *runs and joins her, yelling.* MRS. ROCKETT *sits transfixed, staring at him murderously.*

HENRY [*quietly*]: Three generations. Grandmother, Mother and Kid. Made of the same bones and sinews and muscles and glands, millions of you, millions just like you. You're past it now, Mother, you're past the thick of the fray, you're nothing but a music-hall joke, a mother-in-law with a bit of money put by. Dorrie, the next few years will show whether you've got guts or not. Maybe what I'm doing to you will save your immortal soul in the long run, that'd be a bit of all right, wouldn't it? I doubt it, though, your immortal soul's too measly. You're a natural bully and a cheat, and I'm sick of the sight of you; I should also like to take this opportunity of saying that I hate that bloody awful slave bangle and I always have. As for you, Elsie, you've got a chance, it's a slim one, I grant you, but still it's a chance. If you learn to work and be independent and, when the time comes, give what you have to give freely and without demanding life-long payment for it, there's just a bit of hope that you'll turn into a decent human being. At all events, if you'll take one parting piece of advice from your cruel, ungrateful father, you'll spend the first money you ever earn on having your adenoids out. Good-bye, one and all. Nice to have known you!

The wails of DORIS *and* ELSIE *rise in volume as he goes jauntily out, slamming the door behind him.*

CURTAIN

SHADOW PLAY
A Musical Fantasy

CHARACTERS

VICTORIA GAYFORTH
SIMON GAYFORTH
MARTHA CUNNINGHAM
GEORGE CUNNINGHAM
LENA
SIBYL HESTON
MICHAEL DOYLE
A YOUNG MAN
HODGE—Dresser

Time: The Present.

The scene is a well-furnished, rather luxurious bedroom in the Gayforths' house in Mayfair. There is a bed on the right with a table by the side of it on which are various bottles, books and a telephone.

Below the bed there is a door which leads to the bathroom. On the left there is a door leading to the passage and the rest of the house. Above this is a dressing-table. At the foot of the bed there is a small sofa.

When the curtain rises LENA, VICTORIA's *maid, is bustling about the room. It is about midnight and she is laying out a dressing-gown or negligée on the bed and generally arranging the room for the night.*

VICTORIA *and* MARTHA *come in from the left.* VICTORIA *is about thirty; beautifully gowned. Her manner is bored and irritable.* MARTHA *is slightly older, also well dressed but more tranquil*

VICKY: —It couldn't matter less whether I go to Alice's or not—in fact it would be infinitely more comfortable for everybody concerned if I didn't.

MARTHA: What nonsense!

VICKY: Alice's parties are always dreary, and I don't feel in the mood even for a good party to-night.

MARTHA: What's the matter?

VICKY: I've told you—I've got a headache.

MARTHA: I think you're unwise.

VICKY: What do you mean, darling?

MARTHA: You know perfectly well what I mean.

VICKY [*sitting down at the dressing-table*]: Of course I do, but I'm getting tired of everybody being subtle and hiding behind the furniture—I know that Simon will go without me and I know that Sibyl will be there and I know that if I don't go he will leave with her and if I do go he will leave with me and wish he was leaving with her. I also know that I'm bored stiff with the whole situation—let it rip——

MARTHA: Line of least resistance.

VICKY: Exactly—I have a headache—I feel thoroughly disagreeable—all I want is sleep—no more resisting—just sleep—Lena—give me three Anytal——

LENA: Three, madame?

VICKY: Yes, three—and you can go to bed.

LENA: Yes, madame.

MARTHA: Is the extra tablet a gesture of defiance?

VICKY: Don't be tiresome, Martha.

LENA *brings her three tablets from a bottle by the bed and a glass of water.*

MARTHA: Do you take those things every night?

VICKY [*swallowing the tablets*]: No, darling, I don't. And

[*153*]

even if I did it wouldn't matter a bit—they're perfectly harmless.

LENA: Are you sure that's all, madame?

VICKY: Yes, thank you, Lena—good night.

LENA: Good night, madame.

She goes out.

MARTHA: I don't like seeing people unhappy.

VICKY: I'm not in the least unhappy—just tired.

MARTHA: How much do you mind?

VICKY: Mind what?

She takes the dressing-gown off the bed and goes into the bathroom, leaving the door open.

MARTHA [*firmly*]: About Simon and Sibyl.

VICKY: Heart-broken, dear—— [*She laughs.*] You mustn't be deceived by my gay frivolity, it's really only masking agony and defeat and despair——

MARTHA [*helping herself to a cigarette*]: You're extremely irritating.

VICKY: That's what you wanted, isn't it?

MARTHA: You needn't be suspicious of me, you know—I have no axe to grind—I merely wanted to help——

VICKY: You're a noble, understanding old friend, darling, that's what you are, and I must say I should like to crack you over the head with a bottle.

MARTHA: Thank you, dear.

The telephone rings.

VICKY: Answer that, will you?—it's probably Michael—I'll be out in a minute——

MARTHA: All right. [*She goes to the telephone.*] Hallo—No, it's Martha—She's in the bathroom, she'll be out in a minute—No, she's not—We've been to a play and it was so good that it gave her a headache—Hold on, here she is——

VICKY *comes in in a dressing-gown, flings herself on to the bed and takes the telephone.*

VICKY: Hallo, Michael—No, I'm not—Yes, I've doped myself

[*154*]

to the eyes and I'm about to go off into a coma—Of course you can't, don't be so idiotic—What are you in such a state about?—I thought we'd settled all that—It's no use dropping your voice like that—Martha can hear perfectly well, she's got ears like a hawk——

MARTHA: Perhaps you'd like me to go?

VICKY [*to* MARTHA]: Be quiet, darling—— [*At telephone.*] —I'm tired, Michael, and I've got a headache and so will you kindly shut up—Yes, all right—to-morrow—Good God, no, I shall be sound asleep—Go away, Michael, I can't bear any more—— [*She hangs up.*] It's lovely being loved, isn't it?

She rolls over on the bed face downwards.

MARTHA: You'd better get into bed——

VICKY: Perhaps you'd like to fill a hot-water bottle and take my temperature?

MARTHA [*patiently*]: Have you got a book to read?

VICKY: Yes, but it's unreadable.

MARTHA: Do get into bed.

VICKY: Go to hell, darling, and don't fuss——

MARTHA [*seriously*]: I really wish I could do something——

VICKY [*violently*]: Stop it, I tell you—I don't want your sympathy—I don't want anybody's sympathy—whatever happens, happens—let it—what does it matter——

MARTHA: Very well. [*She turns to go.*]

VICKY [*jumping off the bed and coming to her*]: I'm sorry— I know I'm beastly, but you see it's no use discussing things— the Anytal will begin to work soon and I shall have a nice long sleep and feel much better in the morning—— It was the play that upset me, I think—you were quite right—everybody seemed to be having such a good time, didn't they?—it's a bit tantalising to see everybody having quite such a good time—it would be so much easier, wouldn't it, if we had music when things go wrong—music and a little dancing and the certainty of 'Happy ever after'—I hope you didn't miss the ironic twist at the end when they were married—crashing cords and complete tidiness—very convenient—— Go away, darling—go and collect George and Simon and go on to Alice's—I shall go to sleep in a minute—really I will——

MARTHA: All right—I'll telephone you in the morning——

She kisses her and is about to go, when SIMON *comes into the room. He is wearing a dressing-gown over his evening clothes.*

VICKY [*surprised*]: Simon!

SIMON [*to* MARTHA]: George is waiting for you, Martha—he's getting a bit restive.

VICKY: Aren't you going to Alice's?

SIMON: No, I didn't feel that I could face it.

VICKY: Oh, I see.

MARTHA: Do you want me to make excuses for you both, or just not say anything about it?

VICKY: Say that you haven't seen us, and why aren't we there, and is there any truth in the rumour that we're not getting on very well—— [*She laughs.*]

SIMON: Don't be silly, Vicky.

VICKY: Say that I've gone to Ostend with Michael and that Simon's shot himself—but only in the leg.

SIMON [*bitterly*]: Say that it's definitely true that we're not getting on very well—say that it's due to incompatibility of humour.

MARTHA: I shall say that I don't know you at all—any more.

She goes out.

VICKY [*calling after her*]: Give my love to Sibyl!

SIMON: That was a bit cheap, wasn't it?

VICKY: I thought it was only kind—Sibyl can't live without love—like the woman in the play to-night—don't you remember——? [*She hums.*] 'Nobody can live without loving somebody, nobody can love without leaving somebody!'

SIMON: You mustn't forget to sing that to Michael.

VICKY: Are we going to bicker? There's nothing like a nice bicker to round off a jolly evening.

SIMON: I'm getting a little tired of bickering.

VICKY: Let's not then, let's be absolutely divine to each other—let's pretend.

SIMON: I didn't go to Alice's party on purpose——

VICKY: I didn't think it was a sudden attack of amnesia.

SIMON: I want to talk to you.

VICKY: Do you, Simon? What about?

SIMON: Lots of things.

VICKY: Name fifteen.

SIMON: Seriously.

VICKY: There you are, you see—our moods are clashing again —it really is most unfortunate.

SIMON: I failed to notice during the evening that your spirits were so abnormally high.

VICKY: A sudden change for the better, dear, let's make the most of it.

SIMON: There's something I want to say to you—I've been wanting to say it for quite a while.

VICKY: Take the plunge, my darling—we're alone in the swimming bath.

SIMON: Would you consider divorcing me?

VICKY: Oh, Simon!

SIMON: If I made everything easy——

VICKY: Naming Sibyl?

SIMON: Of course not.

VICKY: You mean you'd prefer to be implicated with a professional homebreaker as opposed to an amateur one?

SIMON: I would like, if possible, to keep this conversation impersonal.

VICKY: We might put on fancy dress for it.

SIMON: I'm serious, Vicky.

VICKY: I'm told that all really funny comedians are serious.

SIMON: You haven't answered my question yet.

VICKY: I thought perhaps I hadn't heard it quite clearly.

SIMON: I want you to divorce me.

VICKY: Yes, now I hear—it's a beastly question, isn't it?

SIMON: Not so very beastly if you analyse it—quite sensible really.

VICKY: It oughtn't to be such a shock—but somehow it is—it makes me feel a little sick.

SIMON: I'm sorry.

VICKY: Don't worry about being sorry—feeling a little sick doesn't matter that much.

SIMON: I've thought it all over very carefully.

VICKY: Oh, Simon, have you? Have you really?

SIMON: Of course I have. It's been on my mind for a long time.

VICKY: How sinister that sounds—surely not for a very long time?

SIMON: Long enough.

VICKY: You're cruelly definite.

SIMON: It's less cruel to be definite—in the long run.

VICKY: It's been an awfully short run—really.

SIMON: You haven't answered me yet.

VICKY: An amicable divorce—everything below board?

SIMON: Yes.

VICKY: Where will you go with your temporary light of love? The South of France, or just good old Brighton?

SIMON: I don't think we need discuss that.

VICKY: It's a nasty business, isn't it—a very nasty business.

SIMON: Not necessarily, if it can be arranged discreetly and without fuss.

VICKY: Do you love her so much? Sibyl, I mean.

SIMON: I'd rather not discuss that either.

VICKY: Perhaps you'd prefer to conduct the whole thing by signs—sort of Dumb Crambo.

SIMON: You're unbelievably irritating.

VICKY: When did you first begin to hate me?—When did I first begin to get on your nerves?—What did I say?—What did I do?—Was it a dress I wore—the way I laughed at somebody's joke?—Was I suddenly gay when you were sad?—Was I insensitive?—Was I dull? When did it start—tell me if you can remember—please tell me.

SIMON: Don't be so foolish.

VICKY: I won't be irritating any more, Simon—I'll try to be sensible—really I will—but I must know why—why things change—I wish to God I hadn't taken those sleeping tablets—my head's going round—I would so love to be clear, just at this moment, but nothing's clear at all——

SIMON: I didn't know you'd taken anything.

VICKY: Don't be alarmed—I'm not becoming a drug fiend—it's an amiable, gentle prescription, just to make me sleep when I have a headache, or when I'm overtired or unhappy——

SIMON: There's the overture—we shall be late.

VICKY: What did you say?

SIMON: —You really ought not to get into the habit of taking things to make you sleep—however harmless they are——

VICKY: We've only been married five years—it seems longer at moments—then it seems no time at all——

The music begins, and, after a few chords, stops again.

SIMON: There it is again—listen.

VICKY: If you really love Sibyl, deeply and truly, it's different, but I have an awful feeling that you don't—anyhow, not enough——

SIMON: "We will wander on together—
      Through the sunny summer weather—
      To our cosy little château
      Like a pastoral by Watteau.

TOGETHER: To our cosy little château on the Rhine."

SIMON: —It isn't that I don't love you—I always shall love you—but this is something else—I don't know what started it, but I do know that it's terribly strong—and then there's Michael —I've been awfully angry about Michael——

VICKY: That's idiotic—Michael doesn't mean a thing to me —you know perfectly well he doesn't——

The music begins again, this time more loudly.

SIMON: There it is again—do hurry. [*He dances a few steps.*]

VICKY [*calling*]: Lena—Lena—hurry up—— I was miserable anyhow to-night—all the time we were in the theatre—everybody was having such a good time—and then they were married in the end—that was funny, wasn't it?—about them being married in the end. . . .

SIMON: —It isn't that I want to make you unhappy, but you must admit we haven't been hitting it off particularly well during the last year—if we're not comfortable together surely it would be much more sensible to separate——

The scene darkens. The side flats move off and up stage away from the centre flat.

VICKY: I feel so sad inside about it—I wish I could make you understand—it was so lovely in the beginning——

SIMON: Things never stay the same—you can't expect what was lovely then to be lovely now——

VICKY [*almost crying*]: Why not—why not?—Then we were happy——

SIMON: But, darling, you must see——

"THEN"

SIMON: Here in the light of this unkind familiar now
     Every gesture is clear and cold for us,
     Even yesterday's growing old for us,
       Everything changed somehow.
       If some forgotten lover's vow
    Could wake a memory in my heart again,
    Perhaps the joys that we knew would start again.
       Can't we reclaim an hour or so
       The past is not so long ago.

VICKY: Then, love was complete for us
     Then, the days were sweet for us
     Life rose to its feet for us

[*160*]

And stepped aside
Before our pride.
Then, we knew the best of it
Then, our hearts stood the test of it.
Now, the magic has flown
We face the unknown
Apart and alone.

SIMON: Hodge—where's Hodge?—I must change—quick—we're going back.

The orchestra swells. FLORRIE [LENA]—*comes hurrying in with an evening gown over her arm and a pair of shoes, a mirror, a powder-puff, etc., in her hands.* VICKY *sinks on to the bed.*

SIMON: You can't sit there—we're going back——

FLORRIE: Here, dear—here's a chair.

VICKY: I'm not sure that I want to—I'm not at all sure—maybe it won't be as lovely as I think it was——

SIMON: Don't be such a fool—grab it while you can—grab every scrap of happiness while you can—Hodge—come on——

HODGE, *a dresser, comes in with a dinner-jacket.* SIMON *takes off his dressing-gown and puts on the dinner-jacket.* VICKY *is changing on the opposite side of the stage. Meanwhile the whole scene is changing. The lights in the foreground fade except for the two spotlights on* SIMON *and* VICKY.

VICKY [*breathlessly*]: Play—go on playing—we must have music——

SIMON *comes down to the footlights and begins to sing to the conductor. He sings.*

"PLAY, ORCHESTRA, PLAY."

SIMON: Listen to the strain it plays once more for us,
There it is again, the past in store for us.
Wake in memory some forgotten song
To break the rhythm—driving us along
And make harmony again a last encore for us.

[*161*]

SHADOW PLAY

Play, orchestra, play
Play something light and sweet and gay
 For we must have music
 We must have music
To drive our fears away.
While our illusions swiftly fade for us,
 Let's have an orchestra score.
In the confusions the years have made for us
 Serenade for us, just once more.
Life needn't be grey,
Although it's changing day by day,
Though a few old dreams may decay,
Play, orchestra, play.

VICKY *joins him and they finish it together. Meanwhile all the lights fade entirely except for two pin-spots on the two of them. The spot on* SIMON *goes out and* VICKY *is left singing almost hysterically "We Must Have Music." The orchestra rises to a crescendo and there is a complete black-out.*

 To measured music and in a pool of light, SIBYL HESTON *appears. She lights a cigarette and glances at her wrist-watch.* SIMON *appears from the opposite side of the stage. He stands a little apart from her. The music stops.*

 SIBYL: I'm waiting—I'm waiting—why don't you tell her?

 SIMON: It will hurt her, you know.

 SIBYL: She can weep on Michael's shoulder—it's a very attractive shoulder.

 SIMON: I don't want to hurt her.

 SIBYL: She'll have to know sooner or later. Nobody can live without loving somebody, nobody can love without leaving somebody.

 SIMON: I saw you in the theatre to-night—you looked marvellous.

 SIBYL: Sweet Simon.

 SIMON: Very cool and green and wise.

[*162*]

SIBYL: Not wise—oh, my dear, not wise at all. I happen to love you.

SIMON: Is that so unwise?

SIBYL: Let's say—indefinite!

SIMON: It's less cruel to be indefinite in the long run.

SIBYL: Tell her the truth—you must tell her the truth.

SIMON: I have been awfully angry about Michael.

SIBYL: Why be angry, darling? It's such a waste of energy.

SIMON: I don't like Vicky making a fool of herself.

SIBYL: I don't like Vicky making a fool of you.

SIMON: I didn't know she took things to make her sleep.

SIBYL: You must tell her the truth—sleep or no sleep.

The music starts again. MICHAEL *walks on. He passes* SIBYL *and* SIMON, *stops, lights a cigarette and glances at his wrist-watch. The music stops.*

MICHAEL: I'm waiting—I'm waiting—why don't you tell her?

SIMON: I don't want to hurt her.

MICHAEL: Give her my love.

SIMON: That was a bit cheap, wasn't it?

SIBYL [*laughing*]: When did she first begin to get on your nerves, Simon? What started it? Was it a dress she wore? Was it the way she laughed at somebody's joke? Was she suddenly gay when you were sad? Was she insensitive? Was she dull?

MICHAEL: Was she dull?

SIBYL: Was she dull?

SIMON: It was so lovely in the beginning.

SIBYL: Things never stay the same—you can't expect what was lovely then to be lovely now.

SIMON: We're going back all the same—it's our only chance——

SIBYL: Was she dull?

MICHAEL: Was she dull?

SIMON: Shut up—shut up both of you—we're going back——

[*163*]

He begins to sing and as he sings the lights fade on SIBYL *and* MICHAEL.

> Life needn't be grey
> Though it is changing day by day.
> Though a few old dreams may decay
> Play Orchestra—Play Orchestra—Play—Orchestra——
> Play——

Black out.
The lights come up on a moonlit garden. There is a stone seat on the left of the stage. VICKY *and a* YOUNG MAN *are sitting on it.*

VICKY: It's nice and cool in the garden.

YOUNG MAN: It's nice and cool in the garden.

VICKY: Country house dances can be lovely when the weather's good, can't they?

YOUNG MAN: Rather—rather—yes, of course—rather.

VICKY: I'm waiting for something.

YOUNG MAN: Country house dances can be lovely when the weather's good, can't they?

VICKY: This is where it all began.

YOUNG MAN: It's nice and cool in the garden.

VICKY: Please hurry, my darling, I can't wait to see you for the first time.

YOUNG MAN: Do you know this part of the country?

VICKY: Intimately. I'm staying here with my aunt, you know.

YOUNG MAN: Does she ride to hounds?

VICKY: Incessantly.

YOUNG MAN: That's ripping, isn't it?—I mean it really is ripping.

VICKY: Yes. She's a big woman and she kills little foxes—she's kind *au fond*, but she dearly loves killing little foxes.

YOUNG MAN: We're getting on awfully well—it's awfully nice out here—I think you're awfully pretty.

VICKY: This is waste of time—he should be here **by now**—walking through the trees—coming towards me.

YOUNG MAN: I think you're an absolute fizzer.

VICKY: Yes, I remember you saying that—it made me want to giggle—but I controlled myself beautifully.

YOUNG MAN: I think you know my sister—she's in pink.

VICKY: I remember her clearly—a beastly girl.

YOUNG MAN: In pink.

VICKY [*suddenly*]:

> "In pink—in pink—
> Your sister's dressed in pink
> It wasn't very wise I think
> To choose that unbecoming shade
> Of pink——"

YOUNG MAN: I'm so glad you like her—you must come and stay with us—my mother's an absolute fizzer—you'd love her.

VICKY: God forbid!

YOUNG MAN: That's absolutely ripping of you.

VICKY: Now—now—at last—you're walking through the trees—hurry——

SIMON *comes through the trees. He is smoking a cigarette.*

VICKY: I thought you'd missed your entrance.

SIMON: Are you engaged for this dance?

VICKY: I was, but I'll cut it if you'll promise to love me always and never let anything or anybody spoil it—never——

SIMON: But of course—that's understood.

YOUNG MAN: Will you excuse me—I have to dance with Lady Dukes.

VICKY: Certainly.

YOUNG MAN: Good hunting.

VICKY: Thank you so much—it's been so boring.

YOUNG MAN: Not at all—later perhaps.

He goes.

SIMON: Well—here we are.

VICKY: The first time—we knew at once, didn't we? Don't you remember how we discussed it afterwards?

SIMON: I saw you in the ballroom—I wondered who you were.

VICKY: My name's Victoria—Victoria Marden.

SIMON: Mine's Simon Gayforth.

VICKY: How do you do?

SIMON: Quite well, thank you.

VICKY: I suppose you came down from London for the dance?

SIMON: Yes, I'm staying with the Bursbys——

VICKY: What do you do?

SIMON: I'm in a bank.

VICKY: High up in the bank? Or just sitting in a cage totting up things?

SIMON: Oh, quite high up really—it's a very good bank.

VICKY: I'm so glad.

SIMON: How lovely you are.

VICKY: No, no, that came later—you've skipped some.

SIMON: Sorry.

VICKY: You're nice and thin—your eyes are funny—you move easily—I'm afraid you're terribly attractive——

SIMON: You never said that.

VICKY: No, but I thought it.

SIMON: Stick to the script.

VICKY: Small talk—a lot of small talk with quite different thoughts going on behind it—this garden's really beautiful—are you good at gardens?——

SIMON: No, but I'm persevering—I'm all right on the more straightforward blooms—you know—Snap-dragons, sweet william, cornflowers and tobacco plant—and I can tell a Dorothy Perkins a mile off.

VICKY: That hedge over there is called Supressus Macrocapa.

SIMON: Do you swear it?

VICKY: It grows terrifically quickly but they do say that it goes a bit thin underneath in about twenty years——

SIMON: How beastly of them to say that—it's slander.

VICKY: Did you know about Valerian smelling of cats?

SIMON: You're showing off again.

VICKY: It's true.

SIMON: I can go one better than that—Lotuses smell of pineapple.

VICKY [*sadly*]: Everything smells of something else—it's dreadfully confusing——

SIMON: Never mind, darling—I love you desperately—I knew it the first second I saw you——

VICKY: You're skipping again.

They sing a light Duet: "*You Were There,*" *after which they dance.*

"YOU WERE THERE"

I

SIMON: Was it in the real world or was it in a dream?
Was it just a note from some eternal theme?
Was it accidental or accurately planned?
　How could I hesitate
　Knowing that my fate
Led me by the hand?

REFRAIN

　You were there
I saw you and my heart stopped beating
　You were there
And in that first enchanted meeting
　Life changed its tune, the stars, the moon came near
　　to me.
　Dreams that I dreamed, like magic seemed to be
　　clear to me, dear to me.
　You were there.

[*167*]

Your eyes looked into mine and faltered.
  Everywhere
The colour of the whole world altered.
  False became true
  My universe tumbled in two
The earth became heaven, for you were there.

2

VICKY: How can we explain it—the spark, and then the fire?
How add up the total of our hearts' desire?
Maybe some magician, a thousand years ago—
Wove us a subtle spell—so that we could tell—so that
  we could know——
You were there—[*etc.*]

*During the dance the lights fade on the scene and they finish
in each other's arms in a spotlight. The spotlight fades and in
the darkness a voice is heard singing "Then they knew the best
of it—then their hearts stood the test of it," etc.*

A spotlight picks up LENA—*singing, holding the tablets and a
glass of water. After song fade again.*

Then love was complete for them
Then the days were sweet for them
Life rose to its feet for them
And stepped aside
Before their Pride.
Then they knew the best of it
Then their hearts stood the test of it.
Now the magic has flown
They face the unknown
Apart and alone.

The lights go up again on the interior of a limousine. MARTHA
and GEORGE CUNNINGHAM *are sitting in it.*

[*168*]

GEORGE: On the whole this has been one of the most uncomfortable evenings I've ever spent.

MARTHA: There, there, dear, I know, but for heaven's sake don't go on about it.

GEORGE [*petulantly*]: Why, if they had to take us to dinner and a play, should they have chosen that particular dinner and that particular play?

MARTHA: What was wrong with the dinner?

GEORGE: Gastronomically speaking it was excellent, but the atmosphere reeked with conjugal infelicity—when people are at loggerheads they should refrain from entertaining—it's bad for the digestive tract.

MARTHA: For an elderly barrister you're unduly sensitive.

GEORGE: I expected the grouse to sit up on its plate and offer me a brief.

MARTHA: Never mind, when we get to Alice's you'll be able to have a nice drink and talk to some lovely young things and feel much better.

GEORGE: And why that play? Sentimental twaddle.

MARTHA: The music was lovely.

GEORGE: That's no good to me. You know perfectly well I can't distinguish "Abide with me" from "God Save the King."

MARTHA: Concentrate on "God Save the King."

GEORGE: I couldn't even go to sleep with those idiotic people loving each other for ever all over the stage.

MARTHA: Well we'll go to a nice soothing gangster picture to-morrow night and you can watch people killing each other all over the screen.

GEORGE: What's wrong with them, anyway?

MARTHA: Who, Simon and Vicky?

GEORGE: Yes.

MARTHA: They're unhappy.

GEORGE: Well, they oughtn't to be—they've got everything they want.

MARTHA: Sibyl Heston's got hold of Simon and Vicky's trying

to pretend that she doesn't mind a bit and everything's in a dreary muddle—women like Sibyl Heston ought to be shot.

GEORGE: Sometimes they are.

MARTHA: Not often enough.

GEORGE: I suppose Vicky's got a young man hanging around, hasn't she?

MARTHA: No, not really—she's been encouraging Michael Doyle a bit but it doesn't mean anything—it's just part of the pretending.

GEORGE: Damn fools—they're all damn fools——

VICKY *runs on from the side of the stage. She is picked up by a blue spotlight.*

VICKY: Go away, you're spoiling it all—I know what you're saying—I know what everybody's saying——

MARTHA: I was only trying to help.

VICKY: I know—I know—you're very kind—but it isn't any use——

GEORGE: People were so much more sensible twenty years ago—take my sister, for instance—look how brilliantly she managed her life—you ought to have known my sister——

VICKY: In pink.

GEORGE: In brilliant pink.

VICKY [*singing*]:

> "In pink—in pink
> Your sister's dressed in pink,
> It wasn't very wise I think
> To choose that unbecoming shade
> Of pink——!"

SIMON *enters and is picked up in a blue spot.*

SIMON: This compartment is reserved—we're going back.

GEORGE: I'm most awfully sorry.

VICKY: There are probably some empty ones farther along the train.

MARTHA: But of course—we quite understand—George, help me with my dressing-case——

SIMON: Allow me——

He helps them to remove imaginary luggage from the rack.

GEORGE: I suppose you don't happen to know what time we reach Milan?

SIMON: I know we arrive in Venice at about six-thirty—I think there's about four hours' difference.

VICKY: It's really charming of you to be so considerate—you see we are on our honeymoon.

MARTHA: Grab every scrap of happiness while you can.

GEORGE: We shall meet later.

SIMON: I hope so.

MARTHA *and* GEORGE *step out of the car and walk off.*

SIMON *and* VICKY *climb in. The spotlights follow them into the cab.*

SIMON: Well, here we are.

VICKY: My name's Victoria.

SIMON: Victoria what?

VICKY: Victoria Gayforth.

SIMON: What a silly name.

VICKY: I adore it.

SIMON: That's because you're sentimental.

VICKY: Fiercely sentimental—over romantic too.

SIMON: Dearest darling.

VICKY: The wedding went off beautifully, didn't it?

SIMON: Brief, to the point, and not unduly musical.

VICKY: Didn't mother look nice?

SIMON: Not particularly.

VICKY: Oh, Simon!

SIMON: It was her hat, I think—it looked as though it were in a hurry and couldn't stay very long.

VICKY: Was that man who slapped you on the back your uncle?

SIMON: Yes, dear—that was my uncle.

[*171*]

VICKY: I'm so sorry.

SIMON: He ran away to sea, you know, when he was very young, and then, unfortunately, he ran back again.

VICKY: Your sister looked charming.

SIMON: In pink.

VICKY: In pink—in pink——

SIMON: Stop it—stop it—you'll wake yourself up.

VICKY: It was that rhyme in the play to-night—it keeps coming into my mind.

SIMON: Do concentrate—we're on our honeymoon.

VICKY: Happy ever after.

SIMON: That's right.

VICKY: Do you think that those people we turned out of the carriage ever loved each other as much as we do?

SIMON: Nobody ever loved each other as much as we do with the possible exception of Romeo and Juliet, Héloïse and Abélard, Paolo and Francesca, Dante and Beatrice——

VICKY: I wish she hadn't been called Beatrice—it's such a smug name.

SIMON: Anthony and Cleopatra, Pelleas and Melisande——

VICKY: I've always felt that Melisande was rather a silly girl—so vague.

SIMON: All right—wash out Melisande.

VICKY [looking out of the window]: Look at all those little houses flashing by—think of all the millions of people living in them—eating and drinking—dressing and undressing—getting up and going to bed—having babies——

SIMON: When I was a young bride I never mentioned such things on my honeymoon.

VICKY: Things never stay the same.

SIMON: It was considered immodest to do anything but weep gently and ask for glasses of water.

VICKY: I'm abandoned, darling—I can't wait to be in your arms——

SIMON: Dear heart——

He takes her in his arms.

VICKY [*struggling*]: No no—this isn't right—my clothes are all wrong—I must go——

SIMON: Don't go.

VICKY: I must—this dressing-gown's all wrong I tell you—when we arrived in Venice I was wearing a blue tailor-made—and then later we dined—and I was in grey——

SIMON: In grey—in grey
　　　Your dress was soft and grey
　　　It seems a million years away
　　　The ending of that sweet and happy day.

VICKY: Oh darling——

SIMON: Don't go——

VICKY: I must—I must——

She steps out of the carriage and disappears into the darkness.

SIMON *left alone, sings a reprise of "You Were There," and the lights fade completely.*

When the lights go up SIMON *and* VICKY *are sitting at a little table with a shaded light on it. They are just finishing dinner.*

SIMON: We can sit on the piazza for a little and then we can drift . . .

VICKY: Let's call the gondola right away and cut out the piazza—I'm a big drifting girl.

SIMON: I think the band on the piazza will be awfully disappointed.

VICKY: It's funny, isn't it, to be so frightfully in love that you feel as if you were going mad?

SIMON: Ever so funny.

VICKY: Do you think our front gondolier is nicer than our back one?

SIMON: Not altogether—he has better teeth, of course, but then he's about fifty years younger.

VICKY: Let's come here again in fifty years' time.

SIMON: All right.

[*173*]

VICKY: We can arrange to be carried on to the train—it will be quite simple.

SIMON: It won't be a train, darling—it will be a pointed silver bullet leaving Croydon at four and arriving here at twenty-past three.

VICKY: Oh dear!

SIMON: What's the matter?

VICKY: We haven't quarrelled yet.

SIMON: Never mind.

VICKY: We'll have a nice quarrel when we get back to London, won't we?

SIMON: I shall sulk for the first few days, anyhow—I'm the sulky type, you know.

VICKY: That's why I married you.

SIMON: Oh, darling—I'm going to be terribly serious for a minute—will you bear with me?

VICKY: Of course.

SIMON: There's something I want to say to you—I've been wanting to say it for quite a while——

VICKY [*with panic in her voice*]: Oh, Simon, don't—what is it? What is it?

SIMON: I love you.

VICKY [*putting her head down on the table*]: You mustn't make people cry on their honeymoons—it's not cricket.

SIMON [*tenderly*]: Dearest—everything's cricket if only you have faith.

VICKY: When did you know you loved me—the very first minute, I mean?

SIMON: In the garden—during the dance—I saw you and my heart stopped beating——

VICKY: It was a most enchanted meeting.

SIMON: Life changed its tune—the stars and moon came near to me——

VICKY: Dreams that I'd dreamed, like magic seemed to be clear to me—dear to me——

[*174*]

SIMON: False became true—my universe tumbled in two—the earth became heaven—for you were there——

VICKY: Stop it—stop it—it's that damned musical comedy again—going round and round in my head—listen—before the dream breaks say what you said that night in Venice—say it from your heart as you said it then—say it, please—please——

SIMON: I'm not sure that I can remember—it's a long while ago——

VICKY: Please, Simon—please——

SIMON: It's this, darling—we're here together close as close and it's the beginning—but we're going to be together for a long time—probably all our lives, so we must be careful—I want to reassure you now about later on—about any tricks the future might play on us—I know I love you with all my heart—with every bit of me—it's easy now, because it's summer weather and there isn't a cloud in the sky and we're alone—but there'll be other people presently—we can't live our whole lives on this little island—other people are dangerous—they spoil true love, not consciously because they want to, but because they're themselves—out for all they can get—mischievous—you do see what I mean, don't you——?

VICKY: You mean they might make us want them one day instead of each other.

SIMON: Yes, but only a little—not like this—not all the way round——

VICKY: I can't imagine even that—I'm very single-tracked.

SIMON: Don't look sad—don't even have a flicker of unhappiness not for ages yet, anyway—but whenever you do—if I'm bad or foolish or unkind, or even unfaithful—just remember this, because this is what really matters—this lovely understanding of each other—it may be a jumping-off place for many future journeys—but however long the journey one's got to come back some time, and this is the white cliffs of Dover—hang on to the white cliffs of Dover——

VICKY: I'll try——

[*175*]

They hold hands for a moment across the table.

There is a burst of music which dies away on a discord. Then a dance tune starts and keeps up a steady rhythm during the ensuing scene. The light on SIMON *and* VICKY *fades a little. They are sitting quite still gazing at each other.* SIBYL HESTON *and* MICHAEL DOYLE *dance on together out of the shadows. They are in a brilliant spotlight.*

MICHAEL: We're a bit early, aren't we? They're still on their honeymoon.

SIBYL: Nonsense. The curtain will be lowered between scenes two and three to denote a lapse of four years——

The light on SIMON *and* VICKY *goes out completely.*

MICHAEL [*over his shoulder*]: I'm so sorry.

SIBYL: It's impossible to dance here.

MICHAEL: They put so many tables on the floor.

SIBYL: There's no room at all.

MICHAEL: Let's go on to the Florida.

SIBYL: And the Cocoanut Grove.

MICHAEL: And the Four Hundred.

SIBYL: And the Blue Train.

SIMON *and* VICKY *dance on in another spotlight.*

SIMON: There's always the Florida.

VICKY: And the Cocoanut Grove.

SIMON: And the Four Hundred.

VICKY: And the Blue Train.

The rhythm gets slightly faster. The two couples circle round each other.

SIBYL: The Florida.

SIMON: The Cocoanut Grove.

MICHAEL: The Four Hundred.

VICKY: The Blue Train.

SIBYL: The Florida.

VICKY: The Cocoanut Grove.

MICHAEL: The Four Hundred.

SIMON: The Blue Train.

[*176*]

SHADOW PLAY

The music gets faster still. They change partners. SIMON
dances with SIBYL *and* MICHAEL *with* VICKY—*then they change
back to each other again*—*then once more*—*all saying together;*
"The Florida," "The Cocoanut Grove," "The Four Hundred,"
"The Blue Train." MICHAEL *and* VICKY *disappear and* SIBYL *and*
SIMON *are left dancing round and round together, faster and
faster. From the darkness can be heard voices shouting rhyth-
mically: "The Florida," "The Cocoanut Grove," "The Four
Hundred," "The Blue Train," coming to a crescendo and then
a black out.*

LENA *appears on the right-hand side of the stage with a telephone.* MARTHA *appears on the opposite side, also with a
telephone. Both in spotlights.*

MARTHA: Hallo—who is it?

LENA: It's Lena, madame.

MARTHA: Oh, Lena—yes—what is it?

LENA: Mr. Gayforth asked me to telephone to you, madame——

MARTHA: Is anything wrong?

LENA: It's Mrs. Gayforth, madame—those sleeping tablets—
Mr. Gayforth wants to know if you can leave the party and
come at once——

MARTHA: Good heavens! Is she ill?

LENA: Yes, madame—that is—she's not exactly ill but——

MARTHA: Have you sent for a doctor?

LENA: No, madame—Mr. Gayforth didn't want to send for
a doctor until he'd seen you.

MARTHA: I'll come at once.

LENA: It was that extra Anytal tablet, madame—I knew she
shouldn't have taken it——

MARTHA: I'll be there in a few minutes—in the meantime—
give her some strong black coffee——

The lights fade.

In the darkness VICKY's *voice is heard.*

VICKY: Simon, Simon—where are you?—I'm lonely—I'm

[177]

frightened—don't go away from me yet—in spite of what they say there is still time if only we're careful——

SIMON: There's something I want to say to you—I've been wanting to say it for quite a while——

VICKY: Don't say it—don't say it yet.

SIMON: I would like if possible to keep this conversation impersonal.

VICKY: I would so love to be clear at this moment. But nothing's clear at all——

SIMON: I didn't know you had taken anything——

VICKY: It was only to make me sleep—whenever I'm tired or unhappy, oh, Simon—Simon—come back—the White Cliffs of Dover—I'm trying so hard—I'm trying to hold on—don't leave me—don't leave me——

SIMON: Give her a little more, Lena.

LENA: Yes, sir.

SIMON: You don't think we ought to send for a doctor?

MARTHA: No, she'll be all right.

SIMON: It was awfully sweet of you to come back, Martha—I got in a panic—you were the only one I could think of——

VICKY: I shall be sick if I have any more of that damned coffee.

SIMON: That's a very good idea—be sick.

VICKY: No, no—I hate being sick—it's mortifying—I'm perfectly all right now—really I am.

The lights slowly go up on the bedroom.

VICKY *is sitting on the edge of the bed.* SIMON *is sitting by her side with one arm round her, holding a cup of coffee in his other hand.* MARTHA *is kneeling on the floor at her feet.* LENA *is standing anxiously at the foot of the bed holding a coffee pot.*

SIMON: There, darling—won't you lie down a bit?

VICKY: Don't fuss.

SIMON: You ought to be ashamed of yourself.

VICKY: What are you rolling about on the floor for, Martha? It looks very silly.

MARTHA [*rising*]: You may well ask.

VICKY: I think I should like a cigarette.

SIMON: Then you will be sick.

VICKY: No, it's passed off.

LENA [*handing her a cigarette*]: Here, madame.

VICKY: Thank you, Lena. Match, please.

SIMON: Here, Martha, take this cup, will you?

He gives MARTHA *the coffee cup and lights* VICKY's *cigarette.*

VICKY: That's lovely. [*She puffs.*]

SIMON: It's all right, Lena—you can go to bed again.

LENA: Are you sure, sir?

SIMON: Yes, thank you, Lena.

LENA: Good night, sir.

SIMON: Good night.

LENA *goes out.*

VICKY: Now perhaps somebody will explain. What happened to me?

SIMON: You just went mad, that's all—raving.

VICKY [*interested*]: Did I froth at the mouth?

SIMON: I don't know—I was too agitated to notice.

MARTHA: I think I'd better go back to Alice's.

VICKY: Alice's! Oh yes, of course. Oh, Simon—I remember now.

SIMON: Don't think of anything—just relax.

MARTHA [*kissing her*]: Good night, darling.

VICKY [*absently—her thoughts a long way away*]: Good night.

MARTHA: Good night, Simon.

SIMON: Thanks awfully, Martha.

MARTHA *goes out.*

VICKY: I'm so sorry, Simon—I'm feeling quite tranquil now— let's talk about the divorce in the morning.

SIMON: Divorce? What do you mean?

VICKY: You asked me to divorce you, didn't you?

SIMON: Certainly not.

[*179*]

VICKY: Are you trying to make me believe that that was part of the dream?

SIMON: I don't know what you're talking about.

VICKY: It's sweet of you to lie—but it won't wash.

SIMON *sits on the bed again and puts his arms round her.*

SIMON: Please forgive me.

VICKY [*sleepily*]: We'll talk it all over calmly—to-morrow.

SIMON: All right.

VICKY [*resting her head on his shoulder*]: If you really love her all that much I'll try not to be beastly about it——

SIMON: I don't love anybody that much.

VICKY: What did I do when I went mad? I'm so interested.

SIMON: You talked a lot—I thought it was nonsense at first and then I realised that it was true—then you began dancing about the room—then you really did go mad—and I got very frightened and told Lena to ring up Martha——

VICKY: It was certainly a very strange feeling——

She closes her eyes and the music starts again very softly.

SIMON: It will be all right now—it really will—I promise.

VICKY: The music's beginning again.

The music swells. SIMON *lifts her gently on to the bed and covers her over with the counterpane. Then he kisses her, disentangles her cigarette from her fingers, tip-toes across the room and switches off the lights, all but a little lamp by the bed, and stretches himself on the sofa at her feet.*

The music reaches a crescendo as——

THE CURTAIN FALLS

TONIGHT AT 8.30
III

WAYS AND MEANS
A Light Comedy in Three Scenes

CHARACTERS

STELLA CARTWRIGHT
TOBY CARTWRIGHT
OLIVE LLOYD-RANSOME
LORD CHAPWORTH (Chaps)
NANNY
MURDOCH
STEVENS
PRINCESS ELENA KRASSILOFF
GASTON

The action of the play takes place in a bedroom in the Lloyd-Ransomes' house, Villa Zephyre, on the Côte d'Azur.

The time is the present.

SCENE I.   *11.30 a.m. on an April morning.*
SCENE II. *1.30 a.m. the following morning.*
SCENE III. *Two hours later.*

SCENE I

The Scene is a bedroom in the Villa Zephyre on the Côte
d'Azur. The Villa Zephyre belongs to Mrs. Lloyd-Ransome,
who is excessively rich, comparatively pleasant and entirely idle,
the bedroom therefore is luxurious and tastefully appointed. On
the right there is a dressing-table with, above it, a door leading
to the bathroom. On the left there is a French window leading
on to a small verandah, above that, in the back wall, is a door
leading to the passage and the rest of the house. There is a
slight recess in the back wall containing a very wide and com-
fortable bed.

This is occupied at the rise of the curtain by STELLA *and* TOBY
CARTWRIGHT. *They are an attractive couple in the thirties.*
Between them there is a breakfast tray. STELLA *is opening and*
reading letters, TOBY *is scanning the* Continental Daily Mail.
A certain amount of pale sunshine is coming through the win-
dow, but this fails to banish from either of their faces an ex-
pression of gloomy dissatisfaction. After a considerable silence,
STELLA *speaks.*

STELLA: Here's a letter from Aunt Hester.

TOBY: Is she well and hearty?

STELLA: Apparently.

TOBY: To hell with her!

There is a further silence.

STELLA [*pensively eating a brioche*]: Why do other people's
breakfasts always taste much nicer than one's own?

TOBY: Probably because they are.

There is another silence.

STELLA: I knew marrying you was a mistake at least seven

[*187*]

years ago, but I never realised the thoroughness of the mistake until now——

TOBY [*reading his paper*]: You will be interested to hear that Mrs. S. J. Pendleton gave a small dinner party for Mr. and Mrs. Hubert Weir at the Hotel Normandie in Le Touquet last night——

STELLA: How thrilling.

TOBY: Among the guests were Lord and Lady Haven, Mrs. George Durlap, the Countess Pantulucci, Mr. Henry Bird, Mr. and Mrs. Harvey Lincoln, Miss Styles——

STELLA: Shut up!

TOBY: I beg your pardon?

STELLA: I said shut up.

TOBY [*continuing*]: —Mr. and Mrs. Sidney Alford have returned from Vichy and are staying at the Crillon——

STELLA: Toby——

TOBY: They are to be joined in a few days by Mrs. Alford's sister, Lady Croker——

STELLA: Toby, please——

TOBY: Prince and Princess Jean Marie de Larichon have left the Hotel George Cinq en route for the Riviera——

STELLA *snatches the paper from him.*

STELLA [*angrily*]: Mr. and Mrs. Toby Cartwright have left the Villa Zephyre under a cloud——

TOBY [*complacently taking some coffee*]: Not yet they haven't——

STELLA: Owing to the idiocy of Mr. Toby Cartwright losing his shirt at the Casino——

TOBY: Oh, God, must we go back over that again!

STELLA: Yes, we must—don't you see—we've got to do something——

TOBY: Darling, what's the use——?

STELLA: Give me the pad and pencil—they're just by you——

TOBY [*taking a pencil and pad from the bedside table*]: So what?

[*188*]

STELLA: Give it to me.

TOBY [*giving it to her*]: Toby lost fifty pounds—Toby lost fifty pounds—Toby lost fifty pounds—write it down quickly, it would be awful if you happened to forget it——

STELLA [*near tears*]: Oh, Toby!

TOBY [*relenting*]: All right, darling—I am sorry—really I am. *He leans towards her, nearly upsetting the breakfast-tray.*

STELLA: Look out!

TOBY: Damn——

STELLA: It isn't that I want to rub in about the fifty pounds—really it isn't—but we are in the most awful jam, and we've got to concentrate.

TOBY: We concentrated up until four-thirty this morning and nothing came of it——

STELLA: Will you promise not to take offence at anything I say for ten minutes?

TOBY: That means you're going to be absolutely bloody.

STELLA: Promise.

TOBY: All right—I promise.

STELLA: We must face facts. Now then. Our combined incomes amount to seven hundred and fifty pounds a year——

TOBY: Until Aunt Hester dies.

STELLA: Aunt Hester will not die—she's outwitted life for seventy years and is now determined to outwit death.

TOBY: It's indecent.

STELLA: Never mind about that now—our combined over-drafts amount to roughly thirteen hundred pounds—in addition to which, you owe about three thousand——

TOBY: What about you?

STELLA [*writing*]: Two thousand.

TOBY: I can't understand why you don't get a job of some sort—look at Liza Herrick—she at least made some effort—she opened a hat shop.

STELLA: And shut it again.

[*189*]

TOBY: No talent—that's what's wrong with you—no marketable talent whatsoever.

STELLA: You seem to forget that on a certain bleak day in 1928 I gave my life into your keeping.

TOBY: Marriage is a sacrament, a mystic rite, and you persist in regarding it as a sort of plumber's estimate.

STELLA: Be quiet. Where was I?

TOBY: Wandering along the paths of memory, dear, with a singularly nasty expression.

STELLA: You will admit, I suppose, that we live beyond our income?

TOBY: You have a genius for understatement.

STELLA: Having managed to rake up seventy-two pounds in order to stay—God knows why—in this over-elaborate house——

TOBY: I don't agree. I think Olive, considering her innate vulgarity, has done this house with remarkable restraint.

STELLA: Olive is not vulgar—she's one of my oldest friends. She was at school with me, and——

TOBY: Well, let's just say that she was at school with you.

STELLA: Now look here, Toby——

TOBY: Go on—concentrate.

STELLA: You're maddening.

TOBY: Go on, write—write down the truth—face facts—put down our congenital idiocy in black and white—write down that we were brought up merely to be amiable and pleasant and socially attractive—that we have no ambition and no talent—except for playing games.

STELLA [*sharply*]: And not enough of that.

TOBY: Toby lost fifty pounds—Toby lost fifty pounds——

STELLA: I wrote that down first—but what I didn't write down was that you were a silly, selfish, careless, bloody fool to do it——

TOBY [*furiously*]: Look here, Stella——

He makes a violent movement.

STELLA: Look out!

[*190*]

TOBY: Damn!

STELLA: It's no use quarrelling. The fifty pounds has gone—we've already stayed over our time here—the Lorings are expecting us in Venice—we have, at the moment, one hundred and fourteen francs—and we are down two thousand four hundred francs in the Bridge Book.

TOBY: That's entirely your fault—you play Bridge too merrily, Stella.

STELLA: My merriment is entirely a social gesture. I loathe Bridge.

TOBY: That is no excuse for playing it as though it were lacrosse.

STELLA: I don't know what you mean.

TOBY: Your bids have a certain girlish devil-may-care abandon —you whoop through every rubber like a games' mistress.

STELLA: What do you mean, whoop?

TOBY: What I say—whoop—W-H-O-O-P.

STELLA: Oh, do be quiet! What was I saying?

TOBY: You were saying that we were down two thousand four hundred francs in the Bridge Book. What you should have said was, that owing to your——

STELLA: Never mind about that now—within the next week we shall be asked definitely to leave—Olive was dropping hints all over the dinner-table last night.

TOBY: We can't leave.

STELLA: We'll have to.

TOBY: Chaps owes you some money, doesn't he?

STELLA: Yes. Backgammon—seven thousand francs.

TOBY: Thank God for that!

STELLA: If we travel to Venice second-class and send Nanny home——

TOBY: I can't think why you had to bring her in the first place; I don't have to have a valet, why should you have a maid?

STELLA: Nanny's not a maid—Nanny's saved our lives a million times.

TOBY: Wrongly.

STELLA: Anyhow——

There is a knock on the door and GASTON *enters. He is a neatly dressed French valet.*

GASTON: Bon jour, monsieur.

TOBY: Bon jour, Gaston.

GASTON: Bon jour, madame.

STELLA: Bon jour.

GASTON: Lord Chapworth wish to speak to you.

TOBY: Is he there?

STELLA: Tell him to come in. [*She calls.*] Come in, Chaps!

GASTON *stands aside to let* LORD CHAPWORTH *enter.* LORD CHAPWORTH *is an amiable-looking young man.*

GASTON *goes out.*

CHAPS: Good morning—how d'you feel?

TOBY: Frightful.

CHAPS: So do I.

TOBY: Good!

STELLA: You look very sweet, Chaps darling, and very dapper—why are you up so early?

CHAPS: It's after eleven. I came to say good-bye——

STELLA: Of course, you're leaving to-day—I'd forgotten. Are you going to May Bainbridge?

CHAPS: Yes—Guy's picking me up.

STELLA: You must find out all about the chauffeur scandal and wire us immediately.

CHAPS: What chauffeur scandal?

STELLA: Don't be silly, darling, the whole coast is buzzing with it.

CHAPS: Oh, that!—I always thought it was a valet.

TOBY: Chauffeur-valet—a combined occupation rife, apparently, with the most delirious opportunities——

CHAPS: Do you think it's true?—I mean, do you think May really did——?

STELLA: Certainly—you only have to look at her.

TOBY: Don't be catty, Stella.

STELLA: As May Bainbridge has been consistently odious to me for years I really don't see why I shouldn't be as catty as I like.

TOBY: After all, Chaps is going to stay with them.

STELLA: Serve him right.

CHAPS: Oh, old May's not bad—she just has an unfortunate manner.

STELLA: To be not bad with an unfortunate manner is not enough——

CHAPS: You seem a bit scratchy this morning.

TOBY: Compared with what took place in the night, this is purring.

CHAPS: Well, it's a nice sunny day, anyhow.

STELLA: It had better be.

CHAPS: I had an awful evening—I got stuck with Pearl Brandt —she insisted on playing at the big table and I lost a packet.

TOBY: You what?

CHAPS: Just dropped about four hundred pounds—cleaned myself out.

STELLA: Oh, Chaps!

CHAPS: She kept on asking me to go in with her, she never ran a hand more than two coups except once, then she passed it after the fourth and it ran eleven times.

TOBY: Did it occur to you to strike her in the face?

CHAPS: So I wondered if you'd mind waiting for that seven thousand francs I owe you, Stella, until I get my allowance?

TOBY: When do you get your allowance?

CHAPS: First of May.

STELLA [*hurriedly*]: Of course I don't mind, Chaps—it doesn't matter a bit.

TOBY: God is love, there is no pain.

CHAPS: It's awfully sweet of you.

STELLA: Don't be silly.

OLIVE LLOYD-RANSOME's *voice is heard, outside.*

OLIVE [*outside*]: Can we come in?

STELLA [*calling*]: Of course!

TOBY: Send for a Bridge table and the Corinthian Bagatelle—don't let's waste a moment.

OLIVE LLOYD-RANSOME *and* PRINCESS ELENA KRASSILOFF *enter.* OLIVE *is smartly dressed and dark.* ELENA *is fair and rather vague.*

OLIVE: Good morning, everybody—I'm suicidal.

STELLA: Why—what's the matter?

OLIVE: Everything's the matter. I went down twenty mille last night, Precious Bane's got distemper and I had to send him off to the vet. at seven o'clock this morning, and on the top of that I've had a telegram from Nicky and Vera to say they're arriving to-morrow.

TOBY: To-morrow!

OLIVE: It's the most awful bore—it means that I shall have to turn you out, which I absolutely loathe—it also means that I shall have to put off Dolly, because she and Vera aren't speaking and——

STELLA: Why don't you put off Nicky and Vera?

OLIVE: Bob would never forgive me—he worships Nicky. They talk about international finance—also I've already put them off once—I feel absolutely dreadful about the whole business.

TOBY: Don't worry about us—we've got to go to the Lorings anyhow.

OLIVE: But I do—I adore you being here—you're the nicest guests I've ever had in my life.

ELENA [*scrutinising the breakfast-tray*]: Do you mind if I take one of your lumps of sugar?

TOBY: Not at all—take the whole bowl.

ELENA: Angel!

She sits down quietly with the bowl of sugar and devours several lumps.

OLIVE: And to-night we've got the Brandt dinner party—nobody wants to go—I tried to hint that we'd all rather stay in, but they're absolutely set on it—it's something to do with being American, I think, that passion for entertaining in restaurants.

TOBY: That means the Casino again?

STELLA: Yes, dear, that's what that means.

CHAPS: Have you got any messages for May, Olive?

OLIVE [*laughing*]: None that I could possibly send her.

ELENA: He was lovely that chauffeur—he wore his cap bravely as though he wasn't afraid.

OLIVE: Wasn't afraid of what, darling?

TOBY: George Bainbridge.

ELENA: Anything—anything in the world. I remember he drove me to the station once, and I knew the back of his neck reminded me of someone, and who do you think it was?

STELLA [*wearily*]: Who?

ELENA [*triumphantly*]: Dimitri.

OLIVE: Everybody reminds you of Dimitri, darling.

ELENA: I loved him dreadfully. [*At the dressing-table*] Do you mind if I take a little of your scent?

STELLA [*with false enthusiasm*]: Do, dear!

ELENA *sprays herself lavishly.*

OLIVE: We're going up to Vence to lunch—do you want to come?

STELLA: We shan't be ready in time.

OLIVE: I'll leave the small car for you—Irving and Pearl want to buy some of that awful pottery.

MURDOCH *enters through the open door. He is a very correct English butler.*

MURDOCH: Excuse me, madame.

OLIVE: What is it, Murdoch?

MURDOCH: Mr. Guy Forster has arrived, madame, for Lord Chapworth.

CHAPS: I must go.

OLIVE: Has his lordship's luggage gone down?

MURDOCH: Yes, madame.

ELENA: I love Guy, he's an angel. Where is he, Murdoch?

[*195*]

MURDOCH: In the bar, madame.

ELENA: I'll come down.

MURDOCH *exits*.

CHAPS: Good-bye, Stella—Good-bye, Toby.

STELLA: Good-bye.

TOBY: Good-bye.

CHAPS: It's awfully sweet of you to hold that over. Good-bye, Olive.

OLIVE: I'll see you off—don't forget to write in the book—give Guy a drink.

CHAPS: He's probably had three already—come on, Elena.

ELENA *and* CHAPS *go out*.

OLIVE: I do feel so horrid about turning you out.

STELLA: Don't be silly, darling—we've overstayed frightfully, but we were having such a lovely time.

OLIVE: If it were anyone else but Vera and Nicky I'd tell them to go to hell, but Bob really has to discuss business with Nicky and—oh, well, I know you understand perfectly.

TOBY: Of course we do—when are they arriving?

OLIVE: To-morrow afternoon—I must pop down and see Chaps off. The car will be waiting for you at twelve-thirty; we'd better meet in the main square.

STELLA: All right.

OLIVE: You *do* understand, don't you?

She kisses her hand to them and goes out.

There is silence for a moment.

STELLA: Dear Olive!

TOBY: She's done everything but throw us into the drive!

STELLA: We must think—we must think.

TOBY: What's the use of thinking—we haven't even enough to tip the servants.

STELLA: Oh, don't!

TOBY: If we asked Olive to lend us five thousand francs, do you think she would?

STELLA: Of course she would, and she'd dine out on it for a

week—I'd rather die than ask her. Anyway, five thousand francs wouldn't be enough—not nearly enough. We've got to pay our train fares—Nanny's fare home—our Bridge debts—the servants—— Oh, God!

There is a knock on the door.
Yes, who is it?

MURDOCH: Murdoch, madame.

TOBY: Come in!

MURDOCH *enters.*

MURDOCH: Mrs. Lloyd-Ransome asked me to come and see you, madame, about your reservations.

STELLA: Reservations?

MURDOCH: On the afternoon train to-morrow. I took the liberty of telephoning in to the hall porter of the Majestic about them.

TOBY: How thoughtful of you, Murdoch.

STELLA: Why the hall porter at the Majestic?

MURDOCH: He happens to be a personal friend of mine, madame—he does a lot of odd jobs.

TOBY: This one may be odder than he bargained for.

MURDOCH: I beg your pardon, sir?

STELLA [*hurriedly*]: When did you order these reservations, Murdoch?

MURDOCH: Last night, madame, directly Mrs. Lloyd-Ransome told me.

STELLA [*with an attempt at lighthearted naturalness*]: What have you got for us?

MURDOCH: Two single sleepers and one for your maid—that is what Mrs. Lloyd-Ransome told me you required.

TOBY: It's a pity they don't have sitting-rooms on Continental trains.

STELLA: I'm afraid you'll have to change them, Murdoch. You see, we're not going back to London—we're going to Venice.

MURDOCH: That's all right, madame, Mrs. Lloyd-Ransome told me that, too.

STELLA: She didn't happen to mention in passing that my sister was going to have a baby in July?

MURDOCH: I'll send the tickets up to you the moment they arrive; there's a small laundry bill as well—I've given that to your maid.

TOBY: You think of everything, Murdoch.

MURDOCH: Thank you, sir.

STELLA: Thank *you,* Murdoch.

MURDOCH *bows and goes out.*

TOBY: Dear Olive!

STELLA: Last night—she had it all arranged last night.

TOBY [*pensively*]: I think I should like something quite dreadful to happen to Olive, you know—something really humiliating, like being sick at a Court Ball.

STELLA: How dare she!

TOBY: It's unsufferable.

STELLA: After all, she badgered us to come.

TOBY: Now she's badgering us to go.

STELLA: Isn't there anyone we could cable to?

TOBY: Don't be silly, dear—we've exhausted every possible telegraphic saviour years ago.

STELLA: Do you think I could do a little light prostitution in the Casino to-night?

TOBY: You'd have to work hard to raise ten thousand francs by to-morrow morning.

STELLA: There's no need to be rude.

TOBY: If you'd thought of that at the beginning of our stay things might have been much easier.

STELLA: You have the moral standards of a wart hog.

TOBY: Think—think—there must be some way out.

STELLA: There isn't—it's no use—nothing's any use.

TOBY: Listen, darling, this is desperate—we've got to take a chance.

STELLA: What do you mean?

TOBY: Your bracelet.

STELLA: Don't be so absurd—it wouldn't fetch fifteen pounds.

TOBY [*ringing the bell*]: We'll send Nanny into Cannes with it this afternoon.

STELLA: But I tell you——

TOBY: Shut up. Listen, at worst we can get a couple of thousand francs on it.

STELLA: I bet we couldn't.

TOBY: With my waistcoat buttons we could.

STELLA: Even then—what's the use?

TOBY: This is the use—listen—I'll gamble to-night.

STELLA: Oh, no, Toby—no!

TOBY: It's our only chance. I'll be careful, I promise. We'll have enough for three goes of the minimum at the big table——

STELLA: Oh, not the big table!

TOBY: The biggest——

He springs out of bed and goes over to the dressing-table.

NANNY enters. She is a capable-looking, middle-aged woman.

STELLA: Nanny, we're in the most awful trouble!

NANNY: I don't wonder—lying about in bed on a lovely morning like this.

TOBY [*springing at her with the bracelet and buttons*]: Here, Nanny——

NANNY: What's this?

TOBY: Go into Cannes this afternoon and pop them.

NANNY: Oh, I couldn't—I really couldn't!

TOBY: You must.

NANNY: That lovely bracelet your Aunt Agnes left you.

STELLA: Listen, Nanny, we've got to leave to-morrow and we haven't got any money at all—we owe a lot as well—you must do this for us—go in by the twelve o'clock bus—please, Nanny.

NANNY: I could let you have a little, you know.

TOBY: We wouldn't hear of it, Nanny.

STELLA: Anyhow, a little's no good—we've got to have a lot.

NANNY: I shan't get much on these.

STELLA: Get what you can—promise you will, Nanny.

[*199*]

NANNY: That man in the pawnshop will split his sides when he sees me again.

TOBY: Never mind, Nanny—please!

NANNY: Won't you let me advance you a little?—I could go up to seven pounds.

TOBY: I tell you, Nanny, we couldn't possibly dream of such a thing.

NANNY: Oh, very well.

STELLA: How much do we owe you already?

NANNY: Three hundred and forty-two pounds all told.

STELLA: Oh, dear! [*She collapses on to the bed in helpless laughter.*]

TOBY: Go on, Nanny—go like the wind.

He pushes her out of the room. GASTON *enters and crosses over to run the bath—he disappears into the bathroom.* TOBY *gets into bed again.*

STELLA: It's madness—stark, staring madness!

TOBY *casually starts to read the paper again.*
You'll lose it, I know you will. Oh, God, I wish I could play the damned game——

There is a pause.

TOBY [*reading*]: Mr. and Mrs. Eugene B. Oglander arrived yesterday at the Hotel Maurice with their daughters Margaret and Helen——

STELLA: It's too humiliating—I wish I were dead!

TOBY: I wonder what the B stands for?

STELLA [*bitterly*]: I *know!*

THE LIGHTS FADE

SCENE II

The Scene is the same.
TOBY *is lying on the bed, smoking. He is in his dressing-gown*

and pyjamas. STELLA, *in a negligee, is doing her face at the dressing-table.*
The time is about 1.30 *a.m.*

TOBY: Is there no justice in the universe? No decency?

STELLA: Absolutely none, dear. I remember remarking that to Nanny only the other day when the stopper came out of my nail varnish and made the inside of my handbag look like Bortsch.

TOBY: There was no reason in what happened—it had nothing to do with the law of logic or the law of compensation or the law of anything—it was just low, senseless bad luck.

STELLA: Never mind, darling.

TOBY: Mind! I shall mind to the end of my days. The whole beastly scene is etched on to my brain in blood. [*Reconstructing his despair.*] I went up to the table—seven, my lucky number, was miraculously vacant—I sat down and waited for the shoe to come round—just as it was two away from me that New Jersey hag tapped me on the shoulder. "It's terrible," she said, "I can't find a place anywheres—will you be a dear and let me have yours just for a little while? I'm feeling so lucky tonight."

STELLA: She was right.

TOBY: Right! She ran the bank seventeen times—collected one hundred and seventy thousand francs with all the delicacy of a starving jaguar let loose in a butcher's shop—and graciously gave me back my place.

STELLA: Whereupon you proceeded to lose our two thousand francs in the brief space of four minutes, borrow five hundred francs from Bertie Gifford, who will never let us forget it, lose that too, and join me in the bar wearing what might be moderately described as a 'set look.'

TOBY: Correct. Have you anything more to say?

STELLA: Not for the moment.

TOBY: Good! Then we might talk of something else.

STELLA: I can't see any necessity to talk at all.

TOBY: That is only because you are temporarily exhausted by your own verbosity. Your natural flow will return in a minute.

STELLA: I was fond of Aunt Agnes and she was fond of me.

TOBY: That rather cloying relationship belongs mercifully to the days before I met you.

STELLA: She left me that bracelet in her will.

TOBY: It seems odd that she should symbolise her almost incestuous love for you by such an undistinguished little trinket.

STELLA: You have a disgusting mind, Toby.

TOBY: I said almost.

STELLA: Aunt Agnes was the most generous woman in the world.

TOBY: I suspect that your memory of her has been softened by time. To the impartial observer she appears to have been a mean old bitch.

STELLA: Toby!

TOBY: If it's all the same to you, I would prefer to leave Aunt Agnes where she rightly belongs, warbling through eternity with the Feathered Choir.

STELLA: It seems a pity that you can't turn your devastating wit to a more commercial advantage—you should write a gossip column.

TOBY: I haven't got a title.

STELLA: Oh, shut up!

TOBY: That was merely rude.

STELLA: There's no sense in going on like this—snapping at each other—we've got to face facts——

TOBY [rolling over]: Oh, God!

STELLA [turning round]: Toby, don't you see——

TOBY: Your passion for facing facts is rapidly becoming pathological. You'll go mad, that's what you'll do, and spend your declining years being led about some awful institute by a keeper —facing the fact that you're the Empress Eugénie.

STELLA: Don't be so idiotic.

TOBY: I'm sick of facing facts; in future I shall cut every fact I meet stone dead—I intend to relax, to live in a lovely dream world of my own where everything is hilariously untrue. After all, at least three-quarters of the civilised world do it, why shouldn't I?

STELLA: Why shouldn't you what?

TOBY: Delude myself! I'm going to start deluding myself this very minute. I'm going to begin with the Old Testament and believe every word of it—I'm going to believe in Jehovah and Buddha and Krishna and Mahomet and Luther and Mary Baker Eddy and Aimée Semple Macpherson—I'm even going to believe in Aunt Agnes!

STELLA: Will you shut up about Aunt Agnes!

TOBY: It is possible, in my present state of splendid detachment, that I might go off into a Yogi trance and stay upside down for several days—in that case all our troubles would be over—even Olive's social conscience would jib at one of her guests being carried out of the house in a sort of sailor's knot.

STELLA: Darling, darling Toby!

She rushes to him and flings her arms round his neck.

TOBY: Look out—you're strangling me.

STELLA: I've been wanting to strangle you for hours and now I'm doing it—it's heaven!

TOBY: This might lead to almost anything.

STELLA [*in his arms*]: Fiddling while Rome's burning—that's what we're doing.

TOBY: In the present circumstances fiddling sounds singularly offensive.

STELLA: I didn't mean that sort of fiddling.

TOBY: Really, Stella——

STELLA: Oh, darling, what are we to do?

TOBY: Let's go quietly but firmly along the passage and murder Pearl Brandt.

STELLA: We should be hanged.

TOBY: It would be worth it.

STELLA: She sleeps alone, you know—Irving is separated from her by the bathroom—it would be deliciously easy.

TOBY [*wistfully*]: I hate her so. There's a certain austere scientific beauty about my hatred for that shrill harpy—like higher mathematics.

STELLA: I'd like to fasten that wad of thousand franc notes to her nose with a safety-pin.

TOBY: I had other plans for them.

STELLA: Hush, darling.

TOBY [*jumping up and striding about the room*]: I can't bear it—I really can't!

STELLA: Well, now let's talk about something else. I consider this particular topic exhausted and I don't want to get angry again.

TOBY: Angry!—Again! I shall never stop being angry until the end of my days.

STELLA: Being angry is very bad for you—I believe that when you are angry all the red corpuscles in your blood fight with the white ones.

TOBY: If that's so, my circulation at the moment would make the battle of Mons look like a Morris dance.

STELLA: It's dreadfully late, we'd better go to sleep.

TOBY: I shall never sleep again.

STELLA: Nonsense!—go and brush your teeth.

TOBY: We must think of something.

STELLA: No, we mustn't—we're worn out—go on.

TOBY: But, darling——

STELLA: Go on—leave the door open—the noise of your gargling will give me a sense of security, as though everything was all right.

TOBY *goes into the bathroom, leaving the door open.* STELLA *gives a few final pats to her face and tries to spray herself with scent, but there isn't any left.*
Toby!

TOBY: What?

STELLA: Were Russians always predatory—even before the Revolution, I mean?

TOBY: I expect so. Why?

STELLA: Elena's splashed herself from head to foot with the last precious drops of my scent this morning.

TOBY: Personally, I'm very glad—I never cared for it.

STELLA: That's beside the point.

TOBY: It smells like bad salad dressing.

STELLA: Smelt, dear—you can use the past tense now.

TOBY: Good—from now onwards I intend to live in the past anyhow—the present is too unbearable. I intend to go back to the happy scenes of my boyhood.

STELLA: I'm sorry I'm not a rocking-horse.

TOBY: You underrate yourself, darling.

STELLA [*getting into bed*]: Witty to the last.

TOBY [*after a pause, during which the sound of gargling is heard*]: Stella!

STELLA: What?

TOBY: What are we going to do?

STELLA: I told you just now—I refuse to discuss it—I'm too tired.

TOBY: If you broke your leg we should have to stay, shouldn't we?

STELLA: I have no intention of breaking my leg.

TOBY: Modern women have no courage—in olden times women did brave things for their menfolk every day of the week.

STELLA: I don't look upon you as my menfolk.

TOBY: Think of the girl who put her arm through the latches of the door to save Bonnie Prince Charlie.

STELLA: In my opinion a misguided ass.

TOBY: I won't hear a word against Flora Macdonald.

STELLA: It wasn't Flora Macdonald.

TOBY: Don't be so ignorant, of course it was. Flora Macdonald never stopped doing things like that.

[205]

STELLA: It was not.

TOBY: Who was it, then?

STELLA: I don't know who it was, but it was *not* Flora Macdonald.

TOBY [*appearing with a toothbrush*]: I suppose you'll tell me it was Grace Darling in a minute.

STELLA: I see no reason for you to suppose any such thing.

TOBY: It was Flora Macdonald.

STELLA: It's a matter of supreme indifference to me whether it was Nell Gwynn or Marie Antoinette.

TOBY: Well, we're getting on—by a process of tedious elimination—we might ultimately arrive at who you think it was.

STELLA: I tell you I don't know who it was, I only know who it wasn't, and it wasn't Flora Macdonald.

TOBY: Oh, God!

He slams into the bathroom in a rage. There is a moment's pause, then a crash. Then TOBY *gives a wail of pain.*

STELLA: What's happened?

TOBY: I'm hurt.

STELLA: What sort of hurt?

TOBY: Badly hurt.

STELLA: Oh, darling!

She jumps out of bed and rushes into the bathroom. The following dialogue takes place off stage.

TOBY [*groaning*]: It was the door of that blasted little cupboard——

STELLA: My poor sweet!

TOBY: Do something—it's bleeding.

STELLA: Where's the iodine?

TOBY: How do I know?

STELLA: Wait a minute—no, that's eye-drops—here——

TOBY: It's agony.

STELLA: Stand still.

TOBY: I don't want to stand still—I want to jump out of the window. This is the end——

STELLA: Don't be so silly!

TOBY: Cotton-wool.

STELLA: There isn't any.

TOBY: There ought to be.

STELLA: Wait a minute—I've got some.

She comes running in and goes to the dressing-table. She rummages in the drawers for a moment and produces some cotton-wool. TOBY *comes in carrying a bottle of iodine. There is an enormous bruise on his forehead which is bleeding slightly.* Here we are.

TOBY: God, what a crack!

STELLA: Stand still.

TOBY: Do stop telling me to stand still.

STELLA: Don't be so irritable.

TOBY [*as she dabs him with iodine*]: Ow!—hell!—ow!——

STELLA: Stand still.

TOBY: Shut up!

STELLA: I'm doing my best—don't be so childish. There!

TOBY [*looking in the glass*]: For this to happen—on top of everything else—it's too much!

STELLA: Never mind, darling.

TOBY: It's not even bad enough to keep us here.

STELLA: You might pretend it had given you concussion and behave very peculiarly to-morrow morning.

TOBY: I couldn't carry it through—I'm too depressed.

STELLA: Get into bed, darling.

TOBY: The light's on in the bathroom.

STELLA: I'll turn it out.

She goes into the bathroom and does so, while he takes off his dressing-gown and gets into bed. STELLA *returns.*

TOBY: You don't think we ought to bandage it?

STELLA: No—let the air get to it.

TOBY: Open the window.

STELLA: All right—I was just going to.

[207]

TOBY: If you're beastly to me I swear to God I'll yell the place down.

STELLA *opens the window, switches out all lights except one by the bed, and gets into bed.*

STELLA: Does it hurt?

TOBY: Was that question merely rhetorical or do you really care?

STELLA: Of course I care—it's horrid for you.

TOBY: It does hurt, Stella—it hurts dreadfully.

STELLA: Try to forget about it.

TOBY: That remark was just plain silly.

STELLA: Do you want to read?

TOBY: Read! I doubt if I shall ever be able to read again.

STELLA: I'll turn out the light then.

TOBY: It would make no appreciable difference to me if the light of the world went out. My mind is a trackless waste of impenetrable darkness.

STELLA: That's right, dear.

There is a pause. STELLA *switches out the bed light.*

TOBY: Stella—what *are* we to do?

STELLA: We'll deliver ourselves over to Olive bound and gagged in the morning. We'll meet her delighted, patronising contempt with fortitude—we'll humiliate ourselves without flinching—we'll add up how much we need and borrow it from her gaily, as though we enjoyed it—no matter how broken we are we'll never let her see——

TOBY [*drowsily*]: Like Flora Macdonald.

STELLA: It was *not* Flora Macdonald!

THE LIGHTS FADE

SCENE III

The scene is the same about two hours later. Moonlight is streaming into the room.

[208]

TOBY *and* STELLA *are fast asleep. There is a slight noise on the verandah, a shadow falls across the moonlight. A man steps softly into the room. His face is muffled. He tiptoes across and trips over the stool in front of the dressing-table.*

TOBY [*switching on the light*]: Who's there?

STELLA [*waking*]: Oh, dear!

STEVENS [*covering them with a revolver*]: Keep quiet.

TOBY: Scream, dear, he wouldn't dare to shoot.

STELLA: Scream yourself.

STEVENS: Oh yes, I would.

TOBY: What do you want?

STEVENS: I want you to keep quiet.

TOBY: Naturally you do—I meant apart from that.

STEVENS: Where's your jewellery?

TOBY: Number 18, Rue Mirabeau, Cannes.

STELLA: We haven't a thing here—you've chosen probably the worst room to burgle in the whole world.

STEVENS: Come on—tell me where it is.

STELLA *makes a sudden movement; he switches his gun towards her.* TOBY *throws a pillow and knocks it out of his hand—he leaps out of bed, there is a scuffle and* TOBY *gets the revolver—he covers the man with it.*

TOBY: Now then!

STEVENS: Look out—it's loaded!

TOBY: I should damn well hope it was.

STELLA: Why aren't you French? We're in France—you ought to be French.

TOBY: Take off his muffler, Stella. [*To* STEVENS.] Keep your hands up.

STELLA [*approaching*]: Excuse me.

TOBY: Keep them up.

STELLA *undoes the scarf from round his mouth.*

STELLA: There now!

TOBY: Turn on the other lights, Stella.

STELLA [*doing so*]: It's a very expensive scarf. [*She looks at the man.*] My God, it's Stevens!

STEVENS: Oh, madame!

STELLA: Stevens, how *could* you!

TOBY: You ought to be ashamed of yourself.

STEVENS: I had no idea, sir—madame—I didn't realise you was staying here.

STELLA: Did you really mean to burgle this house?

STEVENS: Yes, madame.

STELLA: But why? You can't suddenly become a burglar all in a minute—you were a respectable chauffeur last week.

STEVENS: That was before the crash came, madame.

TOBY: You mean it was before George Bainbridge threw you out.

STEVENS: Yes, sir.

STELLA [*reproachfully*]: Oh, Stevens!

STEVENS: He sacked me straight away—without even a reference.

STELLA: You should have applied to Mrs. Bainbridge.

TOBY: Stella!

STEVENS: I'm desperate, madame—I haven't got a bob.

STELLA: That's no excuse for becoming a criminal.

STEVENS: It's the usual excuse—begging your pardon, madame.

STELLA: Do you mean to tell me Mrs. Bainbridge didn't give you so much as a——

TOBY: Stella, be quiet—your behaviour is in the worst possible taste.

STELLA: I think it's a dirty shame—you have my sympathy, Stevens.

STEVENS: Thank you, madame.

TOBY: You'd better get out, Stevens—I'll keep the gun, if you don't mind.

STEVENS: It belongs to Meadows, sir—Mr. Bainbridge's butler —I pinched it. If you wouldn't mind returning it to him I should be much obliged.

TOBY: We ought to hand you over to the police.

STEVENS: Oh, please don't do that, sir. I've had an awful time I've got a wife and child in Walthamstow, I've got to get back somehow.

STELLA: We can't help you—we would if we could, but——

TOBY: Be quiet, Stella.

STEVENS: Thank you, madame—you're very kind.

TOBY: Go on—get out as quickly as you can.

STEVENS: Yes, sir. Thank you, sir.

TOBY: Go on.

STEVENS *goes to the window.*

STELLA: Stop!

TOBY: Stella!

STELLA: Come back a minute.

TOBY: Don't be an idiot, Stella.

STELLA: Leave this to me—I know what I'm doing.

TOBY: What are you talking about?

STELLA: Sit down, Stevens.

TOBY: Have you gone mad?

STELLA: Shut up—sit down, Stevens.

STEVENS [*bewildered*]: Yes, madame. [*He sits down.*]

STELLA: Now then——

TOBY: Look here——

STELLA: Put that gun down, Toby, and don't keep on waving it about like pampas grass—Stevens may be a potential thief, but he isn't a murderer and even if he were, he wouldn't murder us, he likes us, don't you, Stevens?

STEVENS: Very much, madame.

STELLA: You seem to forget, Toby, that when we were staying with the Bainbridges in Scotland last September, Stevens lent you seven pounds.

TOBY: I paid it back.

STEVENS: You certainly did, sir; within the month.

STELLA: Do you trust us, Stevens?

STEVENS: Trust you, madame?

STELLA: Yes—I mean will you trust us if we trust you?

STEVENS: I don't understand, madame.

STELLA: I'll explain. We're broke—cleaned out.

STEVENS: Yes, madame.

STELLA: You're broke, too—in addition to which you've involved yourself in one of the juiciest scandals the Riviera has known for years.

STEVENS: It wasn't my fault, madame—I——

STELLA: I never imagined for one moment that it was.

TOBY: Look here, Stella—what is the use——?

STELLA: Toby, don't be such a fool—don't you see!

TOBY: See what?

STELLA: God sent Stevens to us to-night, Toby—or it may have been Buddha, or Mahomet or Mary Baker Eddy, but whoever it was he's here hale and hearty and ready to help us—you are ready to help us, aren't you, Stevens!

STEVENS: Help you, madame?

STELLA: If you can help yourself at the same time.

STEVENS: Anything you say, madame—you can rely on me.

TOBY [at last realising what she means]: Stella—we can't!

STELLA: We can—and we will.

TOBY: You're raving.

STELLA: I'd rather face prison than Olive's patronising sneer to-morrow morning.

STEVENS [noticing TOBY's wound]: Oh, sir, what have you done to your head?

TOBY: Never mind about that now.

STELLA: Mind about it—it's the most important thing in the world. You did it, Stevens—you knocked him out——

STEVENS: Oh, madame, I'd never do such a thing.

STELLA: Yes, you would—if you were an intelligent professional burglar you would—you'd knock him out; then you'd bind and gag us both—then you'd burgle the house and get away with the swag.

STEVENS: Swag, madame?

STELLA: That's what it's called.

STEVENS: What what's called, madame?

STELLA: The money that you're going to take from this house to-night.

STEVENS [*rising*]: Oh, madame!

STELLA: Sit down and listen.

STEVENS *sinks back again.*

A few yards away from this room there is wrapped in plebeian slumber a lady from New Jersey called Mrs. Irving Brandt——

TOBY: Go on, darling—I'm with you.

STELLA: In the top right hand drawer of her dressing-table, just to the left of the door, there is a bundle of one hundred and seventy thousand francs——

STEVENS: Oh, dear!

STELLA: Halves, Steven, halves!

STEVENS: Oh, madame—I don't think I dare.

TOBY: Be a man, Stevens.

STELLA: Go now—it's the last door on the right at the end of the passage.

TOBY: The carpet is ostentatiously soft, so you won't be heard.

STELLA: If by any chance she wakes up and screams, double back here and out of the window—I'll scream, too, and bathe my husband's head. If, on the other hand, you get away with it—come back here, give us half, tie us both up and get out.

STEVENS: All right, madame—I'll do it.

TOBY: Think of Walthamstow.

STELLA: Go on—last door on the right—dressing-table on left of the door—top right hand drawer.

TOBY [*holding out his hand*]: Good luck.

STEVENS *shakes it.*

STELLA [*also shaking his hand*]: Good luck, Stevens.

TOBY: Turn out the lights.

STELLA [*doing so*]: There.

STEVENS *slips out of the room. They listen anxiously for a moment.*

[*213*]

STELLA [*in a whisper*]: Quick—get the bedclothes off the bed
—and your dressing-gown cord——

TOBY [*also in a whisper*]: My feet are cold.

STELLA [*wrestling with the bedclothes*]: Put on your slippers.

TOBY [*doing so*]: Handkerchiefs for gags.

He rummages in the dressing-table drawers.

STELLA: Don't make such a row.

TOBY: My God!

STELLA: What is it?

TOBY: Stevens might bind and gag us and then take all the
money.

STELLA: Don't be so absurd—he's utterly honest—you only have
to look at him. His moral values may wobble a bit on the sex
side, but otherwise I'm certain his integrity is beyond question.
Why, he was a valet before he was a chauffeur—he's been
trained as a gentleman's gentleman—they're always much more
reliable than gentlemen.

TOBY: Hush!—did you hear anything?

STELLA: He's coming back.

They stand in silence for a moment. STEVENS *creeps back into
the room. He closes the door softly after him.*

Got it?

STEVENS: Yes.

STELLA: Switch on the bed-light, Toby.

TOBY [*doing so*]: Was she asleep?

STEVENS: Snoring, sir.

STELLA: I'm *glad!*

STEVENS: Here you are, madame.

He flings the wad of notes on to the bed.

TOBY: Come on—help divide them.

STEVENS: I'd rather not, sir, if you don't mind—I'd rather you
had the money. I happened to find these on the dressing-table
—they'll do me nicely.

*He produces several diamond bracelets, some rings and a
jewelled cigarette-case.*

[*214*]

STELLA: Stevens, for shame!—take them back at once!

TOBY: They can be traced.

STEVENS: I'll manage all right, sir.

STELLA: You must take half the money.

STEVENS: I'd really rather not.

TOBY: It's extraordinarily generous of you, Stevens.

STEVENS: You and Madame have always been very nice to me, sir—it feels somehow as if we was old friends.

STELLA: Thank you, Stevens.

TOBY [*giving him some bills*]: Here, you must take these, for travelling expenses.

STEVENS: Very well, sir—if you insist.

TOBY: Where shall I put the rest?

STELLA: Put eleven thousand in the drawer and the rest in the inside pocket of your dinner-jacket.

STEVENS: Allow me, sir.

TOBY: Thank you, Stevens.

STEVENS *puts some notes in the dressing-table drawer and stuffs the rest into* TOBY's *dinner-coat; he then proceeds to fold it neatly and lay it on the chair.*

STELLA: Never mind about that now, Stevens—bind and gag us.

The following dialogue takes place while they are being bound and gagged.

TOBY: Do you intend to go direct to England?

STEVENS: Yes, sir. I thought of going by boat from Marseilles. I've never seen Gibraltar.

TOBY: It's very impressive.

STELLA: The P. & O. boats always stop at Marseilles, don't they? I remember Blanche came home on one.

STEVENS: I think I shall try another Line this time, madame. I once went P. & O. as far as Egypt with Mr. Bainbridge—and I didn't fancy it.

TOBY: Why not, Stevens?

STEVENS: All them bugles got me down, sir—it was like being in the army all over again.

STELLA: You must look us up when you come to London—we might be able to help you to find a job.

STEVENS: Thank you, madame.

TOBY: We're in the book.

STEVENS: As a matter of fact, I've been thinking for a long time of giving up domestic service—I'd rather get a job that was more steady—more respectable, if you know what I mean.

STELLA: I couldn't know better.

STEVENS: I think my brother will be able to help me.

TOBY: Oh—what does he do?

STEVENS: He's got a very nice position in Barclay's Bank, sir.

TOBY: Oh, I see.

By this time they are both successfully tied to two chairs.

STEVENS: Now for the gags.

STELLA: They're on the dressing-table.

STEVENS *politely gags them.*

STEVENS: Let me know if they're too tight.

TOBY: They ought to be pretty tight.

STEVENS: I think we might allow ourselves a little poetic license, don't you, sir?

TOBY: Thank you, Stevens.

STEVENS [*regarding them*]: Quite comfy?

They both nod.

Light on or off?—One nod for on—two nods for off.

They both nod once.

Well, I'll be getting along now—thank you very much, sir and madame—it's been a great pleasure meeting you again. Good night.

He bows politely and goes out of the window.

They are left tied to the chairs. Behind their gags it is apparent that they are convulsed with laughter. STELLA *loosens her gag enough to speak.*

STELLA: If I'd been May Bainbridge, I'd have married him!

CURTAIN

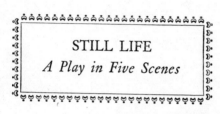

STILL LIFE
A Play in Five Scenes

CHARACTERS

(In the order of their appearance)

LAURA JESSON
MYRTLE BAGOT
BERYL WATERS
STANLEY
ALBERT GODBY
ALEC HARVEY
YOUNG MAN
BILL
JOHNNIE
MILDRED
DOLLY MESSITER

The action of the play takes place in the refreshment room of Milford Junction Station.

Time: The present.

SCENE I

The scene is the refreshment room of Milford Junction Station. On the left of the stage is a curved counter piled with glass cases containing sandwiches, rock cakes, etc. There are rows of tea-cups and glasses symmetrically arranged, an expression of the fanciful side of MYRTLE's *imagination. Schweppes' bottles of soda and Tonic water have been placed in circles and squares. Even the rock cakes mount each other on the glass stands in a disciplined pattern. There is a metal machine which gushes hot tea, a sort of cylindrical samovar.*

For drinking hours there are the usual appurtenances for the drawing of draught beer, and the wall behind the counter, except for a door upstage, is lined with looking-glass shelves supporting bottles, packets of chocolate, packets of cigarettes, etc.

There are two windows in the back wall. Their lower panes are frosted and their upper ones tastefully plastered with stained glass paper. There is another similar window on the right-hand wall which is at a slight angle. In this there is also a door leading on to the platform. There are three tables against the back wall, a stove in the corner, and two more tables against the right-hand wall, then the door and another table set below it. There are several advertisements and calendars in frames, and artificial flowers.

MYRTLE BAGOT *herself is a buxom and imposing widow. Her hair is piled high, and her expression reasonably jaunty except on those occasions when her strong sense of refinement gets the better of her.*

BERYL WATERS, *her assistant, is pretty but dimmed, not only by* MYRTLE's *personal effulgence, but by her firm authority.*

[221]

STILL LIFE

When the curtain rises it is about 5.25 p.m. on an evening in April. The evening sunlight streams through the right-hand window illuminating gaily the paraphernalia on the counter.

A YOUNG MAN *in a mackintosh is finishing his tea at one of the upstage tables and reading an evening paper.*

LAURA JESSON *is sitting at the downstage table having tea. She is an attractive woman in the thirties. Her clothes are not particularly smart but obviously chosen with taste. She looks exactly what she is, a pleasant, ordinary married woman, rather pale, for she is not very strong, and with a definite charm of personality which comes from natural kindliness, humour and reasonable conscience. She is reading a Boot's library book at which she occasionally smiles. On the chair beside her there are several parcels as she has been shopping.*

STANLEY *enters from the platform. He wears a seedy green uniform and carries a tray strapped to his shoulders. He goes to the counter. He addresses* MYRTLE *with becoming respect,* BERYL, *however, he winks at lewdly whenever the opportunity.*

STANLEY: I'm out of "Marie's," Mrs. Bagot, and I could do with some more Nestlé's plain.

MYRTLE [*scrutinising the tray*]: Let me see.

STANLEY: An old girl on the 4.10 asked if I'd got an ice-cream wafer. I didn't 'arf laugh.

MYRTLE: I don't see that there was anything to laugh at—a very natural request on a faine day.

STANLEY: What did she think I was, a 'Stop me and buy one?'

BERYL *sniggers.*

MYRTLE: Be quiet, Beryl—and as for you, Stanley, don't you be saucy—you were saucy when you started to work here, and you've been getting saucier and saucier ever since. Here you are—— [*She gives him some packets of biscuits and Nestlé's chocolate.*] Go on now.

STANLEY [*cheerfully*]: Righto.

He winks at BERYL *and goes out.*

[222]

MYRTLE: And see here, Beryl Waters, I'll trouble you to remember you're on duty——

BERYL: I didn't do anything.

MYRTLE: Exactly—you just stand there giggling like a fool —did you make out that list?

BERYL: Yes, Mrs. Bagot.

MYRTLE: Where is it?

BERYL: I put it on your desk.

MYRTLE: Where's your cloth?

BERYL: Here, Mrs. Bagot.

MYRTLE: Well, go and clean off Number 3. I can see the crumbs on it from here.

BERYL: It's them rock cakes.

MYRTLE: Never you mind about the rock cakes, just you do as you're told and don't argue.

BERYL *goes over to clean No. 3 table.*

ALBERT GODBY *enters. He is a ticket inspector, somewhere between thirty and forty. His accent is north country.*

ALBERT: Hullo!

MYRTLE: Quite a stranger, aren't you?

ALBERT: I couldn't get in yesterday.

MYRTLE [*bridling*]: I wondered what had happened to you.

ALBERT: I 'ad a bit of a dust-up.

MYRTLE [*preparing his tea*]: What about?

ALBERT: Saw a chap getting out of a first-class compartment, and when he come to give up 'is ticket it was third-class, and I told 'im he'd 'ave to pay excess, and then he turned a bit nasty and I 'ad to send for Mr. Saunders.

MYRTLE: Fat lot of good he'd be.

ALBERT: He ticked him off proper.

MYRTLE: Seeing's believing——

ALBERT: He's not a bad lot Mr. Saunders, after all you can't expect much spirit from a man who's only got one lung and a wife with diabetes.

MYRTLE: I thought something must be wrong when you didn't come.

ALBERT: I'd have popped in to explain but I had a date and 'ad to run for it the moment I went off.

MYRTLE [*frigidly*]: Oh, indeed!

ALBERT: A chap I know's getting married.

MYRTLE: Very interesting, I'm sure.

ALBERT: What's up with you, anyway?

MYRTLE: I'm sure I don't know to what you're referring.

ALBERT: You're a bit unfriendly all of a sudden.

MYRTLE [*ignoring him*]: Beryl, hurry up—put some coal in the stove while you're at it.

BERYL: Yes, Mrs. Bagot.

MYRTLE: I'm afraid I really can't stand here wasting my time in idle gossip, Mr. Godby.

ALBERT: Aren't you going to offer me another cup?

MYRTLE: You can 'ave another cup and welcome when you've finished that one. Beryl'll give it to you—I've got my accounts to do.

ALBERT: I'd rather you gave it to me.

MYRTLE: Time and Taide wait for no man, Mr. Godby.

ALBERT: I don't know what you're huffy about, but whatever it is I'm very sorry.

MYRTLE: You misunderstand me—I'm not——

ALEC HARVEY *enters. He is about thirty-five. He wears a moustache, a mackintosh and a squash hat, and he carries a small bag. His manner is decisive and unflurried.*

ALEC: A cup of tea, please.

MYRTLE: Certainly. [*She pours it out in silence.*] Cake or pastry?

ALEC: No, thank you.

MYRTLE: Threepence.

ALEC [*paying*]: Thank you.

He takes his cup of tea and goes over to a table. He takes off his hat and sits down. LAURA *glances at the clock, collects her parcels in a leisurely manner and goes out on to the platform* BERYL *returns to her place behind the counter.*

BERYL: Minnie hasn't touched her milk.

MYRTLE: Did you put it down for her?

BERYL: Yes, but she never came in for it.

MYRTLE: Go out the back and see if she's in the yard.

ALBERT [*conversationally*]: Fond of animals?

MYRTLE: In their place.

ALBERT: My landlady's got a positive mania for animals—she' got two cats, one Manx and one ordinary, three rabbits in a hutch in the kitchen, they belong to her little boy by rights, and one of them foolish-looking dogs with hair over its eyes.

MYRTLE: I don't know to what breed you refer.

ALBERT: I don't think it knows itself——

There is a rumbling noise in the distance, and the sound of a bell.

MYRTLE: There's the boat train.

There is a terrific clatter as the express roars through the station.

ALBERT: What about my other cup? I shall have to be moving —the five-forty-three will be in in a minute.

MYRTLE: Who's on the gate? [*She pours him out another cup.*]

ALBERT: Young William.

MYRTLE: You're neglecting your duty, you know—that's what you're doing.

ALBERT: A bit of relaxation never did anyone any harm——

LAURA *enters hurriedly holding a handkerchief to her eye.*

LAURA: Please could you give me a glass of water—I've got something in my eye and I want to bathe it.

MYRTLE: Would you like me to have a look?

LAURA: Please don't trouble. I think the water will do it.

[225]

MYRTLE [*handing her a glass of water*]: Here.

MYRTLE *and* ALBERT *watch her in silence as she bathes her eye.*

ALBERT: Bit of coal dust, I expect.

MYRTLE: A man I knew lost the sight of one eye through getting a bit of grit in it.

ALBERT: Painful thing—very painful.

MYRTLE [*as* LAURA *lifts her head*]: Better?

LAURA [*obviously in pain*]: I'm afraid not—oh!

ALEC *rises from his table and comes over.*

ALEC: Can I help you?

LAURA: Oh, no, please—it's only something in my eye.

MYRTLE: Try pulling down your eyelid as far as it'll go.

ALBERT: And then blowing your nose.

ALEC: Please let me look. I happen to be a doctor.

LAURA: It's very kind of you.

ALEC: Turn round to the light, please—now—look up—now look down—I can see it. Keep still—— [*He twists up the corner of his handkerchief and rapidly operates with it.*] There——

LAURA [*blinking*]: Oh, dear—what a relief—it was agonising.

ALEC: It looks like a bit of grit.

LAURA: It was when the express went through—thank you very much indeed——

ALEC: Not at all.

There is the sound of a bell on the platform.

ALBERT [*gulping down his tea*]: There we go—I must run.

LAURA: How lucky for me that you happened to be here.

ALEC: Anybody could have done it.

LAURA: Never mind, you did and I'm most grateful. There's my train. Good-bye.

She puts out her hand and he shakes it politely. She goes out followed at a run by ALBERT GODBY.

ALEC *looks after her for a moment and then goes back to his table. There is the noise of the train rumbling into the station as the lights fade.*

SCENE II

The scene is the same and the time about the same.

Nearly three months have passed since the preceding scene, and it is now July.

MYRTLE *is resplendent in a light overall.* BERYL'S *appearance is unaltered. The tables are all unoccupied.*

MYRTLE [*slightly relaxed in manner*]: It's all very faine, I said, expecting me to do this that and the other, but what do *I* get out of it? You can't expect me to be a cook-housekeeper and char rolled into one during the day, and a loving wife in the evening just because you feel like it. Oh, dear no. There are just as good fish in the sea, I said, as ever came out of it, and I packed my boxes then and there and left him.

BERYL: Didn't you ever go back?

MYRTLE: Never. I went to my sister's place at Folkestone for a bit, and then I went in with a friend of mine and we opened a tea-shop in Hythe.

BERYL: And what happened to him?

MYRTLE: Dead as a door-nail inside three years!

BERYL: Well, I never!

MYRTLE: So you see, every single thing she told me came true —first them clubs coming together, an unexpected journey, then the Queen of diamonds and the ten—that was my friend and the tea-shop business. Then the Ace of spades three times running——

STANLEY *enters.*

STANLEY: Two rock and an apple.

MYRTLE: What for?

STANLEY: Party on the up platform.

MYRTLE: Why can't they come in here for them?

STANLEY: Ask me another. [*He winks at* BERYL.]

MYRTLE: Got something in your eye?

STANLEY: Nothing beyond a bit of a twinkle every now and again.

BERYL [*giggling*]: Oh, you are awful!

MYRTLE: You learn to behave yourself, my lad. Here are your rock cakes. Beryl, stop sniggering and give me an apple off the stand.

BERYL *complies.*

Not off the front, silly, haven't you got any sense. Here—— [*She takes one from the back of the stand so as to leave the symmetry undisturbed.*]

STANLEY: This one's got a hole in it.

MYRTLE: Tell 'em to come and choose for themselves if they're particular—go on now.

STANLEY: All right—give us a chance.

MYRTLE: What people want to eat on the platform for I really don't know. Tell Mr. Godby not to forget his tea.

STANLEY: Righto!

He goes out as ALEC *and* LAURA *come in.* LAURA *is wearing a summer dress,* ALEC, *a grey flannel suit.*

ALEC: Tea or lemonade?

LAURA: Tea, I think—it's more refreshing, really. [*She sits down at the table by the door.*]

ALEC *goes to the counter.*

ALEC: Two teas, please.

MYRTLE: Cakes or pastry?

ALEC [*to* LAURA]: Cakes or pastry?

LAURA: No, thank you.

ALEC: Are those bath buns fresh?

MYRTLE: Certainly they are—made this morning.

ALEC: Two, please.

MYRTLE *puts two bath buns on a plate, meanwhile* BERYL *has drawn two cups of tea.*

MYRTLE: That'll be eightpence.

ALEC: All right. [*He pays her.*]

MYRTLE: Take the tea to the table, Beryl.

[*228*]

ALEC: I'll carry the buns.

BERYL *brings the tea to the table.* ALEC *follows with the buns.*

ALEC: You must eat one of these—fresh this morning.

LAURA: Very fattening.

ALEC: I don't hold with such foolishness.

BERYL *returns to the counter.*

MYRTLE: I'm going over my accounts. Let me know when Albert comes in.

BERYL: Yes, Mrs. Bagot.

BERYL *settles down behind the counter with "Peg's Paper."*

LAURA: They do look good, I must say.

ALEC: One of my earliest passions—I've never outgrown it.

LAURA: Do you like milk in your tea?

ALEC: Yes, don't you?

LAURA: Yes—fortunately.

ALEC: Station refreshments are generally a wee bit arbitrary, you know.

LAURA: I wasn't grumbling.

ALEC [*smiling*]: Do you ever grumble—are you ever sullen and cross and bad-tempered?

LAURA: Of course I am—at least not sullen exactly—but I sometimes get into rages.

ALEC: I can't visualise you in a rage.

LAURA: I really don't see why you should.

ALEC: Oh, I don't know—there are signs, you know—one can usually tell——

LAURA: Long upper lips and jaw lines and eyes close together?

ALEC: You haven't any of those things.

LAURA: Do you feel guilty at all? I do.

ALEC [*smiling*]: Guilty?

LAURA: You ought to more than me, really—you neglected your work this afternoon.

ALEC: I worked this morning—a little relaxation never did anyone any harm. Why should either of us feel guilty?

[229]

LAURA: I don't know—a sort of instinct—as though we were letting something happen that oughtn't to happen.

ALEC: How awfully nice you are!

LAURA: When I was a child in Cornwall—we lived in Cornwall, you know—May, that's my sister, and I used to climb out of our bedroom window on summer nights and go down to the cove and bathe. It was dreadfully cold but we felt very adventurous. I'd never have dared do it by myself, but sharing the danger made it all right—that's how I feel now, really.

ALEC: Have a bun—it's awfully bad for you.

LAURA: You're laughing at me!

ALEC: Yes, a little, but I'm laughing at myself, too.

LAURA: Why?

ALEC: For feeling a small pang when you said about being guilty.

LAURA: There you are, you see!

ALEC: We haven't done anything wrong.

LAURA: Of course we haven't.

ALEC: An accidental meeting—then another accidental meeting—then a little lunch—then the movies—what could be more ordinary? More natural?

LAURA: We're adults, after all.

ALEC: I never see myself as an adult, do you?

LAURA [*firmly*]: Yes, I do. I'm a respectable married woman with a husband and a home and three children.

ALEC: But there must be a part of you, deep down inside, that doesn't feel like that at all—some little spirit that still wants to climb out of the window—that still longs to splash about a bit in the dangerous sea.

LAURA: Perhaps we none of us ever grow up entirely.

ALEC: How awfully nice you are!

LAURA: You said that before.

ALEC: I thought perhaps you hadn't heard.

LAURA: I heard all right.

ALEC [*gently*]: I'm respectable too, you know. I have a home

[*230*]

and a wife and children and responsibilities—I also have a lot of work to do and a lot of ideals all mixed up with it.

LAURA: What's she like?

ALEC: Madeleine?

LAURA: Yes.

ALEC: Small, dark, rather delicate——

LAURA: How funny! I should have thought she'd be fair.

ALEC: And your husband? What's he like?

LAURA: Medium height, brown hair, kindly, unemotional and not delicate at all.

ALEC: You said that proudly.

LAURA: Did I? [*She looks down.*]

ALEC: What's the matter?

LAURA: The matter? What could be the matter?

ALEC: You suddenly went away.

LAURA [*brightly*]: I thought perhaps we were being rather silly.

ALEC: Why?

LAURA: Oh, I don't know—we are such complete strangers, really.

ALEC: It's one thing to close a window, but quite another to slam it down on my fingers.

LAURA: I'm sorry.

ALEC: Please come back again.

LAURA: Is tea bad for one? Worse than coffee, I mean?

ALEC: If this is a professional interview, my fee is a guinea.

LAURA [*laughing*]: It's nearly time for your train.

ALEC: I hate to think of it, chugging along, interrupting our tea party.

LAURA: I really am sorry now.

ALEC: What for?

LAURA: For being disagreeable.

ALEC: I don't think you could be disagreeable.

LAURA: You said something just now about your work and ideals being mixed up with it—what ideals?

ALEC: That's a long story.

LAURA: I suppose all doctors ought to have ideals, really—otherwise I should think the work would be unbearable.

ALEC: Surely you're not encouraging me to talk shop?

LAURA: Do you come here every Thursday?

ALEC: Yes. I come in from Churley, and spend a day in the hospital. Stephen Lynn graduated with me—he's the chief physician here. I take over from him once a week, it gives him a chance to go up to London and me a chance to observe and study the hospital patients.

LAURA: Is that a great advantage?

ALEC: Of course. You see I have a special pigeon.

LAURA: What is it?

ALEC: Preventive medicine.

LAURA: Oh, I see.

ALEC [*laughing*]: I'm afraid you don't.

LAURA: I was trying to be intelligent.

ALEC: Most good doctors, especially when they're young, have private dreams—that's the best part of them, sometimes though, those get over-professionalised and strangulated and —am I boring you?

LAURA: No—I don't quite understand—but you're not boring me.

ALEC: What I mean is this—all good doctors must be primarily enthusiasts. They must have, like writers and painters, and priests, a sense of vocation—a deep-rooted, unsentimental desire to do good.

LAURA: Yes—I see that.

ALEC: Well, obviously one way of preventing disease is worth fifty ways of curing it—that's where my ideal comes in—preventive medicine isn't anything to do with medicine at all, really—it's concerned with conditions, living conditions and common-sense and hygiene. For instance, my specialty is pneumoconiosis.

LAURA: Oh, dear!

ALEC: Don't be alarmed, it's simpler than it sounds—it's nothing but a slow process of fibrosis of the lung due to the inhalation of particles of dust. In the hospital here there are splendid opportunities for observing cures and making notes, because of the coal mines.

LAURA: You suddenly look much younger.

ALEC [*brought up short*]: Do I?

LAURA: Almost like a little boy.

ALEC: What made you say that?

LAURA [*staring at him*]: I don't know—yes, I do.

ALEC [*gently*]: Tell me.

LAURA [*with panic in her voice*]: Oh, no—I couldn't, really. You were saying about the coal mines——

ALEC [*looking into her eyes*]: Yes—the inhalation of coal dust —that's one specific form of the diseases—it's called Anthracosis.

LAURA [*hypnotised*]: What are the others?

ALEC: Chalicosis—that comes from metal dust—steel works, you know——

LAURA: Yes, of course. Steel works.

ALEC: And Silicosis—stone dust—that's gold mines.

LAURA [*almost in a whisper*]: I see.

There is the sound of a bell.

There's your train.

ALEC [*looking down*]: Yes.

LAURA: You mustn't miss it.

ALEC: No.

LAURA [*again the panic in her voice*]: What's the matter?

ALEC [*with an effort*]: Nothing—nothing at all.

LAURA [*socially*]: It's been so very nice—I've enjoyed my afternoon enormously.

ALEC: I'm so glad—so have I. I apologise for boring you with those long medical words——

LAURA: I feel dull and stupid, not to be able to understand more.

[*233*]

ALEC: Shall I see you again?

There is the sound of a train approaching.

LAURA: It's the other platform, isn't it? You'll have to run. Don't worry about me—mine's due in a few minutes.

ALEC: Shall I see you again?

LAURA: Of course—perhaps you could come over to Ketchworth one Sunday. It's rather far, I know, but we should be delighted to see you.

ALEC [*intensely*]: Please—please——

The train is heard drawing to a standstill.

LAURA: What is it?

ALEC: Next Thursday—the same time——

LAURA: No—I can't possibly—I——

ALEC: Please—I ask you most humbly——

LAURA: You'll miss your train!

ALEC: All right. [*He gets up.*]

LAURA: Run——

ALEC [*taking her hand*]: Good-bye.

LAURA [*breathlessly*]: I'll be there.

ALEC: Thank you, my dear.

He goes out at a run, colliding with ALBERT GODBY, *who is on his way in.*

ALBERT: 'Ere—'ere—take it easy now—take it easy—— [*He goes over to the counter.*]

LAURA *sits quite still staring in front of her as the lights fade.*

SCENE III

It is now October. Three months have passed since the preceding scene.

The refreshment room is empty except for MYRTLE, *who is bending down putting coal into the stove.*

ALBERT GODBY *enters. Upon perceiving her slightly vulnerable position, he slaps her lightly on the behind—she springs to her feet.*

MYRTLE: Albert Godby, how dare you!

ALBERT: I couldn't resist it.

MYRTLE: I'll trouble you to keep your hands to yourself.

ALBERT: You're blushing—you look wonderful when you're angry, like an avenging angel.

MYRTLE: I'll give you avenging angel—coming in here taking liberties——

ALBERT: I didn't think after what you said last Monday you'd object to a friendly little slap.

MYRTLE: Never you mind about last Monday—I'm on duty now. A nice thing if Mr. Saunders had happened to be looking through the window.

ALBERT: If Mr. Saunders is in the 'abit of looking through windows, it's time he saw something worth looking at.

MYRTLE: You ought to be ashamed of yourself!

ALBERT: It's just high spirits—don't be mad at me.

MYRTLE [*retiring behind the counter*]: High spirits indeed!

ALBERT [*singing*]:
"I'm twenty-one to-day—I'm twenty-one to-day,
 I've got the key of the parlour door—
 I've never been twenty-one before——"

MYRTLE [*retiring behind the counter*]: Don't make such a noise—they'll hear you on the platform.

ALBERT [*singing*]:
"Picture you upon my knee and tea for two and two for tea."

MYRTLE: Now look here, Albert Godby, once and for all, will you behave yourself!

ALBERT [*singing*]:
"Sometimes I'm 'appy—sometimes I'm blue-oo——" [*He breaks off.*] This is one of my 'appy moments——

MYRTLE: Here, take your tea and be quiet.

ALBERT: It's all your fault, anyway.

MYRTLE: I don't know to what you're referring, I'm sure.

ALBERT: I was thinking of to-night——

MYRTLE: If you don't learn to behave yourself there won't be a to-night—or any other night, either——

ALBERT [*singing*]:
"I'm in love again, and the spring is coming.
  I'm in love again, hear my heart-strings humming——"

MYRTLE: Will you hold your noise?

ALBERT: Give us a kiss.

MYRTLE: I'll do no such thing.

ALBERT: Just a quick one—across the counter. [*He grabs her arm across the counter.*]

MYRTLE: Albert, stop it!

ALBERT: Come on—there's a love.

MYRTLE: Let go of me this minute.

ALBERT: Come on, just one.

They scuffle for a moment, upsetting a neat pile of cakes on to the floor.

MYRTLE: Now look at me Banburys—all over the floor.

ALBERT *bends down to pick them up.* STANLEY *enters.*

STANLEY: Just in time—or born in the vestry.

MYRTLE: You shut your mouth and help Mr. Godby pick up them cakes.

STANLEY: Anything to oblige. [*He helps* ALBERT.]

ALEC *and* LAURA *come in.* LAURA *goes to their usual table.* ALEC *goes to the counter.*

ALEC: Good afternoon.

MYRTLE [*grandly*]: Good afternoon.

ALEC: Two teas, please.

MYRTLE: Cake or pastry?

ALEC: No, thank you—just the tea.

ALBERT [*conversationally*]: Nice weather.

ALEC: Very nice.

ALBERT: Bit of a nip in the air, though.

[*236*]

MYRTLE, *having given* ALEC *two cups of tea, and taken the money for it, turns to* STANLEY.

MYRTLE: What are you standing there gaping at?

STANLEY: Where's Beryl?

MYRTLE: Never you mind about Beryl, you ought to be on Number 4, and well you know it.

ALBERT [*reflectively*]: Love's young dream!

ALEC, *meanwhile, has carried the two cups of tea over to the table and sat down.*

STANLEY: There's been a run on the Cadbury's nut milk this afternoon; I shall need some more.

MYRTLE [*looking at his tray*]: How many have you got left?

STANLEY: Only three.

MYRTLE: Take six more then, and don't forget to mark 'em down.

STANLEY: Righto.

STANLEY *goes behind the counter and collects six packets of chocolate, then he goes out whistling.*

ALEC: I didn't mean to be unkind.

LAURA: It doesn't matter.

A YOUNG MAN *comes in and goes to the counter.*

YOUNG MAN: Cup of coffee, please, and a beef sandwich.

MYRTLE: We're out of beef—will ham do?

YOUNG MAN: Yes—ham'll do.

ALBERT *winks at* MYRTLE *over his tea-cup.* MYRTLE *draws a cup of coffee for the* YOUNG MAN *and takes a sandwich out of one of the glass stands.*

ALEC: We can't part like this.

LAURA: I think it would be better if we did.

ALEC: You don't really mean that?

LAURA: I'm trying to mean it—I'm trying with all my strength.

ALEC: Oh, my dearest dear——

LAURA: Don't—please don't——

MYRTLE [*to* YOUNG MAN]: Fourpence, please.

[237]

YOUNG MAN: Thank you. [*He pays, and carries his coffee and sandwich over to the table near the stove.*]

ALBERT: It is all right about to-night, isn't it?

MYRTLE: I'll think about it.

ALBERT: It's Claudette Colbert, you know.

MYRTLE: Fat chance I shall get of enjoying Claudette Colbert with you hissing in me ear all the time.

ALBERT: I'll be as good as gold.

BERYL *enters in a coat and hat—she goes behind the counter.*

ALEC: It's no use running away from the truth, darling—we're lovers, aren't we? If it happens or if it doesn't, we're lovers in our hearts.

LAURA: Can't you see how wrong it is? How dreadfully wrong!

ALEC: I can see what's true—whether it's wrong or right.

BERYL [*taking off her hat and coat*]: Mr. Saunders wants you, Mr. Godby.

ALBERT: What for?

BERYL: I don't know.

MYRTLE: You'd better go, Albert, you know what he is.

ALBERT: I know 'e's a bloody fool, if that's what you mean.

MYRTLE: Be quiet, Albert—in front of Beryl.

BERYL: Don't mind me.

MYRTLE: Go on—finish up your tea.

ALBERT: No peace for the wicked——

MYRTLE: Go on——

ALBERT: I'll be back——

MYRTLE: That'll be nice, I'm sure——

ALBERT *goes.*

MYRTLE *retires to the upper end of the counter.* BERYL *goes off and comes on again laden with various packages of comestibles. She and* MYRTLE *proceed to stack them on the upstage end of the counter.*

ALEC [*urgently*]: There's no chance of Stephen getting back until late—nobody need ever know.

LAURA: It's so furtive to love like that—so cheap—much better not to love at all.

ALEC: It's too late not to love at all—be brave—we're both in the same boat—let's be generous to each other.

LAURA: What is there brave in it—sneaking away to someone else's house, loving in secret with the horror of being found out hanging over us all the time. It would be far braver to say good-bye and never see each other again.

ALEC: Could you be as brave as that? I know I couldn't.

LAURA [*breathlessly*]: Couldn't you?

ALEC: Listen, my dear. This is something that's never happened to either of us before. We've loved before and been happy before, and miserable and contented and reckless, but this is different—something lovely and strange and desperately difficult. We can't measure it along with the values of our ordinary lives.

LAURA: Why should it be so important—why should we let it be so important?

ALEC: We can't help ourselves.

LAURA: We can—we can if only we're strong enough.

ALEC: Why is it so strong to deny something that's urgent and real—something that all our instincts are straining after —mightn't it be weak and not strong at all to run away from such tremendous longing?

LAURA: Is it so real to you? So tremendous?

ALEC: Can't you see that it is?

LAURA: It's so difficult, so strained. I'm lost.

ALEC: Don't say that, darling.

LAURA: Loving you is hard for me—it makes me a stranger in my own house. Familiar things, ordinary things that I've known for years like the dining-room curtains, and the wooden tub with a silver top that holds biscuits and a water-colour of San Remo that my mother painted, look odd to me, as though they belonged to someone else—when I've just left you, when I go home, I'm more lonely than I've ever been before. I passed the house the other day without noticing and had to turn back, and when I went in it seemed to draw away from me—my whole life seems to be drawing away from me, and—and I don't know what to do.

ALEC: Oh, darling——

LAURA: I love them just the same, Fred I mean and the children, but it's as though it wasn't me at all—as though I were looking on at someone else. Do you know what I mean? Is it the same with you? Or is it easier for men——

ALEC: I don't know.

LAURA: Please, dear, don't look unhappy. I'm not grumbling, really I'm not——

ALEC: I don't suppose being in love has ever been easy for anybody.

LAURA [*reaching for his hand*]: We've only got a few more minutes—I didn't mean to be depressing.

ALEC: It isn't any easier for me, darling, honestly it isn't.

LAURA: I know, I know—I only wanted reassuring.

ALEC: I hold you in my arms all the way back in the train— I'm angry with every moment that I'm not alone—to love you uninterrupted—whenever my surgery door opens and a patient comes in, my heart jumps in case it might be you. One of them I'm grateful to—he's got neuritis, and I give him sun-ray treatment—he lies quite quietly baking, and I can be with you in the shadows behind the lamp.

LAURA: How silly we are—how unbearably silly!

ALEC: Friday — Saturday — Sunday — Monday — Tuesday — Wednesday——

LAURA: Thursday——

ALEC: It's all right, isn't it?

LAURA: Oh, yes—of course it is.

ALEC: Don't pass the house again—don't let it snub you. Go boldly in and stare that damned water-colour out of countenance.

LAURA: All right—don't bake your poor neuritis man too long —you might blister him.

The continuation of their scene is drowned by the noisy entrance of two soldiers, BILL *and* JOHNNIE. *They go to the counter.*

BILL: Afternoon, lady.

MYRTLE [*grandly*]: Good afternoon.

BILL: A couple of splashes, please.

MYRTLE: Very sorry, it's out of hours.

JOHNNIE: Come on, lady—you've got a kind face.

MYRTLE: That's neither here nor there.

BILL: Just sneak us a couple under cover of them poor old sandwiches.

MYRTLE: Them sandwiches were fresh this morning, and I shall do no such thing.

BILL: Come on, be a sport.

JOHNNIE: Nobody'd know.

MYRTLE: I'm very sorry, I'm sure, but it's against the rules.

BILL: You could pop it into a couple of tea-cups.

MYRTLE: You're asking me to break the law, young man.

JOHNNIE: I think I've got a cold coming on—we've been mucking about at the Butts all day—you can't afford to let the army catch cold, you know.

MYRTLE: You can have as much as you want after six o'clock.

BILL: An 'eart of stone—that's what you've got, lady—an 'eart of stone.

MYRTLE: Don't you be cheeky.

JOHNNIE: My throat's like a parrot's cage—listen! [*He makes a crackling noise with his throat.*]

MYRTLE: Take some lemonade then—or ginger-beer.

BILL: Couldn't touch it—against doctor's orders—my inside's been most peculiar ever since I 'ad trench feet—you wouldn't give a child carbolic acid, would you? That's what ginger-beer does to me.

MYRTLE: Get on with you!

[*241*]

JOHNNIE: It's true—it's poison to him, makes 'im make the most 'orrible noises—you wouldn't like anything nasty to 'appen in your posh buffay——

MYRTLE: May licence does not permit me to serve alcohol out of hours—that's final!

JOHNNIE: We're soldiers we are—willing to lay down our lives for you—and you grudge us one splash——

MYRTLE: You wouldn't want to get me into trouble, would you?

BILL: Give us a chance, lady, that's all—just give us a chance. *They both roar with laughter.*

MYRTLE: Beryl, ask Mr. Godby to come 'ere for a moment, will you?

BERYL: Yes, Mrs. Bagot.

She comes out from behind the counter and goes on to the platform.

BILL: Who's 'e when 'e's at home?

MYRTLE: You'll soon see—coming in here cheeking me.

JOHNNIE: Now then, now then—naughty naughty——

MYRTLE: Kaindly be quiet!

BILL: Shut up, Johnnie——

JOHNNIE: What about them drinks, lady?

MYRTLE: I've already told you I can't serve alcoholic refreshment out of hours——

JOHNNIE: Come off it, mother, be a pal!

MYRTLE [*losing her temper*]: I'll give you mother, you saucy upstart——

BILL: Who are you calling an upstart!

MYRTLE: You—and I'll trouble you to get out of here double quick—disturbing the customers and making a nuisance of yourselves.

JOHNNIE: 'Ere, where's the fire—where's the fire!

ALBERT GODBY *enters, followed by* BERYL.

ALBERT: What's going on in 'ere!

MYRTLE [*with dignity*]: Mr. Godby, these gentlemen are annoying me.

BILL: We 'aven't done anything.

JOHNNIE: All we did was ask for a couple of drinks——

MYRTLE: They insulted me, Mr. Godby.

JOHNNIE: We never did nothing of the sort—just 'aving a little joke, that's all.

ALBERT [*laconically*]: 'Op it—both of you.

BILL: We've got a right to stay 'ere as long as we like.

ALBERT: You 'eard what I said—'Op it!

JOHNNIE: What is this, a free country or a bloody Sunday school?

ALBERT [*firmly*]: I checked your passes at the gate—your train's due in a minute—Number 2 platform—'Op it.

JOHNNIE: Look 'ere now——

BILL: Come on, Johnnie—don't argue with the poor little basket.

ALBERT [*dangerously*]: 'Op it!

BILL *and* JOHNNIE *go to the door.* JOHNNIE *turns.*

JOHNNIE: Toodle-oo, mother, and if them sandwiches were made this morning, you're Shirley Temple——

They go out.

MYRTLE: Thank you, Albert.

BERYL: What a nerve talking to you like that!

MYRTLE: Be quiet, Beryl—pour me out a nip of Three Star— I'm feeling quite upset.

ALBERT: I've got to get back to the gate.

MYRTLE [*graciously*]: I'll be seeing you later, Albert.

ALBERT [*with a wink*]: Okay!

He goes out.

A train bell rings. BERYL *brings* MYRTLE *a glass of brandy.*

MYRTLE [*sipping it*]: I'll say one thing for Albert Godby—he may be on the small side, but 'e's a gentleman.

She and BERYL *retire once more to the upper end of the counter and continue their arrangement of bottles, biscuits, etc. There is the sound of a train drawing into the station.*

LAURA: There's your train.

ALEC: I'm going to miss it.

LAURA: Please go.

ALEC: No.

LAURA [*clasping and unclasping her hands*]: I wish I could think clearly. I wish I could know—really know what to do.

ALEC: Do you trust me?

LAURA: Yes—I trust you.

ALEC: I don't mean conventionally—I mean really.

LAURA: Yes.

ALEC: Everything's against us—all the circumstances of our lives—those have got to go on unaltered. We're nice people, you and I, and we've got to go on being nice. Let's enclose this love of ours with real strength, and let that strength be that no one is hurt by it except ourselves.

LAURA: Must we be hurt by it?

ALEC: Yes—when the time comes.

LAURA: Very well.

ALEC: All the furtiveness and the secrecy and the hole-in-corner cheapness can be justified if only we're strong enough—strong enough to keep it to ourselves, clean and untouched by anybody else's knowledge or even suspicion—something of our own for ever—to be remembered——

LAURA: Very well.

ALEC: We won't speak of it any more—I'm going now—back to Stephen's flat. I'll wait for you—if you don't come I shall know only that you weren't quite ready—that you needed a little longer to find your own dear heart. This is the address.

He scribbles on a bit of paper as the express thunders through the station. He gets up and goes swiftly without looking at her again. She sits staring at the paper, then she fumbles in her bag and finds a cigarette. She lights it—the platform bell goes.

MYRTLE: There's the 5.43.

BERYL: We ought to have another Huntley and Palmer's to put in the middle, really.

MYRTLE: There are some more on the shelf.

BERYL *fetches another packet of biscuits and takes it to* MYRTLE. *There is the noise of the 5.43—*LAURA's *train—steaming into the station.* LAURA *sits puffing her cigarette. Suddenly she gets up—gathers up her bag quickly, and moves towards the door. She pauses and comes back to the table as the whistle blows. The train starts, she puts the paper in her bag and goes quietly out as the lights fade.*

SCENE IV

The time is about 9.45 on an evening in December.
There are only two lights on in the refreshment room as it is nearly closing time.
When the scene starts the stage is empty. There is the noise of a fast train rattling through the station.
BERYL *comes in from the upstage door behind the counter armed with several muslin cloths which she proceeds to drape over the things on the counter. She hums breathily to herself as she does so.* STANLEY *enters, he has discarded his uniform and is wearing his ordinary clothes.*

STANLEY: Hallo!
BERYL: You made me jump.
STANLEY: Are you walking home?
BERYL: Maybe.
STANLEY: Do you want me to wait?
BERYL: I've got to go straight back.
STANLEY: Why?
BERYL: Mother'll be waiting up.
STANLEY: Can't you say you've been kept late?
BERYL: I said that last time.
STANLEY: Say it again—say there's been a rush on.
BERYL: Don't be so silly—Mother's not that much of a fool.
STANLEY: Be a sport, Beryl—shut down five minutes early

[245]

and say you was kept ten minutes late—that gives us a quarter of an hour.

BERYL: What happens if Mrs. Bagot comes back?

STANLEY: She won't—she's out having a bit of a slap and tickle with our Albert.

BERYL: Stan, you are awful!

STANLEY: I'll wait for you in the yard.

BERYL: Oh, all right.

STANLEY *goes out.*

BERYL *resumes her song and the draping of the cake stands.* LAURA *enters—she looks pale and unhappy.*

LAURA: I'd like a glass of brandy, please.

BERYL: We're just closing.

LAURA: I see you are, but you're not quite closed yet, are you?

BERYL [*sullenly*]: Three Star?

LAURA: Yes, that'll do.

BERYL [*getting it*]: Tenpence, please.

LAURA [*taking money from her bag*]: Here—and—have you a piece of paper and an envelope?

BERYL: I'm afraid you'll have to get that at the bookstall.

LAURA: The bookstall's shut—please—it's very important—I should be so much obliged——

BERYL: Oh, all right—wait a minute.

She goes off.

LAURA *sips the brandy at the counter, she is obviously trying to control her nerves.* BERYL *returns with some notepaper and an envelope.*

LAURA: Thank you so much.

BERYL: We close in a few minutes, you know.

LAURA: Yes, I know.

She takes the notepaper and her brandy over to the table by the door and sits down. She stares at the paper for a moment, takes another sip of brandy and then begins to write. BERYL *looks at her with exasperation and goes off through the upstage door.* LAURA *falters in her writing, then breaks down and buries*

[246]

her face in her hands. ALEC *comes in—he looks hopelessly round for a moment, and then sees her.*

ALEC: Thank God—oh, darling!

LAURA: Please go away—please don't say anything.

ALEC: I can't let you go like this.

LAURA: You must. It'll be better—really it will.

ALEC [*sitting down beside her*]: You're being dreadfully cruel.

LAURA: I feel so utterly degraded.

ALEC: It was just a beastly accident that he came back early— he doesn't know who you are—he never even saw you.

LAURA: I listened to your voices in the sitting-room—I crept out and down the stairs—feeling like a prostitute.

ALEC: Don't, dearest—don't talk like that, please——

LAURA [*bitterly*]: I suppose he laughed, didn't he—after he got over being annoyed? I suppose you spoke of me together as men of the world.

ALEC: We didn't speak of you—we spoke of a nameless creature who had no reality at all.

LAURA [*wildly*]: Why didn't you tell him the truth? Why didn't you say who I was and that we were lovers—shameful secret lovers—using his flat like a bad house because we had nowhere else to go, and were afraid of being found out! Why didn't you tell him we were cheap and low and without courage —why didn't you——

ALEC: Stop it, Laura—pull yourself together!

LAURA: It's true—don't you see, it's true!

ALEC: It's nothing of the sort. I know you feel horrible, and I'm deeply, desperately sorry. I feel horrible, too, but it doesn't matter really—this—this unfortunate, damnable incident—it was just bad luck. It couldn't affect us really, you and me—we know the truth—we know we really love each other—that's all that matters.

LAURA: It isn't all that matters—other things matter, too, self-respect matters, and decency—I can't go on any longer.

ALEC: Could you really—say good-bye—not see me any more?

LAURA: Yes—if you'd help me.

There is silence for a moment. ALEC *gets up and walks about— he stops and stands staring at a coloured calendar on the wall.*

ALEC [*quietly, with his back to her*]: I love you, Laura—I shall love you always until the end of my life—all the shame that the world might force on us couldn't touch the real truth of it. I can't look at you now because I know something—I know that this is the beginning of the end—not the end of my loving you—but the end of our being together. But not quite yet, darling—please not quite yet.

LAURA: Very well—not quite yet.

ALEC: I know what you feel—about this evening, I mean— about the beastliness of it. I know about the strain of our different lives, our lives apart from each other. The feeling of guilt— of doing wrong is a little too strong, isn't it? Too persistent —perhaps too great a price to pay for the few hours of happiness we get out of it. I know all this because it's the same for me, too.

LAURA: You can look at me now—I'm all right.

ALEC [*turning*]: Let's be careful—let's prepare ourselves—a sudden break now, however brave and admirable, would be too cruel—we can't do such violence to our hearts and minds.

LAURA: Very well.

ALEC: I'm going away.

LAURA: I see.

ALEC: But not quite yet.

LAURA: Please not quite yet.

BERYL *enters in hat and coat.*

BERYL: I'm afraid it's closing time.

ALEC: Oh, is it?

BERYL: I shall have to lock up.

ALEC: This lady is catching the 10.10—she's not feeling very well, and it's very cold on the platform.

BERYL: The waiting-room's open.

ALEC [*going to counter*]: Look here—I'd be very much obliged if you'd let us stay here for another few minutes.

BERYL: I'm sorry—it's against the rules.

ALEC [*giving her a ten-shilling note*]: Please—come back to lock up when the train comes in.

BERYL: I'll have to switch off the lights—someone might see 'em on and think we were open.

ALEC: Just for a few minutes—please!

BERYL: You won't touch anything, will you?

ALEC: Not a thing.

BERYL: Oh, all right.

She switches off the lights. The lamp from the platform shines in through the window so it isn't quite dark.

ALEC: Thank you very much.

BERYL *goes out by the platform door, closing it behind her.*

LAURA: Just a few minutes.

ALEC: Let's have a cigarette, shall we?

LAURA: I have some. [*She takes her bag up from the table.*]

ALEC [*producing his case*]: No, here. [*He lights their cigarettes carefully.*] Now then—I want you to promise me something.

LAURA: What is it?

ALEC: Promise me that however unhappy you are, and however much you think things over that you'll meet me next Thursday as usual.

LAURA: Not at the flat.

ALEC: No—be at the Picture House café at the same time. I'll hire a car—we'll drive out into the country.

LAURA: All right—I promise.

ALEC: We've got to talk—I've got to explain.

LAURA: About going away?

ALEC: Yes.

LAURA: Where are you going? Where can you go? You can't give up your practice!

ALEC: I've had a job offered me—I wasn't going to tell you—

I wasn't going to take it—but I must—I know now, it's the only way out.

LAURA: Where?

ALEC: A long way away—Johannesburg.

LAURA [*hopelessly*]: Oh God!

ALEC [*hurriedly*]: My brother's out there—they're opening a new hospital—they want me in it. It's a fine opportunity, really. I'll take Madeleine and the boys, it's been torturing me for three weeks, the necessity of making a decision one way or the other—I haven't told anybody, not even Madeleine. I couldn't bear the idea of leaving you, but now I see—it's got to happen soon, anyway—it's almost happening already.

LAURA [*tonelessly*]: When will you go?

ALEC: In about two months' time.

LAURA: It's quite near, isn't it?

ALEC: Do you want me to stay? Do you want me to turn down the offer?

LAURA: Don't be foolish, Alec.

ALEC: I'll do whatever you say.

LAURA: That's unkind of you, my darling. [*She suddenly buries her head in her arms and bursts into tears.*]

ALEC [*putting his arms around her*]: Oh, Laura, don't, please don't!

LAURA: I'll be all right—leave me alone a minute.

ALEC: I love you—I love you.

LAURA: I know.

ALEC: We knew we'd get hurt.

LAURA [*sitting up*]: I'm being very stupid.

ALEC [*giving her his handkerchief*]: Here.

LAURA [*blowing her nose*]: Thank you.

The platform bell goes.

There's my train.

ALEC: You're not angry with me, are you?

LAURA: No, I'm not angry—I don't think I'm anything, really —I feel just tired.

[*250*]

ALEC: Forgive me.

LAURA: Forgive you for what?

ALEC: For everything—for having met you in the first place—for taking the piece of grit out of your eye—for loving you—for bringing you so much misery.

LAURA [*trying to smile*]: I'll forgive you—if you'll forgive me——

There is the noise of a train pulling into the station. BERYL *enters.* LAURA *and* ALEC *get up.*

ALEC: I'll see you into the train.

LAURA: No—please stay here.

ALEC: All right.

LAURA [*softly*]: Good night, darling.

ALEC: Good night, darling.

She goes hurriedly out on to the platform without looking back.

ALEC: The last train for Churley hasn't gone yet, has it?

BERYL: I couldn't say, I'm sure.

ALEC: I'll wait in the waiting-room—thank you very much.

BERYL: I must lock up now.

ALEC: All right. Good night.

BERYL: Good night.

The train starts as he goes out on to the platform.

BERYL *locks the door carefully after him, and then goes off upstage as the lights fade.*

SCENE V

The time is between 5 and 5.30 on an afternoon in March. MYRTLE *is behind the counter.* BERYL *is crouching over the stove putting coals in it.* ALBERT *enters.*

ALBERT [*gaily*]: One tea, please—two lumps of sugar, and a bath bun, and make it snappy.

[*251*]

MYRTLE: What's the matter with you?

ALBERT: Beryl, 'op it.

MYRTLE: Don't you go ordering Beryl about—you haven't any right to.

ALBERT: You heard me, Beryl—'Op it.

BERYL [*giggling*]: Well, I never!

MYRTLE: Go into the back room a minute, Beryl.

BERYL: Yes, Mrs. Bagot.

She goes.

MYRTLE: Now then, Albert—you behave—we don't want the whole station laughing at us.

ALBERT: What is there to laugh at?

MYRTLE: Here's your tea.

ALBERT: How d'you feel?

MYRTLE: Don't talk so soft—how should I feel?

ALBERT: I only wondered—— [*He leans toward her.*]

MYRTLE: Look out—somebody's coming in.

ALBERT: It's only Romeo and Juliet.

LAURA *and* ALEC *come in.* LAURA *goes to the table,* ALEC *to the counter.*

ALEC: Good afternoon.

MYRTLE: Good afternoon—same as usual?

ALEC: Yes, please.

MYRTLE [*drawing tea*]: Quite Springy out, isn't it?

ALEC: Yes—quite.

He pays her, collects the tea and carries it over to the table— something in his manner causes ALBERT *to make a grimace over his tea-cup at* MYRTLE. ALEC *sits down at the table, and he and* LAURA *sip their tea in silence.*

ALBERT: I spoke to Mr. Saunders.

MYRTLE: What did he say?

ALBERT: 'E was very decent as a matter-of-fact—said it'd be all right——

MILDRED *comes in hurriedly. She is a fair girl wearing a station overall.*

MILDRED: Is Beryl here?

MYRTLE: Why, Mildred, whatever's the matter?

MILDRED: It's her mother—she's bad again—they telephoned through to the Booking Office.

MYRTLE: She's inside—you'd better go in. Don't go yelling in at her now—tell her gently.

MILDRED: They said she'd better come at once.

MYRTLE: I thought this was going to happen—stay here, Mildred. I'll tell her. Wait a minute, Albert.

MYRTLE *vanishes into the inside room.*

ALBERT: Better get back to the bookstall, hadn't you?

MILDRED: Do you think she's going to die?

ALBERT: How do I know?

MILDRED: Mr. Saunders thinks she is—judging by what the doctor said on the telephone.

ALBERT: 'Ow do you know it was the doctor?

MILDRED: Mr. Saunders said it was.

ALBERT: She's always being took bad, that old woman.

MILDRED: Do you think Beryl would like me to go along with her?

ALBERT: You can't, and leave nobody on the papers.

MILDRED: Mr. Saunders said I might if it was necessary.

ALBERT: Well, go and get your 'at then, and don't make such a fuss.

MYRTLE *comes back.*

MYRTLE: She's going at once, poor little thing!

ALBERT: Mildred's going with her.

MYRTLE: All right, Mildred—go on.

MILDRED [*half-way to the door*]: What about me 'at?

MYRTLE: Never mind about your 'at—go this way.

MILDRED *rushes off upstage.*

MYRTLE: Poor child—this has been hanging over her for weeks. [*She puts her head round the door.*] Mildred, tell Beryl she needn't come back to-night, I'll stay on.

[253]

ALBERT: 'Ere, you can't do that, we was going to the Broadway Melody of 1936.

MYRTLE: For shame, Albert—thinking of the Broadway Melody of 1936 in a moment of life and death!

ALBERT: But look 'ere, Myrtle——

MYRTLE: I dreamt of a hearse last night, and whenever I dream of a hearse something happens—you mark my words——

ALBERT: I've got reserved tickets——

MYRTLE: Send Stanley to change them on his way home. Come in 'ere when you go off and I'll make you a little supper inside.

ALBERT [*grumbily*]: Everybody getting into a state and fussing about——

MYRTLE: You shock me, Albert, you do really—go on, finish up your tea and get back to the gate. [*She turns and goes to the upper end of the counter.*]

ALBERT *gulps his tea.*

ALBERT [*slamming the cup down on the counter*]: Women! *He stamps out on to the platform.*

ALEC: Are you all right, darling?

LAURA: Yes, I'm all right.

ALEC: I wish I could think of something to say.

LAURA: It doesn't matter—not saying anything, I mean.

ALEC: I'll miss my train and wait to see you into yours.

LAURA: No—no—please don't. I'll come over to your platform with you—I'd rather.

ALEC: Very well.

LAURA: Do you think we shall ever see each other again?

ALEC: I don't know. [*His voice breaks.*] Not for years, anyway.

LAURA: The children will all be grown up—I wonder if they'll ever meet and know each other.

ALEC: Couldn't I write to you—just once in a while?

LAURA: No—please not—we promised we wouldn't.

ALEC: Please know this—please know that you'll be with me for ages and ages yet—far away into the future. Time will wear

down the agony of not seeing you, bit by bit the pain will go
—but the loving you and the memory of you won't ever go—
please know that.

LAURA: I know it.

ALEC: It's easier for me than for you. I do realise that, really I
do. I at least will have different shapes to look at, and new
work to do—you have to go on among familiar things—my
heart aches for you so.

LAURA: I'll be all right.

ALEC: I love you with all my heart and soul.

LAURA [*quietly*]: I want to die—if only I could die.

ALEC: If you died you'd forget me—I want to be remembered.

LAURA: Yes, I know—I do, too.

ALEC: Good-bye, my dearest love.

LAURA: Good-bye, my dearest love.

ALEC: We've still got a few minutes.

LAURA: Thank God——!

DOLLY MESSITER *bustles into the refreshment room. She is a
nicely dressed woman, with rather a fussy manner. She is laden
with parcels. She sees* LAURA.

DOLLY: Laura! What a lovely surprise!

LAURA [*dazed*]: Oh, Dolly!

DOLLY: My dear, I've been shopping till I'm dropping—that
sounds like a song, doesn't it? My feet are nearly falling off,
and my throat's parched. I thought of having tea in Spindle's,
but I was terrified of losing the train. I'm always missing trains,
and being late for meals, and Bob gets disagreeable for days at
a time. Oh, dear—— [*She flops down at their table.*]

LAURA: This is Doctor Harvey.

ALEC [*rising*]: How do you do!

DOLLY [*shaking hands*]: How do you do! Would you be a
perfect dear and get me a cup of tea! I don't think I could
drag my poor old bones as far as the counter. I must get some
chocolates for Tony, too, but I can do that afterwards—here's
sixpence——

[255]

ALEC [*waving it away*]: No, please———

He goes drearily over to the counter, gets another cup of tea from MYRTLE, *pays for it and comes back to the table, meanwhile* DOLLY *continues to talk.*

DOLLY: My dear—what a nice-looking man. Who on earth is he? Really, you're quite a dark horse. I shall telephone Fred in the morning and make mischief—that is a bit of luck. I haven't seen you for ages, and I've been meaning to pop in, but Tony's had measles, you know, and I had all that awful fuss about Phyllis—but of course you don't know—she left me! Suddenly upped and went, my dear, without even an hour's warning, let alone a month's notice.

LAURA [*with an effort*]: Oh, how dreadful!

DOLLY: Mind you, I never cared for her much, but still Tony did. Tony adored her, and—but, never mind, I'll tell you all about that in the train.

ALEC *arrives back at the table with her tea—he sits down again.* Thank you so very much. They've certainly put enough milk in it—but still it's wet and that's all one can really ask for in a refreshment room—— [*She sips it.*] Oh, dear—no sugar.

ALEC: It's in the spoon.

DOLLY: Oh, of course—what a fool I am—Laura, you look frightfully well. I do wish I'd known you were coming in to-day, we could have come together and lunched and had a good gossip. I loathe shopping by myself, anyway.

There is the sound of a bell on the platform.

LAURA: There's your train.

ALEC: Yes, I know.

DOLLY: Aren't you coming with us?

ALEC: No, I go in the opposite direction. My practice is in Churley.

DOLLY: How interesting! What sort of a doctor are you? I mean, are you a specialist at anything or just a sort of general family doctor?

ALEC: I'm a general practitioner at the moment.

[256]

LAURA [*dully*]: Dr. Harvey is going out to Africa next week.

DOLLY: But, my dear, how thrilling! Are you going to operate on the Zulus or something? I always associate Africa with Zulus, but I may be quite wrong.

There is the sound of ALEC's *train approaching.*

ALEC: I must go.

LAURA: Yes, you must.

ALEC: Good-bye.

DOLLY: Good-bye.

He shakes hands with DOLLY, *looks at* LAURA *swiftly once, then presses her hand under cover of the table and leaves hurriedly as the train is heard rumbling into the station.* LAURA *sits quite still.*

DOLLY: He'll have to run—he's got to get right over to the other platform. How did you meet him?

LAURA: I got something in my eye one day, and he took it out.

DOLLY: My dear—how very romantic! I'm always getting things in my eye and nobody the least bit attractive has ever paid the faintest attention—which reminds me—you know about Harry and Lucy Jenner, don't you?

LAURA [*listening for the train to start*]: No—what about them?

DOLLY: My dear—they're going to get a divorce—at least I believe they're getting a conjugal separation, or whatever it is to begin with, and the divorce later on.

The train starts, and the sound of it dies gradually away in the distance.

It seems that there's an awful Mrs. Something or other in London that he's been carrying on with for ages—you know how he was always having to go up on business. Well, apparently Lucy's sister saw them, Harry and this woman, in the Tate Gallery of all places, and she wrote to Lucy, and then gradually the whole thing came out.

There is the sound of a bell on the platform.

Is that our train? [*She addresses* MYRTLE.] Can you tell me, is that the Ketchworth train?

MYRTLE: No, that's the express.

LAURA: The boat train.

DOLLY: Oh, yes—that doesn't stop, does it? Express trains are Tony's passion in life—he knows them all by name—where they start from and where they go to, and how long they take to get there. Oh, dear, I mustn't forget his chocolate. [*She jumps up and goes to the counter.*]

LAURA *remains quite still.*

[*At counter.*] I want some chocolate, please.

MYRTLE: Milk or plain?

DOLLY: Plain, I think—or no, perhaps milk would be nicer. Have you any with nuts in it?

The express is heard in the distance.

MYRTLE: Nestlé's nut milk—shilling or sixpence?

DOLLY: Give me one plain and one nut milk.

The noise of the express sounds louder—LAURA *suddenly gets up and goes swiftly out on to the platform. The express roars through the station as* DOLLY *finishes buying and paying for her chocolate. She turns.*

DOLLY: Oh! where is she?

MYRTLE [*looking over the counter*]: I never noticed her go.

DOLLY *comes over to the table,* LAURA *comes in again, looking very white and shaky.*

DOLLY: My dear, I couldn't think where you'd disappeared to.

LAURA: I just wanted to see the express go through.

DOLLY: What on earth's the matter—do you feel ill?

LAURA: I feel a little sick.

DOLLY: Have you any brandy?

MYRTLE: I'm afraid it's out of hours.

DOLLY: Surely—if someone's feeling ill——

LAURA: I'm all right, really.

The platform bell goes.

That's our train.

DOLLY: Just a sip of brandy will buck you up. [*To* MYRTLE.]
Please——

MYRTLE: Very well. [*She pours out some brandy.*]

DOLLY: How much?

MYRTLE: Tenpence, please.

DOLLY [*paying her*]: There!

She takes the brandy over to LAURA, *who has sat down again at the table.*

Here you are, dear.

LAURA [*taking it*]: Thank you.

As she sips it the train is heard coming into the station. DOLLY *proceeds to gather up her parcels as the Curtain falls.*

FAMILY ALBUM
A Victorian Comedy with Music

CHARACTERS

JASPER FEATHERWAYS
JANE, his wife
LAVINIA FEATHERWAYS
RICHARD FEATHERWAYS
HARRIET WINTER
CHARLES WINTER
EMILY VALANCE
EDWARD VALANCE
BURROWS

The action of the play passes in the drawing-room of the Featherways' house in Kent on an Autumn evening in the year 1860.

The scene is the drawing-room of the Featherways' house in Kent not very far from London.

It is an Autumn evening in the year 1860.

When the curtain rises the entire family is assembled. They are all in deep mourning. The music plays softly; an undercurrent to grief. The family group would be static were it not for an occasional slight movement from one or other of them. Apart from the music there is silence for quite a while. EMILY, *who is by the window, breaks it.*

EMILY: It has stopped raining.

RICHARD [*moving to the window*]: Not quite, Emily, but it is certainly clearing.

LAVINIA: It was fitting that it rained to-day. It has been a sad day and rain became it.

JASPER: True, very true.

JANE: A little sunshine would have been much pleasanter nevertheless.

JASPER: Lavinia has a tidy mind. She likes life to be as neat as her handkerchief drawer.

HARRIET: I hope Mr. Lubbock reached London safely.

JANE: Dear Mr. Lubbock.

LAVINIA: Really Jane!

JANE: I think he's a sweet man. He read the will with such sympathy.

HARRIET: He coughed a great deal, I thought. I wanted to give him one of my pastilles.

CHARLES: I'm glad you didn't, my dear, they have an alarming flavour and he was already considerably nervous.

HARRIET: They're very efficacious.

EMILY [*pensively—at the window*]: I wonder if he knew.

EDWARD: What was that, my love?

EMILY: Papa—I wonder if he knew it was raining?

LAVINIA: Perhaps he was watching—from somewhere above the trees.

HARRIET: Oh! Do you suppose he was!

LAVINIA: I like to think it.

JANE: Do you, Lavinia?

LAVINIA: Of course.

JANE: When I die I hope I shall go swiftly and not linger

[265]

above familiar trees. It must be painful to watch those you have left, in black and weeping.

EMILY: Oh, don't, Jane, don't! [*She weeps.*]

EDWARD [*comforting her*]: There, there, my dear.

HARRIET: Poor Papa.

EMILY: Poor dear Papa.

The door opens quietly and BURROWS, *a very aged butler, enters staggering under the weight of a heavy tray on which is a decanter containing Madeira, and the requisite number of glasses.*

RICHARD *goes quickly and relieves him of it.*

RICHARD: Oh, Burrows, you should have let Martin carry the tray, it's too heavy for you.

BURROWS [*cupping his ear with his hand*]: Pardon, Master Richard?

JASPER [*bending down to him and speaking clearly*]: You should have let Martin carry the tray, Burrows, it's too heavy for you.

BURROWS: Martin is young, Mr. Jasper. He would have been out of tune with the evening's melancholy. His very bearing would have been an intrusion.

LAVINIA: Thank you, Burrows, that was very considerate of you.

BURROWS: I beg your pardon, Miss Lavvy?

LAVINIA [*loudly*]: I said thank you, Burrows, that was very considerate of you.

BURROWS: Your servant to the grave, Miss Lavvy.

JANE: Oh, Burrows!

BURROWS: I beg your pardon, Ma'am?

JANE [*loudly*]: I only said 'Oh, Burrows,' Burrows.

BURROWS: Very good, Ma'am.

BURROWS *goes out.*

HARRIET: Poor Burrows looks very depressed.

JASPER: Burrows has looked depressed for at least thirty years.

JANE: One could scarcely expect him to be hilarious now.

[266]

LAVINIA: Hilarious! Really, Jane.

HARRIET: I think sorrow has increased his deafness.

JASPER: He was just as deaf last Christmas really, and that was a gay occasion.

JANE [*with meaning*]: Gay!

JASPER [*reprovingly*]: Hush, Jane.

HARRIET: A bereavement in the house must affect the servants profoundly, although I must admit I heard Sarah singing in the pantry this morning.

EMILY [*horrified*]: This morning!

HARRIET: It was quite early.

LAVINIA: Disgraceful.

HARRIET: She was singing very softly, and it *was* a hymn.

LAVINIA: Nevertheless, I hope you scolded her.

HARRIET: I hadn't the heart, she has such a pretty voice.

CHARLES: What hymn was it?

HARRIET: 'For those in peril on the sea.'

LAVINIA: Most inappropriate.

JASPER: Sarah's young man is a sailor, you know, he's on the *Brilliant*.

CHARLES [*with interest*]: That's a Three Decker.

EDWARD: She carries 114 thirty-two pounders, 2 sixty-eight pounders and 4 eighteen pounders.

EMILY: Oh, Edward, how clever of you to know.

RICHARD: A fine ship, I have seen her at anchor.

CHARLES: Surely not a hundred and twenty guns?

EDWARD: Yes, she is the same class as the *Britannic* and the *Prince Regent*.

RICHARD: Cast-iron muzzle loaders, I presume?

EDWARD [*enthusiastically*]: Yes, their recoil is checked by stout rope breechings.

CHARLES: How are they elevated?

EDWARD: Quoins—and trained by handspikes.

RICHARD: Oh—handspikes.

JANE [*with slight mockery*]: Handspikes, Lavinia—do you hear that?—they're trained by handspikes!

LAVINIA: I declare I'm more at sea than Sarah's young man.

JANE: Oh, Lavvy—a joke—how sweet!

EMILY [*hugging her*]: Darling Lavvy!

LAVINIA: Behave, Emily—let me alone.

JASPER: It seems odd that the solemnity of this particular family reunion should be dissipated by gunnery.

LAVINIA: Such irrelevance, on such a day.

EDWARD: It was my fault, I apologise.

JANE: With so much to be done, so much to be decided.

LAVINIA [*raising her handkerchief to her eyes*]: Oh, dear!

JASPER: Steel yourself, Lavinia—be brave.

LAVINIA: I'll try.

HARRIET: We must all try.

CHARLES *and* RICHARD *go to the table on which* RICHARD *has placed the tray.*

CHARLES: Jane—a little wine?

JANE: Thank you, Charles.

CHARLES: Harriet?

HARRIET: Thank you, Charles.

RICHARD: A little Madeira, Emily?

EMILY: Just a drop, please.

RICHARD: Lavinia?

LAVINIA: No, thank you.

HARRIET: Oh, Lavvy, a little sip would warm you.

LAVINIA: I am not cold.

JASPER [*brusquely*]: Come, Lavvy, don't be annoying.

LAVINIA: How can you, Jasper——

JASPER: I insist—here—— [*He gives her a glass.*]

JANE: We should drink a toast.

LAVINIA: You should be ashamed.

JANE: Don't be alarmed, I meant quite a gentle toast.

RICHARD: An excellent idea.

CHARLES: Why not?

LAVINIA: As though this were a moment for celebrating.

CHARLES: Again—why not?

JASPER [*sternly*]: Charles—behave yourself!

JANE: Charles is right. Why not indeed!

LAVINIA: I am at a loss to understand your behaviour this evening, Jane.

JANE: A billiard room—I heard Charles and Harriet discussing it—they're going to have a billiard room——

HARRIET: It's an extravagance—I told Charles it was an extravagance.

JANE: Never mind, you can afford it now.

CHARLES: That's what I say.

JANE: Isn't it splendid!—Isn't it absolutely splendid?

LAVINIA [*immeasurably shocked*]: What!

JANE: About Charles and Harriet being able to afford a billiard room, about Emily and Edward being able to send John and Curly to Eton, about you, Lavinia, being able to buy a little house anywhere you like, about Jasper and me living here——

RICHARD: What about me?

JASPER: I think Crockford's should be congratulated—that's where all your money goes.

RICHARD: Touché, Jasper—a new black fleece, though, for the blackest of black-sheep.

EMILY: Where will you go, Lavvy?

LAVINIA: I feel this conversation to be abominably out of place.

JANE: Darling, don't be stuffy.

LAVINIA: It is my father who has passed away, remember.

JANE: Jasper's too, and Emily's and Richard's and Harriet's.

JASPER: Leave Lavinia her decorum, Jane, polite grief should be respected.

LAVINIA: Polite! Oh, Jasper!

JASPER: I am your brother, dear, I know your heart.

JANE: Smile, Lavinia—just once.

EMILY: Yes, Lavvy, just one smile.

[269]

LAVINIA: You are disgraceful, all of you—unfeeling and dis-graceful—I am ashamed of you.

JASPER: Smile, then, and you can be ashamed of yourself as well.

HARRIET: Please, Lavvy.

RICHARD: Come along, Lavvy.

JASPER: Think, Lavvy—a little house in some gay country—France or Italy—you've always loved foreigners—a little villa in the sun—you can paint your pictures—blue seas and cypresses—you could take tabby with you, she's an insular cat but I doubt whether French or Italian mice taste so very different——

JANE: We'll all come and stay with you, Lavinia.

RICHARD: Hurrah, Lavinia—smile and say Hurrah!

LAVINIA [*struggling*]: No—no——

EMILY [*flinging her arms round her*]: Yes—yes——

LAVINIA: Be still, Emily—for shame!

HARRIET: Her mouth twitched—I saw it.

JASPER [*tickling the back of her neck*]: Come along, Lavvy——

LAVINIA [*slapping his hand away*]: How dare you, Jasper!

JANE: Think of Mrs. Hodgson's bonnet at the funeral—do you remember?—I nudged you——

LAVINIA [*breaking at last into laughter*]: Oh, dear—how horrid you all are—I hate you—it was the most ridiculous bonnet I ever saw—like a little black pie—oh, dear——

JASPER: Are your glasses charged?

LAVINIA: No, Jasper, no—I don't approve——

JASPER [*raising his glass*]: To Mrs. Hodgson's little black pie!

ALL [*raising their glasses*]: Mrs. Hodgson's little black pie!

JASPER [*triumphantly, as* LAVINIA *drinks*]: There!

LAVINIA *chokes—everyone gathers round her and pats her on the back.*

Some more—quickly, Richard——

RICHARD, CHARLES, EDWARD *and* JASPER *refill all the glasses.*

LAVINIA: This is so wrong—so dreadfully wrong——

JASPER: Another toast—be prepared——

LAVINIA: Please, stop, Jasper—the servants will hear.

JASPER [*raising his glass*]: To ourselves—a closely united family and the dear strangers who have joined us—I allude to you, Jane darling, and Charles and Edward——

CHARLES: Does that mean that we three may not drink?

JASPER: Certainly not—drink to yourselves—to each other—and the happiness of us all.

CHARLES: Good!

HARRIET: Do be quiet, Charles.

JASPER: Where was I?

JANE: The happiness of us all, my dear.

JASPER *sings a short toast to each of them—everybody joins in. The tempo becomes more gay and there is much laughter as each individual is commented upon.*

The gaiety is interrupted by the clock on the mantelpiece striking ten.

The music drops to the minor. Everyone puts down his glass.

LAVINIA: Papa's eight-day clock—he would never allow anyone to wind it but himself—who will wind it now?

She bows her head. EMILY, JASPER, HARRIET *and* RICHARD *all sing sadly together.*

EMILY
JASPER   'Ah, who will wind it now—alack-a-day—who
HARRIET   will wind it now!'
RICHARD

JANE: Jasper, of course—don't be so silly.

JASPER: Richard, be so kind as to ring for Burrows.

RICHARD: Now?

JASPER: Yes, now.

LAVINIA: The box?

JASPER: The box.

RICHARD: Very well.

He pulls the bell-rope by the fireplace.

EMILY: Oh, dear!

[*271*]

There is a gloomy silence for a moment. EDWARD *breaks it.*

EDWARD [*at the window*]: Look—there's a squirrel!

CHARLES [*eagerly*]: Where?

EDWARD: There—by the steps.

RICHARD [*joining them*]: How can you tell—it's so dark.

EMILY: There's only a little moon but enough to see by, look —there he goes—back into the wood.

LAVINIA: Poor Papa—poor dear Papa—he'll never see a squirrel again.

HARRIET: Don't, Lavinia.

JANE: Do you think he would wish to?—I mean—not to see any more squirrels is surely one of the lesser disadvantages of dying.

LAVINIA [*coldly*]: You take me too literally, Jane.

EMILY [*coming away from the window*]: Oh, it's all so dreadful—death is so frightening.

LAVINIA: So lonely.

JASPER: Lonelier even than life.

JANE [*hurt*]: Jasper!

JASPER: Forgive me, my love—it was a generalisation.

BURROWS *enters.*

BURROWS: You rung, Mr. Jasper?

JASPER: We are ready for the box now, Burrows.

BURROWS: Every one of them, Mr. Jasper—regulated to the minute—I did them myself.

JASPER: Not the clocks, Burrows, the box.

BURROWS: I had a mort of trouble with the one in the library— it struck fifteen three times—but I fixed it. [*He gives a slight cackle and then controls himself.*]

JASPER: The box, Burrows—we want the box—I told you to have it brought down from the attic this morning.

BURROWS: Oh, the trunk! Very well, Mr. Jasper.

He goes off.

LAVINIA: It seems callous somehow—so soon to pry upon Papa's secrets.

[272]

JASPER: Callous perhaps, but certainly necessary.

JANE: I observed one of his more open secrets at the back of church this morning.

LAVINIA: What do you mean, Jane?

JANE: Mrs. Wynant.

HARRIET: That creature.

JASPER: Hush, Harriet—we cannot resent her grieving, too—in her own way.

HARRIET: Nevertheless, I do resent it.

LAVINIA: She should not have come.

EMILY: Poor Mrs. Wynant.

LAVINIA: Really, Emily—poor Mrs. Wynant indeed!

EMILY: I was thinking of the will.

RICHARD: It was perfectly just—she had no claim.

JASPER: No legal claim at any rate.

LAVINIA: Jasper!

JASPER: It would be unchristian to deny her a certain moral right.

CHARLES: Moral is hardly the word I should have chosen.

JASPER: Spoken like a soldier, Charles—and also, I'm afraid, like a gentleman.

BURROWS *enters*.

BURROWS: The box is outside, Mr. Jasper—if you and Mr. Richard—I would rather Martin did not enter——

JANE: Why, Burrows, it really wouldn't matter.

BURROWS: It isn't the clatter, Ma'am, it's his face, it's so very hot and red—in this pale room—you understand?

JASPER: Very well, Burrows—come along, Richard.

RICHARD *and* JASPER *go out*.

BURROWS: Will there be any tea required, Ma'am?

JANE: Yes, please, Burrows—a little later.

BURROWS [*cupping his ear with his hand*]: I beg your pardon, Ma'am?

JANE [*shouting*]: A little later, Burrows.

[273]

BURROWS [*respectfully*]: Oh, no, Ma'am—certainly not—not for the world, Ma'am.

BURROWS *goes out.*

JANE: What could he have thought I said?

CHARLES: I fear that we shall never know.

RICHARD *and* JASPER *return with a very dusty little trunk. They put it down.*

JASPER: Sarah has done her best with a duster, but I fear it needs scrubbing.

RICHARD: Never mind.

LAVINIA: The box.

HARRIET: Oh, dear—the box.

JASPER: Yes, there it sits—reproaching us—almost frowning at us.

JANE: That little strap makes it look even more disagreeable than it really is.

JASPER: You have the key, Lavinia. You took it from Father's chain.

LAVINIA: Yes, it's here. [*She hands it to* JASPER.] You're the eldest.

JASPER: Before opening it—before unearthing our dear Father's secrets—I must most earnestly enjoin—complete discretion.

CHARLES: Of course.

JASPER: You, Charles, and Edward, and my dear Jane——

JANE: Open it, Jasper, and don't be silly.

JASPER: You cut me short, Jane, in the most frivolous way.

JANE: Never mind.

CHARLES: We understand, Jasper—complete discretion.

JANE [*impatiently*]: Open it!

JASPER [*on his knees*]: Poor Papa! [*He wrestles with the lock.*] The key doesn't fit—— [*He lifts the lid.*] It's already open—— [*He puts his hand into the box and produces a gilt paper crown.*] It's the wrong box!

LAVINIA: Oh, how stupid of Burrows!

EMILY: A paper crown.

HARRIET: I remember it.

RICHARD: Where's the sceptre—there should be a sceptre, too —I made it myself from Uncle William's walking-stick—— [*He searches in the box.*]

EMILY: He was very angry.

RICHARD [*finding it*]: Here it is.

LAVINIA: There was a scarf with beads on it from India—I wore it when I was the Queen—— [*She goes on her knees too, and searches in the box.*]

HARRIET: And there were four swords—flat ones—but one was broken——

She joins LAVINIA *and searches in the box.*

EMILY [*rushing to the box*]: Princes and Princesses—oh, how lovely!

JANE: What on earth are you talking about?

JASPER [*smiling*]: Princes and Princesses—it was a dressing-up game—we played it when we were children——

HARRIET: On Sundays—only on Sundays——

They sing a foolish little tune: 'Princes and Princesses.' They act a little too, fragments of the game they remember. LAVINIA *is crowned with the paper crown.* JASPER *and* RICHARD *fight a brisk duel with the swords. At the end* LAVINIA *tears off her crown and throws it on to the floor.*

LAVINIA: This is wicked—wicked—I shall never forgive myself to the end of my days——

She sinks on to a sofa, in tears. The others look at her mutely. RICHARD *rises from the floor where he has been lying since being killed in the duel and dusts himself down.*

JASPER: Don't cry, Lavvy—please don't.

LAVINIA [*tearfully*]: —God must surely punish us for this heartlessness, dancing and singing and playing, with Father not yet cold in his grave.

JASPER: That is an emotional statement, my dear, understandable in the circumstances, but hardly accurate.

EMILY: The cemetery really is very exposed, Lavinia.

LAVINIA: Forgive us, Papa, forgive us——

RICHARD: A little more Madeira, Charles, our sister is becoming hysterical.

CHARLES *pours out some Madeira and hands it to* RICHARD, *who takes it to* LAVINIA.

Here, my dear.

LAVINIA: No, no—I don't want it.

JASPER: Drink it, Lavinia, it will calm you.

JANE: I think I should like a little more, too.

CHARLES [*pouring it for her*]: Very well—Harriet?

HARRIET: Yes, please.

JASPER [*to* LAVINIA]: Come along, dear.

LAVINIA [*sipping the wine*]: How shameful—oh, how shameful!

CHARLES: Emily, some more wine?

EMILY: May I, Edward?

EDWARD: Yes, my love, but only a little.

CHARLES: There is only a little left.

RICHARD: We had better ring for some more.

LAVINIA: No, Richard, no—I forbid it.

RICHARD: As you say, Lavvy, but my throat is cruelly dry.

CHARLES: Mine too—Jasper?

JASPER: Dry as dust.

LAVINIA [*bursting into tears again*]: Dust! Oh, Jasper!

The door opens discreetly and BURROWS *enters bearing another decanter of Madeira. Everyone looks at him in silence as he places it ceremoniously on the tray. He looks enquiringly at* CHARLES *who is holding the empty decanter.* CHARLES *gives it to him. He bows politely and goes to the door. He turns and regards them all lovingly for a moment then, from his cuff, he produces a large white handkerchief with which he wipes his eyes, but it is difficult to tell whether he is laughing or weeping.*

He goes out, closing the door behind him.

JASPER: With every advancing year Burrows grows wiser.

HARRIET: And kinder.

[276]

RICHARD: And more understanding.

JASPER: Surely, among ourselves, a little private toast to Burrows would not be entirely without grace?

CHARLES: Hear, hear!

EMILY: I think Papa would have wished it.

EDWARD: Well spoken, my love.

LAVINIA: Papa would not have approved at all—Jasper—I appeal to you——

HARRIET: Oh, Lavvy, I know he would——

RICHARD: Tinge your grief with tolerance, Lavinia.

CHARLES: What harm is there, Lavinia?

JANE: Don't be silly, Lavinia.

JASPER: The 'Ayes' have it—charge your glasses.

Everybody refills their glasses.

[*Raising his glass.*] To Burrows—our first friend—don't you remember, Lavinia? He made us toys in the woodshed. He read us stories when we were ill; he gave us forbidden sweets from the pantry. He loved us all—you particularly, Lavinia—have you forgotten his tenderness when Mother died? Have you forgotten his welcoming smile when we came home from school? Surely this small gesture of affection to him can only be a pale sin in the eyes of heaven. To Burrows, Lavinia.

LAVINIA [*rising to her feet*]: To Burrows! [*She drinks.*]

ALL: To Burrows! [*They drink.*]

CHARLES: That was delicious.

RICHARD: I think it must have come from Papa's special cellar.

EMILY: I believe I should like a little more.

EDWARD: No, Emily.

EMILY [*gaily*]: Spoilsport—I defy you!

She quickly pours herself out another glassful and drinks it before anyone can stop her.

HARRIET: Emily!

LAVINIA: Behave, Emily.

JASPER: You shock me appallingly, Emily—I'm almost sure you do.

EMILY: Nonsense!

EDWARD: I apologise—I apologise to you all. Come to bed, Emily.

EMILY: Papa liked wine—he liked it to excess—I expect this is hereditary. [*She giggles.*]

EDWARD: Come to bed immediately.

EMILY: I shall do no such thing, my love, so there! I want to see what more there is in the box—— [*She kneels on the floor beside it and begins to rummage about in it.*]

JANE: Poor Edward, I fear the grape has robbed you of your marital authority.

RICHARD: Vanquished, Edward—be a man and admit it.

LAVINIA: I feel a little faint—the heat, I think, and everyone behaving so strangely——

HARRIET [*going to her*]: My dear——

JANE: Would you like me to take you upstairs?

LAVINIA: No, no, it will pass—it's nothing.

RICHARD: Some salts—some vinegar?

LAVINIA: No, no—I think perhaps a thimbleful more of that wine——

CHARLES [*pouring her out some*]: Here, my dear——

LAVINIA: Thank you, Charles—how kind. [*She accepts it weakly.*]

JANE: I feel very curious myself.

JASPER: Beloved!

HARRIET: Open the window.

JANE: No—the air is damp—it would be dangerous——

RICHARD: Some wine?

JANE: Perhaps—perhaps that would revive me.

CHARLES [*pouring her out some*]: Here, my dear.

JANE [*smiling gaily*]: Thank you, Charles.

They all casually take a little more wine.

EMILY [*at the box*]: Oh, look—look——!

JASPER: What is it?

EMILY: The musical box—don't you remember?

RICHARD: I thought it had dropped to pieces years ago.

LAVINIA: Aunt Heathcote gave it to us—it was a Christmas present.

HARRIET: Papa forbade us to play it.

EMILY [*placing it on the table and winding it*]: He can't forbid us now!

EDWARD [*reprovingly*]: Emily!

EMILY: Shh! Be still—listen——

They all listen—no sound comes from the musical box.

JASPER: It's old and tired, it's forgotten how to play.

RICHARD: No, no—there was a little catch—I'm sure there was——

EMILY: Make it play, Richard—please try——

RICHARD *tinkers with it and it strikes one note. They all sing 'Let's play a tune on the music box.' They stop singing and the music box tinkles out a tinny little melody.*

RICHARD: There!

EMILY [*clasping her hands ecstatically*]: Oh, how sweet—how sweet!

HARRIET: The red schoolroom curtains—I can suddenly see them—blowing out in the draught——

RICHARD: The hard pink sugar on the edge of the cake—I can suddenly taste it.

JASPER: Your hand in mine, Jane, when you were brought over to tea by your governess—I can suddenly feel it.

JANE [*taking his hand*]: Oh, darling——

EMILY: Again, again—make it play again—I want to remember, too——

RICHARD *tinkers with it again. It plays the same sticky little melody.*

EMILY *begins to sing—they all join in—little snatches of melody come back to them out of their childhood.*

HARRIET: There was another tune as well—I remember distinctly—it played another tune——

RICHARD: We mustn't ask too much of it.

JASPER: Try the little catch again.

HARRIET: It was a waltz.

JANE [*looking at* JASPER]: Of course it was—a waltz—don't you recall it, my dear love? We danced to it years later—at a ball—just before we were married—it was this—it was this——

She starts to sing—RICHARD *is still at work on the music box— suddenly it begins to play again—the tune that* JANE *is singing.*

EMILY: It's remembered—oh, how clever of it!

RICHARD: Hush, Emily—that was their love song——

JASPER *and* JANE *sing to each other the love song of their youth. The others join in, humming very softly, as they dance together. At the end of it* JANE *sinks to the floor in a deep curtsy,* JASPER *bows over her, taking her hand.*

JASPER: I love you, my heart.

JANE: 'Till death us do part——'

He raises her to her feet and takes her in his arms.

LAVINIA *sinks on to the sofa once more in tears.*

RICHARD: Oh, Lavvy!

LAVINIA: Don't mock me—these are true tears.

JASPER: Not sad ones though, I beg of you——

LAVINIA: Mama died when we were little, Papa died four days ago, but life isn't dead, is it—is it?

JASPER: Never, as long as it's gay, as long as it's happy.

EMILY: Poor Papa—poor dear Papa!

LAVINIA: To hell with Papa!

HARRIET: Lavinia!

RICHARD: Lavinia!

EMILY: Oh, Lavvy, how can you!

JASPER: Bravo, Lavvy!

LAVINIA: I mean it—give me some more Madeira, Charles.

CHARLES: Good Heavens!

LAVINIA: I hated Papa, so did you, Jasper, and Harriet and Richard and Emily——

EMILY: Oh, Lavvy—don't—don't——

LAVINIA: He was cruel to Mama, he was unkind to us, he was profligate and pompous and worse still, he was mean——

CHARLES [*handing her some wine*]: Here, my dear—drink this.

LAVINIA [*taking it*]: Certainly I will—— [*She raises her glass.*] Now I will propose a toast—To Papa—and to the truth, too—Papa and the truth together—for the first time.

JASPER: I do hope you will not regret this in the morning, Lavinia.

HARRIET: Don't you think you had better retire to bed?

EMILY: I feel frightened.

LAVINIA: This may be wicked. I expect it is—I expect I shall be punished for it—but I don't care. You escaped—all of you —you found husbands and wives and lives of your own—but I had to stay here—with him—— For years he has scarcely spoken to me—I've counted the linen—I've added up the bills —I've managed the house—years ago I said good-bye to someone I loved because my miserable unkind conscience told me that it was my duty. I've sat here in this house week after week, month after month, year after year, while he insulted me and glowered at me and betrayed our name with common village loves. The will—the happy will which was read to us to-day was made ten years ago—you realize that, do you not?

JASPER: Lavinia—what in heaven's name——

LAVINIA: What you do not realise is that he made another— a week before he died——

HARRIET: What are you saying?

RICHARD: Lavinia—are you mad?

EMILY [*wailing*]: Oh, Lavvy!

LAVINIA: None of us were even mentioned in it. Five thousand pounds was left to Mrs. Wynant. Six thousand pounds to Rose Dalton. Three thousand pounds to Mrs. Waterbury—I can only gather that she was less satisfactory than the others— and the rest to a fund for the erection of a new church containing a memorial of himself in black marble!

[*281*]

JASPER: Lavinia—are you sure of this?

LAVINIA: Quite sure. Burrows witnessed it.

JASPER: And would it be trespassing too far on your indiscretion to ask what became of it?

LAVINIA: Seven and a half minutes after Papa breathed his last, Burrows and I burnt it.

JASPER: Ring the bell, Richard.

RICHARD: Very well. [*He goes to the bell and pulls it.*]

EMILY: I think, Edward dear, another sip of wine would be pardonable in the circumstances.

HARRIET: I agree.

JANE: Black marble—how very nasty.

RICHARD: Black clay would have been more appropriate.
They all pour themselves out a little more Madeira.

EMILY: Poor Mrs. Waterbury.

JANE: Think of the humiliation she has been spared.

HARRIET: I wonder where Rose Dalton is now?

JASPER: In Scotland, I believe—she married a Baptist.

EDWARD: Do you suppose Mrs. Wynant suspects?

JASPER: Suspects what, Edward?

EDWARD: About the—er—about your father—about what Lavinia has just told us?

LAVINIA: I observed an expensive diamond brooch fastening her cloak in church to-day. That, I think, should be a sufficient reward for services rendered.

JASPER: How hard you are, Lavinia.

JANE: And how right.

BURROWS *enters.*

BURROWS: You rang, Mr. Jasper?

JASPER: Yes, Burrows.

RICHARD: We wish to ask you a question, Burrows.

BURROWS: Much better, thank you, Master Richard. A little herb tea sooths all disharmony.

JASPER: A question, Burrows.

BURROWS: Very well, Mr. Jasper.

JASPER: Miss Lavinia gives me to understand that you witnessed my late father's last Will and Testament.

BURROWS [*cupping his ear with his hand*]: I beg your pardon, sir?

JASPER: Did you or did you not witness my late father's last Will and Testament?

BURROWS: My affliction is increasing bad, Mr. Jasper, I shall never be able to hear that particular question.

LAVINIA [*softly*]: Thank you, Burrows.

BURROWS: Not at all, Miss Lavinia.

RICHARD: Some Madeira, Burrows?

He holds up the decanter.

BURROWS: I should be honoured, Master Richard.

RICHARD [*pouring him some*]: Here, then.

BURROWS [*accepting it*]: At your service always.

JASPER: Thank you, Burrows.

BURROWS [*catching sight of the musical box*]: Have I your permission for a moment?

JASPER: Certainly—what is it?

BURROWS: There should be a little tune, a little tune from the years that are dead—allow me——

He starts the musical box. It plays the same gay little melody that it played before. He stands beside it, bending down to hear it more clearly, then he stands up with his head nodding to the tune and raises his glass.

BURROWS: I drink to you all—— [*Then to* JASPER *and* JANE.] And to you, sir, and ma'am—this house was happy when there were children in it——

He drinks. EMILY *and* JANE *and* HARRIET *start to sing. All the others join in. The tune becomes gayer and swifter until they are all hand in hand and dancing round* BURROWS *as—*

THE CURTAIN FALLS

[*283*]

CONVERSATION PIECE

CAST OF CHARACTERS

Sophie Otford	SYLVIA LESLIE
Martha James	MOYA NUGENT
Mrs. Dragon	BETTY SHALE
Paul, Duc de Chaucigny-Varennes	PIERRE FRESNAY
Melanie	YVONNE PRINTEMPS
Rose	MAIDIE ANDREWS
The Marquis of Sheere	CARL HARBORD
Duchess of Beneden	WINIFRED DAVIS
Duke of Beneden	ATHOLE STEWART
Lady Julia Charteris	IRENE BROWNE
Hannah	JILL ANTHONY
Miss Goslett	PHYLLIS HARDING
Miss Mention	EILEEN CLIFTON
Lord St. Marys	GEORGE SANDERS

Soldiers, guests, milliners, children.

ACT I

SCENE I

*At the end of the overture, the curtain rises disclosing a
painted curtain, which depicts, in pastel colours, the Brighton
of the Regency.*

*SOPHIE and MARTHA, with MRS. DRAGON, come in, exquisitely
dressed in the fashion of 1811, and each carrying a little mask
on an ivory stick. They stand, formally, side by side, with their
masks held before their eyes. They lower them in order to
speak and retire behind them again when they are silent.*

BOTH: Ladies and Gentlemen.
SOPHIE: A Prologue to a play is out of date,
    A leisurely technique of past decades,
    So please regard us as two friendly shades
    Returning down the years to indicate,
    More by our presence, than by what we say,
    The atmosphere and tempo of this play.
MARTHA: My friend has explained it most concisely,
    She always was one to put things nicely!
SOPHIE: We represent the fine but faded flower
    Of that old "Demi Monde" that used to be
    At Vauxhall, and at Brighton by the sea
    Before the pure in heart came into power,
    Before a great but sanctimonious Queen
    Firmly rang down the curtain on our scene.
MARTHA: Please don't suppose *our* flowers were faded;
    Others were pushed, *we* were persuaded!

[289]

SOPHIE: The interruptions of my friend are meant
To clarify for you our "Status Quo,"
A social level neither high nor low,
With which we were entirely content,
And which provides the background, may I say,
Of this polite but faintly raffish play.
To music, and with great dignity, they part the curtains on the first scene.

SCENE II

The scene is part of the Parade at Brighton. There is a railing running the whole length of the stage and, behind it, a row of demure Georgian houses. There is room only for pedestrians to pass between the railing and the houses.

When the curtain rises it is about eleven o'clock on a sunny spring morning. There are two fishermen leaning against the railing with expressions of static resignation. Several people pass and repass along the Parade. Two soldiers in scarlet coats stop and talk to a neat little milliner's assistant with a hat box. A little boy runs across bowling a hoop, and two little girls walk along sedately with their nurse. The whole picture seems fresh and gay and alive, and the orchestra, which plays continually throughout the scene, celebrates the entrance of any particular character with a pleasant little burst of individual melody. Finally, SOPHIE OTFORD and MARTHA JAMES walk on from the left. They are both pretty and charmingly dressed, and a certain manner and quality about them suggest that they are of the superior courtesan class. They walk languidly and chatter with a vivacity that one cannot help feeling is just a trifle artificial. PAUL, the Duc de Chaucigny-Varennes, enters from the right. He is a superbly dressed, neat little man of about forty-five. He appears to exude an aroma of perfection. His gestures possess an authentic grace, and although they are precise they are not in the least overdone. He turns to the front door of

CONVERSATION PIECE

MELANIE's *house and rat-tat-tats briskly on the knocker as the
lights fade.*

SCENE III

The scene is the interior of MELANIE's *house; to be exact, the
living room. It is charmingly furnished, and the windows at the
back open onto a small balcony which looks out over the
Parade and the sea. There are two doors. The one up stage right
leads into a little hall and to the rest of the house. The one
opposite to it up stage left leads to* MELANIE's *bedroom.*

*As the lights rise on the scene the rat-tat-tat of the knocker
can be heard, this rat-tat-tat theme being a motif in the music
which recurs throughout the play. The music continues, and*
ROSE *enters. She is* MELANIE's *English maid, a pretty girl in the
twenties. She casts a careful glance over the room to see that
everything is tidy, and then runs downstairs to open the front
door. After a moment she follows* PAUL *into the room. He walks
in with an air of complete authority and hands her his hat,
gloves, and cane.*

PAUL: Chocolate?
ROSE: All ready, sir.
PAUL: No lumps in it?
ROSE: Not one, sir.
PAUL: Good.
*He goes over to the desk and, placing some glasses upon
his nose, seats himself at it. In a methodical, businesslike man-
ner he looks through a pile of bills and papers.* ROSE *goes out to
fetch the chocolate. She returns in a moment with a neatly
arranged tray which she places on the desk.*
ROSE: You're sure you wouldn't like an egg, sir?
PAUL: Quite sure, thank you.
ROSE: Nor a nice crisp bit of bacon?
PAUL: It would kill me.

[*291*]

ROSE: I see, sir.

PAUL [*pouring himself some chocolate*]: How is Mademoiselle?

ROSE: Gay as a lark, sir.

PAUL: Good. How is her English this morning?

ROSE: I don't know, sir, but my French is improving by leaps and bounds.

PAUL: Then consider yourself dismissed.

ROSE: You don't really mean that, do you, sir?

PAUL: No.

ROSE: I didn't think you did really, sir.

PAUL: But I am very displeased with you. The rule of the house is that no one must speak French to Mademoiselle under any circumstances.

ROSE: I only said "Mon Dieu" when I dropped the nail file.

PAUL: Stick to "My God," it's more blasphemous and far more expressive.

ROSE: Very well, sir.

PAUL: This butcher's bill seems very high.

ROSE: It's the veal, I expect. Mademoiselle dearly loves a bit of veal, and I keep telling her it's unreliable.

PAUL: It isn't its integrity I question, but its cost.

ROSE: Yes, sir.

PAUL: In future no more veal except on special occasions. [*He holds out a bill.*] What does this mean?

ROSE: Humbugs, sir.

PAUL: What are they?

ROSE: Sort of big bull's-eyes.

PAUL [*horrified*]: Bull's-eyes?

ROSE [*laughing*]: Oh, not real ones, sir, they're sweets. You tuck one in your cheek and it keeps you going for hours.

PAUL: Disgusting.

ROSE: Mademoiselle's very partial to them, sir. She saw some in a shop a long time ago, and since then we've 'ad 'em regular.

PAUL: That will be all for the moment, Rose.

[*292*]

ROSE [*curtseying*]: Thank you, sir.

She goes out right. PAUL *continues to check the accounts. After a moment* MELANIE *comes out of her bedroom. She is wearing a négligé and looks radiant, but her face is slightly distorted by an obvious bulge in the left cheek.* PAUL *springs to his feet and bows.*

PAUL: Good-morning, Melanie.

MELANIE [*indistinctly*]: My God!

PAUL: What's the matter?

MELANIE [*gracefully disposing of the humbug in a small handkerchief*]: Mon cher, personne ne m'a dit que——

PAUL [*sternly*]: Anglais.

MELANIE [*demurely*]: I did not know you were here.

PAUL: What were you eating?

MELANIE: A 'oomboog. Tu veux le voir?

PAUL: Non. No, certainly not.

MELANIE: They are delicious. Good-morning.

PAUL: You slept well?

MELANIE: Oui.

PAUL: Yes.

MELANIE: Yes, Paul.

PAUL: You have been speaking French to Rose.

MELANIE: Only a little.

PAUL: You have also been eating too much veal. I am very angry with you.

MELANIE: Please, I am sorry.

PAUL: Veal is unreliable and expensive. Those dreadful sweets are bad for your skin, and unless you learn English quickly we shall have to go away, just as we came, without money, without position, without anything.

MELANIE: Ah, ne sois pas fâché, mon cher, it is so difficult, when I awake the morning comes in at the window and makes me gay and I wish to talk very quick to Rose and say how the waves of the sea are pretty and how the sun shines and I learn better every day, I promise I do, but at the very beginning my

[*293*]

brain does not wake itself enough and I cannot wait to find the stupid English words.

PAUL: It is so important. So very, very important.

MELANIE: Oui, je sais bien c'est important, mais——

PAUL: Anglais.

MELANIE: Zut! Je ne peux pas.

PAUL: You must.

MELANIE: Please do not be angry with me this morning. It is my birthday.

PAUL: Again?

MELANIE: Well, it feels like my birthday.

PAUL: You mean that you feel particularly happy?

MELANIE: Oui—yes.

PAUL: Why?

MELANIE: Je ne sais pas.

PAUL: You feel happy today without reason, just as yesterday you felt miserable without reason. You are a creature entirely lacking in balance.

MELANIE: I was an acrobat once.

PAUL: Kindly remember that you are my ward, the daughter of my dear friend the Marquis de Tramont, and that you have never seen an acrobat, let alone been one.

MELANIE: Allez Oop! [*She performs an acrobat's pose.*]

PAUL: Melanie!

MELANIE: Oh, comme vous êtes fastueux ce matin. Je parie que c'est encore à cause de votre foie.

PAUL: Mon foie est en parfaite santé.

MELANIE: Alors! Pourquoi cet air de bravache? C'est affolant. Vous m'accusez d'être heureuse sans raison, mais vous, mon ami, vous êtes âpre et désagréable également sans raison.

PAUL: Vous me désespérez.

MELANIE: Pourquoi?

PAUL: J'insiste que vous parliez en anglais.

MELANIE: Je ne peux pas et je ne veux pas quand j'ai quelque chose d'important à dire vite, et à ce moment j'ai beaucoup

[*294*]

à dire vite. Je travaillerai très fort. Je ferai tout ce que vous dites, mais pas quand vous êtes sévère, pas quand vous refusez de rigoler avec moi. Je vous défie!

PAUL: Soyez raisonnable, ma chère. [*He goes to her, pleading.*]

MELANIE: Riez! Allez riez!

PAUL: Non.

MELANIE: Allons, un tout petit peu. Allez-y pour me faire plaisir.

PAUL: J'ai dis non.

MELANIE: Bon. Je ne parlerai pas un mot d'anglais jusqu'à ce que vous souriez. [*She sits with decision.*]

PAUL [*without mirth*]: Ha, ha, ha!

MELANIE: That is better.

PAUL: How can I make you realize that life is serious?

MELANIE: Because it is not serious.

PAUL: Look at these bills.

MELANIE: I see them.

PAUL: We have been here a month.

MELANIE: Yes, Paul.

PAUL: Nothing has happened at all.

MELANIE [*she rises and walks away*]: We have enough money for three months.

PAUL: Not at this rate.

MELANIE [*turning on him*]: What would you have me do? Have no food, have no clothes? Go out into the street in rags and say, "Marry me. Marry me," to every man I see?

PAUL: Don't be ridiculous.

MELANIE: Listen. I will be sensible, even in English I will try to be sensible, but you must not ask me to be serious. This adventure must be gay and funny. We will cheat and lie and pretend to everyone because that is agreed, but there must be truth between us, ourselves.

PAUL [*smiling*]: Entendu!

She indicates the sofa. He sits at the end.

MELANIE: Have you ever had a dear friend called the Marquis de Tramont?

[295]

PAUL: No.

MELANIE: Did he ever have a daughter?

PAUL: No.

MELANIE: Did you ever by chance visit a café called Le Petit Girondin?

PAUL: Oui.

MELANIE: Anglais!

PAUL: Yes.

MELANIE: It was very dirty, and there was sand on the floor, and men got drunk and spat onto the sand; sometimes they were sick——

PAUL [*sharply*]: That is enough.

MELANIE: And there was a girl who sang and danced and made acrobatics like this—— [*She does a trick.*] Do you remember?

PAUL [*admonishing*]: Melanie! I remember an old grey château with a walled garden, and a sweet fair-haired little girl feeding the swans——

MELANIE: Liar!

PAUL: And there was peace inside the garden, and memories of much happiness, but outside the walls there were horror and bloodshed and revolution, and presently the walls crumbled, and the father and mother of the little girl were led away to die——

MELANIE: Stop, please. That is too near your own truth. It has nothing to do with mine.

PAUL: If you insist on truth you shall have it. [*He firmly places her on the sofa.*] You are uneducated, illiterate, a child of the gutter, aren't you?

MELANIE: Yes.

PAUL: Penniless?

MELANIE: Yes.

PAUL: I am a ci-devant aristocrat, and old.

MELANIE [*quickly*]: No.

PAUL: Middle-aged, then.

MELANIE: Yes.

PAUL: Educated, cultured, and useless.

[296]

MELANIE: Yes.

PAUL: And equally penniless.

MELANIE: Yes.

PAUL: But fortunately possessed of an inherent talent for obtaining credit.

MELANIE: Fortunately.

PAUL: You are my only possible business asset.

MELANIE: Let us talk of something else.

PAUL [*continuing*]: Attractive, young, and, surprisingly enough, a virgin.

MELANIE: Please stop now. I will be good, really I will.

PAUL: You are my ward, are you not? The forsaken daughter of my dear old friend the Marquis de Tramont?

MELANIE: Yes, Paul.

PAUL: You spent your lisping, carefree childhood in an old grey château, didn't you?

MELANIE: What's "lisping"?

PAUL: Never mind. [*He stalks round the room, engrossed in the story.*] You have never been to Paris in your life, have you?

MELANIE: No, Paul.

PAUL: What is Le Petit Girondin?

MELANIE: I suppose it must be a very little man from Bordeaux.

PAUL: Correct. [*He goes to the table, places a chair for her to sit.*] Come! Business! Now then, what did Lord Sheere say to you last night?

MELANIE [*seated*]: Not very much, but he was very ardent.

PAUL: Good. He is coming here this morning.

MELANIE: This morning?

PAUL: Yes. I wrote him a little note from you. I will receive him, and when I have talked to him for a little he will propose marriage.

MELANIE: He seemed last night to wish for something a little less binding.

PAUL: Never mind. When he proposes, you will accept him.

MELANIE: When may I love somebody, please?

PAUL: Not until you are safely married, and then only with the greatest discretion.

MELANIE [*quietly*]: I see.

PAUL [*after a slight pause*]: What's the matter?

MELANIE: It doesn't feel like my birthday any more. [*Singing*]

> A cloud has passed across the sun,
> The morning seems no longer gay.

PAUL [*speaking*]: I want to get on with these bills. You had better go and dress.

MELANIE [*listlessly*]: Very well—— [*Singing*]

> With so much business to be done,
> Even the sea looks grey.

PAUL [*speaking*]: Don't be silly.

MELANIE [*singing*]:

> C'est vrai. C'est vrai.
> It seems that all the joy has faded from the day
> As though the foolish world no longer wants to play.

PAUL [*speaking*]: Go and dress.

MELANIE [*speaking*]: What shall I wear? A black crêpe with a little bonnet?

PAUL: What on earth is the matter with you this morning?

MELANIE: White, white for a bride. But the sun ought to shine on a bride.

PAUL: You're not a bride yet.

MELANIE: But I shall be soon, shall I not? A very quiet aristocratic bride with a discreet heart! [*Singing*]

> You ask me to have a discreet heart
> Until marriage is out of the way,
> But what if I meet
> With a sweetheart so sweet
> That my wayward heart cannot obey
> A single word that you may say?

CONVERSATION PIECE

PAUL [*speaking*]: Then we shall have to go away.
MELANIE [*singing*]:

> No.
> For there is nowhere we could go
> Where we could hide from what we know
> Is true.

PAUL [*speaking*]: Do stop talking nonsense.
MELANIE [*speaking*]: It is not sense. You are so sure that everything in life can be arranged just so, like arithmetic.
PAUL: Why not? Emotion is so very untidy.
MELANIE: The sun has come out again. I feel a little better.
PAUL [*writing something on one of the bills*]: Good.
MELANIE [*goes to the window humming, then returns to the desk and, leaning across it, pats PAUL's hand*]: I'm sorry.[*Singing*]

> Don't be afraid I'll betray you
> And destroy all the plans you have made,
> But even your schemes
> Must leave room for my dreams
> So when all I owe to you is paid
> I'll still have something of my own,
> A little prize that's mine alone.
> I'll follow my secret heart
> My whole life through.
> I'll keep all my dreams apart
> Till one comes true.
> No matter what price is paid,
> What stars may fade
> Above,
> I'll follow my secret heart
> Till I find love.

When she has sung this waltz refrain she goes into her room.
PAUL *rings a little bell on the desk.* ROSE *enters.*

[299]

PAUL: Rose, prenez le plateau——

ROSE *takes up the tray.*

PAUL: I am expecting the Marquis of Sheere. He should be here at any moment.

ROSE [*raising her eyebrows*]: Oh!

PAUL: Why do you say "Oh" like that?

ROSE: It seems funny a gentleman of his position calling in the morning.

PAUL: Why funny?

ROSE: In my last place the gentlemen always called in the evening.

PAUL: I think the sooner you wipe your last place from your mind the better.

ROSE: Yes, sir.

There is a rat-tat-tat on the door downstairs, and ROSE, *with a knowing look in her eye, goes out.* PAUL *rises as* ROSE *reënters.*

ROSE [*announcing*]: The Marquis of Sheere.

The MARQUIS OF SHEERE [EDWARD] *comes in quickly, wearing an air of expectancy, which changes to slight confusion when he sees* PAUL. *He is a good-looking, romantic young man in the twenties.*

PAUL [*going to him*]: Lord Sheere?

EDWARD: Yes.

ROSE *goes out.*

PAUL: Allow me to introduce myself. I am the Duc de Chaucigny-Varennes.

EDWARD: Oh, how do you do?

They shake hands.

PAUL: Melanie, my ward, will be here in a moment.

EDWARD [*relieved but puzzled*]: Oh, I'm so glad.

PAUL: In the meantime, can I offer you a little wine?

EDWARD: No, thank you.

PAUL: At least I beg you will be seated. [*He indicates the sofa and draws up a chair for himself.*]

EDWARD [*sitting down*]: Thank you.

[300]

PAUL: Tell me, do you speak French?

EDWARD: Oui, un peu.

PAUL: I never think that's enough, do you?

EDWARD [*slightly crestfallen*]: I suppose not.

PAUL [*charmingly*]: Never mind, we will talk English. In the old days before the Revolution my mother engaged an English governess for all of us. I remember she had a very pink nose, but her syntax was above reproach.

EDWARD: I'm so glad.

PAUL: It is not a matter for unrestrained jubilation, but we will leave it for the moment, as we have things of more importance to discuss.

EDWARD: Have we?

PAUL: I understand that you wish to marry my ward?

EDWARD [*rising, extremely startled*]: What! I beg your pardon?

PAUL: You seem embarrassed?

EDWARD [*floundering*]: Well—I—er—I——

PAUL [*sententiously*]: Ah, Love, Love, that fond foolish ecstasy! It ties the tongue in knots as well as the heart, does it not?

EDWARD: Yes, but you see—I really feel——

PAUL: Come, now, there is no need to look so confused. I am a man of the world, old enough to be your father—you can be perfectly frank with me. Please sit down again.

EDWARD *sits*.

EDWARD: I had no idea that Melanie, Mademoiselle de Tramont, had a—a——

PAUL: Guardian.

EDWARD [*gulping*]: Guardian.

PAUL: She is the daughter of my dear old friend the Marquis de Tramont. The whole family was wiped out, father, mother, five sons, and four daughters.

EDWARD: A large family.

PAUL: Very large. Melanie alone escaped. She was smuggled out of the château by one of the serving maids, a rude homely

[*301*]

girl, who, after many vicissitudes, managed to convey her to me in Amiens, where I was in hiding.

EDWARD: How old was she?

PAUL: A mere child.

EDWARD: I see.

PAUL [*leaning forward*]: I have watched over her and cared for her all these years. I have seen her grow from childhood to girlhood, from girlhood to womanhood. We have wandered together lonely exiles, through strange countries. Her youth and sweetness have kept my heart alive when everything I loved was dead, and now you come, a stranger, and wish to take her from me——

EDWARD: You misunderstand, sir, I assure you——

PAUL [*holding up his hand*]: No, no, do not protest. I understand only too well. I have known that this would happen. It is the penalty of age to be lonely, and I am quite prepared.

EDWARD [*firmly*]: I have not proposed marriage to Melanie.

PAUL: That does credit both to your upbringing and your personal integrity. I unfortunately am not in a position to put your fears entirely at rest. I cannot tell for certain whether or not she really loves you, but, if you will take the advice of an old man, don't give up hope, don't despair too soon. [*He rings the bell on the desk.*]

ROSE *enters very quickly, having obviously been listening at the door.*

ROSE: You rang, sir?

PAUL: Ask Mademoiselle if she would be kind enough to come here.

ROSE: Yes, sir.

She goes into the bedroom.

PAUL: You understand, her happiness is all that matters to me. I have naturally taken care to make discreet inquiries as to your character and way of life. Forgive my being frank, but, as a foreigner, such precautions I think may be excused. You may rest assured that at the earliest possible moment I shall give myself the honour of calling upon your parents.

EDWARD [*terrified*]: For God's sake, don't do that!

PAUL [*smiling fondly*]: Foolish boy!

MELANIE *comes in from the bedroom, very beautifully dressed and rather pale. She curtseys to* PAUL.

MELANIE: Bonjour, mon oncle.

PAUL [*sweetly*]: Fie donc, Melanie. Anglais, je t'en prie. N'oublie pas ta promesse.

MELANIE: Non. I am sorry. [*She curtseys to* EDWARD.] Good-morning, Monsieur le Marquis.

EDWARD: Good-morning, Mademoiselle!

PAUL: There is no need to be so formal, my dear. We all understand one another. Lord Sheere and I have had a little talk.

MELANIE [*slightly apprehensive*]: Oh—vraiment?

PAUL [*taking both her hands*]: My little Melanie.

MELANIE [*drawing back—suspiciously*]: Qu'est-ce qu'il y a?

PAUL: Qu'est-ce qu'il y a? [*In a very beautiful voice*] Be gentle with him, my Melanie, gentle and kind. True love is oversensitive. I will leave you for a while.

MELANIE: No, Paul—please stay——

PAUL: It is better that I should go. [*He places his hand upon* EDWARD's *shoulder and gazes searchingly into his eyes for a moment.*] My boy!

PAUL *bows gracefully and goes out, leaving behind him an atmosphere of considerable embarrassment.* MELANIE *and* EDWARD *stand staring at each other until she can bear it no longer and breaks the strain by going to the window.*

MELANIE [*at window*]: It is a very nice day, is it not?

EDWARD: Very nice.

MELANIE: So pretty—everything here in England looks so fresh and clean—regardez ce petit bateau à voiles—sailboat?

EDWARD [*coming also to the window*]: Yes—that's a sailing boat.

MELANIE: Léger sous le soleil, comme un papillon blanc——

EDWARD: Yes. Oh, yes, indeed——

A hand organ begins to play softly in the street below.

MELANIE: Music too.

EDWARD [*staring at her*]: Yes—music too——

MELANIE: Why do you look like that?

EDWARD: It's true.

MELANIE: What is true? Je ne comprends pas——

EDWARD: What he said—your guardian—about love.

MELANIE [*turning away*]: Oh.

EDWARD: I didn't understand.

MELANIE: The music is too loud.

EDWARD: Why not? Why shouldn't it be loud? It plays every-where, doesn't it—that sort of music—all over the world?

MELANIE: You speak so quickly—please do not speak so quickly.

EDWARD: Who are you, really?

MELANIE [*she sits on the sofa, closing her eyes as though re-peating a lesson*]: I am Melanie de Tramont, the daughter of the Marquis de Tramont, he—my father—was killed in the Revolution—my mother also, and my little brother Armand——

EDWARD: And your other brothers and sisters?

MELANIE: All dead.

EDWARD: What were their names?

MELANIE: Je ne comprends pas.

EDWARD: How many were there?

MELANIE: Many—a great many.

EDWARD: You loved them?

MELANIE: Yes, they were very nice.

EDWARD: And your mother and father?

MELANIE: Very nice indeed.

EDWARD: Guillotined?

MELANIE: Please—I cannot bear to speak of it.

EDWARD: I'm sorry.

MELANIE: It is long ago now, but I can never quite forget.

EDWARD: And your guardian—you love him?

[*304*]

MELANIE: Yes.

EDWARD: I see.

MELANIE: As a father.

EDWARD: Who are you—really?

MELANIE: Oh—go away—please go away.

EDWARD: Who are you—really?

MELANIE: I do not know.

EDWARD [*suddenly he sits next to her*]: I love you.

MELANIE [*painfully*]: No.

EDWARD: Before, when I have seen you in the distance, and last night when I talked to you, I wanted you—but now—now I love you——

MELANIE: No, no——

EDWARD: It's true, I know it—it happened suddenly a moment ago—it feels strange, as though I were not quite awake, and yet at the same time more awake than I have ever been before. You see I am not very old, not very experienced yet, and it's—it's the first time.

MELANIE [*she rises, walks away, clasping and unclasping her hands*]: Oh—this is very uneasy.

EDWARD: Why? Didn't you expect it?

MELANIE: No—not like this.

EDWARD: You know—you wanted me to love you, didn't you? Both you and your—your guardian—wanted me to love you——

MELANIE [*retreating from him*]: No, no——

EDWARD: You see I am not quite so young as all that, not quite a fool—my eyes are wide open—there is a lot that I don't understand, a trick, some sort of trick, I feel it with all my instincts, but I don't care—I feel more than that—I feel that you are very lovely, and very sweet too, and that is enough—will you, please—please, be my wife?

MELANIE [*sinking into a chair and covering her face with her hands*]: Laissez-moi, je vous en supplie, laissez-moi——

EDWARD: Look at me.

MELANIE: Non, non——

[*305*]

EDWARD [*gently taking her hands away from her face*]: Melanie.

MELANIE [*whispering*]: Go away—please, please, go away.

EDWARD: Very well. [*He smiles rather tremulously.*] But I shall come back.

MELANIE: Yes, come back—but think a little before you come back—see me once again from the distance——

EDWARD: I am afraid it is too late for that.

MELANIE [*curtseying, with her eyes averted from him*]: Thank you, Monsieur le Marquis.

EDWARD [*bowing*]: Mademoiselle!

He looks at her for a moment and then goes out swiftly. When he has gone she goes to the window and sings very softly, "I'll follow my secret heart" as the lights fade on the scene.

SCENE IV

QUARTETTE:

"Regency Rakes."

Verse

You may think,
Looking at the four of us,
Food and drink
Constitute the core of us.
That may be,
But still you'll see
Our names on posterity's page.
You will read
Histories galore of us,
Strutting England's stage.
We represent,
To a certain extent,
The ineffable scent
Of our Age.

[306]

CONVERSATION PIECE

Refrain

We're Regency Rakes,
And each of us takes
A personal pride
In the thickness of hide
Which prevents us from seeing
How vulgar we're being
Without making us wince.
We're ruthless and rude
And boast of a crude
And lordly disdain
Both for mind and for brain.
Tho' obtuse and slow-witted,
We're not to be pitied,
For we follow the Prince.
Every orgy
With our Georgie
Lasts till dawn without a lull.
We can venture
Without censure
To be noisy, drunk, and dull!
We revel in Sport,
Madeira, and Port,
And when we pass out
With Sclerosis and Gout,
All our children will rue our mistakes,
Roistering Regency Rakes.

2nd Refrain

We're Regency Rakes,
And each of us makes
A personal issue
Of adipose tissue;
But still, notwithstanding,
Our stomachs' expanding,

[*307*]

CONVERSATION PIECE

We all yearn for romance.
We frequently start
Affairs of the heart,
Sublimely unheeding
That long overfeeding
Has made so disgusting
Our loving or lusting
That girls eye us askance,
Tho' we wonder,
As we blunder
Into this or that bordel,
Whom we know there,
Why we go there,
But we're far too drunk to tell,
Tho' overjocose,
Unfunny and gross,
We don't lose a fraction
Of self-satisfaction.
Complacency never forsakes
Roistering Regency Rakes!

SCENE V

The scene is MELANIE's *room again. It is about three o'clock in the afternoon.*

When the curtain rises, the room is empty. Presently ROSE *ushers in* SOPHIE OTFORD, MARTHA JAMES, *and* MRS. DRAGON. MRS. DRAGON *is an ample lady attired austerely in black, enlivened here and there by an occasional glitter of jet.*

ROSE: Mademoiselle will be with you in a moment.
SOPHIE: Thank you.
ROSE: I will inform Mademoiselle that you are here.
MARTHA: Thank you.

[*308*]

CONVERSATION PIECE

SOPHIE [*conversationally*]: Such a nice little house. Which is the Duc de Varennes' room?

ROSE: Monsieur le Dook don't live here.

MARTHA [*triumphantly*]: There you are.

She goes up to examine the quality of the wineglasses on the sideboard.

SOPHIE: He just visits Mademoiselle, I suppose?

ROSE: Yes, every morning.

MARTHA: Only in the morning?

She tests one of the glasses with a snap of her finger—it rings clearly.

SOPHIE: Don't be crude, Martha.

ROSE: Monsieur le Dook is Mademoiselle's guardian.

SOPHIE: That's right, my dear. You're a very good girl.

MARTHA: Have you been with Mademoiselle long?

ROSE: Ever since she arrived in England, madame.

MARTHA: I seem to know your face. Have I ever seen you before?

ROSE: I don't think you could have, madame.

SOPHIE: Where do you come from?

ROSE: I was brought up in Wales, madame. In a little village by the sea.

MARTHA: You haven't got a Welsh accent.

ROSE: I know. That's what's so funny. My mother and father never 'ave been able to understand it.

SOPHIE: Well, if they can't, nobody can.

MARTHA: Were you engaged by Monsieur le Duc or by Mademoiselle herself?

SOPHIE: Martha!

MARTHA: Well, I want to know.

ROSE: I was engaged through a friend.

SOPHIE: Who?

ROSE [*exasperated*]: Mrs. Edwards, the one who arranged your little affair with Lord Meadowfield.

SOPHIE: Don't be impudent.

ROSE: Well, mind your own business, then.

She goes out.

MARTHA: I thought as much. Do sit down, Dragon.

MRS. DRAGON *sits down.*

SOPHIE: Guardian, indeed!

MARTHA: None of my gentlemen have ever spoken to her alone yet.

SOPHIE: Not even his Grace?

MARTHA: Not even his Grace.

ROSE *returns from the bedroom, and the visitors invent charming conversation until* ROSE *goes out the other door.*

SOPHIE: There's something fishy about it.

MARTHA: There's always something fishy about the French!

MELANIE *enters. Everyone curtseys with great enthusiasm.*

MELANIE: Ah, chères mesdames, mes chères mesdames, comme je suis enchantée de vous voir——

SOPHIE: This is Mrs. Dragon.

MELANIE: 'Ow do you do!

MRS. DRAGON *curtseys but doesn't say anything.*

MARTHA: We've been admiring your charming house.

MELANIE: I am so glad. Please sit you down, and the tea will be here soon.

The guests sit on the sofa.

SOPHIE [*with an effort*]: Est-ce que vous trouvez que Brighton est joli?

MELANIE [*smiling gaily*]: Ah, ça, c'est défendu. Monsieur le Duc ne me permet pas de parler un mot de français, parce que, enfin, c'est absolument nécessaire que je fasse des progrès en anglais.

SOPHIE: Oh—er—oui—je vois, je vois.

They all laugh.

MELANIE: Mais je souffre, ah, mon Dieu, comme je souffre! Quand je tâche de chercher les phrases, je me sens perdu. C'est idiot!

SOPHIE [*giving up*]: There now.

CONVERSATION PIECE

MELANIE: Mais vous savez je fais des progrès, mais quand
même je continue à dire des bêtises affreuses, surtout lorsque
je me trouve dans une situation délicate. C'est vraiment inouï.
Ma langue fourche, et je dis des choses que je ne devrais pas,
et Paul, Monsieur le Duc, me regarde d'un petit air narquois,
et je veux cacher ma tête comme une autruche.

SOPHIE: I always love the Austrians.

MARTHA: Such charming manners.

ROSE *enters with the tea things, which she sets up on a little
table.*

MELANIE: Please take the tea?

SOPHIE: Thank you.

They all sit round the table.

MELANIE [*dispensing tea*]: It was so kind of you to arrive.

SOPHIE: Martha and I are giving a little party this evening,
just cards and conversation and a few friends. His Grace the
Duke of Twickenham has promised to honour us, we would be
so pleased if you would come too.

MELANIE: It would delight me, but I fear I cannot.

MARTHA: What a shame! You have another engagement?

MELANIE: No, I have to work in the evening with Monsieur
le Duc.

SOPHIE: As well as the morning? How tiring!

MELANIE: Another time I should be so glad if you will invite
me.

MARTHA: But, of course, we would like to know you better.
When we spoke to you the other day on the Steyne we thought
you looked so nice and so lonely, with only your maid for
company.

SOPHIE: That was a delightful bonnet you were wearing.

MELANIE: The green plush?

SOPHIE: Yes.

MELANIE: I have two new ones, more pretty, and a cramoisie
dress, velvet, for walking—you would like to see?

MARTHA: Oh, yes.

MELANIE: They all came from the little shop of Mrs. Baxter
—Rose, please bring the boxes from my room.

ROSE: Yes, mademoiselle.

She curtseys and goes out.

SOPHIE: Mrs. Baxter is very expensive.

MELANIE: Alas, yes, but the line she makes is good.

MARTHA: Are you staying here long?

MELANIE: I do not really know. My guardian has the business
to make. When that is done, we will return.

SOPHIE: What is his business?

MARTHA *and* DRAGON *are "all ears."*

MELANIE: It is financial—I do not know words to explain
correctly, but there must be a—a—transaction. That I know
very well.

SOPHIE: I see.

MARTHA: Were you born in Paris?

MELANIE: Oh, no, I lived as a child on the Loire—an old grey
château, with a small water where there were swans——

SOPHIE: Very pretty.

MELANIE: Yes, it was pretty; I spent all my early days lisping
there.

MARTHA: You haven't got a lisp now.

MELANIE: No, I lost it in the Revolution.

ROSE *enters from bedroom carrying several dress and hat boxes.*

ROSE [*putting them down*]: There, mademoiselle.

MELANIE: Merci, Rose. [*To* SOPHIE] You wish to see? [*To*
ROSE] The mull dress with marabout and the turban——

ROSE *opens one of the boxes and takes out a turban.* SOPHIE
and MARTHA *give appropriate cries of appreciation.* ROSE *opens
another box and takes out a dress. The music, which has been
playing softly throughout the scene, falls into a more set rhythm,
and* ROSE, MARTHA, SOPHIE, *and* MELANIE *sing a quartette while
they all try on different garments and hats. In course of this, a
fife-and-drum band is heard outside on the Parade, and they all
run to the window to wave to the soldiers marching by. To-*

wards the end of the song, there is a rat-tat-tat at the front
door. None of them hears except ROSE, *who runs down to an-*
swer it.

QUARTETTE:

SOPHIE: Charming! Charming! Charming!

ROSE: This gown is for the morning,
When Mademoiselle goes out.
As Madame sees,
In the slightest breeze
The feathers float about.

SOPHIE: ⎫
MARTHA: ⎬ Charming! Charming! Charming!

ROSE: This jacket is for driving,
Or strolling beside the sea.

SOPHIE: Pretty as it seems to be,
It's a little too full in the sleeves for me.

ALL: Ah la la la—la la—la la.

SOPHIE: Pretty as it seems to be,
It's a trifle full in the sleeves for me.

MELANIE: This dress is for the evening,
To wear when I meet my dear,
Whenever that may chance to be.
In the moment that he looks at me
The skies will suddenly clear.
I'll know him then for my destiny,
And so, through each changing year,
I shall leave him never, forevermore.

ROSE: Don't you think these pinks and blues are sweet?
This stuff is sent specially from France.

MELANIE: Oh, please, please, say you think these satin shoes
are sweet—
They make me feel I want to dance.

Danser—Danser—La Vie est gaie,
Je me sens libre, abandonnée.

[*313*]

CONVERSATION PIECE

Le chant trouble mon cœur
Qui donc m'envoie ce doux bonheur,
Mon corps, mes pieds, ensorcelés
Légers, ailes, vont s'envoler.
Tra la la la la—la la la—la la la la la,
Tra la la la la la—la la la—lalalalala la—la—la

SOPHIE:
MARTHA: Look for a love that's gay and sweet.
ROSE: Music to guide your dancing feet.
MELANIE:

Follow your secret strain
And you won't be living in vain,
SOPHIE: Treat your desire by word and deed
MARTHA: Lightly—lightly—
ROSE: And if at first you don't succeed
Try and try again.

MELANIE: Mon corps, mes pieds, ensorcelés
Légers, ailes, vont s'envoler.
Tra la la la la—la la la—la la la—la—la
Tra la la la la la—la la la——

SOPHIE [*speaking*]: Soldiers!

MARTHA [*rushing to window*]: Quickly—let's see——

ROSE [*also rushing to window*]: I do love soldiers.

MELANIE [*joining them*]: Oh, they are so pretty, so pretty in their red coats.

SOPHIE: They're some of the guards from the Pavilion.

ROSE [*singing*]: When I see the soldiers marching by
With fife and drum
Beneath a summer sky,

SOPHIE:
MARTHA: Little dears who love to do and die,

ROSE: My spirit sings
And spreads its wings to fly.

SOPHIE [*spoken*]: Nicely put, my girl, but a trifle affected.

ROSE: Well, it's true.

[*314*]

CONVERSATION PIECE

MARTHA: Look at the officer leading them.

SOPHIE: I must admit he could leave his shoes under my bed any time he liked.

ROSE [*singing*]: Think of all the battles they have won,

MELANIE [*singing*]: So brave and strong,
                 They march along
                 Like little boys
                 Who play with toys
                 For fun.

SOPHIE: }
MARTHA: } Little boys who frolic in the sun.

ROSE: Right—right—right left right——

ALL: Right—right—right left right left——
         March, little soldiers, we all adore you,
         We'd swoon before you
         If we thought that you would care,
         Whate'er befalls you,
         Where duty calls you,
         We should love to be there,
         To share
         All your troubles, but we'd never dare,
         But we're quite prepared to cheer you to victory,
         To joy or despair,
         Joy or despair,
         That's only fair.
         Dear little soldiers,
         Should you admire us
         And feel desirous
         On returning from the fray,
         We'd soon surrender,
         You'd find us tender
         And sublimely unresisting
         In assisting
         You to spend
         Your soldiers' pay pay pay.

CONVERSATION PIECE

At the end of the song, when MELANIE, MARTHA, *and* SOPHIE *are twirling gaily about the room,* ROSE *reënters and announces in rather gloomy tones: The* DUKE *and* DUCHESS OF BENEDEN. *The music stops dead as they enter. They are elderly, haughty, and grim.*

DUCHESS [*stiffly*]: Mademoiselle de Tramont?

MELANIE [*curtseying*]: Oui!

DUCHESS: I am the Duchess of Beneden. Please forgive us for calling upon you so—so unexpectedly. I believe you are acquainted with my son, Lord Sheere?

DUKE: A moment, my love, just a moment, do not rush matters.

MELANIE: I think you do not know Mrs. James and Mrs. Otford.

DUCHESS [*icily*]: I do not.

MELANIE [*charmingly*]: Then it is easy that you should, because they are here.

She indicates them with a polite gesture; they both curtsey low. The DUCHESS *bows almost imperceptibly.*

SOPHIE: This is Mrs. Dragon.

MARTHA: Of Dorset.

DUCHESS [*without the faintest sign of recognition*]: Indeed?

SOPHIE [*after a slight pause*]: Nice weather, taken all in all?

MELANIE: Will you not sit yourselves down?

DUCHESS: No, thank you.

MELANIE: Perhaps you would like the tea.

DUCHESS [*with an atrocious accent*]: Non, merci. Je pense qu'il serait mieux si nous parlons en français.

MELANIE: Au contraire, madame, my friends do not understand French.

MARTHA [*with great refinement*]: Oh, please, don't bother about us, we shall have to go now, anyhow.

MELANIE: Oh, no, please stay a little longer.

SOPHIE: We really must go, we have an appointment with the

Duke of Twickenham. [*Pertly to the* DUCHESS] He is your cousin, I believe.

The DUCHESS *turns away without answering.*

MARTHA: Come on, Dragon. [*She goes to the door.*]

SOPHIE: Good-bye, my dear Duke—it's ages since we last met, isn't it? Do you remember? That New Year's party at Mrs. Johnstone's—a very gay evening, wasn't it? [*She turns to* MELANIE.] Au revoir, mademoiselle. [*She curtseys.*]

MARTHA [*also curtseying*]: We must meet again very soon.

SOPHIE: Et merci beaucoup!

MELANIE: Au revoir.

MRS. DRAGON *does a slightly abortive curtsey to everyone, and the three of them go out, followed reluctantly by* ROSE. *When the door has closed behind them the* DUCHESS *turns.*

DUCHESS: As I said before, I believe you are acquainted with my son.

MELANIE: Yes.

DUCHESS: You would be doing my husband and myself a great service if you discontinued that acquaintance.

MELANIE: You are come here to ask a service?

DUKE: Yes, mademoiselle, we have.

MELANIE [*to the* DUCHESS]: Then I do not understand how your manner is so unpolite.

DUKE: My wife is upset, naturally upset.

MELANIE: Pourquoi?

DUKE: Edward is our only son.

MELANIE: Is that not more your fault than mine?

DUCHESS: It is no use bandying words, Frederick, and wasting time. [*To* MELANIE] I am a woman of the world, mademoiselle, and I fully realize your position.

The DUKE *looks appraisingly at* MELANIE *through his quizzing glass.*

MELANIE: I fear I do not understand.

DUCHESS: Things may be different in France, I am sure I do not know about that since that dreadful Bonaparte has ruined the country, but here in England there are still two distinct worlds. You belong to one, and my son belongs to the other. Those two worlds do not mix.

MELANIE: I would prefer that you speak to my guardian of these things.

DUCHESS [*sniffing*]: Guardian.

MELANIE: Monsieur le Duc de Chaucigny-Varennes.

DUKE: Perhaps, my love, that, after all, would be a better plan.

DUCHESS: Please, Frederick, allow me to deal with this. [*To* MELANIE] My son is infatuated with you, but he is young, and that infatuation will not last. It must not last. I wish you to give me your word that you will never see him again. My husband and I are fully prepared to compensate you within reason.

MELANIE: Compensate? Que-ce que c'est ça—compensate?

DUCHESS [*laconically*]: Money.

MELANIE: Money! You will pay me money?

DUCHESS: Yes.

MELANIE: To see your son never again?

DUCHESS: Yes.

MELANIE: If I love him, what then?

DUCHESS: That is beside the point.

MELANIE: I think you will perhaps go away now.

DUCHESS: Five hundred pounds.

MELANIE: He is very charming, your son, and his eyes are very clear and true. I think he will be angry.

DUCHESS: A thousand pounds.

MELANIE [*ringing the bell on the desk*]: I am tired, madame. I cannot sit down until you go.

DUKE: Mademoiselle, I beg of you—my wife is distrait——

MELANIE: That is not of interest to me.

DUCHESS [*losing control slightly*]: I would like to make one thing clear to you. My son is not yet of age. If he marries without his parents' consent he will not have a penny. Not a penny! Do you understand that?

DUKE: Georgina, Georgina—please——

MELANIE: He would make a very sweet husband, your son, even without a penny, because he is kind.

ROSE *enters and stands by the door.*

DUKE: Come, Georgina.

The DUCHESS *looks at* MELANIE *furiously for a moment in silence, and then, without a word, turns her back on her and sweeps out of the room, followed by the* DUKE. *The* DUKE *turns at the door and bows with the suspicion of a smile.* ROSE *follows them out, and* MELANIE *runs to the window to peep through the curtains at them. In a moment or two* ROSE *returns.*

MELANIE: Ça y est!

ROSE: What's that?

MELANIE: Some Madeira, quickly, my legs will not stand. [*She sinks down on the sofa.*]

ROSE *runs to a little side table and pours her out a glass of Madeira.*

ROSE: My goodness! Her face when she went out!

MELANIE: Mon Dieu! Her face when she came in.

ROSE: That bonnet!

MELANIE [*starting to laugh*]: Like a pheasant.

ROSE: Feathers and all. [*She starts to laugh too.*]

MELANIE [*laughing more wildly*]: The Duke—the poor, poor man——

ROSE: Looked like a corpse, and no wonder——

They are both laughing weakly when PAUL *comes into the room.*

PAUL: Why was the front door open?

ROSE: Oh, dear!

PAUL: What is the matter?

MELANIE [*hysterically*]: Five hundred pounds—a thousand pounds—not enough—not quite enough—but better than nothing!

PAUL: That will do, Rose.

ROSE: Yes, sir.

She goes out, wiping her eyes.

[*319*]

PAUL: Now, what has happened?

MELANIE: Je vous raconterai ce qui vient de passer. On m'a insulté et si cela ne me faisait pas tant rire j'aurais envie de pleurer.

PAUL: Qui vous a insulté? Que voulez-vous dire?

MELANIE: La très charmante mère de Monsieur le Marquis, ils sortent d'ici, le Duc et la Duchesse, je ne suis pas encore assez bien élevée—j'avais envie de lui cracher à la figure—c'est un grossier vieux chameau—elle s'est conduite avec moi comme envers une grue!

PAUL: J'espère que vous ne lui avez pas donné de raison pour vous prendre comme telle.

MELANIE: Du reste tout ceci est de votre faute. Je n'avais aucune envie de connaître tous ces gens. J'étais bien plus heureuse là où j'étais.

PAUL: Ça c'est idiot!

MELANIE: Mais c'est vrai! Vous voulez que je l'épouse votre Marquis? Eh bien, soit: et puis après, vous verrez, il sera sans le sou, et moi, je serai forcée de retourner chanter dans un café —Madame la Marquise au café chantant! Ça sera du joli, et ça sera bien faire pour vous!

There is a rat-tat-tat at the door. MELANIE *runs to the window.* C'est lui, le Duc, et tout seul cette fois.

PAUL: I'll talk to him.

MELANIE: No.

PAUL: But, my dear Melanie——

MELANIE: Go into the bedroom.

PAUL: But I——

MELANIE: Go quickly—listen at the door—and do not come out until I say——

PAUL: You will call me?

MELANIE: I will say, "The sea is so pretty." Go on—quickly——

PAUL *goes into the bedroom.* MELANIE *pushes the boxes to the back of the room.* ROSE *enters.*

ROSE [*with a slight leer*]: The Duke of Beneden.

MELANIE *is now seated, posing for the interview. The* DUKE
enters. He bows with almost overdone politeness. ROSE *goes out.*

DUKE: Mademoiselle, I—I—have returned.

MELANIE: I see you have.

DUKE: I ask your forgiveness.

MELANIE: Thank you.

DUKE: My wife——

MELANIE: She is upset?

DUKE: Yes.

MELANIE: Distrait?

DUKE: Exactly.

MELANIE: Ill-mannered?

DUKE: Yes—er—I mean—well, you understand.

MELANIE: I do not understand.

DUKE [*with a charming smile*]: Please try.

MELANIE: That is better.

DUKE: You are very pretty, mademoiselle, and very charming.

MELANIE: Oh!

DUKE: I am sure that you cannot possibly be hard-hearted.

MELANIE: It is difficult to have the soft heart when one is
insulted.

DUKE: My wife does not understand as I understand.

MELANIE [*averting her eyes*]: Oh, Monsieur le Duc.

DUKE: Do you love my son?

MELANIE [*still looking down*]: I do not know.

DUKE: He loves you?

MELANIE: Yes.

DUKE: Do you wish to marry him?

MELANIE: Please—I do not know.

DUKE: All his money is controlled by his mother; if you did
become his wife, she would cut him off entirely.

MELANIE: I see.

DUKE: Whereas I——

MELANIE [*looking up sharply*]: You?

[321]

DUKE [*with slight embarrassment*]: I find myself in an extremely awkward position.

MELANIE: Why?

DUKE: I do not want to bore you with my troubles, but you are so sympathetic.

MELANIE [*going to him*]: What is it you would say?

DUKE: I have a little house in London, a dear little house, very nicely furnished, just near Berkeley Square, and it is unhappy because it is not lived in; the pretty furniture is covered up, and the blinds are drawn.

MELANIE: How sad!

DUKE: You see I am an old man now.

MELANIE: Non, monsieur.

DUKE: Well, elderly.

MELANIE: Perhaps.

DUKE: And my heart, like the house, is covered up, and the blinds are drawn.

MELANIE [*turning away*]: Your wife, does she know about the little house?

DUKE: No.

MELANIE: And your heart? Does she know about that?

DUKE: No.

MELANIE [*resting her hand lightly on his arm*]: Poor Monsieur le Duc, life is very difficult, is it not?

DUKE: I knew you would understand. [*He holds her hand, almost as though he didn't notice it.*]

MELANIE: What is the rent of the little house?

DUKE: That is all paid.

MELANIE: And is there a little carriage with white horses and a footman on the box?

DUKE: How did you guess?

MELANIE: And every month, the bills of the house? They will be much?

DUKE [*tentatively*]: Two hundred pounds?

MELANIE [*firmly*]: Three hundred pounds.

[*322*]

DUKE [*smiling*]: Three hundred pounds.

MELANIE: On the first day of every month?

DUKE [*pulling her a little towards him*]: On the first day of every month.

MELANIE [*surrendering*]: But I do not yet know about London.

DUKE: It is delightful! You would love it.

MELANIE: But I love it here in Brighton.

He takes her in his arms.

The sea is so pretty.

PAUL *enters from the bedroom. The* DUKE *starts back and hurriedly disentangles himself from* MELANIE.

PAUL [*sternly*]: Melanie!

MELANIE [*terrified*]: Ah, mon Dieu!

PAUL: Monsieur, I do not think I have the pleasure of your acquaintance.

DUKE: I am the Duke of Beneden.

PAUL: Melanie, go to your room.

MELANIE: Mais, mon oncle, je——

PAUL: Immediately. Do as I tell you.

MELANIE: Oui, mon oncle.

She drops a hurried little curtsey to the DUKE, *curtseys to* PAUL, *makes a wry face, and goes out.*

PAUL: Now then, monsieur!

DUKE: I see it all now.

PAUL: You are the father of the Marquis of Sheere?

DUKE: Yes.

PAUL: I see. Good-bye, monsieur.

DUKE: I would like to explain.

PAUL: There is nothing to explain. It is all depressingly clear. [*He rings the bell.*] I will call upon you and the Duchess later, when I have decided what course to take.

DUKE: Look here, sir, I——

PAUL: The Duc de Chaucigny-Varennes. At your service.

ROSE *enters.*

Rose, kindly conduct his Grace downstairs.

ROSE: Yes, sir.

DUKE: I fear you don't quite understand. There is some mistake——

PAUL: There is a very grave mistake, and I understand perfectly. Good-bye. [*He bows abruptly.*]

The DUKE *still hesitates for a moment, then bows stiffly and goes out, followed by* ROSE, *who has the impertinence to wink broadly at* PAUL *over her shoulder.*

The music swells, and MELANIE *puts her head round the bedroom door.* PAUL *beckons to her, and they both tiptoe in time to the music to the window, where, shaking with silent laughter, they peep through the curtains as the lights fade.*

SCENE VI

TRIO: MARTHA, SOPHIE, *and* DRAGON:

"*There's Always Something Fishy about the French.*"

Verse I

SOPHIE: A life of Love is curious
But not injurious
If you are wise,

MARTHA: For you get pleasure,
Leisure,
Knowledge to treasure
After the gay life dies;

SOPHIE: Tho' men we seldom bind to us
They're often kind to us,

MARTHA: And entre nous,

BOTH: English Gentlemen,
Spanish Noblemen,
Indian Merchantmen too,
Always play the game,
Never cause us shame.

[324]

CONVERSATION PIECE

Refrain 1

BOTH: But there's always something fishy about the French!
Whether Prince or Politician,
We've a sinister suspicion
That behind their "savoir faire"
They share
A common contempt
For every mother's son of us.
Tho' they smile and smirk,
We know they're out for dirty work,
So we're most polite
But don't put out the night-light!
Every wise and thoroughly worldly wench
Knows there's always something fishy about the
French!

Refrain 2

BOTH: Oh, there's always something fishy about the French!
As a Race, they're conscientious
But undoubtedly licentious,
Tho' the compliments they pay
Are gay
And ever so nice,
We don't believe a word of them.
They may kiss our hands
And talk to us of foreign lands,
We "Toi" and "Moi"
And watch for "Je ne sais quoi."
Every time their fingers begin to clench—
Well, we know there's something fishy about the
French!

After a short dance they go off left as the lights fade.

SCENE VII

This scene is the Public Gardens.
It is evening, and there are lights in the Pavilion windows.
Down stage on the left is a stone or wooden seat.
When the curtain rises there is a mixed collection of people
on the stage. Residents. Visitors. A few soldiers. A man with
a hurdy-gurdy. Several ladies of the town, some with escorts,
some without. Everyone has his back turned to the audience
and is obviously craning to see somebody pass by. MISS GOSLETT
and MISS MENTION, *two elderly maiden ladies, have actually*
stood upon the seat in order to see better. After a moment or
two, the tune that the band is playing comes to an end with a
little flourish of brass. Everyone relaxes and proceeds to stroll
about. MISS GOSLETT *and* MISS MENTION *climb down off the seat*
and sit on it.

MISS GOSLETT: He's certainly getting very fat.

MISS MENTION: Perhaps it's dropsy.

MISS GOSLETT: Surely not, at his age.

MISS MENTION: A friend of mine died of dropsy when she was only twenty-three. They kept on tapping her and tapping her, but it was no good.

MISS GOSLETT: That poor Princess Caroline, it does seem a shame.

MISS MENTION: Such a common face.

MISS GOSLETT: She can't help that, to be sure.

MISS MENTION: This place is certainly much more lively than Exeter, although I *do* miss the cathedral.

The man with the hurdy-gurdy approaches them, playing busily.

MISS GOSLETT [*fumbling in her reticule*]: I must give him some pence.

MISS MENTION: It will only encourage him.

MISS GOSLETT *hands the man a few pennies, and he goes off.*

[*326*]

The band starts again, this time playing a slightly more senti-
mental tune. The DUKE OF BENEDEN *strolls across accompanied*
by the MARQUIS OF SHEERE.

EDWARD: But, Papa, I assure you, she is different——

DUKE: My dear boy, that sort of woman is never so very
different.

EDWARD [*hotly*]: You cannot possibly tell what sort of woman
she is.

DUKE: I shall make it my business to find out.

They go off. SOPHIE *walks on, accompanied by* LORD KENYON,
an immaculately dressed dandy, who is obviously a little the
worse for drink.

SOPHIE: Not tonight. I have already told you, I have another
engagement.

LORD KENYON: Just a little drive.

SOPHIE: I do not trust your horses.

LORD KENYON: What is wrong with them?

SOPHIE: They make conversation impossible.

They meet MARTHA *with* LORD ST. MARYS.

MARTHA. My dear, I've been searching for you everywhere.

SOPHIE: I can't think why.

MARTHA: Lord St. Marys wants to be presented to Mademoiselle what's-her-name.

SOPHIE [*raising her eyebrows*]: Oh, does he? [*To* LORD ST.
MARYS] For your own benefit or somebody else's?

LORD ST. MARYS: I cannot give away state secrets.

SOPHIE: I thought as much.

MARTHA: I hope this—this commission of yours won't prevent
you from coming to the Assembly Rooms later on?

LORD ST. MARYS: That all depends—neither my heart nor my
soul is my own these days——

They pass out of sight, all four of them, as the DUKE OF BENE-
DEN *and* EDWARD *come on right, in time to meet* LADY JULIA
CHARTERIS, *who is strolling down from the back, accompanied*
only by her maid. She is a handsome, authoritative woman,

exquisitely gowned, middle-aged, and slightly over made up.

DUKE [*bowing*]: My dear Julia! I thought you were in Spain.

JULIA: I'm grateful even for the thought, Frederick. The last ten years have seemed singularly barren without your attentions.

DUKE [*hurriedly*]: This is my son, Julia.

JULIA [*smiling in response to* EDWARD'S *bow*]: We have met before.

EDWARD: Madame—I——

JULIA: Don't look confused. You couldn't possibly remember. It was years ago, in London. We stopped to converse for a moment, your nurse and I, and you were permitted to bite my glove.

EDWARD: I never tasted a more delicious glove.

JULIA: This has been a strange day, my first in England for a long while. A day of ghosts. Out of the past they come, one after the other, looking almost as real as when they were alive. You are the sixth, Frederick, there really should be seven. Seven is my lucky number.

DUKE: You still gamble as much as ever?

JULIA: Yes, with the difference that I know now that it is far too late to win.

They exchange bows. The DUKE *and* EDWARD *stroll off up stage.* JULIA *has just reached the seat on her way off, when* PAUL *hurries on. He is obviously searching for someone. He passes* JULIA *without looking at her.*

JULIA [*stopping dead*]: The seventh!

PAUL [*turning*]: I beg your pardon?

JULIA [*singing softly*]: Au clair de la lune, mon ami Pierrot——

PAUL [*staring at her*]: Julie!

JULIA: I thought you were dead.

PAUL [*warmly kissing her hands*]: Oh, how charming to see you again, how very, very charming.

JULIA: English, too! Almost without an accent.

PAUL: How long ago is it?

[328]

JULIA: Let us both try *not* to remember.

PAUL: It is so difficult—seeing you again so suddenly, so un-expectedly—conjures up so much of the past.

JULIA: The past is dead—perhaps happily.

They sit.

PAUL [*incredulously*]: It isn't true. Do you remember the salon of Madame de Plessier?

JULIA: And Father François, and the little pink cakes with seeds in them——?

PAUL: And the day you cried over the dead dog!

JULIA: I've cried over many dead dogs since then.

At this moment MELANIE *comes on. She goes swiftly up to* PAUL.

MELANIE: Ah, mon cher, enfin! J'ai pensé que vous étiez perdu.

PAUL: Julia, I want to present to you my ward, Melanie de Tramont.

MELANIE *and* JULIA *both curtsey.* JULIA *is palpably very puzzled.*

JULIA: De *Tramont?*

MELANIE: Oui, madame. I am the daughter of the dear old Marquis de Tramont.

JULIA: I shouldn't boast of it, my dear, as he was unmarried.

MELANIE [*to* PAUL]: Je ne comprends pas.

PAUL: I will explain later. Lady Julia Charteris and I are very old friends——

At this moment, MARTHA *appears with* LORD ST. MARYS.

MARTHA: Oh, mademoiselle, will you please allow me to in-troduce a friend of mine, Lord St. Marys.

MELANIE *curtseys,* LORD ST. MARYS *bows.*

MELANIE: Enchantée, monsieur.

LORD ST. MARYS: Please forgive me for imposing myself upon you, mademoiselle, but I have been commanded to approach you on behalf of His Royal Highness, the Prince Regent.

MELANIE: Ah, mon Dieu! Son Altesse?

LORD ST. MARYS: His Royal Highness wishes to know whether

you would do him the honour of taking supper with him this evening.

PAUL: Will you please tell His Royal Highness with our most deep thanks that this evening it would not be possible, as she is a little ill.

JULIA: This situation seems a trifle delicate. I hope to continue our reminiscences very soon, Paul. Au revoir, Mademoiselle de Tramont. Come, Hannah.

She goes off with her maid.

LORD ST. MARYS: I fear that Mademoiselle does not quite understand. My request, coming from such an exalted quarter, amounts practically to a command.

PAUL: Mademoiselle de Tramont, my ward, has not yet had the honour of being presented to His Royal Highness.

LORD ST. MARYS: The fact, His Royal Highness is the first to deplore——

PAUL: Surely, it is a matter soon remedied?

LORD ST. MARYS: If Mademoiselle will allow me to escort her now, I myself will take great pleasure in presenting her.

PAUL: I fear, monsieur, there is some mistake. Will you kindly bear my homage to His Royal Highness, and inform him, with all due respect, that I will be honoured to present my ward to him myself, on a more formal occasion.

LORD ST. MARYS [*stiffly*]: My regrets, monsieur.

PAUL [*amiably*]: And mine.

LORD ST. MARYS *bows abruptly and goes off with* MARTHA, *and* DRAGON *follows.*

MARTHA: Well, really!

PAUL: Come, Melanie.

He crooks his arm, and MELANIE, *after bowing politely to* MARTHA, *takes it. The band strikes up a particularly gay little tune. As they walk away,* MELANIE *turns her head towards* DRAGON, *who winks broadly at her, kicking up the back of her dress, as—*

THE CURTAIN FALLS

[*330*]

ACT II

SCENE I

The painted curtains again.
SOPHIE *and* MARTHA *appear before them as in the Prologue.*

SOPHIE: This play, or, let us say, this pantomime,
    Being too small in scope, too tenuous,
    Too personal to illustrate the strenuous
    And glittering excitements of the time,
    We feel it, in a sense, obligatory
    To hint at what goes on *behind* the story.

MARTHA: My friend, though a trifle too rhetorical,
    Means it should be more historical.

SOPHIE: We ask you to imagine, if you please,
    That just around the corner of the tale,
    Mrs. Fitzherbert and the Prince inhale
    The self-same air, the same urbane sea breeze.
    Imagine that this world is living still
    And passing just beneath the window sill.

MARTHA: You've left out Brummell, the pert impostor,
    And what about Pitt? And the Duke of Gloucester?

SOPHIE: Picture a little further if you will
    The neat Pavilion Gardens, and the Steyne.
    The little band that orchestrates the scene.
    The Fireworks, the Races, the Quadrille,
    And furthermore, the bawdy, merry Hell
    Created by our lordly clientele!

They curtsey and go off, left and right.

[*331*]

SCENE II

The scene is MELANIE'S *room again.*

When the curtain rises it is early afternoon. MELANIE *is seated at a table upon which is a pile of books. She is wearing large horn-rimmed glasses and an expression of rather depressed concentration. She is also sucking a pencil, and there is a paper bag of humbugs on the table by her side. She sings a song, half in French and half in English, dealing entirely with the intricacies of language.*

MELANIE:

"English Lesson"

Verse

The Tree is in the Garden,
The water is in the Pot;
The Little sheep
On the mountain sleep,
The fire is very hot.

Refrain

Oh, c'est dur,
Tous ces mots obscurs
Me rendent triste;
Rien n'existe
Que le malheur qui insiste;
Dieu, je tâche d'apprendre, mais voilà
Je ne peux pas.

Verse 2

The fire is *not* in the garden,
The tree is not in the pot,
The silly sheep

[332]

On the something sleep,
But whether they do or not,
I do not care a jot;
I don't care if they're cold
Or if they're hot.

CHILDREN *sing, "La—la—la," etc., outside the window. She shuts it, and the* CHILDREN *stop singing.*

Refrain 2

Oh! c'est dur,
Tous ces mots obscurs
Me rendent triste;
Rien n'existe
Que le malheur qui insiste
Dieu, je tâche d'apprendre, mais voilà
Je ne peux pas.

At the end of it, she rests her head wearily on her hands and is obviously on the verge of tears. ROSE *enters.*

ROSE: There is a lady downstairs to see you.

MELANIE [*perking up slightly*]: Is it Mrs. James or Mrs. Otford?

ROSE: No. She said the name was Lady Julia Charteris.

MELANIE: Tall, with a painted face?

ROSE: Yes, and very grandly dressed. She come in a curricle.

MELANIE: I do not wish to see her. I do not wish to see anyone.

ROSE: Shall I say you're out?

MELANIE: Yes, please—say I am a long way away.

At this moment LADY JULIA *comes into the room.* MELANIE *jumps to her feet.*

JULIA: Please forgive me, but it was so very draughty in the hall.

MELANIE: I am at my work, madame.

JULIA: So I see. How interesting!

[*333*]

MELANIE: I fear that Monsieur le Duc is not here.

JULIA: I know. It was you I wished to see.

MELANIE [*making the best of the situation*]: I am very happy, madame. Perhaps you will sit yourself?

JULIA [*looking round the room*]: Not just for a moment, thank you. I want to enjoy this charming room. What pretty curtains—and what a lovely view!

MELANIE: Yes, the view is pretty.

JULIA: I believe they are arranging for a new ship to travel between here and Dieppe. That will be so convenient, won't it?

MELANIE: I do not very much like ships.

JULIA: I have so much to talk to you about. Your guardian and I are old friends, you know. We spent a great deal of our childhood together in France.

MELANIE: That is very nice.

JULIA: Is it entirely necessary for your maid to chaperon us?

MELANIE: You will bring the tea please, Rose.

ROSE: Yes, mademoiselle.

She goes out reluctantly, taking the writing table.

JULIA: It was such a pleasant surprise to see Paul—your guardian—again. I had thought he was dead. [JULIA *sits on the sofa.*]

MELANIE: No, he is alive.

JULIA: I suppose you are too young to remember his wife, and his mother and father?

MELANIE: Yes, I was young.

JULIA: I understand that you, too, were bereaved of your parents during the Terror.

MELANIE: What, please, is "bereaved"?

JULIA: I mean that they died. That they were guillotined.

MELANIE: Please, I would rather not speak of it.

JULIA: I understand that perfectly. I knew your father many years ago.

MELANIE: Yes?

JULIA: A most witty and delightful man.

[*334*]

MELANIE: Yes, he was very nice.

JULIA: It was so strange of him to keep his marriage such a secret. Paul, apparently, was the only one who knew anything about it.

MELANIE *sits*.

MELANIE: It was a secret because of the Jesuits.

JULIA: The Jesuits?

MELANIE: Yes—my father made them a promise, when he was very little, that he never would take wife and make marriage with himself.

JULIA: I see.

MELANIE: The Jesuits are very powerful.

JULIA: They must be. Where did you live when you were a child?

MELANIE: A grey-walled château near Bordeaux. It is all very distant in my mind.

JULIA: The Château de Tramont, no doubt?

MELANIE: Yes. There were swans.

JULIA: Graceful creatures, but disagreeable.

MELANIE: Yes, they were very disagreeable.

JULIA: There was a moat, too, I expect, and tall trees, and I suppose you were brought to Paris by your faithful old nurse?

MELANIE: Yes.

JULIA: You were not dressed as a boy, by any chance, were you?

MELANIE: No, why should I be boy?

JULIA: Merely a matter of convention. Perhaps you're really a boy now. Perhaps you're the Dauphin. That's quite an interesting idea.

MELANIE: I think you are laughing.

JULIA: You remember very little about your early life?

MELANIE: It is so far away.

JULIA: So very far away from the truth!

MELANIE [*rising and drawing herself up with great dignity*]: Madame!

[*335*]

JULIA: My dear child, don't be absurd. The whole story is idiotic. You have been very badly rehearsed. Paul should be ashamed of himself.

MELANIE: I do not understand what you speak, madame.

JULIA: Nonsense. You understand perfectly well.

MELANIE: And I do not understand why you come here.

JULIA: I came to find out what you were like. To see what sort of mistress Paul had picked out for himself.

MELANIE: Mistress! I am no mistress.

JULIA: Oh, come, come, you can hardly expect me to believe that.

MELANIE [*furious*]: How dare you speak these words to me!

JULIA [*rising*]: There is no necessity for you to lose your temper, my dear.

MELANIE: Do not please call me "my dear"—do not please call me any name. Go away.

JULIA: Certainly. I have found out all that I wanted to know.

MELANIE: You have found nothing, because what you know is not true.

JULIA: You can hardly blame me for that, as you have been lying steadily to me for the last ten minutes.

MELANIE: You wish to find about me, do you? You wish to tell all your friends and make a joke. I will explain to you more, very much more. Listen—I am the daughter of a mandarin in China—he was my first father—my second father was a Russian Jew in Prague—he sold silks, and little jewelry, and furs for your neck—I lived in Spain—I lived in Italy—I was born in the far Indies—my mother was black, black, black! My brothers and sisters were slaves—no, they were little pigs—they ran about in the fields trying with their big noses to find out things—like you, madame—I am a cocotte from the streets—I am a singer of songs—I am the new wife of Napoleon Bonaparte—take these tales, madame—take them for your friends—but take them very quickly—now, at this moment—because if you do not go away

[*336*]

and leave me alone I will smack your painted face and pull out your dead hair by the roots!

JULIA [*quietly*]: Obviously a guttersnipe.

At this moment PAUL *enters.* MELANIE *runs to him.* PAUL *and* MELANIE *speak to each other from now onwards in French, unless otherwise indicated.*

PAUL: My dear Julia, what a charming surprise——

MELANIE: Dites-lui de s'en aller—elle me rend folle.

PAUL: Melanie—je vous prie de vous surveiller.

MELANIE: Non, je ne me surveillerai pas. J'en ai assez de me surveiller. J'en ai assez de ces vieilles rosses anglaises. Si elles se regorgent tant, si elles relèvent si haut le nez, c'est sans doute pour ne pas sentir la puanteur de leur fausse moralité. . . .

JULIA: I congratulate you, Paul.

PAUL: My dear Julia——

MELANIE: Appelez-la: ma chère; appelez-la ma bien-aimée, si vous voulez, mais que je ne la voie plus.

PAUL: Lady Julia est une vieille amie, et je ne supporterai pas que vous lui parliez sur ce ton.

MELANIE: Je ne me soucie pas de savoir depuis quand elle est votre amie, mais je sais qu'elle n'a pas le droit de venir ici, chez moi, pour m'insulter.

PAUL: Alors chaque fois que je tourne le dos quelqu'un vous insulte—cela devient fatigant.

MELANIE: C'est pourtant vrai—on m'insulte. Cette vieille bête curieuse m'a jeté à la figure que j'étais votre maîtresse—Je ne le supporterai plus—Je ne resterai pas dans ce pays, pas même pour vous—pas même pour l'amour de Dieu. Je retourne chez les miens—chez les honnêtes et braves gens de la rue—Je n'ai pas besoin de leur mentir à eux—Je n'ai pas besoin d'être polie avec eux, ni de leur faire des sourires, quand j'ai envie de les étrangler—Je vous dis que je retourne en France—Je partirai demain, quand je devrais nager jusque là.

She whirls off into the bedroom and slams the door. PAUL *and* JULIA *stand looking after her for a moment; then* JULIA *laughs.*

JULIA: That was all very interesting.

PAUL: I hope, Julia, that since the old days your French has not improved too much.

JULIA: I could understand the gist of what she was saying, if not the actual words.

PAUL: How fortunate!

JULIA: I think, if only on account of our early years, some explanation is required.

PAUL: It was unkind of you to come here and bully the child.

JULIA: I didn't bully her. I merely wanted to find out who and what she was. Then she flew into a strange fury and was extremely rude. I do not like people being rude to me.

PAUL: She shall apologize later on.

JULIA [*grandly*]: That is quite unnecessary.

ROSE *enters with tea. While she is arranging it upon the table,* JULIA *and* PAUL *talk of other things.*

PAUL: I suppose you have been to the Pavilion?

JULIA: Yes. I supped there the other evening. It is quite hideous.

PAUL: Very informal, I believe?

JULIA: Oh, yes, and very agreeable. One plays cards and dances a little. Mrs. Fitzherbert plays very high, but then she always has, hasn't she?

ROSE *goes out.*

PAUL: It is only by shutting the eyes of my mind very tight that I can conjure up the schoolgirl I used to know.

JULIA: Surely that is quite natural. Twenty-five years leaves an adequate margin for change—and decay!

PAUL: Decay? [*Sadly*] Perhaps you are right.

JULIA: Now, tell me, Paul—what does all this mean? Why are you here?

PAUL: It is an odd story, quite fantastic. I think I need you a little.

JULIA: What can I offer you? My heart, my advice, or merely a little tea? [*She goes to the table.*]

[*338*]

PAUL: All three.

JULIA: Surely not the first, when your own is apparently so very much engaged.

PAUL: I fear you misunderstand the situation.

JULIA: I shall be only too pleased to be enlightened. Here is the tea, anyhow. [*She hands him a cup of tea.*]

He stands opposite to her.

PAUL: I feel at a loss—guilty—and yet I have nothing to be guilty about, really.

JULIA: I think it was rather unkind of you to take poor Maurice de Tramont's name and fasten it onto the first little light-of-love you meet.

PAUL *raps his cup sharply on the saucer.*

PAUL. [*icily*]: Melanie is not my light-of-love.

JULIA [*smiling incredulously*]: My dear Paul!

PAUL: It's perfectly true. She has never been anybody's light-of-love. That is her greatest asset.

JULIA: Asset?

PAUL [*he sits*]: Yes. Business asset. She is my plan. My trick to be played upon the world. My livelihood.

JULIA: Have you gone mad?

PAUL: No. I have merely transformed myself, owing to hard circumstances, from an effete aristocrat into a cunning and unscrupulous adventurer.

JULIA: That sounds faintly theatrical.

PAUL [*rising*]: The murder of my wife and child was theatrical enough—the deaths of my mother and father and sister on the guillotine were equally theatrical. My life from then onwards, as a fugitive, was an endless succession of serio-comic stage effects. I was a baker's assistant—a lawyer's clerk—a tutor to the children of nouveaux riches parvenus. Two years ago I found Melanie singing in a café. She seemed to me to be better material than my snivelling little bourgeois pupils, so I took her away from the café and kept us both on my savings. Every now and then I procured for her an engagement to sing at a private house. Five months ago I had a stroke of luck. I managed to sell two pictures from the old house, which somehow or other had been overlooked by the revolutionaries. With that money I brought her here.

JULIA: Why?

PAUL: She is to make a rich marriage.

JULIA: And you take commission?

PAUL: Yes.

JULIA: In England, we describe that as pimping!

PAUL: At that rate, every fondly ambitious mother is a pimp.

JULIA: That is hardly the same thing.

PAUL: Well?

JULIA: Well—I think it is a good joke, in very bad taste.

PAUL: Taste is too expensive a social luxury for a poor man.

JULIA: I suppose the poor little thing is in love with you?

PAUL [startled]: In love with me! What nonsense! [He laughs.]

JULIA: I should have thought it was inevitable.

PAUL: I appreciate the compliment, Julia, but I think it is a trifle far-fetched. This whole plan has been understood completely between us from the first as a business arrangement.

JULIA: How wise!

PAUL: Will you help me?

JULIA: With all your worldly experiences, Paul, you have contrived to remain singularly naïf.

PAUL: At any rate, even if you cannot help, please make me a promise that you will not hinder.

JULIA: Of course, if it's money you want, you could always marry me. I have plenty.

PAUL [shocked]: Julia!

JULIA: We could find some employment for Melanie. She might even be my maid.

PAUL: I see I have made a mistake.

JULIA [rising with decision and patting his shoulder]: No,

[340]

Paul. Don't be afraid. I won't give away your secret, and I'll help you all I can. It should be amusing, at least.

PAUL: How much do you despise me for it?

JULIA: Just a little. If it matters to you.

PAUL: I'm sorry.

JULIA: Cunning, unscrupulous adventurers have no time to waste on conscience. Call her in. We will discuss possibilities.

PAUL: Do you think that is wise?

JULIA: I can manage her.

PAUL: Very well. [*He goes to the bedroom door.*] Melanie. Venez ici.

After a moment MELANIE *comes in. She sees that* JULIA *is still there, and her face hardens immediately.*

PAUL: Melanie, I wish you to apologize to Lady Julia.

MELANIE [*firmly*]: No.

PAUL [*sternly*]: Please do as I tell you.

MELANIE: I have nothing to say.

JULIA: But it is for me to say I am sorry. I was over inquisitive, and I jumped to conclusions too hastily. Mademoiselle, I ask your forgiveness.

MELANIE [*bowing*]: Merci, madame.

JULIA: Shall we be friends?

MELANIE: Je ne comprends pas.

PAUL: You are being very ungracious, Melanie.

MELANIE: I am sorry.

PAUL: I have told Lady Julia everything. She has promised to help us.

MELANIE: You have told her—what?

JULIA: A story. Just a story, mademoiselle, but it is a very interesting story, and I should like, as Paul and I are such old friends, to help to bring it to a happy ending.

MELANIE *looks searchingly from one to the other, and then, with a great effort, smiles.*

MELANIE [*curtseying*]: Merci beaucoup, madame. I understand now.

[*341*]

JULIA *also curtseys.*

JULIA [*briskly*]: Come now—to business.

MELANIE [*with great manner*]: Madame will sit?

JULIA [*sitting down*]: Thank you.

MELANIE [*inquiringly to* PAUL]: What business shall we begin?

PAUL: We can talk quite freely in front of Lady Julia.

MELANIE: That is very nice.

JULIA: In the first place, whom do you know here?

MELANIE [*humming softly*]: Even the sea looks grey.

PAUL: Melanie!

MELANIE [*fiercely singing*]: C'est vrai!

JULIA [*politely*]: I beg your pardon?

MELANIE: It is nothing, madame, but when business is here to be talked——[*Singing*] It seems that all the joy has faded from the day—as though the foolish world no longer wants to play——

JULIA: Really, these vocal outbursts are most disconcerting.

PAUL: Do be good, Melanie.

MELANIE: Very well—I will be good.

PAUL: Lord Sheere is our only definite proposal so far.

JULIA [*to* MELANIE]: Do you like him?

MELANIE [*singing*]:

> I'll follow my secret heart
> My whole life through.
> I'll keep every dream apart
> Till one comes true.
> No matter what price is paid,
> What stars may fade above,
> I'll follow my secret heart
> Till I find—love.

She rises while she is singing this, and walks over to the window. She finishes with her back turned.

PAUL [*irritably*]: Melanie! Will you kindly concentrate?

JULIA: I do see how difficult it must be, for anyone so young and so charming, to banish sentiment entirely.

MELANIE [*turning*]: You are sympathetic, madame, but it is not so very difficult really. Sentiment is very silly. [*She looks at* PAUL, *and her voice hardens.*]

JULIA: How wise!

MELANIE: There is no sentiment in the whole world that is real.

JULIA: Wiser still.

MELANIE: Real enough to waste the time upon—Paul has spoken me that very often.

JULIA: How very sensible of him!

MELANIE: I will be sensible too and make business. [*She puts a chair by the table and sits.*] I have three with which to begin.

JULIA: Three!

MELANIE: Yes, I make the progress. First there is the Prince Regent. He wishes to sleep with me.

PAUL: Melanie!

MELANIE [*quickly*]: Do not be shocked, Paul. That is true, and we are speaking of truth.

JULIA [*laughing*]: Admirable!

MELANIE: If I do that—there is a risk—a risk that I may not stay in the royal heart long enough to gain large money for Paul.

PAUL: I will not have you speaking like that—it is intolerable.

JULIA: She is quite right, Paul. It ill becomes you to be so outraged. Remember how unscrupulous you are.

MELANIE: Then there is the Duke of Beneden. He has a little house with pretty furniture and a coach with white horses and three hundred pounds on the first day of every month—these things would be useful, would they not?

JULIA: Hard work, but a little more lasting than the other.

MELANIE: Then there is Lord Sheere.

JULIA: That's better.

MELANIE: He loves me.

JULIA: Excellent.

MELANIE: But if we marry, there is no money at all.

JULIA: That can soon be remedied if your social position is improved. You must first of all be presented—more or less informally, here—at the Pavilion.

PAUL: But how? Who will present her?

JULIA: I will, but before that you must give a little supper party. I will arrange it and invite the guests. Lord St. Marys must come, and the Benedens, and Lord Sheere, and the Harringfords—they are very useful.

MELANIE [*rising sharply*]: Are they rich? Have they a foolish son? [*She goes to the window.*]

JULIA [*ignoring her, to* PAUL]: You must have cards, and good wine—Mademoiselle might sing a little—she has such a charming voice, but I should suggest songs more closely allied to the classics than to the café chantant.

PAUL [*going over to her*]: I can never begin to express my gratitude, Julia——

JULIA: Not at all. Old friends must be kept from starving. If all else fails, I shall take up a subscription for you.

PAUL: I am still very low in your eyes, I see.

JULIA: You share that position with almost everyone I know. [*Rising*] I will leave you now. Call upon me tomorrow, and we will discuss the party invitations.

PAUL: I will send for a carriage.

JULIA: My curricle is outside. [*She crosses to* MELANIE *and curtseys.*] Au revoir, mademoiselle.

MELANIE: Au revoir, madame.

JULIA: And please accept my admiration. Your common sense is magnificent—— [*She laughs.*] But you will be careful, won't you, not to betray too much hardness of heart. Cynicism in the young is *so* unbecoming.

She sweeps out, followed by PAUL. MELANIE, *when they have gone, picks up* JULIA's *handkerchief from the floor, sniffs it contemptuously, and pitches it into the waste-paper basket—as the lights fade.*

CONVERSATION PIECE

SCENE III

QUARTETTE, FISHERMEN:

"There was once a little village."

There was once a little village by the
    sea,
Where we lived our lives in amiable
    tranquillity.
We were humble in our ways
And we swam through all our days
As little fishes swim—in immobility;
We watched for gales in the evening
    sky,
And we trimmed our sails till the night
    went by,
No less, no more,
Than stones on an English shore.

Then whimsical Fate,
Resenting our state,
Decided to break us
And mould and remake us;
Our sweet isolation
From civilization
Has all vanished away.
We're urban and proud,
Supporting a crowd
Of Doxys and Dandys
And Regency Randys,
Who fiddle and faddle
And piddle and paddle
And turn night into day.
The Pavilion

CONVERSATION PIECE

Cost a million
As a monument to Art,
And the wits here
Say it sits here
Like an Oriental tart!
The dashing "beau monde"
Has ruffled our pond,
And even the turbot
Know Mrs. Fitzherbert.
We're richer than ever before
But Brighton is Brighton no more.

SCENE IV

The scene is a larger room on the ground floor of MELANIE'S
*house. It is circular, and the ceiling is supported by pillars.
There are two sets of double doors up stage right and left.
Down stage, almost on the footlights, there are two curved
benches. There is a buffet on the left side of the stage upon
which are jugs of iced wine and elaborate cakes and other
delicacies. From behind the right-hand double doors comes the
sound of music. There are candles on the buffet and in sconces
on the walls. Hanging in the centre is a large crystal chandelier.
Up at the back of the stage, between the doors, there is a low
dais upon which is a clavisan.*

When the curtain rises the GUESTS *are grouped, with* JULIA
and PAUL *in the centre, forming a beautiful "still" picture. This
attitude is held through a phrase of music, when, at a given
point, the "picture" comes to life, and the party is in progress.*

*Note: Throughout this scene there are musical "stops" to
allow the dialogue to be heard. All guests, etc., not actually
concerned in dialogue remain immovable, in whichever positions they may be.*

There is the sound of laughter and dancing from the ball-

room. GUESTS *are strolling about and chatting to one another. There are several people clustered round the buffet.*

PAUL *and* JULIA *are standing centre. A* BUTLER *flings open the doors left and announces, in succession:*

BUTLER: Lady Mosscrock. The Earl and Countess of Harring-ford.

The HARRINGFORDS *enter, and* PAUL *goes forward to receive them. The conversation is too general for their exact greetings to be heard. They come over to* JULIA *and talk for a little; meanwhile the* BUTLER *announces in succession,* MR. *and* MRS. HAILSHAM, *the* LADY BRACEWORTH, *the* HONOURABLE JULIAN KANE, LORD DOYNING. [Musical stop.]*

LADY H. [*to* JULIA]: What a charming house, and what a lovely party! You must come to tea tomorrow and tell me the name of our host over and over again. I know I shall never remember it.

JULIA: The Duc de Chaucigny-Varennes.

LADY H.: The French do seem to go out of their way to make things hard for us, don't they? All those hyphens.

LORD H.: Where's the girl you told us about? The ward or niece or whatever she is.

JULIA: You shall see her soon. She is very lovely.

Music resumes.

They pass on to talk to someone else. The BUTLER *announces the* DUKE *and* DUCHESS OF BENEDEN. *When they enter,* PAUL *receives them politely but with a certain hauteur. Presently the* DUCHESS *takes* JULIA's *arm and walks her down stage left. They sit for a few moments on the curved bench. [Musical stop.]*

DUCHESS: Julia, I must tell you frankly. I do not understand at all. I am completely at a loss.

JULIA: Why, Georgina?

DUCHESS: Frederick made me come. I still don't approve——

JULIA: You have no reason not to approve. You merely jumped to conclusions too hastily. As usual.

DUCHESS: Do you mean to tell me——

JULIA: I don't mean to tell you anything, Georgina, except that I have known the Chaucigny-Varennes family all my life, and that Paul is one of my oldest friends.

DUCHESS: But the girl—I can't believe——

JULIA: You made a grave mistake, and all I can suggest is that you remedy it as soon as possible. Melanie will be down soon.

The DUKE *joins them.*

DUKE: Is Edward here?

JULIA: I haven't seen him yet.

DUCHESS: He hasn't spoken to me for four days.

JULIA: You really can't be surprised. You both of you made a bad blunder.

DUCHESS: But those dreadful women! Trying on each other's hats.

JULIA: Melanie is a stranger here. How was she to know whom to receive and whom not to receive?

DUCHESS: Very well, Julia, I'll take your word for it, for the time being, but I'm still not convinced.

[*Music resumes—Short phrase—Musical stop.*]

She moves away to talk to LADY HARRINGFORD.

JULIA: Really, Frederick, Georgina is more disagreeable than ever.

DUKE: She is upset.

JULIA: You've been saying that for twenty years.

DUKE: It's been true for twenty years.

JULIA: I don't know how you've stood it.

DUKE: On the contrary, you should know better than anyone.

JULIA [*laughing*]: Yes, Frederick, perhaps I should. Poor Georgina.

DUKE: The years have changed you very little.

JULIA: Thank you, Frederick.

DUKE: Dear Julia. [*He kisses her hand.*]

JULIA: That gesture was reminiscent—almost painfully so.

Fortunately the light is too strong to allow us to deceive ourselves.

DUKE: Deceive ourselves?

JULIA: Into a momentary belief that we were young again.

DUKE: Julia—do you remember——?

JULIA: I remember nothing. That is one of my greatest virtues. Who is your mistress at the moment?

DUKE: Really, Julia!

JULIA: Or have you retired from public love?

[*Music resumes.*]

She curtseys to him rather mockingly and goes over to PAUL. *The* DUKE *moves over to the buffet. There is a general buzz of conversation during which* LORD SHEERE *and* LORD ST. MARYS *are announced and make their entrance.* PAUL *receives them.*

[*Musical stop.*]

MELANIE *comes in quite quietly and unostentatiously, but even so her entrance is the signal for the conversation to die down. People turn, with elaborate casualness, to scrutinize her. She looks pale but very lovely.*

MELANIE [*to* PAUL]: My dress would not manage itself. I am so sorry. [*She curtseys to* JULIA.] Madame.

JULIA: You look delicious, my dear.

MELANIE: Merci, madame.

She curtseys to EDWARD *and* LORD ST. MARYS.

JULIA [*to the* DUCHESS OF BENEDEN]: Georgina—I want to present to you Mademoiselle Melanie de Tramont.

DUCHESS [*stiffly*]: How do you do?

MELANIE [*curtseying low*]: I am honoured, madame.

DUCHESS [*with an effort*]: I am delighted to see you again.

MELANIE: Again? Ah, forgive me, madame, but I am so quite sure that we have never, never met before.

DUCHESS: That is very charming of you, mademoiselle.

The DUKE *comes up.*

PAUL: Ah, Monsieur le Duc, I wish to present my ward, Melanie de Tramont.

[*349*]

CONVERSATION PIECE

The DUKE *bows low, and again* MELANIE *curtseys.*

DUKE: I hope you are enjoying yourself in England, mademoiselle?

MELANIE: Yes, I love it here. The sea is so pretty!

[*Music resumes. Musical stop.*]

The BUTLER *flings open the doors and announces* MRS. JAMES, MRS. OTFORD, *and* MRS. DRAGON. *There is a horrified silence for a moment or two.*

PAUL: Melanie! Did you invite them?

MELANIE: Pourquoi pas? They are my friends.

SOPHIE *and* MARTHA *enter, followed discreetly by* MRS. DRAGON. *They are extravagantly dressed and overbejewelled.*

SOPHIE: My dear, what a *lovely* party!

MARTHA: So sweet of you to ask us!

They curtsey. MELANIE *greets them with enthusiasm.*

JULIA [*to* PAUL]: This is idiotic!

PAUL: We must get rid of them.

JULIA: It's too late now. Oh, what an abysmal mistake!

DUCHESS [*to* PAUL, *sweetly*]: Good-night, monsieur. It has been so delightful.

PAUL: But surely, Duchess, you are not leaving?

DUCHESS: A sudden headache. It will be better in the morning. My husband, I am sure, will be delighted to stay.

She bows coldly to JULIA *and goes out.* LADY HARRINGFORD *comes up to* PAUL.

LADY H.: Good-night, monsieur—I have to drive to London early tomorrow, and I am very tired.

[*Music resumes.*]

PAUL *bows, and she goes off after the* DUCHESS.

Nearly all the women in the room come up in turn to say good-bye to PAUL, *but you do not hear the exact excuses they give because* MELANIE *has led* SOPHIE *and* MARTHA *and* MRS. DRAGON *down stage right to the bench.*

[*Musical stop.*]

JULIA [*to* PAUL]: You see! [*She sits.*]

[350]

SOPHIE: We should scold you, Melanie.

MELANIE: What is "scold"?

MARTHA: Be angry.

MELANIE: Angry! Why?

SOPHIE: We didn't know it was this sort of party.

MELANIE: I do not understand.

SOPHIE: We never like meeting these sort of women.

MARTHA: Most of them are the wives of our gentlemen, you know. It's very awkward.

SOPHIE: Don't stand there twiddling your fingers, Dragon. Go and get yourself some claret.

MRS. DRAGON *goes over to the buffet.*

MELANIE [*noticing what is happening*]: They have all gone away—all the ladies.

SOPHIE. That's our fault.

MELANIE [*suddenly angry*]: I understand now—very, very well—Paul——

PAUL *comes over to her.*

Paul—I do not believe you know Madame Otford and Madame James.

PAUL [*bowing coldly*]: Enchanted.

MELANIE: These ladies have been very kind to me—I should like that you know that—they have made me happy——

PAUL: That is delightful.

SOPHIE: I think we had better go, Martha. I feel quite faint.

MELANIE: If you go, I will go with you.

PAUL: Don't be ridiculous, Melanie.

MELANIE [*to* SOPHIE]: You must not go—you must stay for me to sing—it is all arranged—Lord Sheere—Lord St. Marys——

EDWARD *and* LORD ST. MARYS *come over to her.*

PAUL: Melanie!

MELANIE: This is my party, Paul. I wish to enjoy myself. Lord Sheere, Lord St. Marys—I have something to say to you—where is the Duke?—I have something to say to him also.

JULIA [*rising*]: What is happening?

[*351*]

MELANIE: Nothing, madame, except that I am going to sing—
it was planned that I should sing—because I sing so charmingly,
do I not? [*To* EDWARD *and* LORD ST. MARYS] Messieurs, you will
sit, please, next to my two friends—ah, Monsieur le Duc de
Beneden—I wish that you pay very special favour to a lady much
in my esteem—Mrs. Dragon——

She darts to the buffet and brings MRS. DRAGON *over to the*
DUKE. MRS. DRAGON *looks slightly flustered owing to having a glass
of claret in one hand and a large sandwich in the other. However, she manages to curtsey, a trifle unsteadily.*

Where is Mr. Jones? He is to play—please find Mr. Jones,
Paul——

JULIA [*laughing, none too pleasantly*]: Excellent—the whole
situation is most entertaining.

MELANIE: I am glad if you are gay, madame—I would like that
everybody is gay.

PAUL [*to* MELANIE]: Melanie—écoutez! Je veux vous dire
quelque chose d'importance——

MELANIE: Do not speak in French, Paul—I cannot understand—I can understand only English among my English friends
—ah, there is Mr. Jones—please play for me, Mr. Jones—Mr.
Jones plays very light, very pretty—everybody will please sit—
Monsieur le Marquis—it is from the distance that you see me
now—please for me remember that—Monsieur le Duc—when
you are in your small house in London, with the shutters drawn
—think sweetly of me, because I shall be far away—Lord St.
Marys, you have proposed such kind honours, but I am too little
in life to say Yes or No—I may only say merci——

MR. JONES *begins to play the clavisan. Everybody sits down,
looking faintly bewildered.* PAUL *remains standing, near* JULIA.
MELANIE *starts to sing. First she sings to* EDWARD, *briefly, but
with very genuine sweetness. Then she turns to the* DUKE OF
BENEDEN. *For him, the words she sings are tinged with gentle
malice. She sings to* LORD ST. MARYS *smilingly and with a certain
mocking deference. Last of all she turns suddenly towards* PAUL.

CONVERSATION PIECE

To him she sings in French, an unmistakable love song. Her whole heart is in her voice. PAUL *starts back in horrified amazement.* JULIA's *face hardens into an expression of ill-repressed fury.*

[*Musical Finale.*]

MELANIE: Dear Friends,
      Will you forgive me, pray,
      If many of the words I say
      In English may be wrong.

ALL: She hasn't been in England very long.

MELANIE: A stranger in a foreign land,
      I beg that you will understand
      How gratefully I find
      The gentlemen so very kind,
      So very kind.

[*To the* DUKE OF BENEDEN]
      The offer of protection
      That Monsieur le Duc has made
      I set aside,
      For my foolish pride
      Would feel itself betrayed.

ALL: Charming—Charming—Charming!

MELANIE [*to* LORD ST. MARYS]:
      Monsieur, my Lord St. Marys
      Has made me an offer too.
      Royal though his scheme may be,
      It could never be part of a dream for me.

ALL: Ah la la la—la la—la la.

MELANIE: Handsome though your prince may be,
      He is far too broad in the beam for me.

[*To the* MARQUIS OF SHEERE]
      But there is one, one only,
      Who honours me with his heart,
      Although I'm not the wife for him,
      I shall cherish all my life for him

A feeling somehow apart.
I'd suffer sorrow and strife for him.
Though we may be lovers never,
We're friends forever—forevermore.

[*Spoken*]

Thank you, my dear, for being so sweet to me.

EDWARD [*kissing her hand*]: Melanie!

MELANIE: There is only room for one true love in my heart—my secret heart.

EDWARD: I understand.

MELANIE: I know you do.

JULIA: This is most illuminating.

MELANIE: Paul!

PAUL [*horrified*]: Melanie—please——

MELANIE [*simply*]: It is you I love, I always have, from the very beginning—— [*She sings.*]

C'est assez de mensonge,
Le secret qui me ronge,
Que tout au fond de moi
J'ai tendrement gardé.
Enfin avec franchise
Il faut que je vous dise,
Avouant mon secret,
Que tu n'as pas compris
Plus de cœur discret.
C'est toi qui par l'amour,
Toi qui m'as délivrée,
Je suis à toi toujours.
Esclave de mon cœur,
Me rendras-tu la vie.
Je t'en supplie, crois-moi
Lorsque je dis c'est toi
Plus de cœur discret.
C'est toi qui par l'amour,

[*354*]

Toi qui m'as délivrée,
Je suis à toi toujours.
Esclave de mon cœur,
Me rendras-tu la vie.
Je t'en supplie, crois-moi,
Je t'en supplie, crois-moi,
C'est toi.
Parmi le monde entier c'est toi que j'aime.
Je t'en supplie,
Crois-le si même
Tu ne le veux.
Toi,
Parmi le monde entier c'est toi que j'aime,
Je suis à toi toujours.

At the end of the song MELANIE *swoons. There is an immediate buzz of excited conversation.* SOPHIE *runs forward, followed by* MARTHA. LORD ST. MARYS *hurries forward with a chair.*

SOPHIE: Dragon—fetch some wine—quickly——

MARTHA: Feathers—burn them under her nose—here—— [*She tears some feathers out of her hair.*]

SOPHIE: That's no good.

JULIA: A strange performance.

PAUL [*quivering*]: Please go now—I wish that everyone should go.

All the men start to go.

JULIA: Very well—poor Paul—I am so sorry.

PAUL: Tomorrow—we will talk tomorrow.

JULIA: Frederick!—Edward—will you please see me to my carriage?

JULIA *and the* DUKE *exeunt.*

SOPHIE [*to* MELANIE]: It's all right, dear—we're all going——

MELANIE [*opening her eyes*]: Paul.

MARTHA: Just lie still a minute.

SOPHIE: Come away, Martha.

[*355*]

MARTHA: All right, all right, I'm coming——
They go to the door, call DRAGON, *and all go out.*
During this scene nearly everyone has gone. MELANIE *is sitting on a chair, very white and quite still.* PAUL *sees the last guest,* EDWARD, *out, and closes the door.*
PAUL [*in a cold voice*]: Well—I hope you're satisfied.
MELANIE [*pleadingly*]: Paul!
PAUL: Everything is ruined—everything is finished.
MELANIE: Je vous aime.
PAUL: Ne vous moquez pas de moi.
MELANIE: Non, c'est vrai. Je vous ai toujours aimé.
PAUL: Vous avez d'étranges façons de me témoigner votre amour; en me rendant ridicule.
MELANIE: Est-ce si ridicule d'être aimé de moi?
PAUL: Il ne peut pas y avoir d'amour entre nous; une folie—voilà tout.
MELANIE: Non, c'est vrai.
PAUL: Savez-vous seulement ce qui est vrai? Vous avez manqué à tous vos engagements, vous m'avez menti, vous êtes jouée de moi.
Angrily he crosses to the sofa left.
MELANIE: Et pourquoi m'en serais-je privée? Dans toutes vos adroites combinaisons avez-vous un seul instant—pensé—à moi? Jamais!
PAUL: Pardon—tout était convenu entre nous dès le début. Vous saviez tout et vous aviez tout accepté.
MELANIE: Bien sûr, j'avais tout accepté. Une fille dans la situation où j'étais, aurait été folle de ne pas tout accepter.
PAUL: C'était un contrat d'affaires, et vous y avez manqué.
MELANIE: Pouvais-je répondre de mon cœur?
PAUL: De votre cœur!
MELANIE: Je vous aime, vous entendez. Vous pouvez dire que je suis folle, vous pouvez vous persuader que tout ceci est stupidement romanesque: cela vous met à votre aise, n'est-ce pas?

[356]

PAUL: Je suis parfaitement à mon aise.

MELANIE: Mais c'est vrai, et mon amour est au fond de moi, au plus profond de moi. De ma vie, aucun sentiment n'a poussé en moi des racines si profondes. Regardez-moi maintenant—regardez-moi bien!—je vous en prie, vous qui êtes si sage et si stupidement cruel—vous—l'homme le plus adroit que je connaisse et, de loin, le plus imbécile.

PAUL: Merci!

MELANIE: Vous avez pour toujours renoncé à l'amour, quand votre femme a été tuée, n'est-ce pas? Dieu merci, vous me l'avez assez souvent répété.

PAUL: Melanie, je vous en prie!

MELANIE: Et alors vous pensez pouvoir traverser la vie à l'abri, inaccessible, dans une magnifique sécurité, n'est-ce pas?

PAUL: Je me passerai fort bien de vos conseils.

MELANIE: Vous m'avez ramassée dans le ruisseau et vous m'avez appris la révérence et à faire les manières et à mentir à la vie.

PAUL: C'était bien nécessaire.

MELANIE: Mais voilà que, tout à coup, la vie a pris sa revanche, et elle s'est jouée de vous—et elle s'en jouera toujours. La vie est trop puissante en moi pour que j'accepte vos combinaisons. C'est vrai la vie—et c'est important—plus important que votre tranquillité et que votre cynisme prudent.

PAUL: Vous perdez le sens.

MELANIE: Allez-vous-en, et réfléchissez un peu. Allez-vous-en, et comprenez brusquement quel mal infini vous avez essayé de me faire.

PAUL: C'en est trop!

MELANIE: —et à vous aussi——

PAUL: C'en est trop!

MELANIE: —je t'aime—je t'aime—je t'aime—et toi aussi quelque part au fond de toi—tu m'aimes.

PAUL *starts to go.*

Tout me la crie. Chacun de mes instincts, chaque battement de

CONVERSATION PIECE

mon cœur, chaque bouffée d'air que je respire. Vous allez essayer de m'échapper—cela aussi je le sais—mais vous ne le pourrez pas——

He is just going out of the door and she breaks down completely.

—vous ne le pourrez pas——

She sinks into the chair, sobbing. The last chords of her love song to him crash out in the orchestra as—

THE CURTAIN FALLS

ACT III

SCENE I

The scene is the Steyne, and the time of day is about noon. It is a clear sunny morning, and there are a good many people strolling about. As usual, there is an undercurrent of music to the whole scene, and characters pass as in the First Act.
MISS GOSLETT *and* MISS MENTION *walk slowly across, talking.*

MISS GOSLETT: You don't put the nutmeg on until afterwards.

MISS MENTION: I still don't understand. Surely, if you leave it too long to cool, it gets lumpy.

MISS GOSLETT: Not if you stir it enough in the first place.

MISS MENTION: And why a *wooden* spoon?

MISS GOSLETT: It says so in the recipe.

MISS MENTION: Well, personally I prefer to remain faithful to the ordinary tapioca.

They both pass out of sight.

The LADY BRACEWORTH *enters right with the* DUCHESS OF BENEDEN. *They meet* MRS. HAILSHAM *centre, who has come on from the left.*

DUCHESS: Good-morning, Amelia.

MRS. HAILSHAM: My dear. [*They kiss.*]

LADY B.: Amelia.

MRS. HAILSHAM: My dear. [*They kiss.*]

DUCHESS: How is Mortimer?

MRS. HAILSHAM: Worse, I'm afraid. He had a shivering fit at three this morning. I've been up half the night.

LADY B.: How dreadful!

[*359*]

MRS. HAILSHAM: When he crept into my bed at about six he seemed calmer, but his nose was very hot and dry.

DUCHESS: You really should take him to the Vet.

MRS. HAILSHAM: I intend to this afternoon.

LADY HARRINGFORD *joins them.*

LADY H.: Georgina.

DUCHESS: Ettie. [*They kiss.*]

LADY H.: Amelia!

LADY B.: Good-morning, Ettie. [*They kiss.*]

LADY H.: Louisa!

MRS. HAILSHAM: My dear. [*They kiss.*]

LADY H.: I've had a horrible morning. Nono was sick three times at breakfast.

DUCHESS: Perhaps it's an epidemic.

LADY H.: I shall take him to the Vet. this afternoon.

LADY B.: Is he a really good Vet.?

MRS. HAILSHAM: Charming, my dear, absolutely charming.

LADY B.: Then I shall come with you this afternoon and bring Fifi.

DUCHESS: Is she ill too?

LADY B.: Well, not exactly ill, but moody.

LADY H.: There's probably something in the air here, it's very strong.

DUCHESS: Funnily enough it seems to suit Boney very well. He's much brighter here than in Shropshire.

MRS. HAILSHAM: Shropshire *is* enervating.

DUCHESS: I can't decide whether it's the sea air or the sulphur tablets, but he's certainly a different dog.

LADY B.: I'm so glad, because I never cared for him very much as he was.

DUCHESS: It betrays a small mind, Louisa, to be offended just because he didn't take to you at the very first moment.

MRS. HAILSHAM: I don't like animals to be too friendly.

DUCHESS: At any rate, he is a remarkably good house dog.

LADY B.: I should say more thorough than good.

DUCHESS: Really, Louisa!

MRS. HAILSHAM: How is Frederick?

DUCHESS: I really don't know, he didn't come home until four.

LADY H.: Neither did James.

MRS. HAILSHAM: Nor Robert.

LADY B.: Desmond hasn't come home yet.

LADY H.: It's such a bad example for the children. They ask such difficult questions.

DUCHESS: That dreadful party, and those appalling women. I shall never forgive Julia.

LADY B.: She must be mad.

LADY H.: The French Duke seemed polite, I thought, but peculiar.

MRS. HAILSHAM: My dear, [*to music*] there's always something fishy about the French.

DUCHESS: As a race they're erotic.

LADY B.: And completely idiotic.

LADY H.: Still, they have a certain air.

MRS. HAILSHAM: A "flair."

DUCHESS: Whatever you say, I don't believe a word of it.

They all talk together.

MRS. HAILSHAM: I didn't object to the girl so much—of course she was quite obviously common——

LADY B.: It's all very fine to excuse them on the grounds of being foreigners, but really——

LADY H.: Never in all my life have I had such a shock as when the door opened and those women came into the room——

DUCHESS: It's entirely Julia's fault. She gave me her solemn promise that she had known the Duke for years——

On the last phrase of "Fishy about the French," which the orchestra has been playing softly during this scene, they all sing suddenly together.

ALL FOUR: There's *always* something fishy about the French!

This last line leads them into their quartette, "Mothers and Wives," during which SOPHIE, MARTHA, MRS. DRAGON, *and another courtesan trip gaily across the scene on the arms of the* DUKE OF BENEDEN, MR. HAILSHAM, LORD BRACEWORTH, *and* LORD HARRINGFORD.

QUARTETTE:

"Mothers and Wives."

> In an atmosphere of bawdy jeu d'esprit
> We contrive to be tenaciously conventional,
> Tho' intelligent, we hope,
> Our imaginative scope
> When all is said and done
> Is one-dimensional.
> Our appearance should be ample guarantee
> Of our vigorous and rigorous morality,
> We regard our husbands' gout
> As a proper and devout
> And godly recompense
> For sensuality.
> But when we look at our greying hairs
> We sometimes sigh as we say our prayers,
> Dear Lord,
> We're bored,
> Is virtue enough reward?

Finally, at the end of the quartette, the mothers and wives go disconsolately away, leaving the stage comparatively empty save for a few pedestrians who pass and repass from time to time. JULIA *and* PAUL *enter from the left. During this scene, characters pass by at given moments.*

JULIA: My dear Paul, such sentimentality is utterly ridiculous.

PAUL: That is how I feel.

JULIA: Those feelings may do credit to your heart, but certainly not to your intelligence.

PAUL: It has nothing to do with my heart.

JULIA: Are you sure?

PAUL [*vehemently*]: Quite sure.

[*362*]

JULIA: Then be sensible. This idiotic charade cannot go on any further, you must see that.

PAUL: Yes, I see that.

JULIA: She is a nice little thing and, I am sure, perfectly sincere, but, as is only to be expected when a girl of her class is suddenly plumped down in an entirely different milieu, her values have become hopelessly confused.

PAUL: How can I send her away? She has done her best.

JULIA: It was a business contract between you, and now it is over.

PAUL: I know, but——

JULIA: She made a fool of you last night. She took your pride from you, and your position from you, and those are all that you have left.

PAUL: Not intentionally.

JULIA: Look at me for a moment, Paul, carefully and clearly. I am middle-aged and lonely and, oddly enough, I love you.

PAUL: Julia!

JULIA: Don't affect such surprise. You must know it perfectly well. You must have known that I would not have taken all this trouble to help you with a scheme of which I heartily disapproved if I had not realized, in the first moment of seeing you again, that over all these years, and through all our strange adventures, you are the one man in the whole world that I love and that I have always loved.

PAUL: What can I say to you, Julia?

JULIA: The truth, whatever it may be.

PAUL: I don't believe I know it.

JULIA [smiling]: Dear Paul.

PAUL: Are you laughing at me?

JULIA: Just a little.

PAUL: I am sure you are right to laugh, but please don't, I feel small enough already, and cheap, and of no account.

JULIA: You are worrying about Melanie?

PAUL: Of course.

[363]

JULIA: Listen to me. She is not happy here, she never has been. We will send her back to Paris with enough money to keep her in comfort until she finds a nice husband for herself of her own class.

PAUL: I have no money.

JULIA: I have, a lot.

PAUL: Julia!

JULIA: Please, please, I beseech you to be sensible. Money cannot matter between us, just as the wild ecstasies of passion cannot matter between us. I am rich and, as I said before, lonely. You are poor, and equally lonely. We have still time for many years of happiness together—Paul——

She knocks at the door.

PAUL: If only I could have known before.

JULIA: Fate has offered us a wonderful chance. It would be foolish to allow it to slip away.

PAUL: Perhaps you are right—perhaps this is the truth.

JULIA: The truth is here, very clear and simple. Two very old friends have suddenly, unaccountably, found each other again——

She holds out her hand to him, and he kisses it. During this scene all the lights have faded except on the exact spot where they are standing. As JULIA *turns to go into the house, this light also fades.*

SCENE II

The scene is MELANIE's *room again.*

When the curtain rises MELANIE *and* EDWARD *are discovered clasped tightly in each other's arms. They do not move until* ROSE *enters.*

ROSE: Mademoiselle.

MELANIE [*over* EDWARD's *shoulder*]: Yes?

ROSE: It was only the milkman.

MELANIE [*irritably*]: Oh—— [*To* EDWARD] Then we will sit down again.

ROSE: Do you want some fresh chocolate?

MELANIE [*feeling the chocolate pot on the table*]: No, this is still quite hot.

ROSE *goes out*.

EDWARD: I think I should like a little.

MELANIE [*pouring it out*]: Here—— [*She motions him to sit.*] There is a little cake, too, if you would care.

EDWARD: No, thank you.

MELANIE [*eating one*]: They are delicious.

EDWARD: Very well, I will try one. [*He takes a cake.*]

MELANIE: What will we speak of?

EDWARD: I don't know.

MELANIE [*smiling*]: You are so very sweet.

EDWARD: I don't think we will speak of that, anyhow.

MELANIE: And very, very kind.

EDWARD: No, really I'm not.

MELANIE: And my very, very good friend.

EDWARD: I hope so. I do hope so.

MELANIE: Would you have another small cake?

EDWARD: Yes, please.

MELANIE: I will also.

They both have another cake.

MELANIE: In Paris there are very lovely cakes.

EDWARD: There must be.

There is a rat-tat-tat at the front door. They both put their chocolate cups down hurriedly.

MELANIE: Quickly.

EDWARD: I say, my mouth's full.

MELANIE: Never mind—so is mine.

They fly into each other's arms and stand motionless. Presently ROSE *reënters.*

ROSE: It's only the girl from Mrs. Baxter's, with a bill.

MELANIE: Send her away.

ROSE: I have.

She goes out.

MELANIE [*going to the window*]: I am so very sorry.

EDWARD: He must come soon, mustn't he?

MELANIE: Yes, he is late now.

EDWARD: I wish that you loved me, really.

MELANIE: So do I. You would be so easy to love.

EDWARD: Are you unhappy?

MELANIE: Yes.

EDWARD: Because you love him so much?

MELANIE: Because he does not love me—enough.

EDWARD: Do you think he ever will?

MELANIE: Yes. I know it.

EDWARD: I shall remember you always—whatever happens to me.

MELANIE: I will remember you too. I will remember how you put away your own happiness to help me, and even if we see each other again very little, and even when we become very old people, and even when the day comes when I must die, you will be in my heart truly as a kind and dear friend.

MELANIE:

"Nevermore."

Verse

Dear Friend,
If hearts could only be
Content with love and sympathy,
How sweetly we could live,
We both of us have so much love to give.
No matter how our minds conspire,
Imprisoned by our own desire,
We are not free to choose.
What love we gain,
What love we lose,
We cannot choose.

[*366*]

CONVERSATION PIECE

Refrain

Nevermore. Nevermore,
Can life be quite the same.
The lights and shadows change,
All the old familiar world is strange,
Evermore. Evermore,
Our hearts are in the flame.
Others may regain their freedom,
But for you and me,
Never-nevermore.

EDWARD: Melanie!

He takes her in his arms and kisses her. PAUL *enters quietly and sees them. He looks angry for a moment and then assumes a charming smile.*

PAUL: I hope I am not intruding.

MELANIE [*breaking away*]: Paul!

PAUL: I see that you have returned to reason.

MELANIE: Yes, Paul.

PAUL: I am glad.

MELANIE: Yes, Paul.

PAUL: Lord Sheere, I congratulate you.

EDWARD [*stiffly*]: Thank you.

PAUL: It is so pretty to see Youth—in love.

EDWARD: Love is a very strange sensation, Monsieur le Duc—for Youth, particularly so. When one is young one feels things so strongly. One feels—foolishly perhaps—that the very fact of loving is enough—worth making all sacrifices for. It is sad—almost tragic—to think that with age so much of the best in life loses its savour. You have my sympathy, Monsieur le Duc.

He bows abruptly to both of them and goes out.

PAUL *goes to the writing table.*

PAUL: You should be very happy with him. He seems to be quite suitably unbalanced.

MELANIE: Yes, Paul.

[*367*]

PAUL: You are going to marry him?

MELANIE: Yes, Paul.

PAUL: I am very glad.

MELANIE: Yes, Paul.

PAUL: But I think it is a little vulgar of you to fall into his arms with such abandon so soon after the scene you made last night.

MELANIE: Yes, Paul.

PAUL: The game is over now, so you can speak in French if you like.

MELANIE: Oui, Paul.

PAUL [*irritably*]: Qu'est-ce que vous avez ce matin?

MELANIE: I think I would prefer to talk in English.

PAUL: Pourquoi?

MELANIE: Because it feels more happy—today.

PAUL: You are in love?

MELANIE: Yes, Paul.

PAUL: So am I.

MELANIE: Oh! [*She laughs.*]

PAUL: Why do you laugh?

MELANIE: I thought you would say that.

PAUL: I am going to marry Lady Julia.

MELANIE [*calmly*]: Yes, Paul.

PAUL: Can you say nothing else but "Yes, Paul"?

MELANIE: There is nothing else to say.

PAUL: The whole thing has been a mistake—a ridiculous horrible mistake.

MELANIE: Yes, Paul.

PAUL: When are you going to be married?

MELANIE: Soon—very soon.

PAUL: What about money?

MELANIE: That will not matter. It never does.

PAUL: I will see that you have everything you want.

MELANIE: That is very kind—of Lady Julia.

PAUL: Why do you stare at me like that?

MELANIE: I am sorry.

PAUL: Have you anything to reproach me with?

MELANIE: No.

She shrugs her shoulders and walks away.

PAUL: Melanie—— [*He goes to her.*]

MELANIE: Yes, Paul.

PAUL: I am sorry—very sorry.

MELANIE: No, no, I am good now—you cannot make me cry.

PAUL: I don't want to make you cry. I wish with all my heart for you to be happy.

MELANIE: I will be happy then.

He stirs a cup of chocolate.

PAUL: Will you stay here? The rent is paid for six weeks more.

MELANIE: I do not know.

PAUL: I am going to London.

MELANIE: When?

PAUL: Tomorrow.

MELANIE: So soon.

PAUL: But I will come back—in a little while—to make all arrangements for your marriage.

MELANIE: Very well.

PAUL: Does that satisfy you? [*He drops a spoon noisily.*]

MELANIE: Yes, Paul. [*She turns away.*]

PAUL: Please don't look sad.

She walks away.

MELANIE: It is not a real sadness.

PAUL: All comedies must come to an end.

MELANIE [*turning again*]: I have one thing to ask—it is very small.

PAUL: What is it?

MELANIE: Come once more to see me before you go.

PAUL: No—no——

MELANIE: Please—it is not much to ask—come this evening to a little supper—I will invite Lady Julia also and Edward, my fiancé—it will be to celebrate that we are all so happy.

PAUL: C'est un enfantillage.

[*369*]

MELANIE: It will be very gay, and at the same time it will be a little sad—but please, please, in memory of our happy days together—please say you will come?

PAUL: But, Melanie—my dear child——

MELANIE [*very softly*]: Please?

PAUL: Very well.

MELANIE: Merci, mon cher, cher ami——

She goes up to him quite simply and kisses him on the mouth. He instinctively succumbs to her kiss for a moment, and then, breaking away from her abruptly, he goes hurriedly from the room. She is left standing still for a moment, and then, with an expression of triumph on her face, she runs to the window to see him go. She begins to sing gaily and a trifle hysterically, and she is still singing as she runs towards her room as the lights fade.

SCENE III

The following scene is cued to music.

This scene is the gardens again. It is evening, and although most of the lights are still shining, there are very few people about. Occasionally a couple stroll across and are lost to sight among the shadows. The orchestra plays softly and sentimentally. Presently PAUL *enters. He stands looking about him for a moment, as though he were lost. Two lovers cross in front of him, so engrossed in each other that they do not even notice him. He walks slowly down to the bench left. As he is about to sit down upon it, two more lovers pass. They stop still for a moment in a close embrace and then go on their way.* PAUL *sits down disconsolately. Somewhere in the distance* MELANIE's *voice is heard singing.* PAUL *starts to his feet sharply, and then sinks back again, realizing that the voice is only in his mind. The little boy who bowled the hoop in the first scene comes on, but this time his hoop is looped over his left arm while his right encircles the waist of a little girl. They giggle happily across the*

[370]

stage and disappear. The music swells, and with it MELANIE'S
voice grows louder. PAUL *rises with his hands to his ears and
starts to move away, but wherever he turns he is met by lovers.
The whole scene slides almost imperceptibly into a form of
ballet. Finally with all the lovers circling round him and tor-
menting him, he breaks away and runs off the stage, as the lights
fade.*

SCENE IV

The scene is MELANIE'S *room again. The room has been completely dismantled. There are neither curtains, rugs, nor furniture left. The floor is covered with straw and shavings and
pieces of rope, all the paraphernalia of packing. The windows
are wide open, and strong moonlight floods into the room,
which, itself, is lit only by a few meagre candles. The noise of
the waves on the shingle can be plainly heard. Arranged round
the room are various boxes and trunks and packing cases. At
one of these* ROSE *is kneeling, with a pile of clothes on the floor
beside her.*

There is a knock on the door.

ROSE [*over her shoulder*]: Come in.
EDWARD *enters. He gives a little start of astonishment.* ROSE
rises to her feet.
EDWARD: The front door was open, so I came straight——
ROSE: I left it open on purpose, in case I didn't hear.
EDWARD: What has happened?
ROSE: There is a note for you.
EDWARD: Where is Mademoiselle?
ROSE: She has gone.
EDWARD: Gone!
ROSE: The note will explain everything. Here it is.
*She hands him a note which is lying on one of the packing
cases.*

[*371*]

EDWARD: Thank you. [*He opens it and reads it by the light of one of the candles.*]

ROSE *resumes her packing.*

EDWARD: Where has she gone? She doesn't say.

ROSE: France. She left on the evening boat for Dieppe. You can see its lights out there, the sea is calm, so it isn't going very fast.

He crosses sadly to the opposite window, looks out, then reverently kisses the note. While he is standing looking out of the window there are footsteps on the stairs, and LADY JULIA *sweeps into the room.*

JULIA: Good heavens!

EDWARD: I fear that Mademoiselle is not entertaining this evening after all.

JULIA: Obviously.

EDWARD: She has gone.

JULIA: Do you know, I almost gathered that.

ROSE: There is a note for you, madame.

JULIA: How polite. It would have saved me considerable inconvenience if she had sent it to my house.

ROSE [*curtly*]: Here it is, anyhow.

JULIA [*taking it*]: Thank you.

She, too, reads by the light of one of the candles. When she has finished it, she laughs.

JULIA: Extraordinarily well phrased for a guttersnipe.

EDWARD [*hotly*]: Melanie was not a guttersnipe.

JULIA: I'm so sorry. I had forgotten your great tenderness for her.

EDWARD: I never shall.

JULIA [*smiling*]: Faithful unto death!

EDWARD: Yes. I am her friend, for always.

JULIA: How touching. All the same I cannot help feeling that it is just as well for you that she has gone away.

EDWARD [*turning away*]: I wouldn't expect you to understand, madame.

[372]

JULIA [*loosening her cloak*]: Well, I suppose we had better wait here and break the news to Paul.

ROSE [*still packing*]: That would be waste of time, madame.

JULIA: Why, what do you mean?

ROSE: Monsieur le Dook sailed with Mademoiselle on the evening boat for France.

JULIA [*sharply*]: What!

ROSE: You can still see the lights from the window. They look ever so pretty reflected in the water.

JULIA [*furiously*]: You're lying! Monsieur le Duc couldn't possibly have sailed.

ROSE: That's as may be, but I did happen to see him onto the boat myself. They was very gay—both of them.

JULIA [*controlling herself*]: I see. [*Bitterly*] How very, very amusing.

ROSE: A joke's a joke all the world over, I always say.

JULIA: Lord Sheere, will you kindly escort me to my house?

EDWARD: With pleasure, Lady Julia.

JULIA: I fear my cook will be in bed, but I can offer you a little wine.

EDWARD: Thank you.

JULIA: We can drink a toast—to absent friends!

Without looking at ROSE, *she walks out of the room.* EDWARD *is about to follow her, then he hesitates and comes back.*

EDWARD: Good-bye, Rose.

ROSE [*jumping to her feet and curtseying*]: Good-bye, my lord.

EDWARD [*giving her a little purse of money*]: Will you please keep this in remembrance of me?

ROSE: Oh, yes, my lord—thank you.

He goes to the door and turns.

EDWARD: If—if you should ever see her again—give her my love.

ROSE: Yes, my lord.

EDWARD *goes out.*

ROSE *stands looking after him, and after a moment or two she*

*resumes her packing, humming to herself meanwhile. Presently
there are hurried footsteps on the stairs, and* PAUL *bursts into
the room. His face is white, and he is trembling.*

PAUL: Rose! What's the matter? What is happening?

ROSE [*rising to her feet*]: You've missed them, sir.

PAUL: Missed whom?

ROSE: Lady Julia and Lord Sheere. They just went out.

PAUL: Where is Mademoiselle? [*He rushes toward the bedroom door.*] Where is Mademoiselle?

ROSE: You've missed her too, sir.

PAUL: What do you mean?

ROSE: She has gone.

PAUL: Gone—where—where has she gone?

ROSE: France, sir—she left a note for you—here it is.

*She takes a note from the bosom of her dress and gives it to
him. He takes it mechanically, with an expression on his face of
utter despair.* ROSE *watches him; she starts to sing quietly. When
he has finished reading it, he walks slowly across the stage.*

PAUL [*to* ROSE—*stamping his foot*]: Stop singing! [*Speaking
with great difficulty*] She doesn't give any address—she doesn't
say where I can find her——

*He turns slowly round, goes up to the window, and looks out
at the sea; then, resting his head on his arms, he breaks down
completely.* ROSE *looks at him for a moment and then slams
down the lid of the trunk she has been packing and walks into
the bedroom, her heels clattering sharply on the bare floor. In a
moment or two her footsteps are heard again, but this time it is*
MELANIE *who comes out of the bedroom. She clatters in with the
same tread as* ROSE. *She is dressed for travelling and carries a
paper bag of humbugs in her hand. She looks at* PAUL *in inde-
cision for a second, then she marches across the room and slams
down the lid of another trunk. He does not look round. She
goes to another box and slams down the lid of that. Still he pays
no attention. Finally, when she has slammed the lids of all the
boxes, she goes quietly up to him and sinks onto the floor be-*

[374]

hind him. She takes his hand, which is hanging down by his side, and very tenderly kisses it. He turns slowly, and she proffers him the paper bag.

MELANIE: Mon cher amour—would you like a 'oomboog?

CURTAIN

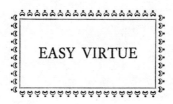

EASY VIRTUE

DRAMATIS PERSONÆ

COLONEL WHITTAKER

MRS. WHITTAKER

JOHN, their son.

MARION, their eldest daughter.

HILDA, their youngest daughter.

SARAH HURST

CHARLES BURLEIGH

PHILIP BORDON

FURBER

MR. HARRIS

NINA VANSITTART

THE HON. HUGH PETWORTH

BOBBY COLEMAN

LUCY COLEMAN

HENRY FURLEY

MARY BANFIELD

MRS. HURST

MRS. PHILLIPS

LARITA WHITTAKER

The action of the play takes place in the hall of COLONEL WHITTAKER'S *house in the country.*

ACT I

The WHITTAKERS' *house is typical of wealthy upper-middleclass England. The furniture is good and the chintz obvious, but somehow right for the atmosphere. There are three French windows down the right-hand wall. A flight of stairs up L., with the lobby leading to the front door. Down L. double doors open into the dining-room. A big bureau where* MRS WHITTAKER *does her accounts, etc., occupies a space between two of the windows. There is a comfortable sofa set in the center, with a table behind it, on which are books and papers and flowers of some sort. A statuette of Venus de Milo on small pedestal L.*

When curtain rises, it is a morning in early April. The hall looks quite gay with spring flowers, but rain can be seen beating against the windows.

MRS. WHITTAKER, *attired in a tweed skirt, shirt-blouse, and a purple knitted sports-coat, is seated at her bureau. She is the type of woman who has the reputation of having been "quite lovely" as a girl. The stern repression of any sex emotions all her life has brought her to middle age with a faulty digestion which doesn't so much sour her temper as spread it. She views the world with the jaundiced eyes of a woman who subconsciously realizes she has missed something, which means in point of fact that she has missed everything.*

MARION *is seated on the sofa, reading her letters. She is largely made and pasty, with big lymphatic eyes. In fifteen years' time she will have the reputation of having been "quite lovely as a girl." Her clothes are slightly mannish.*

COLONEL WHITTAKER *is reading "The Times." He is a grayhaired man of about fifty—his expression is generally resigned.*

[*381*]

MRS. WHITTAKER: I've written a strong letter to Mrs. Phillips.

MARION: What have you said?

MRS. WHITTAKER: Listen. [*She reads.*] "Dear Mrs. Phillips—I feel it my duty to write to you with regard to the advisability of sending the unfortunate Rose Jenkins to London. As you know, she was in my service for a year, and I was quite convinced when I discharged her that a girl of her character could ultimately come to no good. I was therefore extremely surprised when I heard that you had engaged her. As you have appealed to me for advice in the matter, I suggest that you should get rid of her at once, as her presence in the village might quite conceivably corrupt the morals of the other girls. I will endeavor to use my influence with Mrs. Faddle, who, as you know, is a prominent member of the Y. W. C. A., and perhaps later on a respectable berth of some sort may be obtained for her. I sadly fear, however, that our efforts on her behalf will be useless, as recent unpleasant events prove that the wretched girl is entirely devoid of any moral responsibility.

Sincerely yours,
Mabel Whittaker."

MARION: I must go and see Rose Jenkins and have a talk to her.

MRS. WHITTAKER: I'm afraid you wouldn't do any good.

MARION: You never know. A straight-from-the-shoulder chat might make her see things in a better light.

COLONEL: Why not leave the poor girl alone?

MARION: Because, father, if there's any chance of helping some one to see the truth, I consider it shirking to disregard the opportunity.

MRS. WHITTAKER: It's no use arguing with your father, Marion —he doesn't understand.

COLONEL: No, I don't. What is the truth?

MRS. WHITTAKER: The truth is, Jim—that Rose Jenkins, by her immoral behavior, has caused unpleasantness in the village, and therefore must suffer accordingly.

COLONEL: It's her own village—she was born here.

MRS. WHITTAKER: That's not the point.

COLONEL: Yes, it is—it's for her parents to decide what's to be done with her.

MARION: Mother's right, you know, father. It's better for her to be sent to London.

COLONEL: I'm glad you think so.

MRS. WHITTAKER: I wish you wouldn't be so tiresome, Jim dear. I'm sure I've enough worries and responsibilities without——

COLONEL: I fail to see that the Rose Jenkins business is any affair of yours—she isn't in your service any more.

MRS. WHITTAKER: I think we won't discuss it any further.

COLONEL: Very well, dear.

MRS. WHITTAKER: Do you think that letter's all right, Marion?

MARION: Perfectly. You've put it very clearly.

MRS. WHITTAKER: Mrs. Phillips is so hopelessly lacking in stamina. [*She puts letter in envelope and sticks it down.*]

COLONEL: I'm going down to see Jackson for a minute.

MRS. WHITTAKER: You'd better tell him what we decided about that bed in front of the sundial.

COLONEL: All right. I suppose Hilda took the dogs with her to the post office, didn't she?

MRS. WHITTAKER: I expect so—you'll probably meet her.

COLONEL WHITTAKER *goes out.*

MARION: Poor old father.

MRS. WHITTAKER: He's so fearfully annoying about things.

MARION: Edgar's exactly the same. Men never will see.

MRS. WHITTAKER: When is Edgar coming back?

MARION: I don't know—I had a long letter from him this morning. It will mean another four or five months out there, I'm afraid.

MRS. WHITTAKER: Do you think he's really behaving himself?

MARION: I had a straight talk with him the day before he sailed—I think I made him realize things a bit better.

[*383*]

MRS. WHITTAKER: Who would have imagined he'd turn out like that?

MARION: Oh, Edgar's all right—it's his upbringing. We'll always be pals—he's not really a marrying man, you know. I think I realized that all along, and now I've found other things in life to occupy my mind, thank God!

MRS. WHITTAKER: It couldn't have been John's upbringing altogether—could it?

MARION: John's different—he's exactly like father.

MRS. WHITTAKER: Yes, I'm afraid he is.

MARION: He was always weak, you know.

MRS. WHITTAKER: I've tried to shut my eyes to it.

MARION: It's no use doing that, mother—everything must be faced.

MRS. WHITTAKER: I lie awake at nights, wondering what's going to happen eventually.

MARION: You mustn't worry.

MRS. WHITTAKER: Worry! It's on my mind always—naturally I've got over the first shock, to a large extent.

MARION: She may not be so bad, after all.

MRS. WHITTAKER [*bitterly*]: It's the greatest catastrophe that ever happened—your father's affairs were nothing to this—nothing.

MARION: Have you heard from John lately?

MRS. WHITTAKER: Not since that postcard two weeks ago.

MARION: He's bound to bring her home soon.

MRS. WHITTAKER: He's taken good care to explain nothing about her in his letters. If he hadn't been apprehensive of what we should think of her, he would have brought her home at once, instead of waiting three months.

MARION: He did say she was ill.

MRS. WHITTAKER: Ill! Yes, I expect she was.

MARION: I'm glad I shall be here, anyhow.

MRS. WHITTAKER: So am I. I wouldn't have faced it alone—and

[*384*]

Jim's no help; he never has been, especially over anything of this sort.

MARION: Is Sarah coming to-day?

MRS. WHITTAKER: Yes; she's bringing a man over to lunch—they've got a houseful of people.

MARION: I suppose she was broken-hearted when she heard?

MRS. WHITTAKER: She was splendid; she wrote me the sweetest letter—saying that John's happiness was the thing to be considered before anything else, and that she was sure it would all turn out wonderfully.

MARION: That was to comfort you.

MRS. WHITTAKER: Yes.

Enter HILDA. *She possesses all the vivacity of a deficient sense of humor. She is nineteen, and completely commonplace.*

HILDA: Here's a wire, mother—they gave it to me at the post office.

MRS. WHITTAKER [*startled*]: A wire?

HILDA [*giving it to her*]: They were going to send the boy with it, but I said, "Oh no, don't do that, because I'm just going straight through the village and round."

MRS. WHITTAKER *reads it and closes her eyes.*

MARION: What is it? What's the matter? . . . John?

MRS. WHITTAKER [*nodding*]: Yes. [*She gives it to her.*]

HILDA: Let me see—let me see. [*She cranes over* MARION'S *shoulder.*] To-day—this morning—they're arriving this morning!

MARION [*handing the wire back*]: How typical of him.

MRS. WHITTAKER [*bowing her head*]: This is terrible.

MARION: When was it handed in?

HILDA [*snatching the wire from* MRS. WHITTAKER]: Ten-five. They must have sent it just as they were starting.

MRS. WHITTAKER: Ring the bell, Hilda.

HILDA [*jumping up and doing so*]: It's terrifically exciting.

MARION: Why on earth didn't he let you know before? He must be mad! Nothing's ready, or anything.

[385]

MRS. WHITTAKER: I've long ago given up expecting any consideration at Johnnie's hands.

MARION: Are you going to stick to your original plan about the schoolroom?

MRS. WHITTAKER: Yes.—Don't drum your heels, Hilda.

HILDA: I'm thrilled!

Enter FURBER.

MRS. WHITTAKER: Furber, Mr. John is arriving with his wife almost immediately. Will you see that fires are lit in the schoolroom and dressing-room?

FURBER: Yes, ma'am.

MRS. WHITTAKER: If by any chance they're late, we'll wait lunch.

FURBER: Very good, ma'am. [*He goes out.*]

MARION: Sarah! What about Sarah?

MRS. WHITTAKER: What shall we do? Put her off?

MARION: She's bound to meet her sooner or later——

MRS. WHITTAKER: Yes, but we don't know yet—what she's like.

MARION: Sarah doesn't matter—it might be a good thing for her to be here—in one way.

MRS. WHITTAKER: Go and find your father, Hilda.

HILDA: Where is he?

MRS WHITTAKER: With Jackson, I think. Also tell Jackson to send in some flowers at once.

HILDA: All right—lovely! I'll arrange them. [*She rushes off girlishly.*]

MRS. WHITTAKER [*putting out her hand*]: Marion—I shall need your help—badly.

MARION [*patting her*]: Cheer up, mother.

MRS. WHITTAKER: I feel so unequal to it all to-day—I didn't sleep a wink last night, and I woke with a racking headache.

MARION: Shall I get you some aspirin?

MRS. WHITTAKER: No; it wouldn't do me any good—the blow's fallen, you see—the blow's fallen.

MARION: Don't, mother!

[*386*]

MRS. WHITTAKER: I feel as though I were going mad. John—my John—married to this—this—woman! It's unthinkable.

MARION: She may be a good sort.

MRS. WHITTAKER: It's no good bolstering ourselves up—I know in my heart—— [*She cries a little.*]

MARION [*embracing her dutifully*]: It will all come right in the end, mother, if only you have enough faith.

MRS. WHITTAKER: Faith! All my life I've had to battle and struggle against this sort of thing. First your father—and now John—my only son. It's breaking my heart.

MARION: We must just put our trust in Divine Providence, dear. I'll have a straight talk to John. If she really is—well, quite hopeless—something must be done.

MRS. WHITTAKER: Nothing can be done—I tell you I know—she's got him, and she'll stick to him.

MARION: If she's the sort of woman we imagine, she's probably realized her mistake already.

MRS. WHITTAKER: Why should she have married him? Except for what she can get out of him—money and position. He's been made a fool of, just as your father was made a fool of—hundreds of times. We know she's older than John—I don't suppose there was any love, as far as she was concerned; she's just twisted him around her little finger.

MARION: It's no use upsetting yourself *now*—you must pull yourself together and face it bravely.

MRS. WHITTAKER: I thought he would at least have had the decency to give me fair warning.

MARION: I expect they came over from France yesterday.

Enter HILDA *and* COLONEL WHITTAKER.

HILDA: I've told father the news.

COLONEL: I suppose they're motoring down.

MARION: Yes.

HILDA: It was luck me going to the post office like that, wasn't it? I nearly as anything didn't go out at all this morning —what with the rain and everything.

[*387*]

COLONEL: Are their rooms ready?

MRS. WHITTAKER: I've told Furber to have fires lighted.

HILDA: It's too exciting for words—wondering what she'll be like.

MRS. WHITTAKER [*bitterly*]: I wish I could share your feelings.

HILDA: And it's so romantic—the old schoolroom being turned into a boudoir for John's wife.

MRS. WHITTAKER: Sitting-room, not boudoir.

HILDA: Sitting-room, then. Do you think she'll be dark or fair?

MRS. WHITTAKER: I don't know.

MARION: Do be quiet, Hilda.

HILDA: I think fair and larky!

MRS. WHITTAKER: I see no reason to suppose anything of the sort.

HILDA: But guessing at people is such fun—Jackie Coryton and I do it lots—she's awfully good at it. What do *you* think she'll be like, Marion?

MARION: Stop asking absurd questions.

HILDA: I'm dying to see. I wonder if she drinks.

MRS. WHITTAKER [*sharply*]: Hilda!

HILDA: Well, you never know—living abroad like that.

MARION: Can't you see mother's upset and doesn't want to be worried?

COLONEL: I fail to see the object of working yourself up into a state before you've set eyes on her.

MRS. WHITTAKER: You wouldn't see, Jim, because you don't care—you never have cared. As long as you're comfortable you don't mind if your son goes to the dogs.

COLONEL: He had to marry somebody—she's probably a very interesting woman.

MRS. WHITTAKER: I've no doubt you'll find her so.

HILDA: She may be frightfully sweet.

MRS. WHITTAKER: When you've reached my age, Hilda, you'll

[*388*]

probably realize that the sort of women who infest French watering-places are generally far from being "frightfully sweet."

HILDA: Cannes isn't exactly a French watering-place—I mean it's better than that—I mean everyone goes there.

COLONEL: Everything's changing nowadays, anyhow.

MRS. WHITTAKER: I fail to see that that makes the slightest difference.

MARION: Father means that social barriers are not quite so strongly marked now, and perhaps, after all——

MRS. WHITTAKER: I know quite well what your father means.

HILDA: But everybody's accepted so much more—I mean nobody minds so much about people—I mean——

MRS. WHITTAKER: You don't know what you mean—you don't know anything about it.

HILDA: But, mother——

MRS. WHITTAKER: Your attitude towards the whole affair is ridiculous, Hilda, and I'm surprised at you. [*She sniffs.*]

HILDA: Oh, mother, don't cry—it will only make your eyes all red——

FURBER *enters with a tray on which there are some vases, a jug of water and some flowers.*

FURBER: Jackson sent these in just after breakfast, ma'am.

HILDA: These will be enough, mother. I'll arrange them.

MRS. WHITTAKER: Tell Jackson not to pick any more.

FURBER: Very good, ma'am. [*He goes out.*]

HILDA *pounces on the flowers with girlish enthusiasm.*

HILDA: Aren't they lovely?—I expect she's used to orchids and things. These are so fresh—they'll be a gorgeous surprise.

MARION: We ought to warn Sarah—it might be a shock for her.

MRS. WHITTAKER: Yes—you'd better telephone.

MARION: I'll just say that we should like her to come, but if she feels that she'd rather not, we quite understand.

MRS. WHITTAKER: Don't splash that water all over the table, Hilda.

[*389*]

MARION: What's the number?

MRS. WHITTAKER: 60.

MARION [*at telephone*]: Hullo—60, please.

HILDA [*conversationally*]: I saw Mrs. Phillips coming out of Smith's.

MRS. WHITTAKER [*tidying up the papers on bureau*]: Did you?

HILDA: She went over to talk to Mrs. Jenkins. Rose was peeling potatoes in the porch.

MARION: Hullo!—is that you, Sarah? It's Marion. Listen, old girl; prepare yourself for a shock. John's coming home with Larita, or whatever her name is, this morning.—Oh, I thought it would be rather. . . . I'm glad you feel like that, anyhow. We wanted to know if you'd come over to lunch just the same. . . . Yes, of course, bring him. . . . All right. Good-by, old thing. [*She hangs up receiver.*] That's that.

MRS. WHITTAKER: Have you seen my glasses anywhere?

MARION: Aren't they on the desk?

MRS. WHITTAKER: They must have slipped down behind——

HILDA: Did Sarah seem upset?

MARION: She laughed.

MRS. WHITTAKER [*shocked*]: Laughed!

MARION: I think she's pretending—even to herself—that she doesn't mind.

MRS. WHITTAKER: If only everything had been different—it might have been Sarah he was bringing home.

HILDA: It wouldn't have been half so exciting.

MARION: I wish to Heaven it were. She's a damned good sort, that girl.

HILDA: What's the man's name who's coming over with her?

MARION: Charles Burleigh.

HILDA: I'm dying for lunch—it's going to be too thrilling for words.

MARION [*finding glasses*]: Here are your blinkers, mother.

MRS. WHITTAKER [*forcing a wan smile at* MARION's *ebullient phraseology*]: Thank you, Marion.

[*390*]

COLONEL: I wonder how John's looking.

MRS. WHITTAKER [*jumping*]: What a fright you gave me, Jim. I'd forgotten you were here.

COLONEL: The return of the Prodigal is always such a momentous occasion, isn't it?

MRS. WHITTAKER: I wish you wouldn't talk like that—it's not amusing.

COLONEL: I'm sorry. I thought perhaps a little light irony might alleviate the prevailing gloom.

MRS. WHITTAKER: If you think constant reminders of your callousness over the whole affair——

COLONEL: I'm not callous, Mabel; I'm just waiting with a more or less open mind.

MRS. WHITTAKER [*bitingly*]: Open mind!

HILDA: There—those look sweet, don't they? I'll take them up.

MRS. WHITTAKER: Take the tray into the kitchen first.

HILDA: All right. [*She rushes off with the tray.*]

MARION: What's the time?

COLONEL: A quarter past twelve—if I may be so bold.

MARION: They might be here at any minute now.

MRS. WHITTAKER: I'm going upstairs to look at the schoolroom. Tell Hilda to bring that other vase—I'll take these. [*She goes upstairs.*]

COLONEL [*lighting his pipe*]: I'm glad your mother's getting cross. I prefer irritability to hysteria.

MARION: I don't think you're being very decent to mother, father.

COLONEL: You know, Marion, you're the only thoroughly Christian woman I've ever known who has retained her schoolgirl phraseology.

Re-enter HILDA, *breathlessly.*

HILDA: Where's mother?

MARION: She's gone up to the schoolroom with the flowers. Will you take that other vase up?

[*391*]

HILDA: All right. Don't you feel *terrifically* excited, father?

COLONEL: Terrifically.

HILDA *runs joyously upstairs with the vase.*

MARION: Hilda's irrepressible.

COLONEL: How is Edgar?

MARION: He's all right. Why do you ask—suddenly like that?

COLONEL: I have such a friendly feeling for him since you broke off your engagement.

MARION: Do you imagine I don't see when you're sarcastic and bitter, father? It's been growing lately. You're always saying unkind things.

COLONEL: Am I?

MARION: You must be very unhappy.

COLONEL: Perhaps that accounts for it.

MARION: Then you are?

COLONEL: Do you want to have a straight talk to me, Marion?

MARION: I suppose you despise me for trying to help other people?

COLONEL: You and your mother are always trying to help lame dogs over stiles—even if they're not lame and don't want to go.

MARION: You don't appreciate mother.

COLONEL: I appreciate you both enormously.

MARION: Mother's played fair all her life, anyhow.

COLONEL: And I haven't. I quite see that.

MARION: I'm glad you admit it.

COLONEL: I'm surprised that you're glad—it generally annoys people to be agreed with.

MARION: Don't you ever think of other things, father?

COLONEL: What sort of other things?

MARION: You know quite well what I mean.

COLONEL: Don't try to save my soul, Marion. I can defend myself.

MARION: I don't mind your taunts a bit.

COLONEL: Good!

MARION: But mother does.

COLONEL: My dear girl, your mother stood by me through my various lapses from grace with splendid fortitude.

MARION: You realize that?

COLONEL: I realize the fact but distrust the motive.

MARION: What motives could she possibly have had other than loyalty and affection?

COLONEL: I don't believe you know.

MARION: I certainly don't.

COLONEL: Well, I won't disillusion you.

MARION: Father——

COLONEL [*politely*]: Yes?

MARION: She needs your help and support now—badly.

COLONEL: Why?

MARION: You can seriously stand there and ask why?

COLONEL: She has built up in her mind a black-hearted monster of a woman who has enslaved her babe, and she expects me to combine in a superhuman effort to oust her.

MARION: Nothing of the sort, father.

COLONEL: As I said before, I'm waiting with an open mind—and whatever John's wife is or has been, I shall do my utmost to make her happy and comfortable here.

Re-enter MRS. WHITTAKER *and* HILDA.

HILDA: The car's coming up the drive—I saw it from the landing window.

MARION: Now for it!

MRS. WHITTAKER [*appealingly*]: Jim.

COLONEL [*amiably*]: Yes, dear?

MRS. WHITTAKER: Nothing—it doesn't matter.

HILDA: Oh, I wonder what she'll be like—I wonder——

COLONEL: We shall soon see.

They wait in silence. Then JOHN *bursts in. He is young, good-looking, with great charm; his eagerness is perhaps a shade over-done.*

JOHN: Mother! [*He kisses her.*]

MRS. WHITTAKER: But, John, where——

JOHN: She's still in the car—powdering her nose. She said she wanted me to get the first joys of reunion over. Father! [*He shakes hands with the* COLONEL.]

COLONEL: I'm glad you're back, John.

JOHN: I do so hope you'll like her. [*He kisses* MARION *and* HILDA.]

HILDA: I know I shall.

JOHN: I feel terrified. It will be so wonderful if you do like her, and so awful if you don't.

MRS. WHITTAKER: It's a little late to think of that now.

JOHN [*his face falling*]: Mother!

LARITA *comes in. She is tall, exquisitely made-up and very beautiful—above everything, she is perfectly calm. Her clothes, because of their simplicity, are obviously violently expensive; she wears a perfect rope of pearls and a small close traveling-hat.*

MRS. WHITTAKER: How-do-you-do.

LARITA [*taking both her hands*]: How-do-you-do seems so hopelessly inadequate, doesn't it, at a moment like this? But perhaps it's good to use it as a refuge for our real feelings.

MRS. WHITTAKER [*coldly*]: Did you have a nice crossing yesterday?

LARITA [*sensing her attitude and smiling emptily*]: Perfectly horrible.

MRS. WHITTAKER: I'm so sorry. This is my eldest daughter, Marion,—and Hilda. No doubt you've heard John speak of them.

LARITA [*shaking hands with* MARION]: But of course I have—hundreds of times. [*She kisses* HILDA.] You're like Johnnie, you know. [*The family wince at the diminutive.*]

MRS. WHITTAKER: And this is my husband.

LARITA [*shaking hands with the* COLONEL]: You looked dazed —I suppose I'm very unlike what you expected—or perhaps not?

COLONEL: I'm delighted to welcome you home.

LARITA [*gratefully*]: Oh, thank you.

HILDA [*excitedly*]: You're not a bit like what *I* expected.

LARITA: I'm very much older, probably. [*She looks at* MRS. WHITTAKER.] I'm awfully sorry about that.

JOHN: Don't be silly, Lari.

LARITA: There *have* been a good many happy marriages even though——

JOHN: It doesn't matter how many there have or haven't been, as long as ours is.

LARITA: That's right, Johnnie darling.

MRS. WHITTAKER: You must be tired after your journey. Perhaps you'd like to go upstairs.

HILDA [*eagerly*]: We've turned the old schoolroom into a boudoir for you.

LARITA: How divine! It will be full of memories of Johnnie as a grubby little boy.

COLONEL: I'm sure you'd rather smoke one cigarette and get to know us all a little better first. [*He offers her his case.*]

LARITA [*smiling*]: You're right—I should. Do you mind if I smoke one of my own? I have a special kind. Try one. [*She produces a beautiful case.*]

COLONEL [*taking one*]: Thanks.

LARITA [*looking round*]: Would anyone else like one?

MRS. WHITTAKER: No, thank you.

LARITA [*sitting down*]: You know, it's such a relief being here at last. I've been wondering so frightfully what it was going to be like——

The COLONEL *lights her cigarette.*

MRS. WHITTAKER: I'm so sorry it's such bad weather.

LARITA: The house looked fascinating from outside—I'm longing to go all over it.

JOHN: I'll take you after lunch.

LARITA: I want Mrs. Whittaker to show it to me.

JOHN: Oh, Lari darling, not Mrs. Whittaker. It's mother now.

LARITA: Not quite yet, Johnnie—I don't think.

[395]

MARION: Did you get down without any mishaps?

LARITA: Yes, it was a perfect run.

HILDA: Have you ever been in England before?

LARITA: Oh yes, several times. I used to come here a lot with my first husband.

MRS. WHITTAKER: Your first husband?

LARITA: Yes.

MRS. WHITTAKER [*stiffening*]: I never realized you had been married before. John told us so little.

LARITA: That was awfully tiresome of you, Johnnie.

JOHN: He was a perfect brute to her, mother.

MRS. WHITTAKER: How dreadful! It must have been almost a relief when he died.

LARITA: He didn't die—he divorced me.

MARION [*horror-struck*]: Divorced you!

LARITA: Yes, I ran away. I was very young and silly—I should have waited, shouldn't I? and borne it stoically. It would have been braver.

JOHN: I don't see that at all. He was an absolute devil.

HILDA: I think it's the most thrilling thing I've ever heard!

LARITA: It does sound picturesque now.

MRS. WHITTAKER: I suppose you went back to your parents?

LARITA: No—I couldn't go as far as that. They were both dead.

COLONEL [*kindly*]: It's awfully nice of you to tell us this.

LARITA: Johnnie ought to have explained it all, really—it would have cleared the way.

JOHN: You can't write things like that in letters.

MRS. WHITTAKER: No, I suppose not.

LARITA [*to* MRS. WHITTAKER]: You must have been very anxious and surprised and worried. We should have come home at once, only I stupidly got ill—pleurisy, you know. I've had it before —perfectly infuriating.

MARION: Beastly thing, pleurisy.

LARITA: But Johnnie was absolutely wonderful to me, and here we are at last. Can your butler speak French?

MRS. WHITTAKER: I beg your pardon?

LARITA: I say, can your butler speak French? You see, my maid—— Do go and rescue Louise, Johnnie; she's probably having a bad time.

JOHN: All right. Take Lari up, mother. [*He goes off.*]

HILDA: No, let me—do let me.

LARITA: I should love you to.

MRS. WHITTAKER: I hope you'll find everything quite comfortable.

LARITA: I'm sure I shall. Come along, Hilda. [*She takes her hand.*]

HILDA: I've put some flowers up there, but the rooms aren't very warm yet, I'm afraid. You see, the fires have only just been lighted.

MRS. WHITTAKER: I think perhaps I'd better come.

LARITA: No, please don't trouble. Hilda will look after me perfectly all right—won't you, Hilda?

HILDA [*eagerly*]: Rather. Do let me, mother.

MRS. WHITTAKER: Very well. Lunch will be ready quite soon.

LARITA [*as she goes upstairs with* HILDA]: Lovely. I'm ravenous. I was too excited to eat any breakfast. [*They go off. There is silence for a moment.*]

MARION: She seems a good sort—I like her.

MRS. WHITTAKER: Do you, Marion?

MARION: Don't you?

MRS. WHITTAKER: She's exactly what I expected—in every detail. [*She turns away.*]

COLONEL: Surely not in *every* detail? She wasn't drunk——

MRS. WHITTAKER: Jim, please!

MARION: Father—how can you say things like that?

COLONEL: Larita's an extraordinarily pretty name.

MRS. WHITTAKER: Excellent for musical comedy. [*She turns her back and goes over to the window.*]

JOHN *enters, and sees that* LARITA *has gone.*

JOHN [*eagerly*]: Well?

COLONEL: I congratulate you, John.

JOHN [*shaking his hand violently*]: Oh, father, thank you—I—*am* glad!

MARION: I hope you managed the French maid all right?

JOHN: Oh yes. I'm used to her. Mother—— [*He goes to her.*]

MRS. WHITTAKER [*turning and kissing him without warmth*]: Well, John, I hope you'll be very happy.

JOHN: I am, mother—frightfully.

MRS. WHITTAKER: She's very beautiful.

JOHN: Do you think so, honestly?

MRS. WHITTAKER: Yes, of course.

JOHN: And you've no idea what a darling she is. All the time she was ill she was splendid—so brave and everything.

MARION: Is she a Catholic?

JOHN [*nonplused*]: I say—I'm afraid I don't know. You see, we weren't married in church.

MARION: Oh!

JOHN [*pulling himself together*]: What a fool I am! She's a Catholic, of course; I remember now.

MRS. WHITTAKER: Sarah's coming over to lunch.

JOHN: Is she? How ripping. I've been longing to see her again. I want her to meet Lari, too.

MRS. WHITTAKER: The Hursts have been entertaining a lot this winter. Sarah's been very much in demand. They gave a most successful dance in London.

JOHN: Good old Sarah!

MRS. WHITTAKER: If you've got any aspirin in your room, Marion dear, I should like some. My headache's rather bad.

MARION: All right. Will you come up, or shall I fetch it?

MRS. WHITTAKER: I'll come up.

JOHN: I'm so sorry, mother. I suppose I ought to have let you know before that we were coming.

MRS. WHITTAKER: It doesn't matter.

JOHN: I did so want it to be a surprise.

MRS. WHITTAKER: I hope you'll see that your—Larita has everything she wants, John.

JOHN: Rather! Thanks, mother,—of course I will.

MRS. WHITTAKER: That's right. [*She goes upstairs with* MARION.]

JOHN: I suppose mother's upset, isn't she?

COLONEL: A little, I think.

JOHN: You think she'll get over it, though, don't you?

COLONEL: I expect so. Don't worry.

JOHN: It must have been an awful shock for her—for you both.

COLONEL: My dear boy, this sort of thing's always a shock—it's unavoidable.

JOHN: You like Lari, though, don't you, father?

COLONEL: She seems charming.

JOHN: Oh, she is—she's more than that—she's wonderful.

COLONEL: She's older than I thought.

JOHN: Yes, but that doesn't matter really, does it?—I mean if people really care for one another.

COLONEL: I don't know. It might—later on.

JOHN [*haltingly*]: You mean—children?

COLONEL: Not altogether.

JOHN: I don't suppose we shall have any children.

COLONEL: No—I don't suppose you will.

JOHN: But Marion's married, and Hilda will be soon.

COLONEL [*gently*]: That's not quite the same thing, is it?

JOHN: Are you cut up about it?

COLONEL: What's the use of being cut up, John? When a thing's done, you've got to stand by it.

JOHN: Father—I do love her terribly; she's my life's happiness.

COLONEL: That's all right, then. Run up and look after her—she's probably feeling a little shattered.

JOHN: All right. Thanks, father. [*He goes upstairs, two at a time.*]

The COLONEL *sighs, takes "The Times" and goes off into the library.*

FURBER *enters, followed by* SARAH HURST *and* CHARLES BUR-

LEIGH. SARAH *is boyish and modern and attractive.* CHARLES BUR-
LEIGH *is a pleasant-looking man somewhere between thirty and
forty.*

SARAH: Where's everybody, Furber?

FURBER: I don't know, miss. Mr. and Mrs. John have just arrived. They're probably all upstairs. I'll tell them you're here.

SARAH: No, don't do that—we'll wait.

FURBER: Very good, miss.

SARAH: How's your neuritis, Furber?

FURBER: It's been rather bad, miss.

SARAH: I meant to bring you over that stuff, but I forgot. I'll
send it to-night.

FURBER: Thank you very much, miss. [*He goes out.*]

CHARLES: I suppose this is a slightly momentous day in the
lives of the Whittakers.

SARAH: Very momentous.

CHARLES: Is your heart wrung with emotion?

SARAH [*lightly*]: Don't be a beast, Charles.

CHARLES: I think it's spirited of you to come.

SARAH: I want to see her.

CHARLES: I feel secretly embarrassed—as though I oughtn't
to be here at all.

SARAH: Nonsense—you're moral backing for me.

CHARLES: Thank you, Sarah,—it's an attractive rôle.

SARAH: I wasn't really officially engaged to John—it was just a
sort of understood thing.

CHARLES: I see.

SARAH: And I've had a nice three months to get over being upset about it.

CHARLES: And you have?

SARAH: Entirely.

CHARLES: Well, that's a comfort, isn't it?

SARAH: A great comfort.

CHARLES: Shall we be discovered intimately looking over the
Tatler together?

SARAH: No—that would be overdoing it.

CHARLES: Perhaps it would.

SARAH: I'm extremely hungry.

CHARLES: That's a healthy sign.

SARAH: Whatever she's like, you must be awfully nice, and pay a lot of attention to her.

CHARLES: Certainly.

SARAH: I think I'm going to get the giggles.

CHARLES: For Heaven's sake, don't.

SARAH: It is funny, you know.

CHARLES [*gloomily*]: Excruciatingly.

SARAH: You'll realize just *how* funny it is when you see Mrs. Whittaker.

CHARLES: I shall try to control myself.

SARAH: And Marion.—Oh, dear Marion!

CHARLES: Shut up, Sarah—you're unnerving me.

SARAH: I can't help it. [*She giggles hopelessly.*]

CHARLES: Pull yourself together. Some one's coming.

HILDA *rushes downstairs.*

HILDA: Sarah!

SARAH: Hullo!

HILDA [*breathlessly*]: Oh, Sarah, she's too beautiful for words!

SARAH: No, really.

HILDA: And the most heavenly clothes.

SARAH: This is Mr. Burleigh—Hilda Whittaker.

HILDA [*shaking hands*]: How-do-you-do. We're all fearfully excited, you know—John's new wife's just arrived.

CHARLES: Yes; Sarah told me.

HILDA: She's got a scream of a French maid—I nearly died!

SARAH: How's Mrs. Whittaker?

HILDA: She's got a headache. John's talking to her in her room. I've got to dash down to the garage to give a message to the chauffeur—he's a new man. Come with me. [*She proceeds to drag her hand.*]

SARAH: I can't leave poor Charles all alone.

HILDA [*persistently*]: You must—it's only for a minute. I've got such lots to tell you.

SARAH: All right. Do you mind, Charles?

CHARLES: Very much.

HILDA: She shan't be long—honestly. I haven't seen Sarah for ages, and I shan't get another opportunity of talking to her.

SARAH [*laughing*]: Charles is such a timid man, it'll do him good. Come on.

CHARLES: Here, I say—Sarah——

SARAH: We shan't be *very* long! [*She goes off with* HILDA.]

CHARLES [*alone*]: Oh, God!

He wanders about the hall, then finally sits down on the sofa with the "Tatler."

LARITA *comes downstairs, having taken off her hat and generally reinstated herself.*

CHARLES *rises to his feet.*

LARITA: Oh, how-do-you-do.

CHARLES [*shaking hands*]: How-do-you-do.

LARITA: Are you lunching here?

CHARLES: Yes; I came over with Sarah Hurst. I'm staying with them—a few miles away.

LARITA: I've heard Johnnie speak of them.

CHARLES: You've only just arrived, haven't you?

LARITA: Yes, this morning. We came over from Paris yesterday.

There is a slight pause.

CHARLES: It's always rather an anti-climax, isn't it?—arriving anywhere.

LARITA: Why? Do I look bored?

CHARLES: Not at all.

LARITA: I know what you mean, though; one feels sort of dead.

CHARLES: It's only temporary.

LARITA: Oh yes—I hope so.

CHARLES: Do you know if anyone else is lunching?

LARITA: Only you and Miss Hurst, I believe—outside of the family.

[*402*]

CHARLES: Good!

LARITA: Why do you say "Good" so emphatically?

CHARLES: It must be bad enough for you to have to meet a bunch of brand-new relations—let alone total strangers. I feel quite an interloper.

LARITA: Please don't. I don't mind meeting new people a bit—on the contrary, it's rather a comfort, in a way—it eases things a little.

CHARLES [*offering case*]: Will you smoke?

LARITA: I'll smoke one of my own, if you don't mind. I get a bad throat if I change. I smoke far too much. [*She takes a cigarette out of her case.*]

CHARLES [*lighting hers and his own*]: That's an enchanting case.

LARITA: It *is* a darling.

CHARLES: Cartier?

LARITA: No; Lacloche. I've had it for years.

CHARLES: Were you in Paris long?

LARITA: Only a week. I had to get some new clothes and fortify myself.

CHARLES: Naturally.

LARITA: Where is everybody?

CHARLES: I don't know.

LARITA: They're discussing their first impressions of me, I expect. It must be horrid for them.

CHARLES: I don't see why.

LARITA [*smiling*]: You do—perfectly well.

CHARLES: I suppose it's always rather a shock for people when their sons marry.

LARITA: Do you know Johnnie?

CHARLES: No.

LARITA: He's an angel.

CHARLES: I don't know any of them—I'm more of a stranger than you.

LARITA: I'm so glad. It gives us a sort of bond in common, doesn't it?

CHARLES: Yes.

LARITA: Tell me about Sarah Hurst.

CHARLES: How shall I begin?

LARITA: Don't look apprehensive. I know about her and Johnnie—when they were young, and everything.

CHARLES: She's a charming girl—unaffected.

LARITA: Thank God for that.

CHARLES: Not very emotional—and quite a sense of humor.

LARITA: I'm looking forward to seeing her.

CHARLES: Are you?

LARITA: No.

CHARLES [*laughing outright*]: I quite understand.

LARITA: I know you do. Is she pretty?

CHARLES: Not exactly. More attractive than pretty.

LARITA: Dark or fair?

CHARLES: Fairish. She's rather like a young edition of a very old friend of mine. She lives in Paris. I wonder if you've met her.

LARITA: Who?

CHARLES: Cécile de Vriaac.

LARITA [*delighted*]: Cécile! Do you know Cécile?

CHARLES: I've known her for years.

LARITA: How extraordinary! What's your name?

CHARLES: Charles Burleigh.

LARITA: Of course! She has shown me snapshots of you. I knew I recognized your face, somehow. She *is* such fun, isn't she?

CHARLES: I'm devoted to her.

LARITA: And Freddy!

CHARLES: Oh, Freddy! [*They both laugh.*]

LARITA: That's all over now.

CHARLES: No?—Is it?

[*404*]

LARITA: Yes—last August, in Venice—or rather the Lido, to be accurate.

CHARLES: I don't wonder. That beach would kill any passion.

LARITA: You know Zushie Wincott, of course?

CHARLES: Rather! What's become of her?

LARITA: I tremble to think—judging by the way she was behaving in Cannes at Christmas.

CHARLES: With George, I suppose?

LARITA: No, not *with* George—*at* George.

CHARLES: Poor old Zushie! She's rather a dear, really.

LARITA: She's so utterly uncontrolled—always making scenes. I loathe scenes.

CHARLES: You first met John at Cannes, didn't you?

LARITA: Yes. He'd been Banco-ing recklessly and losing everything. I was well up on the day, so I lent him some plaques, and it changed his luck.

CHARLES: In more ways than one.

LARITA: I wonder.

CHARLES: I'm sure of it.

LARITA: It's sweet of you to say so. I'm dreadfully fond of him, you know.

CHARLES: I can see that.

LARITA: Can you? How?

CHARLES: By the way you talk of him.

LARITA: He's awfully young and—well, almost ingenuous sometimes. I think that must have been what attracted me to him at first—it was refreshing.

CHARLES [*nodding*]: Yes.

LARITA: And then we kept on meeting, you know. Cannes is a small place—and I was so tired of everybody.

CHARLES: People run dreadfully in grooves.

LARITA: Always the same faces—and the same expressions and the same motives.

CHARLES: Motives?

LARITA: You know what I mean.

CHARLES: Yes.

LARITA: It's amusing and fun for a little while, and then one begins to realize that perhaps—after all—it's a trifle cheap.

CHARLES: It's certainly astonishing how quickly one becomes disillusioned over everything.

LARITA: Everything?

CHARLES: Well, practically everything.

LARITA [*with a sigh*]: Yes, that's true.

CHARLES: Are you going to live here indefinitely?

LARITA [*slowly*]: I don't know. Through the summer, anyhow.

CHARLES: I hope you'll be very happy.

LARITA: Thank you. [*She looks out of the window.*] I wish it wasn't raining.

CHARLES: There's a ridiculous picture of Harry Leftwich in the *Tatler,* walking along the terrace at Monte Carlo with that dark woman who went to share a studio with Maud Callish in the Rue Bonaparte.

LARITA: Oh, Suzanne—do let me see—Suzanne Fellini—— [*She comes over to the sofa, and they both bend over the "Tatler."*]

CHARLES [*finding it*]: There.

LARITA: Yes, that's Suzanne—doesn't she look fierce? It's so absurd when people are photographed with their legs sticking straight out in front of them like that.

CHARLES [*laughing*]: Poor dears!

LARITA: Oh, do look at her hat. [*They both laugh a good deal.*]

MRS. WHITTAKER *comes downstairs, followed by* JOHN *and* MARION. MRS. WHITTAKER's *face freezes slightly.* CHARLES *gets up.*

MRS. WHITTAKER: How-do-you-do. You are Mr. Burleigh?

CHARLES [*calmly*]: Yes; your youngest daughter came and spirited Sarah away. I don't know where they've gone.

JOHN [*going to* LARITA]: I couldn't think where you were, Larita.

LARITA: I thought everyone was down here.

MRS. WHITTAKER [*to* LARITA]: I suppose you and Mr. Burleigh have introduced yourselves?

LARITA: Oh yes; we've discovered lots of mutual friends.

MRS. WHITTAKER: How nice. [*To* CHARLES] This is my eldest daughter.

CHARLES [*shaking hands*]: How-do-you-do.

MRS. WHITTAKER: And my son.

JOHN: How are you? [*He also shakes hands.*]

HILDA *and* SARAH *re-enter.*

SARAH [*kissing* MRS. WHITTAKER]: Hilda dragged me off to see a perfectly strange chauffeur. Have you all met Charles?

CHARLES: Yes, you're too late—it's all over.

SARAH: Hallo, John—I'm terribly pleased to see you.

JOHN [*taking her hand*]: Sarah, I want you to meet my wife, Larita. I do hope you'll be friends.

LARITA [*shaking hands*]: I hope so, too.

SARAH: Of course we shall. You're utterly different from what I imagined.

LARITA [*smiling*]: Am I really?

SARAH [*laughing*]: Yes—I pictured you fair and fluffy.

LARITA: How absurd!

FURBER *enters.*

FURBER: Lunch is served.

MRS. WHITTAKER: Let's all go in, then. Tell the Colonel, Furber.

FURBER: Yes, ma'am.

The COLONEL *enters.*

HILDA: Come on, father; lunch is ready.

SARAH *takes* LARITA's *arm and walks into the dining-room with her.* LARITA *throws a look over her shoulder at* CHARLES, *who smiles. Everyone goes in talking.* FURBER *waits, and then follows them, closing the folding doors after him.*

CURTAIN

[*407*]

ACT II

Scene: Three months have passed since Act I. It is a warm summer day—warm for England, anyhow—which means that unless you hurl yourself about on tennis-courts or indulge in some sort of strenuous exercise all the time, you get extremely cold. The sun-awning has been let down over the veranda.

LARITA *is lying on the sofa, reading "Sodom and Gomorrah," by Marcel Proust. Outside in the garden tennis noises can be heard, occasional shouts and laughter.* LARITA *throws her cigarette-end out on to the veranda, but it goes on the carpet, so she has to get up and throw it again, which she does with a slight display of temper. She lights herself another and lies down again; then discovers that Marcel Proust has eluded her and is reclining carelessly on the bureau. With an expression of resigned fury she gets up again and fetches it. When she is once more ensconced on the sofa.* MRS. WHITTAKER *enters.*

MRS. WHITTAKER: Why don't you go and watch the tennis, Larita?

LARITA: The excitement's so intense, my nerves won't stand it.

MRS. WHITTAKER [*at window*]: I wish you wouldn't throw cigarette-ends on to the veranda; it looks so untidy. [*She picks it up and throws it into the garden.*]

LARITA: I'm sorry.

MRS. WHITTAKER: Fancy lying indoors on a lovely day like this.

LARITA: It's very chilly outside.

MRS. WHITTAKER: Not in the sun.

LARITA: I get a headache if I sit in the sun.

MRS. WHITTAKER: I wonder you don't play tennis with the others.

[408]

LARITA: I'm so awfully bad that it annoys everybody.

MRS. WHITTAKER: You'd soon improve if you practiced.

LARITA: I don't know that the end would altogether justify the means.

MRS. WHITTAKER: Have you seen Marion?

LARITA: Not since lunch.

MRS. WHITTAKER: I wonder where she is.

LARITA: Upstairs, I think.

MRS. WHITTAKER: She had a letter from Edgar this morning.

LARITA: Did she?

MRS. WHITTAKER: He's coming home.

LARITA: How lovely.

MRS. WHITTAKER [*shooting a suspicious glance at her*]: You've never met him?

LARITA: Never. I meant it was lovely for Marion that he was coming home—not for me.

MRS. WHITTAKER: Where's Jim?

LARITA: He went out, I think.

MRS. WHITTAKER: How irritating! I wanted to talk to him particularly.

LARITA: Perhaps he didn't know.

MRS. WHITTAKER: I think we shall have to get rid of Jackson.

LARITA: What a pity! He seems such a nice man.

MRS. WHITTAKER: He's been neglecting the garden disgracefully.

LARITA: It must be awfully difficult to be a gardener.

MRS. WHITTAKER: I'm worried to death about to-night.

LARITA: I'm so sorry. Why?

MRS. WHITTAKER: If it's wet we can't have the buffet on the veranda.

LARITA: Perhaps it will be fine.

MRS. WHITTAKER: Only half the things I ordered have arrived from Fortnum's.

LARITA: Can I do anything?

MRS. WHITTAKER: No, thank you, Larita. I'm quite used to all

[*409*]

responsibilities of this sort falling on to my shoulders. The children are always utterly inconsiderate. Thank Heaven, I have a talent for organization. [*She goes out with a martyred expression.*]

LARITA, *with a sigh, once more plunges into her book.*

Enter MARION, *down stairs.*

MARION: Hallo! old thing. Why aren't you watching the tennis?

LARITA: I'm afraid of discouraging them.

MARION: Have you seen mother?

LARITA: Yes, she's just gone into the garden.

MARION: I think she's getting a bit fussed about to-night.

LARITA: She has a talent for organization.

MARION: Things are certain to turn out all right, if you don't worry about 'em.

LARITA: That must be a very comforting philosophy.

MARION: You seem a bit snappy, old girl. Has anything upset you?

LARITA [*putting down her book*]: I'm sorry—I didn't mean to be snappy. What shall we talk about?

MARION: I'm afraid I haven't time to talk now—too many things to see to. You know, only half the stuff's arrived from Fortnum's.

LARITA: Why not telephone them?

MARION: I have.

LARITA: Are they sending the rest down?

MARION: Yes.

LARITA: Well, that's all right, then, isn't it?

MARION: Have you seen father?

LARITA: He went out, I think.

MARION: Typical of him to shelve everything on to mother and me.

LARITA: Perhaps he'll come back soon bristling with ideas.

MARION: I think mother's wrong about having the buffet on the veranda—it's sure to rain. [*She goes out.*]

LARITA *lies back and closes her eyes. She is about to read again when* JOHN *rushes in from the garden, very hot.*

JOHN: Hullo! Why don't you come and watch the tennis?

LARITA: There seems to be a conspiracy among everybody to lead me on to that very exposed tennis-court.

JOHN: Well, you needn't come if you don't want to. [*He begins to go upstairs.*]

LARITA: Where are you going?

JOHN: To get Sarah's sweater—she left it in the schoolroom before lunch.

LARITA: You might bring down my fur coat.

JOHN: Fur coat? What on earth for?

LARITA: I'm cold.

JOHN: I don't wonder—lying about indoors all day.

LARITA: Don't be intolerant, darling.

JOHN *goes off.*

LARITA *bites her lip and looks extremely unhappy. After a moment* JOHN *returns, with* SARAH'S *sweater over one arm and* LARITA'S *coat over the other.*

JOHN: Here you are. [*He gives it to her.*]

LARITA: Thank you, Johnnie. [*She puts it on.*]

JOHN: You wouldn't be cold if you took some exercise.

LARITA: Come for a walk with me.

JOHN [*irritably*]: How can I? We're in the middle of a set. [JOHN *goes out.*]

LARITA [*calling*]: Johnnie!

JOHN [*reappearing*]: What is it?

LARITA [*hopelessly*]: Nothing. It doesn't matter.

JOHN *goes out.*

LARITA *sits on the sofa, her fur coat round her and her chin cupped in her hands; her eyes fill with tears, so she takes a handkerchief from her bag and blows her nose.*

COLONEL WHITTAKER *enters. He regards her thoughtfully for a moment.*

COLONEL: Hullo! What's the matter?

[*411*]

LARITA [*jumping*]: Oh—I never heard you.

COLONEL: You seem plunged in gloom.

LARITA [*lightly*]: It's only a mood.

COLONEL: Cheer up.

LARITA: You won't ask me why I'm not watching the tennis, will you?

COLONEL: No, my dear. Nor will I inquire why you are wearing your fur coat—the reasons are obvious: you are bored and cold.

LARITA: Exactly.

COLONEL: Shall we play bézique?

LARITA [*shuddering*]: No, thank you.

COLONEL: Do. It's such a thrilling game.

LARITA: I don't remember how——

COLONEL: Neither do I—that will give it an added piquancy. [*He goes to the bottom drawer of the bureau and produces a bézique set.*]

LARITA [*laughing*]: You really are absurd.

COLONEL: Stay where you are, and I'll bring up this dear little table. [*He does so.*]

LARITA: It is sweet, isn't it?

COLONEL [*sitting down opposite her*]: I forget how to deal. It's either nine or thirteen.

LARITA: I believe it's eleven.

COLONEL [*dealing her two cards and himself two*]: Turn them up.

LARITA [*turning them up*]: Card.

COLONEL [*turning his up*]: Nine.

LARITA: I'm more used to this sort of bézique.

He deals out four more cards. Turning up eight.
Eight.

COLONEL [*passing her the pack*]: There now.

LARITA [*dealing*]: I feel my nostrils quivering like a war-horse.

COLONEL: Card, please.

LARITA [*turning up her cards*]: Useless.

COLONEL: Are you preparing to have a run?

LARITA: Certainly. [*She deals again.*]

COLONEL [*turning up*]: Eight.

LARITA [*also turning up*]: I'm so sorry—nine!

COLONEL: Devil.

LARITA [*dealing again*]: Faites vos jeux.

COLONEL [*turning up*]: Carte.

LARITA: Nine!

COLONEL: Lucky at cards, unlucky——

LARITA: Don't say that to me—it's a malicious treason. [*She deals again.*]

COLONEL: Carte.

LARITA [*giving him one and herself one*]: Now then.

COLONEL: Damn!

LARITA: Nine!

COLONEL: There's something underhand about this.

LARITA: I shall have you turned out of the Casino if you accuse me of cheating.

COLONEL: One more go, please.

LARITA [*dealing*]: There!

COLONEL: Eight.

LARITA [*laughing*]: My poor friend! Nine.

COLONEL [*hurling the pack on to the floor*]: Disgusting.

LARITA: Don't be a cad! [*They both go down on to the floor and proceed to pick up the cards.*]

COLONEL: I should like to get a shoe and a couple of seedy croupiers, and start a gambling-hell in this village.

LARITA: It would be grand.

MRS. WHITTAKER *enters.*

MRS. WHITTAKER: What on earth are you doing?

COLONEL: Gambling.

LARITA: I'm afraid the Colonel forgot he was an English gentleman, and lost his temper.

MRS. WHITTAKER: Have you been down to the village, Jim?

COLONEL: Yes.

[*413*]

MRS. WHITTAKER: Well, all I can say is, you might have told me you were going—you could have seen Harry about fixing the Japanese lanterns.

COLONEL: I did see Harry.

MRS. WHITTAKER: What did he say?

COLONEL: He's coming up at half-past five.

MRS. WHITTAKER: Well, I think you might have let me know. [*She goes upstairs.*]

COLONEL: It is *such* fun giving a dance.

LARITA: You must control your excitement.

COLONEL: There, that's all, I think. [*He rises.*]

LARITA: There's an angry Queen of Hearts secreting herself under the sofa. [*She retrieves it and rises.*] I feel better now, thank you.

COLONEL: Splendid.

LARITA: Who's coming to-night?

COLONEL: The county. You'll see dresses that will make your mouth water.

LARITA: I must be careful—it will be my social début.

COLONEL: What will you wear?

LARITA: Something non-committal and austere.

COLONEL: Not black?

LARITA: No—that would clash with the Dowager's.

COLONEL: White?

LARITA: Too *ingénue*.

COLONEL: There's always lavender.

LARITA: Yes—much more appropriate.

COLONEL: Your friend Charles Burleigh's coming.

LARITA: Yes, I know—I'm awfully glad. He's a nice man.

COLONEL: I tremble for you sometimes.

LARITA: Why?

COLONEL: This life must be so deadly for you.

LARITA: Don't say that.

COLONEL: It is though—isn't it?

LARITA: Now and then—perhaps.

COLONEL: Do you regret everything?

LARITA: What's the good? I must get used to it.

COLONEL: I try my best, with bézique and small-talk, to make things brighter for you.

LARITA: I know you do. You've been a darling all along.

COLONEL: Do you think you'd be happier if you and John settled down in London?

LARITA: I don't know. I feel frightened of making any definite plans. Everything depends on John.

COLONEL: I'll talk to him.

LARITA: No, please don't; let him decide on his own whatever he wants to do.

COLONEL: He must see you're being bored stiff.

LARITA: I'm not—all the time. I just get moods——

COLONEL [*patting her hand*]: I understand.

LARITA: I wouldn't mind how bored and out of place I was— if only——

COLONEL [*gently*]: If only what?

LARITA: If only John were with me a little more.

COLONEL: He's inconsiderate—but he doesn't mean to be.

LARITA: He's getting a bit sick of me, I'm afraid.

COLONEL: What nonsense!

LARITA: I ought to be so much more adaptable—but it's difficult. I've tried terribly hard during the three months I've been here, but I've only succeeded in making everyone more or less used to me. I've established a sort of truce, that's all.

COLONEL: That in itself is an achievement. We're an insular, hidebound set.

LARITA: Nobody really likes me—except you.

COLONEL: Sarah does.

LARITA: Yes, I'd forgotten Sarah. It's queer of her, isn't it?

COLONEL: She places a high value on intelligence where no one else recognizes it.

LARITA: Marion is persistently pleasant because she feels she owes it to her religious views.

COLONEL: Marion—though I says it as shouldn't—is a fool.

LARITA: I've got an unworthy passion for popularity—it hurts my vanity not to be an unqualified success.

COLONEL: Rubbish!—it's nothing to do with your vanity.

LARITA: Please—I want it to be my vanity that's hurt, and nothing else.

COLONEL: You mustn't expect results too soon, you know. Three months is a very short time.

LARITA [*suddenly, with vehemence*]: Oh, what's the use of going on about it?—throwing dust and trying to obscure the truth. You know and I know—it's all a rotten failure! [*She goes upstairs.*]

The COLONEL *shrugs his shoulders and lights a cigarette.*

MARION *comes in from the garden.*

MARION: I think if we had the lanterns just along the veranda and across to the cedar it would be all right, don't you?

COLONEL: Quite. There aren't enough to go further, anyhow.

MARION: Mother thought there ought to be a few round the summer-house.

COLONEL: Fairy lamps would be much better there, and there are more of them.

MARION: I wish you'd tell her what you think. [*She sees* LARITA'S *book and picks it up.*] Hullo! what's this? *Sodom and Gomorrah.* Why does Lari read such silly muck? [*She flings it down again.*]

COLONEL [*gently*]: Don't be sweeping, Marion. Marcel Proust happens to be one of the few really brilliant novelists in the world.

MARION: Pity he chooses such piffling subjects, then.

COLONEL: Have you ever read him?

MARION: No—but all French writers are the same—sex—sex —sex. People think too much of all that sort of tosh nowadays, anyhow. After all, there are other things in life.

COLONEL: You mean higher things, don't you, Marion?—much higher?

[*416*]

MARION: I certainly do—and I'm not afraid to admit it.

COLONEL: You mustn't be truculent just because you've affiliated yourself with the Almighty. [*He goes into the library.*]

MARION *snorts crossly, and* MRS. WHITTAKER *comes downstairs.*

MRS. WHITTAKER [*obviously*]: Oh, there you are, Marion.

MARION: Father's intolerable.

MRS. WHITTAKER: What's the matter?

MARION: He never loses an opportunity of jeering at me.

MRS. WHITTAKER: He's an exceedingly selfish man—he knows perfectly well how rushed and worried I am, and he never attempts to help. I found him in here, on the floor, with Larita.

MARION: On the floor?

MRS. WHITTAKER: Yes; they'd been playing cards, and dropped them, or something.

MARION: I wish Larita wouldn't slack about indoors all day. It isn't healthy.

MRS. WHITTAKER [*seeing "Sodom and Gomorrah"*]: Whose is that book?

MARION: Hers, of course.

MRS. WHITTAKER: Well, please take it up to her room. I don't like that kind of literature left in the hall—especially when there are young people about.

MARION: You'd think she'd make some effort to adapt herself to our ways, wouldn't you? instead of——

MRS. WHITTAKER: Please don't let's discuss her, Marion; you know it upsets me—and Heaven knows I've got enough on my mind to-day.

MARION: I should like to give her a little advice about things.

MRS. WHITTAKER: Do, dear; but wait until after to-night—we don't want a scene.

MARION: I don't think she'd cut up rough if I was tactful. You see, she doesn't quite understand——

MRS. WHITTAKER: How can you expect her to?

MARION: And father's always encouraging her, and saying ridiculous things, and making her laugh.

MRS. WHITTAKER: Your father has a certain horrible streak in him that nothing will eradicate—no one's more aware of that than I. It's caused me years of suffering.

MARION: I know, mother.

MRS. WHITTAKER: Birds of a feather——

MARION [*alarmed*]: But I think Larita's all right—really, mother, don't you? I mean——

MRS. WHITTAKER: My dear Marion, I flatter myself I'm a woman of the world. We have no proof of the sort of life Larita has led, and we don't want any proof—she is John's wife, and as long as he cares for her nothing can be done——

MARION: What do you mean by "nothing can be done"?

MRS. WHITTAKER: This was never anything but a mad infatuation—and mad infatuations don't last.

MARION: But, mother, he's married to her.

MRS. WHITTAKER: There is such a thing as divorce.

MARION: I don't approve of divorce, and I never have.

MRS. WHITTAKER: Neither do I—but in a case like this it's rather different.

MARION: I think she's fond of him, you know.

MRS. WHITTAKER: Time will show.

HILDA *comes in from the garden; she is flushed and hot.*

HILDA: Philip and I won the set. Is there any lemonade, or anything?

MRS. WHITTAKER: You'd better go into the pantry and get some. Furber's very busy.

HILDA: Where's Larita?

MRS. WHITTAKER: I don't know.

HILDA: She was making sheep's eyes at Philip all through lunch.

MRS. WHITTAKER: You mustn't say things like that, Hilda.

HILDA: Well, she was. I nearly *died* of shame.

MARION: You'd better go and fetch the lemonade.

HILDA: You'd think she'd know how to behave at her age.

MRS. WHITTAKER: Hilda, that will do.

[*418*]

HILDA: I'm fed up with her. Look how she went on with Harry Emsworth. She'd better be careful, I can tell you——

Enter JOHN, SARAH *and* PHILIP BORDON—*he is a callow, lanky youth.*

JOHN: Where's the drink?

HILDA: I'm just going to fetch it.

SARAH [*sinking down*]: I'm dead.

PHILIP: It's jolly hot.

JOHN: Why didn't you play, Marion?

MARION: Too busy. Anyhow, you were four.

SARAH: Give me a cigarette, John.

JOHN: I've only got stinkers.

SARAH: I'll take one of Lari's; she won't mind. [*Takes one from* LARI'S *case on the sofa.*]

JOHN *lights it.*

MRS. WHITTAKER: I wonder if two extra girls will be enough, with Furber and Ellen.

MARION: I should think so.

MRS. WHITTAKER: We can get Mrs. Pollock's married daughter, you know. They're only just down the road.

MARION: It won't be necessary.

Re-enter HILDA, *with tray of drinks.*

HILDA: Furber had it all ready.

JOHN: Put it on the veranda, Hilda.

PHILIP: Let me help.

He and HILDA *retire on to the veranda with the drinks.*

MRS. WHITTAKER: Come into the library, Marion, and help me with the dinner list.

MARION: Father's in there.

MRS. WHITTAKER: We'll go up to my room, then. If Harris comes, don't let him go before I've seen him, John.

JOHN: All right, mother.

MRS. WHITTAKER [*as she and* MARION *go upstairs*]: We shall have to put Lady Gibbons next to your father.

MARION: He hates her.

[*419*]

MRS. WHITTAKER: It can't be helped.

They go off.

SARAH: Bring me some lemonade in here, John—it's so nice and cool.

JOHN [*going out on to veranda*]: I wish you were dining too.

SARAH: I've got to be at home and help mother with our party. I ought to be there now, really.

JOHN [*off*]: Wouldn't you rather have ginger beer?

SARAH: No—lemonade, please.

JOHN: Right.

After a moment he returns with lemonade for SARAH *and ginger beer for himself.*

SARAH [*taking it*]: Thanks.

JOHN: Pretty hot player, Philip.

SARAH: He nearly killed me.

JOHN: Keep a lot of dances for me to-night, won't you?

SARAH: Of course.

JOHN: It ought to be fun, if it keeps fine.

SARAH: Where's Lari, I wonder?

JOHN: Reading somewhere, I expect.

SARAH: She looked divine at lunch.

JOHN: It's funny you liking her. I was afraid you wouldn't.

SARAH: Why?

JOHN: Oh, I don't know—she's so utterly different.

SARAH: I expect that's the reason.

JOHN: I wish she wouldn't slack indoors so much.

SARAH: I don't see that it matters, if she wants to.

JOHN: It's all very well in the winter, but in this sort of weather——

SARAH: You mustn't be grumpy just because people don't like doing exactly the same things as you.

JOHN: I'm not grumpy.

SARAH: Yes, you are—a little.

JOHN: It's annoying, though.

SARAH: Don't let it be.

JOHN: You're such a sport, always ready for anything.

SARAH: But I haven't got Lari's beauty or charm or intelligence.

JOHN: Here, I say!

SARAH: I mean that.

JOHN: She is clever, isn't she?

SARAH: Yes, and being clever she's a little bored.

JOHN: She wouldn't be if only she entered into things.

SARAH: Perhaps she can't enter into things. You must remember this sort of life is entirely new to her.

JOHN: Yes, I know, but——

SARAH: You're all right, because you're on your own ground. I think you ought to give a bit more.

JOHN: How do you mean?

SARAH: Do what she wants now and then, instead of only what you want.

JOHN: But I do. I took her for miles in the car yesterday—she said she needed air.

SARAH: That's right.

JOHN: So you see——

SARAH: Don't make excuses; you know what I mean.

JOHN: I don't.

SARAH: Well, I can't explain; it's something you must find out for yourself.

JOHN: I do think it's most frightfully decent of you to stand up for her.

SARAH: That wasn't my object.

JOHN: I say, you have changed lately; you never used to go on like this.

SARAH: Like what?

JOHN: Well, all serious and preachy.

SARAH [*laughing*]: I'm sorry you think I'm preachy; you see, I'm growing up, and you're not.

JOHN: Oh yes, I am.

SARAH: Well, not in the way you should, then.

JOHN: You've got ever so much nicer-looking.

SARAH: Thank you.

JOHN: Are you going to marry, too?

SARAH: Certainly.

JOHN [*anxiously*]: Who? Charlie?

SARAH: Good Heavens, no! He's much too old.

JOHN: Oh!

SARAH [*repentantly*]: I'm awfully sorry. I didn't mean that exactly.

JOHN: It's all right.

SARAH: He's not my type at all; if I loved him, I wouldn't care how old he was.

JOHN: I can't imagine you married.

SARAH: What a pity! I have a vivid mental picture of it.

JOHN: Is there anybody you *are* in love with?

SARAH: Not at the moment, but I'm keeping my eyes open.

JOHN: I've often meant to ask you something, but I hadn't the courage.

SARAH: Well, don't then.

JOHN: I must.

SARAH: Give me a cigarette first.

JOHN: Stinker?

SARAH: Yes; anything.

JOHN [*giving her one*]: Here.

SARAH: Thanks. Go ahead.

JOHN: Did you think I behaved like a cad, marrying Lari like that, without letting you know?

SARAH: Of course not.

JOHN: Are you sure?

SARAH: Quite. I understood perfectly.

JOHN: It's been on my mind rather.

SARAH: You took your opportunity and married for love, John, and I respect you for it. If we'd married, it would have been for friendship and convenience.

JOHN: Would it?

SARAH [*firmly*]: Yes—we knew one another far too well.

JOHN: Do you think that's a disadvantage?

SARAH: In married life, certainly.

JOHN: I don't.

SARAH: It would have been so dull and ordinary—no excitement at all.

JOHN: I don't want excitement.

SARAH: I do. I want thrills and glamour and passionate love-letters—all the trappings.

JOHN: I could have written you love-letters.

SARAH: Well, why didn't you?

JOHN: I don't know. I——

SARAH [*triumphantly*]: The fact that you didn't proves that you couldn't—you didn't feel that way about me, ever.

JOHN: It was a different sort of feeling.

SARAH: Don't be a hypocrite, John, and try and deceive yourself.

JOHN: I did love you, all the same.

SARAH [*rising*]: How touching.

JOHN: I do still.

SARAH: Shut up, John!

JOHN: You see, I'm beginning to realize I've made rather a mess of things. [*He puts his face in his hands.*]

SARAH [*furiously*]: Shut up, I tell you, or I'll never speak to you again. That's behaving like a cad, if you like—an utter cad!

JOHN [*miserably*]: Sarah——

SARAH: You ought to be ashamed of yourself! Haven't you got any sense of decency? Let me tell you one thing—you're not fit to wipe Lari's boots.

LARITA *appears at the top of the stairs in time to catch the last sentence.*

LARITA [*lightly; coming down*]: Hallo!—what are you two squabbling about?

SARAH: John's infuriating—he always gets bad-tempered when he loses a set.

[*423*]

LARITA: I ought to have watched, after all, to keep him in order.

SARAH: I stole a cigarette out of your rich and rare case, Lari.

LARITA: That was revolting of you. I don't think I can forgive it.

HILDA *and* PHILIP *come in from veranda.*

HILDA: Aren't you going to play any more, John?

JOHN [*eagerly*]: Yes, rather.

SARAH: I should stay and talk to Lari if I were you, John— you've neglected her shamefully.

PHILIP: I'll stay with Mrs. John.

LARITA: You're all very kind and considerate—I really only want some one to hold my knitting. [*She makes a gesture of winding wool.*]

HILDA: I want Philip to play.

LARITA: I'll come and glare at you all with eyes starting out of my head like prawns.

SARAH: No, don't. There's nothing so hideously dull as watching people play games you're not particularly interested in. Come on, Hilda—you and I will play Philip. He can beat us easily.

HILDA [*satisfied*]: All right.

SARAH: Come along.

LARITA [*lightly*]: Thanks, Sarah darling. [*She blows a kiss to her.*]

SARAH, HILDA, *and* PHILIP *go off.*

JOHN [*noticing* LARITA *is still wearing her coat*]: Are you still cold?

LARITA: No, not really. I'll take this off if it annoys you. [*She does so.*]

JOHN: I don't mind.

LARITA: What shall we do? Go for a nice drive in the motor?

JOHN: Would you like to?

LARITA: No, dear—don't look so scared; I should hate it.

[424]

JOHN: I'm sorry if you think I've been neglecting you lately, Lari.

LARITA: Sarah put that into your head; I didn't.

JOHN: But have I?

LARITA: No. I think I've been neglecting you.

JOHN: I'm afraid I've been thoughtless and beastly.

LARITA [*smiling*]: Dear Johnnie. [*She pats his hand.*]

JOHN: I say, you have got some strong scent on.

LARITA: It's very good, though, isn't it? [*She leans forward so that he can smell it better.*]

JOHN [*with forced enthusiasm*]: Lovely.

LARITA: Why are you looking so depressed?

JOHN: I'm not depressed.

LARITA: I hope you haven't been overtiring yourself—at tennis?

JOHN: Of course I haven't.

LARITA [*seriously*]: Kiss me, Johnnie.

JOHN: All right. [*He does so.*]

LARITA: I think I'd better put on my fur coat again.

JOHN: What's the matter with you to-day, Lari?

LARITA: Don't you know?

JOHN: No.

LARITA: We're married.

JOHN: What do you mean?

LARITA: That's what's the matter with both of us.

JOHN: There's nothing the matter with me.

LARITA: Isn't there?

JOHN: I feel a bit tired, that's all.

LARITA: Yes, I believe you do.

JOHN: I think you were right—I *have* been rather strenuous to-day.

LARITA: Poor darling!

JOHN: And we've got this awful dance to-night.

LARITA: Aren't you looking forward to it?

JOHN: Not particularly.

LARITA: Let's run away secretly to Deauville.

JOHN: How can we?

LARITA [*smiling*]: It's all right. I didn't mean it; that was a joke.

JOHN: Oh, I see.

LARITA: You mustn't be dull. [*She laughs.*]

JOHN: Oh, do stop twitting me!

LARITA: Twitting! What a ridiculous expression.

JOHN: You're always in some mood or another.

LARITA: Surely that's quite natural?

JOHN: I suppose it's my fault, really, for leaving you alone so much. But still, I *do* think——

LARITA: If you're going to be magnanimous, do it gracefully.

JOHN: There you are, you see. Whenever I try——

LARITA [*sharply*]: You weren't trying hard enough.

JOHN: Anyone would think I'd been deliberately planning to annoy you.

LARITA: Deliberately or not—you've succeeded.

JOHN: I don't see what I've done.

LARITA: You play tennis eternally—tennis—tennis—tennis! Such a pretty game.

JOHN: It's healthier than sitting indoors, anyway.

LARITA: I believe it develops the muscles to an alarming extent.

JOHN: You don't want me to be flabby, do you?

LARITA: Mentally or physically?

JOHN: Lari, look here, I——

LARITA: I'm getting flabby mentally—and I can't bear it.

JOHN: Well, it's not my fault.

LARITA: Yes, it is.

JOHN: How?

LARITA: Come away—come abroad again.

JOHN: We can't—you know we can't—possibly.

LARITA: Why?

JOHN: It's unfair of you to ask me.

LARITA: Yes, it is—I suppose.

JOHN: After all, this is my life, and it always will be.

LARITA: Will it?

JOHN: Of course.

LARITA: And mine?

JOHN: Naturally.

LARITA: How secure that sounds.

JOHN: Secure?

LARITA: Yes. Words are such silly things. When you said "Naturally" like that it sounded like everything I want in the world; but I know in my heart it meant nothing.

JOHN: I don't understand.

LARITA: That's why it meant nothing.

JOHN: Are you really dissatisfied?

LARITA: Yes.

JOHN: You're not happy here at all?

LARITA: No.

JOHN: Why?

LARITA: Because you've stopped loving me.

JOHN [startled]: Lari!

LARITA: It's true.

JOHN: But you're wrong—I haven't stopped loving you.

LARITA [lightly]: Liar!

JOHN: Look here, you're hysterical and upset because I've been neglecting you.

LARITA: No, dear, it isn't that.

JOHN: I've never heard anything so ridiculous in my life.

LARITA: Neither have I.

JOHN: Why, we've only been married six months.

LARITA: It might be six years.

JOHN: It looks more as though you'd stopped loving me.

LARITA: Oh, John, don't be *silly*.

JOHN [hotly]: I'm not silly! You're always irritable and snappy these days—you never used to be.

LARITA: I'm sorry.

JOHN: If you were a bit more interested in everything here and didn't retire into your shell so much, you'd be far happier.

LARITA: Does your mother want me to be interested?

JOHN: Of course she does.

LARITA: Then why does she snub me and discourage me whenever I make the slightest effort?

JOHN: She doesn't mean to. You're too sensitive.

LARITA: Sensitive! [*She laughs.*]

JOHN: Yes, you think everybody's against you.

LARITA: So they are—except your father and Sarah.

JOHN: Marion's been sweet to you, and Hilda——

LARITA: Hilda evinced a high-school passion for me when I first arrived—which has since reacted into black hatred.

JOHN: Rot!

LARITA: It isn't rot. Marion is gratuitously patronizing.

JOHN: She's nothing of the sort.

LARITA: Her religious views forbid her to hate me openly.

JOHN: It's beastly of you to say things like that.

LARITA: I'm losing my temper at last—it's a good sign.

JOHN: I'm glad you think so.

LARITA: I've repressed it for so long, and repression's bad. Look at Marion.

JOHN: I don't know what you mean.

LARITA: No—you wouldn't.

JOHN: But I suppose it's something unpleasant.

LARITA: Quite right—it is.

JOHN: Well, will you please remember that Marion is my sister.

LARITA: I shouldn't think of her at all if she weren't.

JOHN: You're behaving like a child.

LARITA: I can't tell you what a wonderful relief it is.

JOHN: It's damned inconsiderate.

LARITA: Yes—my turn now!

JOHN: Look here, Lari——

LARITA: Don't try and stop me. Let me go on and on—or I shall burst.

JOHN: Don't talk so loudly.

LARITA: Why not? No one would be in the least surprised to find me rolling about on the floor, soaked in drugs and hiccoughing. They almost expect it of me. Surely a little shouting won't matter—it will gratify their conception of my character.

JOHN: I've never seen you like this before.

LARITA: No, it doesn't happen often.

JOHN: Thank God for that!

LARITA: Splendid! Repartee helps. I like you to play up. This is our first row, you know.

JOHN [*sullenly*]: I hope it will be our last.

LARITA: It may be—quite possibly.

JOHN: As far as I can see, you're just thoroughly bad-tempered because I haven't been dancing attendance on you all the time.

LARITA: If you can only see as far as that, you're extraordinarily short-sighted.

JOHN: All the same, I'm right.

LARITA: How I wish you were!

JOHN: If things have been upsetting you for so long, why on earth didn't you tell me before?

LARITA: I was hoping against hope that you'd see for yourself.

JOHN [*turning away irritably*]: Oh, what's the use of arguing and bickering like this? It doesn't lead anywhere.

LARITA: You never know—it might lead to the end of everything.

JOHN: Do you want it to?

LARITA: Do you?

JOHN: No, I don't. All I want is peace and quiet.

LARITA: You're far too young to make a remark like that seriously.

JOHN: I can't help my age.

LARITA: You said just now that you loved me still.

JOHN: I certainly don't when you go on like this.

LARITA: I wanted to see how much it would stand.

JOHN: Wasn't that rather silly?

LARITA: No, it *wasn't* silly. Three months ago you'd never have spoken to me as you have to-day. Whatever I'd done. I've been watching your passion for me die. I didn't mind that so much; it was inevitable. Then I waited very anxiously to see if there were any real love and affection behind it—and I've seen the little there was slowly crushed out of you by the uplifting atmosphere of your home and family. Whatever I do now doesn't matter any more—it's too late.

JOHN: Look here, Lari——

LARITA: I've shown myself to you quarrelsome and cheap and ugly for the first time—and it hasn't hurt you; it's only irritated you. You're miles away from me already.

JOHN: You're utterly unreasonable—you imagine things.

LARITA: Do I?

JOHN: I realize that I'm to blame for leaving you alone so much—and, honestly, I'm sorry.

LARITA: Do you really believe that that accounts for it all?

JOHN: Yes.

LARITA: Well, let's pretend it's true—for a little longer.

JOHN: There's no need to pretend.

LARITA: Give me my handkerchief, will you?—it's in my bag.

JOHN [*finding it*]: Here you are.

LARITA: Thanks. [*She dabs her eyes and blows her nose.*] I hope I'm not going to have a cold.

JOHN: I'll see that you don't get miserable and upset any more.

LARITA [*half smiling*]: Will you, Johnnie?

JOHN: Yes—and I'll talk to mother.

LARITA: No, don't do that.

JOHN: I will. I don't think she's been quite fair.

LARITA: Please don't say a word—promise me you won't. It wouldn't do the slightest good. She's your mother, and I do see her point, you know.

JOHN: As a matter of fact, I should rather like to go abroad again in September—Venice or somewhere.

LARITA: It would be lovely. [*She laughs.*]

JOHN [*suspiciously*]: Why are you laughing?

LARITA: Because I feel happier.

JOHN: Or Algiers—I've never been to Algiers.

LARITA: If we went to Algiers, we could stay with the Lessings.

JOHN: I don't know them.

LARITA: They're darlings. She's an American. She used to design people's houses. We had great fun in New York.

JOHN: I never knew you'd been to New York.

LARITA: I must have told you—I was there for ages.

JOHN: You didn't. Was it before you married?

LARITA: No; after.

JOHN: I thought you lived in Paris all the time.

LARITA: Not all the time.

JOHN: Why did you go?

LARITA: Oh, I don't know—the tall buildings and the champagne air—so fascinating.

JOHN: Did you go alone?

LARITA: Yes—but the boat was crowded.

JOHN: Why didn't you tell me?

LARITA: I thought I had. It doesn't matter though, does it?

JOHN: What did you do there?

LARITA: Really, Johnnie—nothing particular.

JOHN: You never told me much, you know—about anything.

LARITA: I'll write my memoirs one day; then all will be disclosed.

JOHN: Is Francis alive now?

LARITA: Oh yes; he's kicking about somewhere.

JOHN: You never hear from him?

LARITA: Of course not. I don't consider it chic to receive chatty letters from ex-husbands.

JOHN: I only wondered.

LARITA: Well, you needn't have.

JOHN: Mother's always trying to pump me about your early
life.

LARITA: And what do you say?

JOHN: Nothing. I feel rather a fool.

LARITA: Never mind, dear.

JOHN: It's natural that she should be curious, I suppose.

LARITA: Oh, quite.

JOHN: And that I should be, too.

LARITA: I never realized you were.

JOHN: You are my wife, after all.

LARITA: Yes, isn't it lovely?

JOHN: Do you regret anything?

LARITA: Hundreds of things.

JOHN: But seriously——

LARITA: The home atmosphere is certainly having its effect on
you.

JOHN: How do you mean?

LARITA: You never cross-questioned me before.

JOHN: I'm not cross-questioning you.

LARITA: Yes, you are—a little.

JOHN: I'm sorry. I won't any more.

LARITA: It betrays a certain lack of trust.

JOHN: Lari, how can you!

LARITA: You see, when we married, we married because we
loved one another—no explanations were necessary on either
side.

JOHN: They're not necessary now, only——

LARITA: Only you're feeling a little uncomfortable—is that it?

JOHN: No, not exactly.

LARITA: It's all a question of values.

JOHN: Values?

LARITA: Yes, the scales are awfully erratic. When we met and
fell in love, nothing else mattered as long as we were together.
But when the first fine careless rapture wears off, other things
begin to obtrude themselves—one has to readjust oneself to see

clearly. What had happened to either of us in the past didn't count a bit at first—why should it?—everything was new and exciting. Now it's not new and exciting any more; we've grown used to one another, so to alleviate the monotony we start prying about behind the scenes—trying to find out things about each other that haven't any real bearing on the case at all. It's inevitable with such a hideously intimate relationship as marriage.

JOHN: I don't want to find out anything.

LARITA: You may not want to, but you'll persevere until you do. It's human nature.

JOHN: I'd hoped there was nothing to find.

LARITA: There's always something—somewhere.

JOHN: Don't let's say any more about it.

LARITA: Very well. [*She takes out her powder-puff and powders her nose.*]

JOHN: I trust you absolutely.

LARITA: Whatever happens in the future, dear, I want you to remember one thing—I've never deceived you and I've never lied to you. There are many things that I've purposely left unexplained, because they don't concern you in the least and don't apply in any sense to our life together.

JOHN: Darling! [*He kisses her very sweetly, and she smoothes his hair.*]

LARITA: You've rubbed all the powder off my nose.

JOHN: I don't care a bit.

LARITA: Go and play some more tennis—you've been in the house far too long; it isn't healthy.

JOHN: Don't be a beast.

LARITA: Away with you—I'm going to rest before tea.

JOHN: I'll come and rest too.

LARITA: No, you won't. We should go on talking and talking and talking until our heads fell off.

JOHN: Oh, all right. [*He kisses his hand lightly and goes into the garden.*]

LARITA *is about to go upstairs when* MARION *comes down.*

[433]

MARION: Hallo! old girl.

LARITA: Hallo!

MARION: Are you going upstairs?

LARITA: I *was*. I thought of lying down a little.

MARION: You're always lying down.

LARITA: Yes, isn't it strange? I expect there's something organically wrong with me.

MARION [*anxiously*]: I hope there isn't.

LARITA [*beginning to go*]: Well, I'll see you later on——

MARION [*touching her arm*]: Don't go. I've been wanting to talk to you.

LARITA: To me? Why—what about?—anything important?

MARION: No; just everything.

LARITA: That ought to take several years.

MARION [*laughing forcedly*]: I didn't mean it literally.

LARITA: Oh, I see.

MARION: Have you got a cigarette on you?

LARITA: Yes, certainly. Here. [*She hands her case.*]

MARION [*taking one*]: Thanks.

LARITA [*amiably*]: Why aren't you watching the tennis?

MARION [*insensible of irony*]: I've been too busy all the afternoon.

LARITA: How are all the preparations for to-night going?

MARION: All right. You're sitting next to Mr. Furley.

LARITA: Splendid. Is he nice?

MARION: He's a damned good sort—rather High Church, you know; almost ritualistic.

LARITA: He won't be ritualistic at dinner, will he?

MARION: And you've got Sir George on the other side of you.

LARITA: Sir George who?

MARION: Sir George Bentley. He's awfully well up in dead languages and things.

LARITA: I do hope I shall be a comfort to him.

MARION: Very interesting man, George Bentley.

LARITA: How many are dining altogether?

MARION: Only twelve—we haven't really room for more comfortably.

LARITA: I hope it will all be an enormous success.

MARION: You won't be offended if I ask you something—just between ourselves?

LARITA: That depends, Marion. What is it?

MARION: Speaking as a pal, you know.

LARITA [*vaguely*]: Oh yes—well?

MARION: Don't encourage father too much.

LARITA: In what way—encourage him? I don't understand.

MARION: Well, you know—you and he are always getting up arguments together.

LARITA: Why shouldn't we?

MARION: It annoys mother so when he tries to be funny.

LARITA: I've never noticed him trying to be funny—he's a very intelligent man.

MARION: Sometimes when you're discussing certain subjects, he says things which are not quite——

LARITA: You say "certain subjects" in rather a sinister way, Marion. What subjects do you mean particularly?

MARION: Well, sex and things like that. You were talking about the Ericson divorce case the other day at lunch, when Harry Emsworth was here——

LARITA: It's an extraordinarily interesting case.

MARION: Yes, but one doesn't discuss things like that openly in front of strangers—I mean to say, it doesn't matter a bit when we're by ourselves; no one could be more broad-minded than I am—after all, what's the use of being in the world at all if you shut your eyes to things?

LARITA [*crisply*]: Exactly.

MARION: You're not angry, are you?

LARITA: Angry?—no.

MARION: You see, I like you, Lari; we get on well together. I grant you we see things from different points of view, but that's only natural.

[435]

LARITA: Yes—oh yes.

MARION: I knew you'd be a sport about it and not mind. You see, my philosophy in life is frankness. Say what you've got to say, and have done.

LARITA: In other words—moral courage.

MARION: Yes, that's it.

LARITA: Why didn't you attack the Colonel on these little breaches of etiquette? He seems to be more to blame than I.

MARION: A woman always understands better than a man.

LARITA: Surely that's a little sweeping.

MARION: It's true, all the same. I knew you'd see.

LARITA: You weren't by any chance afraid that he'd laugh at you?

MARION: Good Heavens, no! I don't mind being laughed at.

LARITA: How extraordinary! I hate it.

MARION: What does it matter? If you've got something to say, say it.

LARITA: According to your code, the fact of having spoken like that about your father doesn't strike you as being disloyal in any way, does it?

MARION: Not between pals like us.

LARITA: Of course, yes—pals. I keep forgetting.

MARION: I believe you *are* angry.

LARITA: I'm not—but I'm very, very interested.

MARION: Look here, Lari, it's like this. Father's been a bit of a dog in his day. Mother's had a pretty bad time with him, and she's **stood** by him through thick and thin.

LARITA: How splendid!

MARION: Some men are like that—no moral responsibility. Edgar, you know, was just the same.

LARITA: You say "was." Has he reformed?

MARION: I think I've made him see—but it's been a tough struggle.

LARITA: What have you made him see?

MARION: I've made him see that nothing matters if you keep your life straight and decent.

LARITA: There are so many varying opinions as to what is straight and decent.

MARION: God admits of no varying opinions.

LARITA: Your religion must be wonderfully comforting. It makes you so sure of yourself.

MARION: If you're going to take up that tone, we won't discuss it.

LARITA: No—we'd better not.

MARION [*gently*]: You mustn't jeer at religion, old girl. [*She puts her hand on her arm.*]

LARITA [*shaking her off*]: I don't jeer at religion—but I jeer at hypocrisy.

MARION: *I'm* not a hypocrite—if that's what you mean.

LARITA [*quietly*]: I'm afraid you are, Marion—and a disloyal one, too, which makes it all the more nauseating.

MARION: How dare you speak to me like that!

Enter PHILIP BORDON *from the garden.*

PHILIP [*to* LARITA]: Hallo!—I wondered if you were still here.

LARITA: You must be exhausted. You've been at it steadily all the afternoon.

PHILIP: John and Sarah are playing a single now, and Hilda's sitting on the steps, scoring.

MARION, *livid with rage, takes a writing-block off the bureau and marches into the library.*

Looks after her in some surprise.
What's up?

LARITA: We've been arguing about the dinner guests—it's all very difficult.

PHILIP: I wish I was dining.

LARITA: But you're coming directly afterwards, aren't you?

PHILIP: Rather! About ten of us.

LARITA: Good Heavens!

PHILIP: Will you keep a dance for me?

LARITA: Certainly.

PHILIP: What number?

LARITA: I don't know.

PHILIP: Three?

LARITA: Perhaps you won't be here in time.

PHILIP: Say five, then, and six.

LARITA [*laughing*]: Not two running! We should be bored stiff with each other.

PHILIP: Five and seven, then?

LARITA: All right.

PHILIP: You won't forget?

LARITA: Of course not.

PHILIP: I'm sure you dance wonderfully.

LARITA: Why?

PHILIP: Because of the way you move.

LARITA: Oh, thank you very much.

PHILIP: I mean it.

LARITA: Well, it's very sweet of you. [*She sits on sofa.*]

PHILIP: May I sit next to you?

LARITA: Certainly, if you like. [*She makes room for him.*]

PHILIP [*sitting down*]: I'm afraid I'm awfully hot and sticky.

LARITA [*laughing out loud*]: I don't mind as long as you keep your end.

PHILIP: Don't laugh at me.

LARITA: I'm sorry—but you are rather funny.

PHILIP [*gloomy*]: Everyone says that.

LARITA: Never mind. Be frank—speak straight from the shoulder—say what you have to say, and have done.

PHILIP [*surprised*]: I beg your pardon?

LARITA: It's all right—I was only quoting.

PHILIP: Oh, I see.

LARITA: You must forgive me if I'm a little distrait—I've had a rather trying afternoon.

PHILIP: Everybody fussing round, I suppose, over the dance?

LARITA: Yes—more or less.

PHILIP: People take things so damned seriously.

LARITA: You don't think it's a good plan to take things seriously?

PHILIP: Oh, sometimes, of course, but——

LARITA: I'm inclined to agree with you.

PHILIP: Life's too short to worry over things.

LARITA: It *is* miserably short, isn't it?

PHILIP: Rather!

LARITA: I sometimes wonder why we're here at all—it seems such a waste of time.

PHILIP: You're laughing again.

LARITA: Not altogether.

PHILIP: No one ever thought old John would marry anyone like you.

LARITA: Do you know that remark positively made me jump.

PHILIP: You're so different and so alive. He's a lucky devil.

LARITA: You must be careful with your compliments. If you go peppering them about like that they'll lose value.

PHILIP: They're not compliments—they're true.

LARITA: Do you always go on like this?

PHILIP: Of course not. I wouldn't dare.

LARITA: Forgive me for asking—but do you lead a straight and decent life?

PHILIP [*alarmed*]: What!

LARITA: It's *so* important. Whenever you feel yourself slipping, think of me.

PHILIP: I don't quite understand.

LARITA: On second thoughts, it would be better if you thought of Marion.

PHILIP: I'd rather think of you.

LARITA: Good! I must leave you now—I've been trying to get to my room for the last hour. [*She rises.*]

PHILIP [*catching her hand*]: Please don't go yet.

HILDA *bounces in in time to see* LARITA *withdrawing her hand from* PHILIP'*s grasp.*

[*439*]

LARITA: I must, really.

HILDA [*furiously*]: Oh!

PHILIP [*rising*]: Hallo! Have they finished?

HILDA: I wondered where you were—I might have known. [*She shoots a malignant glance at* LARITA.]

LARITA [*frowning*]: Hilda!

HILDA: I hope I'm not intruding.

LARITA [*irritably*]: This is too much!

HILDA: Yes, it is!

LARITA: If you adopt that rather rude tone to me, Hilda, I'm afraid I shall have to poach on Marion's preserves and have a straight talk to you.

PHILIP: Look here, Hilda——

HILDA: Don't speak to me!

FURBER *enters with various tea-things.* MRS. WHITTAKER *comes downstairs.*

MRS. WHITTAKER: Has anyone seen my little blue notebook? I can't think where I left it.

FURBER *finds it on the bureau.*

FURBER: Is this the one, ma'am?

MRS. WHITTAKER: Yes—thank you, Furber. It's really too annoying, Harris has never come—you'd better send down after tea.

FURBER: Very good, ma'am.

SARAH *and* JOHN *come in.*

JOHN [*to* LARITA]: Did you get your rest, darling?

LARITA: No—but it doesn't matter.

SARAH: Mrs. Whittaker, Philip and I must really go now. I've left mother all alone with herds of strange people.

MRS. WHITTAKER: Won't you have some tea first? It's all ready.

SARAH: No, honestly!—I daren't. She'll be cross as it is.

MRS. WHITTAKER: Very well. Be in good time to-night.

SARAH: I don't intend to miss one dance. Come along, Philip.

PHILIP [*shaking hands with* MRS. WHITTAKER]: Good-by, and thanks awfully.

MRS. WHITTAKER: Until to-night.

PHILIP: Rather! [*He goes to* LARITA.] I say—— [*He looks at* HILDA, *who glowers at him.*]

LARITA: Good-by for the moment—you must make me laugh some more to-night.

PHILIP: Remember—five and seven.

LARITA: I won't forget.

SARAH: Come *on,* Philip! See you later, Lari.

LARITA: Yes. Good-by.

SARAH *and* PHILIP *go off.* FURBER *brings in the teapot.*

JOHN: I'm going up to have a bath—I don't want any tea.

MRS. WHITTAKER: Oh, John—just one cup.

JOHN: No, mother. I've had tons of ginger beer during the afternoon. Come up after, Lari.

LARITA: All right, dear.

JOHN *bounds off upstairs.*

MARION *and the* COLONEL *come in from the library.* MARION *is fuming.*

COLONEL: If you don't like my opinions, you shouldn't ask for them.

MARION: I'm not used to having that sort of thing said to me.

MRS. WHITTAKER [*with a look towards* FURBER]: Marion, please!

MARION [*flopping down*]: Father's impossible!

FURBER *goes out.*

MRS. WHITTAKER: I do wish you'd control your temper in front of the servants, Marion.

HILDA: Other people besides Marion ought to control themselves.

MRS. WHITTAKER: What do you mean, Hilda?

HILDA: Ask Lari—she knows what I mean.

MRS. WHITTAKER: Come and sit down and have your tea.

HILDA: Disgusting, I call it!

MARION: What's disgusting?

HILDA: Ask Lari.

LARITA [*quietly*]: Hadn't you better explain yourself, Hilda, instead of referring everyone to me?

[*441*]

HILDA: I pity John—that's all.

COLONEL [*angrily*]: Have you gone mad, Hilda?

MRS. WHITTAKER: What on earth's the matter?

HILDA: I came in suddenly, and found Lari canoodling on the sofa with Philip.

MRS. WHITTAKER: Don't use such expressions, Hilda—I'm surprised at you. Come and sit down, Larita.

LARITA: I think I'll go to my room, if you don't mind.

HILDA: She's frightened because she knows I've found her out.

LARITA *stifles an exclamation of rage.*

COLONEL: Stop, Hilda! I forbid you to say another word.

HILDA [*hysterically*]: I won't stop—I know something you none of you know, only I wasn't going to say anything about it —until after the dance. [*She goes, in dead silence, to the bookcase, takes down a book, and takes a newspaper cutting out of it; she gives it to* MRS. WHITTAKER.] Look at that, mother. I got it from Sir George when I went there on Tuesday—he keeps all the back numbers of *The Times,* in files. I cut it out when he was in the garden.

MRS. WHITTAKER [*reading cutting*]: Marion—Jim—— [*She puts out her hand.*]

MARION *approaches and reads the cutting too. The* COLONEL *turns away.*

LARITA: I should like some bread-and-butter, please.

COLONEL: Here you are, my dear. [*He hands it to her.*]

HILDA: And I'm glad I did—glad.

COLONEL [*ignoring her*]: Do you want any jam with it?

LARITA: No, thanks; I always drop it all over myself.

HILDA [*shrilly*]: It's no use pretending to be so calm. You know the game's up now, don't you?

LARITA [*serenely*]: Specially strawberry—the runny kind.

MRS. WHITTAKER: Hilda, be quiet. [*She sits back and closes her eyes.*]

MARION: We'd better have this out and face it, hadn't we?

LARITA: By all means. What happened?

MARION [*handing her cutting*]: I suppose you don't deny that that's you?

LARITA [*glancing at it and handing it back*]: I've always hated that photograph.

MARION: You'd better read it, father.

COLONEL: Certainly not. I haven't the faintest desire to see it.

LARITA [*taking it and handing it to him*]: Please do—all my friends know about this. I ought to have told you before, really, but it didn't seem necessary.

COLONEL: Really, I'd rather not.

LARITA: Please—it's necessary now.

There is silence while the COLONEL *reads the cutting.* LARITA *drinks a little tea.*

COLONEL: Well, what of it? [*He tears up the cutting.*]

HILDA: Father!

LARITA: That was unkind. Hilda went to such a lot of trouble to get it.

MRS. WHITTAKER: This is appalling!

COLONEL: Why? Larita's past is no affair of ours.

MRS. WHITTAKER: You seem to forget—she's married to our son —our son—— [*She breaks down.*]

MARION [*putting her arm round her*]: Mother, don't give way.

COLONEL: I must apologize for this unpleasant scene, Lari.

LARITA: It had to occur, sooner or later.

MRS. WHITTAKER [*raising her head; to* LARITA, *bitterly*]: I hope you're satisfied.

LARITA: I'm not at all satisfied. I think—with the exception of the Colonel—that you're all behaving ridiculously.

MARION: It's easy to adopt a light tone—when you've brought degradation on to us.

COLONEL: Don't be a fool, Marion.

MARION: I'm not surprised at your attitude, father. Larita's your sort, isn't she?

LARITA: That's one of the nicest things that have ever been said to me.

[*443*]

MRS. WHITTAKER: Don't talk like that, Marion—it's useless.

MARION [*firmly*]: The question is—what's to be done? [*To* LARITA] Does John know about this?

LARITA: Mind your own business.

FURBER *enters.*

FURBER [*announcing*]: Mr. Harris.

MRS. WHITTAKER *gives a gasp of horror, and* HARRIS *enters. He is a thick-set, affable little man.*

HARRIS [*brightly*]: Sorry I couldn't come up before, Mrs. Whittaker, but we've 'ad a busy day down at the White 'Art, what with one thing and another.

There is silence for a moment, then MARION *speaks.*

MARION [*with an effort*]: My mother's not feeling very well, Harris; perhaps you'd call a little later.

HARRIS [*sympathetically*]: Oh, I *am* sorry to 'ear that—but time's getting on, you know—I've got to get back inside of 'arf an hour. If you'd just tell me where you want the fairy lights put, I could run 'em up right away.

MARION [*helplessly*]: I don't really think——

LARITA [*rising*]: I can show you from here——

HARRIS: Oh, thanks very much—if it isn't troubling you——

LARITA: Not at all. Look—[*she moves to the window*]—we want chains—between those four big trees—and some on the arch leading to the rose garden.

HARRIS [*jotting it down*]: Mixed colors, or shall I make it a scheme?

LARITA: Mixed colors would be better, I think.

HARRIS: Right you are.

LARITA: And if you could arrange some round the summer-house—— [*To* COLONEL] Just a few, don't you think?

COLONEL: Oh yes, certainly; it will brighten it up.

HARRIS [*still jotting*]: Rose h'arch—summer-'ouse.—What about the Chinese lanterns?

LARITA: Furber can manage those, I think. We've got them all here.

[*444*]

HARRIS: Righto, then, that's that. I'll get 'em up in no time. It ought to look very pretty and gay.

LARITA: I'm sure it will.

HARRIS: Can I go out this way?

LARITA: Oh yes, by all means.

HARRIS: Thanks very much. Sorry to have troubled you. Hope you'll be feeling better by to-night, Mrs. Whittaker. Good afternoon. [*To* HILDA] Good afternoon, miss.

HILDA [*jumping*]: Oh—good afternoon.

He goes importantly out on to the veranda and out into the garden.

LARITA *sits down again and goes on with her tea.*

MRS. WHITTAKER *has been busy regaining her self-control; her face is slightly suffused with rage.*

MRS. WHITTAKER [*with forced calm*]: Larita, will you oblige me by going to your room, please? We will discuss this later.

LARITA: Certainly not. I haven't finished my tea.

MRS. WHITTAKER: Doubtless you imagine that you are carrying off this—this abominable situation with a high hand, but your callousness only goes to prove that your senses must be blunted to all decent feelings.

LARITA [*quietly*]: Nothing I have ever done warrants your speaking like that.

MRS. WHITTAKER: You have married my son!

LARITA: I married John because I loved him.

MARION: Under false pretenses.

LARITA: There were no false pretenses.

MRS. WHITTAKER: Do you think he'd have married you if he'd known?

LARITA: I expect so.

MARION: Then why didn't you tell him?

LARITA: Because I didn't consider it necessary. We took one another on trust. What happened before I met him concerns no one but myself. I've never let John down in any way—I love him.

[445]

MRS. WHITTAKER: You married John because you wished to break away from your disgraceful life and gain a position to which you were not entitled.

LARITA: It's natural that you should think that, but it's not true.

COLONEL: Larita, please go upstairs, and let me deal with this.

LARITA: No—honestly, I'd rather stay. I understand Mrs. Whittaker's attitude perfectly, and I sympathize with it. It's horrible for her—but I don't want her to labor under any misapprehension.

MARION: In the face of everything, I'm afraid there's very little room for misapprehension.

LARITA: Your life is built up on misapprehensions, Marion. You don't understand or know anything—you blunder about like a lost sheep.

MARION: Abuse won't help you.

LARITA: That's not abuse—it's frankness.

MRS. WHITTAKER: This is beside the point.

LARITA: Not altogether—it's an attitude of mind which you all share.

COLONEL: Instead of jumping to the worst conclusions at once, wouldn't it be better to give Larita a little time to explain? We may be doing her an injustice.

LARITA: That's kind of you. I haven't the faintest intention of making excuses or trying to conceal anything—that newspaper cutting was perfectly accurate—as far as it went. I *was* concerned in that peculiarly unpleasant case. I changed my name afterward for obvious reasons. The papers rather overreached themselves in publishing the number of my lovers—only two of the list really loved me.

MRS. WHITTAKER: You were responsible for a man killing himself.

LARITA: Certainly not. It was his weakness and cowardice that were responsible for that—not I.

MRS. WHITTAKER: It's incredible—dreadful—I can hardly believe it.

LARITA: I felt like that at the time, but it's a long while ago.

MARION: Fifteen years! John was a child.

LARITA: Thank you. I quite realize that.

MRS. WHITTAKER: And how have you lived since this—this—scandal?

LARITA: Extremely well.

MRS. WHITTAKER: Your flippancy is unpardonable.

LARITA: So was your question. I've only explained so far because, as you're John's mother, I felt I owed it to you; but if you persist in this censorious attitude I shall say no more.

MRS. WHITTAKER: Do you realize what you've done?

LARITA: Perfectly, and I regret nothing. The only thing that counts in this instance is my relationship with John. Nothing that has occurred in the past affects that in the least.

MRS. WHITTAKER: Your marrying him was an outrage.

LARITA: Why? I've told you before, I love him.

MRS. WHITTAKER: You prove your love by soiling his name irreparably.

LARITA: Nonsense.

COLONEL: Do you think it's quite fair, Mabel, to set ourselves up in judgment on Larita? We know none of the circumstances which led to these bygone incidents.

MRS. WHITTAKER: You've failed me too often before, Jim, so I'm not surprised that you fail me now.

LARITA: The Colonel's not failing you—it's just as bad for him as for you. You don't suppose he *likes* the idea of his only son being tied up to me, after these—revelations? But somehow or other, in the face of overwhelming opposition, he's managed to arrive at a truer sense of values than you could any of you ever understand. He's not allowed himself to be cluttered up with hypocritical moral codes and false sentiments—he sees things as they are, and tries to make the best of them. He's tried to make the best of me ever since I've been here.

MARION: That hasn't astonished us in the least.

LARITA: No doubt, with your pure and unsullied conception of human nature, you can only find one meaning for the Colonel's kindness to me?

MARION: I didn't say that.

LARITA: You think it, though, don't you? Only this afternoon you asked me not to encourage him.

MRS. WHITTAKER: Marion!

LARITA: You disguised your unpleasant lascivious curiosity under a cloak of hearty friendship—you were pumping me to discover some confirmation of your pretty suspicions. One thing my life has taught me, and that is a knowledge of feminine psychology. I've met your type before.

MARION: How dare you! How dare you!

MRS. WHITTAKER [*rising*]: This is insupportable.

LARITA [*sharply*]: Yes, it is.—Sit down.

MRS. WHITTAKER [*impotently*]: I—I—— [*She sits down.*]

LARITA: I want you to understand one thing—I deny nothing. I have a perfect right to say what I like and live how I choose—whether I've married John or whether I haven't, my life is my own, and I don't intend to be browbeaten.

MARION: I hope God will forgive you.

LARITA: Don't you rather overrate the Almighty's interest in the situation?

MRS. WHITTAKER: In the face of your brazen attitude, there's nothing more to be said.

LARITA: You're wrong. There's a good deal more to be said. According to you, I ensnared John in my toils in order to break away from my old life and better my position. If that were the case, what do you mean by deliberately trying to crush down my efforts to reform myself? How do you reconcile that with your stereotyped views of virtue and charity? But you needn't worry; I didn't marry John to reform myself. I don't consider my position in this house a step up, socially or spiritually. On the contrary, it's been probably the most demoralizing experience that's ever happened to me.

MRS. WHITTAKER: You're a wicked, wicked woman.

LARITA: That remark was utterly fatuous and completely mechanical. You didn't even think before you said it—your brain is so muddled up with false values that you're incapable of grasping anything in the least real. Why am I a wicked woman?

MRS. WHITTAKER: You betrayed my son's honor by taking advantage of his youth and mad infatuation for you. He'd never have married you if he'd known.

LARITA: I suppose you wouldn't consider it betraying his honor if he'd had an affair with me and not married me?

MRS. WHITTAKER: It would certainly have been much more appropriate.

LARITA: Unfortunately, I don't consider John worthy of me in either capacity—I realized a long time ago that our marriage was a mistake, but not from your point of view—from my own.

MARION: It's easy to talk like that now.

LARITA: It isn't easy—it's heartbreaking. I love John more than I can ever say, but it's not blind love—unfortunately—I can see through him. He's charming and weak and inadequate, and he's brought me down to the dust.

MRS. WHITTAKER: How dare you say such vile things! How dare you!

LARITA: It's true. You can't appreciate my feelings about it. I don't expect you to.

MARION: I should think not.

LARITA: Your treatment of all this shows a regrettable lack of discrimination. You seem to be floundering under the delusion that I'm a professional *cocotte*. You're quite, quite wrong—I've never had an affair with a man I wasn't fond of. The only time I ever sold myself was in the eyes of God to my first husband— my mother arranged it. I was really too young to know what I was doing. You approve of that sort of bargaining, don't you? —it's within the law.

MARION [*contemptuously*]: Huh!

LARITA: Why do you make that peculiar noise, Marion? Does it indicate approval, contempt, or merely asthma?

MARION: Do you think this is the moment to be facetious?

LARITA: You're an unbelievable prig.

MARION: I hope you don't imagine that your insults could ever have any effect on me?

LARITA: If you only knew it, I'm at your mercy completely, but you're too silly to take advantage of it—you choose the wrong tactics.

MARION: We're certainly not experienced in dealing with women of your sort, if that's what you mean.

LARITA: It *is* what I mean—entirely. I'm completely outside the bounds of your understanding—in every way. And yet I know you, Marion, through and through—far better than you know yourself. You're a pitiful figure, and there are thousands like you—victims of convention and upbringing. All your life you've ground down perfectly natural sex impulses, until your mind has become a morass of inhibitions—your repression has run into the usual channel of religious hysteria. You've placed physical purity too high and mental purity not high enough, and you'll be a miserable woman until the end of your days unless you readjust the balance.

MARION [*rising impetuously*]: You're revolting—horrible!

LARITA: You need love and affection terribly—you'd go to any lengths to obtain it except the right ones. You swear and smoke and assume an air of spurious heartiness because you're not sure of your own religion and are afraid of being thought a prude. You try to establish a feeling of comradeship by sanctimonious heart-to-heart talks. All your ideals are confused and muddled —you don't know what to ask of life, and you'll die never having achieved anything but physical virtue. And God knows I pity you.

MARION, *with as much dignity as she can command, walks into the library without a word, and slams the door.*

MRS. WHITTAKER: You're achieving nothing by all this.

LARITA: How do you know?

MRS. WHITTAKER: Because you're a moral degenerate—lost to all sense of right and wrong.

LARITA: I respect you for one thing, anyhow—you *are* sure of yourself.

MRS. WHITTAKER: I don't want your respect.

LARITA: You're the only one here with the slightest grip. You've risen up like a phœnix from the ashes of your pride. It's quite, quite excellent—and infinitely pathetic.

MRS. WHITTAKER: I don't wish to speak to you any more—until to-morrow. I shall be very grateful if you will remain upstairs this evening—I will make suitable excuses for your absence.

LARITA: You mean you're frightened that I should make a scene?

MRS. WHITTAKER: That is neither here nor there—I certainly don't desire an open scandal.

LARITA: You've run to cover again. I was afraid you would.

MRS. WHITTAKER: This has been painful beyond belief.

COLONEL: You're right—it has.

MRS. WHITTAKER: I don't feel capable of bearing any more.

LARITA: You intend to confine me to my room like a naughty child?

MRS. WHITTAKER: The simile is hardly appropriate, but I hope you will have the decency to remain there. [*She goes upstairs in silence.*]

COLONEL: Lari——

LARITA: Please go away—I don't want anyone to speak to me at all for a little. I must think—think——

She is trembling hopelessly and making a tremendous effort to control her nerves.

COLONEL: Very well. [*He goes out into the garden.*]

HILDA, *who has been standing aghast throughout the entire scene, suddenly bursts into floods of tears and rushes at* LARITA.

HILDA [*hysterically*]: Lari—Lari—forgive me! I didn't mean it—I didn't mean it——

[451]

LARITA [*pushing her gently away*]: Don't be a little toad, Hilda. Try to have the courage of your convictions.

HILDA *rushes out into the garden, weeping hysterically.*

LARITA *bites her lip; then, still trembling violently, she lights a cigarette and takes "Sodom and Gomorrah" off the bureau. She settles herself on the sofa, obviously exerting every ounce of control, and opens the book methodically; she attempts to read, but her eyes can't focus the page; she is acutely conscious of an imperfect statuette of the Venus de Milo· which is smirking at her from a pedestal by the dining-room doors. Suddenly, with all her force, she hurls the book at it, knocking it to the floor and smashing it.*

LARITA: I've always hated that damned thing!

CURTAIN FALLS

When it rises once, she has buried her face in the sofa cushion, and her shoulders are heaving, whether with laughter or tears it is difficult to say.

ACT III

SCENE: *The same. When the curtain rises the dance is in full swing. The actual dancing takes place in the dining-room, because the floor is better. The hall and library are the sitting-out places; the buffet is on the lower end of the veranda, just out of sight of the audience. The festoons of Japanese lanterns and fairy lights look—as* MR. HARRIS *prophesied—very pretty and gay.*

There is a group of YOUNG PEOPLE *clustered round the buffet; their light-hearted conversation can be heard intermittently. Several people are littered about the hall.* MISS NINA VANSITTART, *attired in a strikingly original rose-taffeta frock, with a ribbon of the same shade encircling her hair the wrong way—giving more the impression of a telephone apparatus than a head ornament —is seated on the sofa, basking enthusiastically in the illuminating conversation of the* HON. HUGH PETWORTH, *healthy young man, whose unfortunate shape can be luckily accounted for by his athletic prowess. He has had the forethought to wear white gloves which have wrinkled up slightly, displaying below his cuffs a mercifully brief expanse of blood-red wrists.*

HUGH: It was a frightful rag.

NINA: I wish I'd been there.

HUGH: If you'd seen old Freddie fall off the roof of the taxi——

NINA [*delightedly*]: I should have *died*—I know I should!

HUGH: And you should have seen the way old Minky Taylor lammed into the commissionaire chap outside the Piccadilly——

NINA [*with whole-hearted sincerity*]: Oh, lovely!

A cherubic boy—BOBBY COLEMAN *by name—approaches them.*

BOBBY: I say, Nina—this is us.

[453]

NINA: What number is it?

BOBBY: Nine.

NINA [*rising*]: I'll leave my bag here. Keep your eye on it, Hughie.

HUGH: I'm supposed to be dancing this with Lucy.

NINA: Never mind; it will be all right there.

HUGH *rises automatically, and subsides again as* BOBBY *and* NINA *go into the dancing-room. Two* YOUNG PEOPLE *walk across and out on to the veranda.*

1ST YOUNG PERSON: Jolly good tune, that.

2ND YOUNG PERSON: Lovely.

1ST YOUNG PERSON: The garden looks awfully pretty, doesn't it?

2ND YOUNG PERSON: Yes, awfully pretty. [*They go off.*]

HILDA *comes out of the library. She is wearing such a pretty blue dress, with stockings to match.*

HILDA [*to* HUGH]: Why aren't you dancing?

HUGH: I'm supposed to be—with Lucy. Have you seen her anywhere?

HILDA: Yes, she's in the library. I'm looking for Philip Bordon. Have you seen him anywhere?

HUGH: No. I'll go and get Lucy. Will you dance later?

HILDA: Missing two.

HUGH: Righto. [*He goes off.*]

HILDA *goes towards the veranda and meets* PHILIP *entering.*

HILDA: Oh, there you are. This is ours.

PHILIP: Oh—is it?

HILDA: Yes—nine. You said so this afternoon.

PHILIP: Where's Larita?—Mrs. John——?

HILDA: She's upstairs with a bad head—she's not coming down at all.

PHILIP [*despondently*]: I say—what a shame!

HILDA [*with meaning*]: Yes, isn't it?

PHILIP [*resigned*]: Come on.

They go into the dancing-room. The music stops, and every-one can be heard clapping. Then it goes on again.

HUGH *comes out of the library with* LUCY, *a pretty girl with badly-bobbed hair; her dress is awfully pretty—yellow, with shoes and stockings to match. They go into the dancing-room. They meet* SARAH *and* CHARLES *coming out, and exchange a few meaningless words.* SARAH *flops down on the sofa.*

CHARLES: Do you want an ice or anything?

SARAH: No, thanks.

CHARLES [*sitting down*]: That dining-room's far too small and hot to dance in. Why didn't they have the band here?

SARAH: The floor's better in there.

CHARLES: I hadn't noticed it.

SARAH: I'm worried, Charles—about Larita.

CHARLES: Yes—I know.

SARAH: I tried to slip up and see her when we arrived, but Marion stopped me; she said she'd asked particularly to be left alone.

CHARLES: I'm extremely disappointed—I wanted to see her too.

SARAH: Something's happened—I'm sure of it.

CHARLES: What could have?

SARAH: I don't know exactly, but I've got a feeling.

CHARLES: What shall we do about it?

SARAH: Nothing, yet—but I mean to see her somehow, before we go.

CHARLES: John seems quite happy.

SARAH: Mrs. Whittaker doesn't, though, and I haven't seen the Colonel.

CHARLES: They're a tiresome family.

SARAH: Very.

CHARLES: Have you danced with John?

SARAH: Yes—just after we got here.

CHARLES: Did he say anything?

SARAH: Only that she'd got a racking headache and was in bed.

CHARLES: You'd have been able to tell from his manner if anything was wrong.

[455]

SARAH: He's either being cleverer than I thought him, or he just doesn't know.

CHARLES: She seemed all right this afternoon, didn't she?—You were here?

SARAH: Yes—more or less.

CHARLES: How do you mean—more or less?

SARAH: I'm furious with John.

CHARLES: Why?

SARAH: He's making her utterly wretched.

CHARLES: That was inevitable.

SARAH: I don't see why.

CHARLES: She's all wrong here—right out of the picture.

SARAH: I know, Charles; but he oughtn't to let her down—it's filthily mean of him.

CHARLES: He can't help it—he doesn't see anything.

SARAH: But he should see. If she's unhappy here, he must take her away.

CHARLES: That wouldn't do any good—ultimately.

SARAH: It was all a fiasco, from the first. I knew that directly I saw her. But still, he ought to play up and stand by her.

CHARLES: I can't imagine anyone of her intelligence being silly enough to marry him.

SARAH: She adores him.

CHARLES: Yes, but—she might have known it would end badly.

SARAH: It hasn't ended badly yet.

CHARLES: It will.

SARAH: Don't be so certain.

CHARLES: You're just as certain.

SARAH: Oh, Charles, I wish she'd been a cheap, loud-voiced cat—it would have been funny then.

CHARLES: Would it?

SARAH: Well, less difficult, anyhow. There would be some excuse for John.

CHARLES: That's what's worrying you, is it?

SARAH: Of course. I used to be awfully fond of him, but he's shrunk over this beyond all recognition—gone tiny.

CHARLES: An observant mind is painful sometimes, isn't it?

SARAH: Damnably.

CHARLES: Would you like to marry me, Sarah?

SARAH: Don't make me laugh, Charles—just now.

CHARLES: I believe I mean it.

SARAH: You're a darling—but you don't. The intoxicating atmosphere of this revelry has gone to your head.

CHARLES: Perhaps.

SARAH: You're not in the least in love with me.

CHARLES: I don't know.

SARAH: But it is frightfully sweet of you to ask me, and I do appreciate it.

CHARLES: We might be awfully happy together.

SARAH: We probably should, but something would be wrong somewhere.

CHARLES: I wonder.

SARAH: You know perfectly well——

CHARLES: I've been paying pretty marked attentions to you during the last six months—surely that proves something?

SARAH: It proves that you like being with me very much, and I like being with you.

CHARLES: Well, then——?

SARAH: Marriage would soon kill all that—without the vital spark to keep it going.

CHARLES: Dear, dear, dear. The way you modern young girls talk—it's shocking, that's what it is!

SARAH: Never mind, Charles dear, you must move with the times.

CHARLES: I didn't know you thought so highly of the vital spark, anyhow.

SARAH: Of course I do. It's a fundamental instinct in everybody. Being modern only means twisting things into different shapes.

[457]

CHARLES [*rising*]: The garden looks awfully pretty, doesn't it?

SARAH [*also rising*]: Oh, yes, frightfully pretty.

CHARLES [*as they move away*]: All those colored lights and everything—so attractive.

SARAH: Terribly sweet!

CHARLES: It's extraordinary how pretty a garden *can* look.

SARAH: Oh, shut up! [*They go off on to the veranda.*]

FURBER *crosses the hall, with a tray of clean glasses. The music stops, and desultory clapping can be heard. Several couples belch out of the dining-room, among them* MARION *with* HENRY FURLEY, *an earnest young man with a pinched face and glasses.* MARION, *for some obscure reason, is in white, with a black Indian scarf speckled with gold, and gold shoes which hurt her a little. They walk across, talking.* MARION *is being painfully jolly and gay—she slaps* PHILIP BORDON *heartily on the back in passing.*

MARION: We'll have you turned out if you twirl about like that, you know.

PHILIP [*with equal jocularity*]: I shan't go quietly.

MARION: I bet you won't.

Several people laugh at this volley of wit, including the perpetrators of it.

[*To* MR. FURLEY] Damned good tune that.

FURLEY: Yes, I enjoyed it.

MARION: You lugged me round like a Trojan.

FURLEY [*politely*]: Not at all.

MARION: You know some tricky steps—we'd do well on the stage.

FURLEY [*laughing*]: Yes, wouldn't we?

MARION: Be a good chap and get me a glass of something—I'm dry as a bone.

FURLEY: Claret-cup?

MARION: Yes, rather. That'll do. I'll wait here. [*She sits down, up-stage, and fans herself with her hand.*]

MR. FURLEY *departs in search of claret-cup.*

Two YOUNG PEOPLE *who have been sitting on the stairs rise.*

[458]

GIRL: You really are awful—I don't believe a word of it.

BOY: It's true—I swear it is.

They both go into the dancing-room, where the music has re-started.

MRS. WHITTAKER *comes in, wearing a good many brooches on a mauve dress; she also has a diamanté butterfly in her hair. She is accompanied by* MRS. HURST, *a tall, handsome woman in black.*

MRS. WHITTAKER: But you really mustn't—it's quite early yet.

MRS. HURST: I'm just going to slip away without anybody noticing. Sarah can collect our party and come home when she wants to.

MRS. WHITTAKER: Of course, if you're really tired——

MRS. HURST: I'm so sorry your daughter-in-law is so seedy.

MRS. WHITTAKER: It is tiresome, isn't it?—Poor Larita.

MRS. HURST: Tell her how disappointed I was not to have seen her, won't you?

MRS. WHITTAKER: Certainly.

MRS. PHILLIPS, *a pale white-haired woman, approaches.*

MRS. PHILLIPS [*effusively*]: There you are, Mrs. Whittaker! It's all going off most successfully, isn't it?

MRS. WHITTAKER: Yes; I think the young people seem to be enjoying themselves.

MRS. PHILLIPS: So fortunate that it kept fine.

MRS. WHITTAKER: I've been on absolute tenterhooks all day.

MRS. HURST: I was just saying what a pity poor Mrs. John is missing it all.

MRS. PHILLIPS: I know—it's dreadful. What *is* wrong with her, exactly?

MRS. WHITTAKER: A blinding headache—she has them, you know, quite often. I'm always trying to make her go to a specialist.

MRS. PHILLIPS: Poor dear! It *is* a shame—to-night of all nights.

JOHN *comes in with* MARY BANFIELD, *a dark girl with whom he has been dancing.*

[459]

MRS. WHITTAKER: But still, it's much better, if you do feel ill, to stay quite quiet.

MRS. PHILLIPS: Oh, much, much! Do tell her how sorry I am, won't you?

CHARLES *and* SARAH *wander in from the veranda.* MARION *has been rejoined by* MR. FURLEY, *and is sipping her claret-cup.* JOHN *and* MARY BANFIELD *sit on the bottom step of the stairs and light cigarettes.*

MRS. HURST: Sarah, dear, I'm just going to slip away. When you come home, you will remember to lock up and turn out all the lights, won't you?

SARAH [*joining the little group with* CHARLES]: All right, mother.

MRS. PHILLIPS: The Chinese lanterns look so pretty, don't they?

CHARLES [*amiably*]: Perfectly charming—quite Venetian.

SARAH: Mrs. Whittaker, I'm so sorry about Lari. Do you think I could run up and see her?

MRS. WHITTAKER [*hurriedly*]: No, dear, really—she asked particularly to be left alone; you know what these headaches are——

SARAH: Yes, but——

MRS. WHITTAKER: The only thing to do is just rest and keep quiet.

SARAH: Poor darling!

MRS. WHITTAKER: She may have dropped off to sleep by now.

At this moment LARITA *appears at the top of the stairs. Her dress is dead-white and cut extremely low; she is wearing three ropes of pearls, and another long string twined round her right wrist. Her face is as white as her dress and her lips vivid scarlet. Her left arm positively glitters with diamond, ruby and emerald bracelets; her small tiara of rubies and diamonds matches her enormous earrings; she also displays a diamond anklet over her cobweb fine flesh-colored stocking. She is carrying a tremendous scarlet ostrich-feather fan. There is a distinct gasp from everybody.* MARION *rises and drops her glass of claret-cup.*

[460]

CHARLES: Marvelous—marvelous.

MRS. PHILLIPS: Well.

LARITA: Get out of the way, Marion dear, or I shall tread on you.

MARION: Larita—I——

MRS. WHITTAKER: My dear Larita, this is a surprise.

LARITA: Why?

MRS. WHITTAKER: We thought you weren't coming down.

LARITA: I've been dressing and doing my face, it always takes me hours.

MRS. WHITTAKER: We understand you had a bad headache.

LARITA: Forgive me but that is quite untrue—you didn't understand anything of the sort.

MARION [*flustered*]: Larita—I——

LARITA: If you have been building up a few neat social lies on my account, it is very unwise of you—I don't live according to your social system.

SARAH [*kissing her*]: You look perfectly lovely, Lari, and I'm frightfully glad to see you.

LARITA: I'm dying for something to eat—I didn't feel inclined for any dinner and now I'm starving—Oh, get me a sandwich or something, Johnnie. There's a darling.

JOHN: What's the matter—I don't understand——

LARITA: And some champagne—[*There is a blank pause.*] If there isn't any, plain water will do.

JOHN: Oh, all right.

LARITA: How divine the garden looks. Hello, Charles Burleigh, I hoped you were coming—I haven't seen you for ages.

MRS. PHILLIPS: We were just sending you up messages of sympathy—we understood you were prostrate.

LARITA: So I was—my maid has been massaging me—perfect agony.

MRS. WHITTAKER: Well, anyhow I'm sure I'm glad you're better now—and changed your mind about coming down.

LARITA: Why do you persist in this ridiculous fallacy of my

[461]

being ill? This afternoon you had the impertinence to command me to remain in my room. That was quite unpardonable and you must take the consequences. I have nothing more to say to you. [JOHN *enters with sandwich.*] Thank you, Johnnie.

MRS. WHITTAKER: Marion, I'm sure the band ought to be given something to eat and drink—they've been playing for such a long time.

MARION: Righto, mother—I'll see Furber about it. [*She looks at* LARITA *contemptuously.*]

LARITA: How charming you look, Marion—and what a lovely scarf. I'm sure it came from India.

MARION, *ignoring her, goes on to the veranda.*

MRS. HURST: I really must be off now.

MRS. PHILLIPS: I don't think I can tear myself away—yet——

MRS. HURST: Good-by and thank you so much.

MRS. PHILLIPS [*seating herself beside* LARITA]: I must stay a little longer.

MRS. WHITTAKER: Please do—It's so early. [*She walks towards the door with* MRS. HURST.]

LARITA [*to* MRS. PHILLIPS]: How is your girl, Rose Jenkins, progressing in London, Mrs. Phillips? You seemed so worried about her when you came to tea last week.

MRS. PHILLIPS: I really don't know—I'm afraid she's a hopelessly bad character.

LARITA: I'm sure she'll get on in the profession you've sent her to.

MRS. PHILLIPS [*stiffly*]: I sent her to no profession.

LARITA: How stupid of me! I thought you had.

MRS. PHILLIPS, *sensing underlying meaning, moves away.*

JOHN: Lari, why on earth are you dressed up like this?

LARITA: I just felt like it, Johnnie. I'm wearing all the jewelry I've got in the world—it's a heavenly sensation. [*She jingles her bracelets.*]

JOHN: It looks ridiculous.

LARITA: Don't be an ass, John.

[462]

JOHN: But it does—honestly.

LARITA [*brushing him with her fan*]: Run away and dance if you can't be pleasant to me.

JOHN: But look here, Lari——

LARITA [*with suppressed fury*]: Perhaps you don't realize that I'm serious?

JOHN: Oh, all right—if you're going on like that. [*He slams off in a rage.*]

LARITA: John's lost grip of things terribly lately, hasn't he?

SARAH: Lari dear, what's happened?

LARITA: Lots and lots and lots of things.

SARAH: Are you upset?

LARITA: You don't suppose I should do this—ordinarily—do you?

SARAH: Tell me.

LARITA: Not yet, Sarah—later on.

PHILIP BORDON *rushes up.*

PHILIP: I *am* glad you're all right.

LARITA: Thank you.

PHILIP: You've cut both the dances you promised me by coming down late.

LARITA: I'm so sorry. Let's have this one.

PHILIP: Rather!

LARITA [*to* SARAH]: Later on, dear.

CHARLES: Next dance, please.

LARITA: Missing eight.

CHARLES: No—the next one.

LARITA: All right. [*She goes into the dancing-room with* PHILIP.]

CHARLES: You must say she's magnificent.

SARAH: She's wretched.

CHARLES: I've never seen such an entrance in my life.

SARAH [*smiling*]: Poor Mrs. Whittaker.

CHARLES: Serve her right.

SARAH: I wonder what Lari's object is—in all this.

CHARLES: Swan song.

SARAH: Charles—what *do* you mean?

CHARLES: Wait and see.

SARAH: Come and dance, then.

CHARLES: I feel pleasantly thrilled.

SARAH: Well, you ought to be ashamed of yourself.

They go into the dance-room. NINA VANSITTART *and* HUGH PET-WORTH *are standing by the dancing-room door.*

NINA: That's her in white.

HUGH: Phew!

NINA: I've never seen anything like it.

HUGH: Look at her pearls.

NINA: Downright vulgar, I call it.

HUGH: Come on in. [*They go in.*]

MRS. WHITTAKER *intercepts* MARION *coming from the veranda, and draws her aside.*

FURBER *goes into the dance-room with drinks for the band.*

MRS. WHITTAKER: This is outrageous! How dare she!

MARION: Nothing can be done.

MRS. WHITTAKER: I'm so ashamed.

MARION: If I can get her alone I'll give her a piece of my mind.

MRS. WHITTAKER: No, no; ignore her—don't say a word. We don't want a repetition of this afternoon.

MARION: We shall never hear the last of it. Did you see Mrs. Phillips' face?

MRS. WHITTAKER: I'm sure I don't know what I've done to be so humiliated.

MARION [*fearing a breakdown*]: Mother—for Heaven's sake——

HILDA *rushes in from the dance-room.*

HILDA [*frantically*]: Mother—Lari's come down! She's dancing!

MARION: Yes, yes, we know.

HILDA: I've been telling everybody she was ill.

MRS. WHITTAKER: Don't speak so loudly, Hilda.

[464]

HILDA: She looks a sight. What are we to do?

MRS. WHITTAKER: Nothing. Ignore her completely—behave as if she wasn't there at all, and don't discuss her with anybody.

HILDA: But everybody's talking about her.

MARION: I don't wonder.

HILDA: It's too awful.

FURBER *approaches them.*

FURBER: The sit-down supper's ready in the tent now, ma'am.

MRS. WHITTAKER: Well, tell everybody. You'd better stop the band.

MARION: No, there won't be room if they all troop out. I'll go in and just tell some of them.

MRS. WHITTAKER: Yes, do.

HILDA: I'll come too.

MRS. WHITTAKER: Remember, Hilda—don't be aware of anything unusual at all.

HILDA: All right.

HILDA *and* MARION *go into the dance-room.*

MRS. WHITTAKER *passes her hand hopelessly across her forehead.*

JOHN *comes in.*

JOHN: Mother—I'm fearfully sorry about this.

MRS. WHITTAKER: Don't, John—don't.

JOHN: But I don't understand—it's so unlike Lari to make an exhibition of herself like this.

MRS. WHITTAKER [*bitterly*]: Unlike her!

JOHN: Something's happened. What is it?

MRS. WHITTAKER: Don't worry me now, John; can't you see I'm at my wit's end?

JOHN: I mean to find out.

Several people come in, among them SARAH *and* CHARLES.

MRS. WHITTAKER *goes out to the supper-tent.*

SARAH [*lightly*]: Don't look so gloomy, John.

JOHN: Something's happened to Lari—what is it?

SARAH: She's dancing at the moment with Philip Bordon.

JOHN: Why did she pretend to have a headache, and not come down to dinner or anything?

SARAH: She didn't feel like it, I suppose.

JOHN: I'm going to find out what's wrong.

SARAH [*taking his arm*]: No, you're not; you're going to give me some supper. Come along, or there won't be any room.

JOHN: But, Sarah——

SARAH: Come *along*.

She drags him off, throwing a meaning look at CHARLES *over her shoulder.* CHARLES *nods, and lights a cigarette.*

BOBBY COLEMAN *walks across with a* GIRL.

BOBBY: I think she looks jolly attractive.

GIRL: Fancy all those bracelets, though! [*They go off.*]

LARITA *comes in with* PHILIP, *followed at a discreet distance by* HILDA, *scowling malignantly.*

LARITA: No—I couldn't eat a thing at the moment. If I'd known supper was so close I should never have had that sandwich. [*She sits down on sofa.*]

PHILIP: Can I get you anything to drink?

LARITA: No, thanks—nothing. Go and have supper with poor little Hilda, and we'll dance again afterwards.

PHILIP: But, I say——

LARITA: Please! I want to rest for a minute.

PHILIP: Oh, very well.

HILDA *marches out, with her head in the air.* PHILIP *follows despondently.*

LARITA [*to* CHARLES]: Come and talk to me.

CHARLES: I've been wanting to do that.

LARITA: How sweet of you. Where's Sarah?

CHARLES: With John—having supper.

LARITA: Oh! [*She opens her cigarette-case and offers him one.*]

CHARLES: Thanks. [*He lights hers and his own.*]

LARITA: Such a good floor, don't you think?

CHARLES: Perfectly awful.

[466]

LARITA: I wonder if your attention has been called to those fascinating Japanese lanterns?

CHARLES: Several times.

LARITA: You must admit it's a fine night, anyhow.

CHARLES: How you've changed.

LARITA: Changed?

CHARLES: Yes. Meeting you just now and then, as I've done, makes it easier to observe subtle differences.

LARITA: In what way have I changed?

CHARLES: You're dimmer.

LARITA: Dimmer!—with all these? [*She jingles her bracelets.*]

CHARLES: Yes, even with those.

LARITA: You wouldn't have thought me dim if you'd seen me this afternoon.

CHARLES: Why, what happened?

LARITA: Several things.

CHARLES: I don't want you to think I'm angling for your confidence, but I *am* interested.

LARITA: I know that. It's interesting enough. Do you remember saying, the first day I met you, that one was disillusioned over everything?

CHARLES: You've been disillusioned lately?

LARITA: Yes—I didn't know I was capable of it.

CHARLES: That's one of the greatest illusions of all.

LARITA: You've been awfully nice to me.

CHARLES: Why not? We speak the same language.

LARITA: Yes—I suppose we do.

CHARLES: And naturally one feels instinctively drawn—particularly in this atmosphere.

LARITA: English country life. [*She smiles.*]

CHARLES: Yes, English country life.

LARITA: I wonder if it's a handicap having our sort of minds?

CHARLES: In what way?

LARITA: Watching ourselves go by.

[*467*]

CHARLES: No, it's a comfort in the end.

LARITA: I'm face to face with myself all the time—specially when I'm unhappy. It's not an edifying sensation.

CHARLES: I'm sorry you're unhappy.

LARITA: It can't be helped—you can't cope adequately with your successes unless you realize your failures.

CHARLES: It requires courage to do either.

LARITA: I've always had a definite ideal.

CHARLES: What is it?

LARITA: One should be top-dog in one's own particular sphere.

CHARLES: It's so difficult to find out what *is* one's own particular sphere.

LARITA: I'm afraid that's always been depressingly obvious to me.

CHARLES: You feel you've deviated from your course.

LARITA: Exactly—and it's demoralized me.

CHARLES: Why did you do it?

LARITA: Panic, I believe.

CHARLES: What sort of panic?

LARITA: A panic of restlessness and dissatisfaction with everything.

CHARLES: That's a black cloud which descends upon everyone at moments.

LARITA: Not everyone—just people like us.

CHARLES: When you live emotionally you must expect the pendulum to swing both ways.

LARITA: It had swung the wrong way with a vengeance when I met John. Marrying him was the most cowardly thing I ever did.

CHARLES: Why did you?

LARITA: I loved him quite differently. I thought that any other relationship would be cheapening and squalid—I can't imagine how I could have been such a fool.

CHARLES: Neither can I.

LARITA: Love will always be the most dominant and absorbing

subject in the world because it's so utterly inexplicable. Experience can teach you to handle it superficially, but not to explain it. I can look round with a nice clear brain and see absolutely no reason why I should love John. He falls short of every ideal I've ever had—he's not particularly talented or clever; he doesn't *know* anything, really; he can't talk about any of the things I consider it worth while to talk about; and, having been to a good school—he's barely educated.

CHARLES: Just a healthy young animal.

LARITA: Yes.

CHARLES: Perhaps that explains it.

LARITA: If my love were entirely physical, it would; but it isn't physical at all.

CHARLES: That *is* a bad sign.

LARITA: The worst.

CHARLES: What do you intend to do?

LARITA: I haven't decided yet.

CHARLES: I think I know.

LARITA: Don't say that.

CHARLES: Very well; I'll tell you afterwards if I guessed right.

LARITA: Go, and send Sarah to me—alone; will you?

CHARLES [*rising*]: All right.

LARITA [*putting out her hand*]: We shall meet again, perhaps, some day.

CHARLES: I *was* right.

LARITA [*putting her finger to her lips*]: Sshhh!

CHARLES *goes out*.

People have passed backward and forward during this scene, talking and laughing. Now the hall is practically deserted. HUGH PETWORTH *and* BOBBY COLEMAN *appear on the veranda. Seeing* LARITA *alone, they whisper and nudge each other. Finally* HUGH *comes in.*

HUGH: I say, Mrs. John, will you dance?

LARITA: No, thank you—I'm rather tired.

HUGH: It's a jolly good band.

[469]

LARITA: Do you know, I don't believe I've ever met you before.

HUGH: Well, as a matter of fact, we haven't been introduced officially. My name's Hugh Petworth.

LARITA: Really. How much would you have won from your little friend if I had agreed to dance with you?

HUGH [*flummoxed*]: Here, I say, you know—I——

LARITA: You're far too young and nice-looking to be so impertinent. If I were you, I should run away and recover yourself.

HUGH [*blushing*]: I'm awfully sorry.

LARITA: Don't apologize—it's quite all right.

HUGH PETWORTH *bows awkwardly, and goes hurriedly out to rejoin* BOBBY, *who has disappeared. He cannons into* SARAH, *who is coming in.*

HUGH: I beg your pardon.

SARAH: Not at all. Hullo! Lari.

LARITA: I want to talk to you, Sarah—importantly. There isn't much time.

SARAH: Why? What do you mean?

LARITA: I'm going away—to-night.

SARAH: Lari!

LARITA: For good.

SARAH: Oh, my dear!—what on earth's the matter?

LARITA: Everything. Where's John?

SARAH: In the supper-tent.

LARITA: Listen. There was a dreary family fracas this afternoon.

SARAH: What about?

LARITA: Hilda had unearthed a newspaper cutting, disclosing several of my past misdemeanors——

SARAH: The unutterable little beast! I made her swear——

LARITA: You knew about it?

SARAH: Yes, she showed it to me three days ago.

LARITA [*slightly overcome*]: Oh, Sarah!——

SARAH: I said I'd never speak to her again if she showed it to anybody, and I shan't.

LARITA: It was all very unpleasant. The Colonel stood by me, of course—John wasn't there—he doesn't know anything yet.

SARAH: But, Lari dear, don't give in like this and chuck up everything.

LARITA: I must—you see, they're right; it's perfectly horrible for them. I'm entirely to blame.

SARAH: But what does it matter? The past's finished with.

LARITA: Never. Never, never, never. That's a hopeless fallacy.

SARAH: I'm most frightfully sorry.

LARITA: I wouldn't give in at all—unless I was sure. You see, John's completely sick of me—it was just silly calf-love, and I ought to have recognized it as such. But I was utterly carried away—and now it's all such a hopeless mess.

SARAH: John's behaved abominably.

LARITA: No—not really. I expected too much. When you love anybody, you build in your mind an ideal of them—and it's naturally terribly hard for them to play up, not knowing——

SARAH: But, Lari, don't do anything on the impulse of the moment.

LARITA: It isn't the impulse of the moment—I realized it weeks ago.

SARAH: It may all come right yet.

LARITA: Be honest, Sarah—how can it?

SARAH: Where are you going?

LARITA: London to-night, and Paris to-morrow. I've ordered a car. Louise is packing now.

SARAH: Where will you stay?

LARITA: The Ritz. I always do.

SARAH: I wish I could do something.

LARITA [pressing her hand]: You can.

SARAH: What?

LARITA: Look after John for me.

SARAH [turning away]: Don't, Lari.

LARITA: I mean it. You're fond of him—you ought to have married him, by rights. He needs you so much more than me. He's frightfully weak, and a complete damn fool over most things, but he has got qualities—somewhere—worth bringing out. I'm going to arrange for him to divorce me, quietly, without any fuss.

SARAH: I don't love him nearly as well as you do.

LARITA: All the better. Women of my type are so tiresome in love. We hammer at it, tooth and nail, until it's all bent and misshapen. Promise me you'll do what I ask.

SARAH: I can't promise; but if circumstances make it possible, I'll try.

LARITA: All right—that'll do.

SARAH: Shall I see you again—ever?

LARITA: Yes, please.

SARAH: Well, we won't say good-by, then.

LARITA: It's such a silly thing to say. [*She gets up.*]

SARAH: Good luck, anyhow.

LARITA: I'm not sure that that's not sillier.

JOHN *comes in.*

JOHN: Sarah, I've been looking for you everywhere.

SARAH: Well, you've found me now.

JOHN: Lari, I'm sorry I was beastly just now—about your dress. You are rather a Christmas tree, though, aren't you?

LARITA: It was done with a purpose.

JOHN: What purpose?

LARITA: It was a sort of effort to re-establish myself—rather a gay gesture—almost a joke!

JOHN: Oh!

SARAH: You'll find me in the garden, John.

LARITA [*quickly*]: Don't go, Sarah—please. [SARAH *stops.*] I'm rather tired, so I'll say good night.

JOHN: The dance will go on for hours yet—this is only a lull.

LARITA: Yes, I know; but I'm dead.

JOHN: Oh, very well.

LARITA: Good night, darling. [*She kisses him.*]

JOHN: I'll try not to disturb you.

LARITA: I'm afraid you won't be able to help it.

SARAH: Come and dance, John.

JOHN: What's the matter, Lari? Why are you looking like that?

LARITA: I think I'm going to sneeze.

BOBBY COLEMAN *and* NINA *rush across, laughing; he's delving into her bag and she's trying to recapture it.*

JOHN *and* SARAH *go into the dance-room.*

FURBER *enters from the veranda.*

LARITA: Is the car ready, Furber?

FURBER: Yes, ma'am. Your maid is waiting in it.

LARITA: Get my cloak from her, will you, please?

FURBER: Very good, ma'am. [*He goes off.*]

LARITA, *left quite alone, leans up against one of the windows and looks out into the garden. The light from the lanterns falls on her face, which is set in an expression of hopeless sadness. She fans herself once, then lets her fan drop.*

FURBER *re-enters with her cloak, and helps her on with it.*

LARITA: Thank you very much, Furber. You won't forget what I asked you, will you?

FURBER: No, ma'am.

LARITA: Then good-by.

FURBER: Good-by, ma'am.

He holds open the door for her, and she walks out. There is a burst of laughter from the veranda. The band continues to play with great enthusiasm.

CURTAIN

POINT VALAINE

CAST OF CHARACTERS

Stefan	ALFRED LUNT
May	ALBERTA PERKINS
Lola	RUTH BOYD
Major Tillett	FRED LESLIE
Mrs. Tillett	GRAYCE HAMPTON
Mrs. Birling	LILLIAN TONGE
Elise	PHYLLIS CONNARD
Mortimer Quinn	OSGOOD PERKINS
George Fox	BROD CRAWFORD
Ted Burchell	PHILIP TONGE
Linda Valaine	LYNN FONTANNE
Mrs. Hall-Fenton	GLADYS HENSON
Phyllis	MARGARET CURTIS
Gladys	PHYLLIS HARDING
Sylvia	VALERIE COSSART
Hilda James	EVERLEY GREGG
Martin Welford	LOUIS HAYWARD

ACT I

SCENE I. *The verandah of the Point Valaine Hotel. Morning.*
SCENE II. *Linda's sitting room. Afternoon.*
SCENE III. *The verandah. Late afternoon.*

ACT II

SCENE I. *Linda's sitting room. Afternoon. Four days later.*
SCENE II. *The verandah. Evening. The next day. During this scene the curtain is lowered to denote lapse of a few hours.*

ACT III

SCENE I. *Linda's sitting room. Night.*
SCENE II. *The verandah. The next morning.*

Time: The Present

ACT I

SCENE I

Point Valaine is a small island situated a mile or so south of one of the larger British West Indies. In the evening and the morning, when the light is clear, the coast of Venezuela can be seen, dim and mysterious, like a bank of clouds on the horizon.

The verandah of the Point Valaine Hotel is spacious and shabbily comfortable. There are several long chairs covered with faded chintz lined up against the balustrade in order that the guests of the hotel can sit back in comfort and admire the exceedingly beautiful view, with their feet up. A corrugated tin roof covers the verandah, and around the poles that support it circular tables have been built. One of these is used as a dumb waiter at meal times. Another has a portable gramophone on it, a lot of records, and a pile of old illustrated weeklies. There are two doors on the right-hand side of the stage, the lower one leading to the bedrooms and the rest of the hotel, and the upper one leading to the bar and the kitchen. On the left-hand side, downstage, is a door leading to LINDA VALAINE's *private apartments. In the middle of the balustrade at the back there are steps leading down to the landing stage and the swimming pool. Profuse tropical foliage can be seen over the edge of the verandah at the back, and beyond it, on the right, the open sea. On the left, a mile away, is the main island, to and from which the hotel launch journeys twice daily.*

All round the verandah there are rather battered green shutters which are let down when it rains, imparting to everything an atmosphere of strange gloom, almost as though one were at the bottom of the sea. During the rainy season this faintly

[479]

obvious simile is used several times a day by the majority of the guests.

When the curtain rises it is about 8:30 A.M. MAJOR *and* MRS. TILLETT, MRS. BIRLING, ELISE BIRLING, *and* MORTIMER QUINN *are finishing breakfast. The tables are set along the left side of the stage, close to the balustrade.* STEFAN, LOLA, *and* MAY *are waiting on them. It is a steamy, oppressive morning in June. There is no sun as yet, owing to the rainy season being in full swing, but there is always the hope that in a little while it may burst through the clouds for an hour or so.* MAJOR *and* MRS. TILLETT *are a conventional elderly couple.* MRS. BIRLING *is vague with rather a whining voice.* ELISE, *her daughter, is an anæmic girl in the twenties.* MORTIMER QUINN *is an eminent writer of about forty-five. There is a certain dry aloofness in his manner, but in spite of his enviable detachment he is quite amiable and polite.* LOLA *and* MAY *are coloured girls, products of the island.* STEFAN *is a Russian. He might be any age between thirty and fifty. He speaks briefly and seldom, with a strange Russian-American accent. He is quiet and unobtrusive, even slightly servile at moments, but in his movements there is always a suggestion of controlled force, again detachment, but different from* MORTIMER QUINN's *in that it is animal rather than intellectual.*

MRS. TILLETT: Don't have any more coffee, Bertie, we don't want to waste time, and it will only make you livery.

MAJOR TILLETT: There's only a drain left in the pot.

MRS. TILLETT: I mean don't order any more, you haven't packed your suitcase yet.

MAJOR TILLETT: I mustn't leave without giving you back your ointment, Miss Birling.

ELISE: Oh, you can keep it if you like, you might need it on the voyage. I've got another tube, anyhow.

MRS. BIRLING: It's really wonderful stuff, isn't it?

MAJOR TILLETT: Extraordinary—absolutely extraordinary, the little beggars won't come near it.

ELISE: I only got it as a sample to begin with. Mr. Harrison told me about it, and so off I went to the chemists'—you know that one just near the Royal—and they gave me a little tiny tube no bigger than that——[*She measures in the air a minute tube of mosquito ointment.*]

MRS. TILLETT: No smell, that's what I like about it—no smell at all.

MRS. BIRLING: It will seem funny to be home again, won't it? I mean, where you don't have to worry about insects or anything.

MAJOR TILLETT: Oh, I don't know about that. We get pretty bad gnats in Horsham.

MRS. BIRLING: Yes, but gnats are different, I mean they're not dangerous.

MRS. TILLETT: A friend of ours once got blood-poisoning from a gnat, she couldn't put her leg to the ground for three weeks.

GEORGE FOX *and* TED BURCHELL *come running up the verandah steps. They are wearing bathing trunks, and bath towels over their shoulders. They are both sugar planters, but* GEORGE *is American and* TED *is English.*

TED: Good-morning, everybody.

GEORGE: Good-morning.

Everybody replies with polite "good-mornings."

MRS. BIRLING: How is the water?

TED: A bit soupy.

GEORGE: I think Mrs. Valaine ought to have the net tightened, there was a whale of a jellyfish by the steps.

MRS. TILLETT: A whale of a jellyfish, doesn't that sound funny? [*She laughs immoderately.*]

TED: They slip in over the top at high tide.

ELISE: I hope it will have gone by eleven o'clock.

TED: It's gone now, I scooped it out with the canoe paddle.

MRS. TILLETT: I must go and finish packing—hurry up, Bertie.

MAJOR TILLETT: I'm ready.

MRS. TILLETT: The launch will be here in a minute.

GEORGE [*to* MORTIMER]: Are you working this morning or do you want to come fishing with Ted and me?

MORTIMER: How far are you going?

GEORGE: Just off Mother Amos, the wind's wrong for going right round.

MORTIMER: I shall leave it to the weather. If it rains, I stay; if it doesn't rain, I go.

GEORGE: Good—come on, Ted.

TED: All right.

They go off upstairs to dress.

MRS. TILLETT [*to the* BIRLINGS]: Will you still be here when we come down?

MRS. BIRLING: Oh yes—I'm not going to let Elise bathe until eleven.

ELISE: I'm not sure I want to bathe anyhow.

MRS. BIRLING: We'll be on the landing stage to wave you good-bye.

MAJOR TILLETT: Splendid—splendid.

MRS. TILLETT: Come along, Bertie—hurry up.

MAJOR TILLETT: All right, all right——

They go off upstairs to finish their packing.

The BIRLINGS *get up from their table and move over to the balustrade right.* MRS. BIRLING *sits in a chair, and* ELISE *perches on the edge. She picks up the binoculars which are always lying about and gazes out to sea.* STEFAN, LOLA, *and* MAY *clear away the vacant tables and fold them up.*

MORTIMER: Bring me some fresh coffee, will you, Stefan?

STEFAN: Yes, sir. [*He goes off right.*]

ELISE: There's a ship coming in.

MRS. BIRLING: A big one?

ELISE: One of the French Line, I think.

MRS. BIRLING [*taking the glass from her*]: Let me see.

ELISE: I expect it's the *Colombie*—she's due today.

MRS. BIRLING [*putting down the glass*]: Don't forget to take your iron jelloids.

[482]

ELISE: I took them just now, at breakfast.

STEFAN *comes back with a pot of fresh coffee for* MORTIMER.

MORTIMER: Are you going over to the mainland today, Stefan?

STEFAN: I go tomorrow.

MORTIMER: Can you remember to get me some typewriter rubber?

STEFAN: Eraser?

MORTIMER: Yes, if you prefer it.

STEFAN: I will bring it.

MORTIMER: Thank you.

ELISE: Here it comes—here comes the rain——

There is a spatter of rain on the roof which rapidly swells into a downpour. STEFAN, LOLA, *and* MAY *let down the blinds all round the verandah.* STEFAN *goes off,* MAY *and* LOLA *tidy up a few things rather aimlessly, obviously waiting for* MORTIMER *to finish his coffee so that they can get the table out of the way.*

MRS. BIRLING: How tiresome.

ELISE: It won't last long.

MORTIMER [*with a glint in his eye*]: It feels exactly as though one were at the bottom of the sea, doesn't it?

MRS. BIRLING: That's what I always say.

MORTIMER: It's all right, Lola, you can snatch away the table now if you want to—I'll finish my coffee in a chair.

LOLA [*giggling*]: Yes, sir.

MORTIMER *settles himself in a chair and takes a cigarette.* STEFAN *appears suddenly with a match and lights it for him and disappears again.* GEORGE *and* TED *reënter dressed in old flannel trousers and sweaters.*

TED: This is cheerful, isn't it?

ELISE: It won't last long.

GEORGE [*calling*]: Stefan—Stefan——

TED [*looking out to sea round one of the blinds*]: The fish are jumping, anyway.

STEFAN *enters.*

GEORGE: Did you put any gas in the boat?

[*483*]

STEFAN: Two tins of gas.

GEORGE: Fine.

TED [*to* MORTIMER]: Coming?

MORTIMER: God has sent rain so that I shall not be tempted to go fishing and leave my work. God is very domineering.

ELISE [*laughing*]: Oh, you are awful, Mr. Quinn! Isn't Mr. Quinn awful, Mother?

MRS. BIRLING: It must be lovely to be a writer—I mean to be able to work whenever you feel like it.

MORTIMER: It is lovely. Awful and lovely.

GEORGE: Oh, come on, we can be back in time for lunch.

MORTIMER: No, I shall go and sit on my balcony, very sadly, with the blinds down, and meditate.

TED: You can meditate in the boat.

MORTIMER: I've tried that, it's no good.

ELISE: The rain will stop soon—it never lasts long.

MORTIMER [*in a sinister whisper to* GEORGE]: Has it ever struck you, George, that when it is raining and the blinds are down it feels just as though one were at the bottom of the sea?

GEORGE [*cheerfully*]: Not at all. It feels as though one were on top of a mountain.

MORTIMER [*still whispering*]: That's what I always say. [*He goes off upstairs.*]

The noise of a motor launch is heard, then two blasts of a Klaxon horn.

ELISE: There's the launch.

TED [*to* GEORGE]: Shall we wait and say good-bye to the Tilletts, or slip away now?

GEORGE: Let's go now.

They are about to go when LINDA VALAINE *enters from the left. She is a handsome red-haired woman somewhere between thirty-five and forty-five. She wears heelless sand shoes, bare legs, a cheap faded cotton dress which is almost an overall, a short, vividly coloured Chinese jacket, and horn-rimmed glasses.*

LINDA [*brusquely*]: Good-morning.

TED: Good-morning, Mrs. Valaine.

The BIRLINGS *and* GEORGE *also murmur "good-mornings."*

LINDA [*to* GEORGE *and* TED]: Are you taking the *Maria?*

GEORGE: Yes.

LINDA: Don't go round Mother Amos—it's not safe today: the wind's too strong.

TED: We won't go further than the point.

GEORGE: If the motor doesn't conk out before then.

ELISE: Mr. Fox says there was a jellyfish in the pool this morning.

LINDA: Tell Stefan to take it out.

GEORGE: I took it out myself.

LINDA: Good.

MRS. BIRLING: Don't you think the net ought to be tightened? I mean if a jellyfish could get in, a barracuda could get in, or even a shark—I mean—it's a little dangerous, isn't it?

LINDA: The net is examined carefully every few days. A moray might conceivably squeeze in through the wire—there's no preventing that; but there's no fear of either sharks or barracudas.

MRS. BIRLING: Jellyfish are bad enough: they can be very poisonous.

LINDA [*absently*]: They are.

MRS. BIRLING: Well—I mean—I do think——

LINDA [*patiently*]: The tides are always abnormally high at this time of the year, Mrs. Birling, and if jellyfish float in over the net, the best thing is not to bathe until they've floated out again.

GEORGE [*laughing*]: That sounds reasonable.

LINDA [*calling*]: Lola—May——

TED: We'll be getting along.

LOLA *enters.*

LINDA [*at table*]: Fetch the book, Lola, and refill this inkpot.

The TILLETTS *come bustling down the stairs followed by* MAY *and* STEFAN *with their luggage.*

MRS. TILLETT: Ah, there you are, Mrs. Valaine. We've enjoyed our time here so much.

MAJOR TILLETT: Best holiday I've ever had, far and away the best.

LINDA: I'm so glad. You'd better take down the luggage, Stefan.

MRS. TILLETT: Good-bye, Mr. Fox. Good-bye, Mr. Burchell.

GEORGE: Good-bye.

TED: Have a nice journey.

There are general good-byes, and handshakings all round.

LINDA: Don't forget to write in the book.

MAJOR TILLETT: Of course—of course——

MAY *comes running in with the visitors' book and an inkpot.*

LINDA: It's stopped raining. Pull up the blinds, May.

MAY: Yes, ma'am.

MAY *goes round pulling up the blinds. The* TILLETTS *write in the visitors' book.* GEORGE *and* TED *go off down the steps.*

TED [*as they go*]: Give my love to England—good-bye——

ELISE: Come on, Mother, let's go down to the landing stage.

MRS. BIRLING [*to* MAJOR TILLETT]: What time does your boat sail?

MAJOR TILLETT: Four o'clock.

ELISE: It ought to pass here about half-past five—don't forget to wave.

MRS. BIRLING *and* ELISE *go off down the steps.*

MRS. TILLETT: Well, good-bye, Mrs. Valaine.

LINDA [*shaking hands*]: Good-bye.

MAJOR TILLETT: If ever we come out to the Islands again, we shall come straight here.

LINDA: I shall expect you.

MRS. TILLETT: And if those snapshots turn out well you will send them on to us, won't you?

LINDA: Of course. You left your permanent address?

MRS. TILLETT: It's in the book.

MAJOR TILLETT: Well, good-bye again. [*He shakes hands.*]

MRS. TILLETT: Come along, Bertie.

They go off down the steps.

LINDA *stands looking after them.* STEFAN *comes up the steps and onto the verandah. He passes* LINDA *and is about to go off.*

LINDA [*without turning*]: Stefan.

STEFAN: Yes, ma'am.

LINDA: Get Farrell's boy up to go over the shark net thoroughly.

STEFAN: Last week only he did it.

LINDA: Tell him to do it again.

STEFAN: Yes, ma'am.

LINDA [*coming down to the table*]: Mrs. Hall-Fenton and her daughters are arriving this evening, also Miss James and a Mr. Welford. Miss James had better have her usual room, the Hall-Fentons, the suite, and you can put Mr. Welford in number seven.

STEFAN: There is a hole in number seven mosquito net.

LINDA: Tell Lola to darn it before tonight; if Lola's too busy, old Mamma Dangan can do it.

STEFAN: Yes, ma'am.

LINDA: And when you next go into town, for God's sake, get some new magazines—these are weeks old. [*She goes off left.*]

STEFAN [*looking after her*]: Yes, ma'am.

There is again the sound of a Klaxon from the launch, and a faint chorus of good-byes and bon voyages from the landing stage. STEFAN *goes off to the kitchen, and the lights fade.*

SCENE II

The scene is LINDA VALAINE'S *private sitting room. On the right there is a doorway hung with a bead curtain. This leads into a small passage which in turn leads to the left-stage door of the preceding scene.*

On the left there is another door with two shallow steps lead-

[487]

ing up to it. This opens into LINDA's *bedroom. At the back there is a wide verandah which looks out on to a few rocks in the foreground and beyond them the open sea. Old-fashioned wooden shutters fold right across the window opening at night time. The room itself is not particularly tidy. There are a few chintz covered cane chairs, a chaise-longue, a writing desk, and a few pictures and photographs on the walls. There is a low table by the chaise-longue, and a very battered basket chair and foot rest on the verandah.*

When the curtain rises it is the afternoon of the same day. LINDA *is sitting at the desk, writing. She is dressed in the same clothes as in Scene I.*

There is the sound of an accordion being played in the distance.

LOLA *enters from the right.*

LOLA: Please, ma'am.

LINDA: What is it?

LOLA: Mr. Quinn, ma'am. He wants to see you.

LINDA: Tell him to come in.

LOLA: Yes, ma'am. [*She goes out.*]

LINDA *shuffles some bills into a pile and puts a paper-weight on them, then she takes off her glasses and gets up as* MORTIMER QUINN *comes into the room.*

QUINN: Am I disturbing you?

LINDA: Not at all.

QUINN: I want some more information.

LINDA [*smiling*]: Very well. Do sit down.

QUINN: Thank you. [*He sits.*]

LINDA [*at table*]: Cigarette?

QUINN: Yes, please.

She hands him one and takes one herself. He lights them both.

LINDA: Have you been working all the morning?

QUINN: Yes, but rather aimlessly—it kept on raining and stopping and raining again—very distracting.

[488]

LINDA [*sitting on chaise-longue*]: This is a distracting time of year.

QUINN: You always appear to be very tranquil.

LINDA: I am. It's monotonous.

QUINN: Why is this time of year so distracting?

LINDA [*vaguely*]: Oh, I don't know—the rain, I suppose, and the sudden storms.

QUINN: Everything overemphasized.

LINDA: Yes.

QUINN: It's a strange life, really.

LINDA: Mine?

QUINN: Yes.

LINDA: What is there strange about it?

QUINN: I don't know actually, but I sort of feel it.

LINDA: You're wrong. My life is perfectly ordinary, a routine—year in, year out—the same routine.

QUINN: Perhaps it's the setting that makes it seem strange.

LINDA: Was the information you wanted about me?

QUINN: Have I been impertinent?

LINDA: No.

QUINN: If I have, will you forgive me?

LINDA: Yes.

QUINN: That's all right, then.

LINDA: Yes, that's all right.

QUINN: When did white people first come to this island?

LINDA: Fourteen ninety-two—I told you that the other day.

QUINN: When did your parents come here?

LINDA: I told you that too.

QUINN: I know—I merely wanted to check up, to be absolutely accurate.

LINDA: Am I in the story you are writing?

QUINN: You may be.

LINDA: You don't know me.

QUINN: An imaginary figure based on fact, what could be better than that?

LINDA: Shall I tell you folk tales about the islanders? I know lots of them.

QUINN: No, thank you.

LINDA: There's Mother Amos and the pirate ship, and Captain Laralde's escape from Fever Island, and there's the cave legend——

QUINN: I've read all those in that beastly little book.

LINDA: You're very hard to please.

QUINN: I have no feeling for the past: legends bore me.

LINDA: I wish he'd learn another tune.

QUINN: Stefan?

LINDA: Yes.

QUINN: I like this one.

They both listen for a moment to the distant accordion.

LINDA: Well?

QUINN: Well what?

LINDA: What do you want me to tell you? In what way can I help with this book of yours?

QUINN: I'll tell you a secret.

LINDA: What is it?

QUINN: I'm not writing a book at all.

LINDA: Oh!

QUINN: But don't be disappointed. I shall, eventually. At the moment, however, I'm just sitting and thinking and absorbing and finding out things.

LINDA: I see.

QUINN: One of the greatest advantages of being a writer is the excuse it provides——

LINDA: For not writing?

QUINN [*smiling*]: For being alone when you want to.

LINDA: I am alone too much to be able to appreciate that.

QUINN: Yes, you are, aren't you?

LINDA: I heard your typewriter clicking all the morning.

QUINN: Letters, jolly chatty letters to my friends.

LINDA: You needn't be frightened. I don't mind you writing anything you like about me.

QUINN: You're rather unfriendly today.

LINDA: I'm sorry. I don't mean to be.

QUINN: What's the matter?

LINDA: Nothing's the matter.

QUINN: New arrivals this evening?

LINDA: Yes. [*With a gleam of malice*] One of them is coming especially to see you.

QUINN: Who?

LINDA: Hilda James, she wants to interview you for the *Comet*.

QUINN: I don't mind, she can if she wants to.

LINDA: She's a very go-ahead girl, I'm sure you'll like her.

QUINN: Your unfriendliness seems to be changing rapidly to hatred.

LINDA [*softening*]: I really did try to put her off, but it was no good.

QUINN: Who else is coming?

LINDA: Mrs. Hall-Fenton and her brood, and a strange man I've never heard of. Someone must have told him about the place: he's coming in today from Venezuela on the *Colombie*.

QUINN: New blood for the Birlings. New opportunities for cascades of small talk.

LINDA: Don't you like the Birlings?

QUINN: I worship them.

LINDA: I'm sorry for Elise—her fiancé sailed away and left her in the lurch: that's very seriously mortifying in a small island.

QUINN: All the same, I see his point.

LINDA: That's cruel.

QUINN: I'm all for him. Good luck to him! He was very nearly caught, but he escaped in the nick of time.

LINDA: Woman hater?

QUINN: With reservations.

LINDA: What is it you hate about women?

QUINN: I think I despise most their lack of emotional balance.

[*491*]

LINDA: I see.

QUINN: Do you agree?

LINDA: No.

QUINN: I also dislike their fundamental dishonesty.

LINDA: Poor things.

QUINN: You don't agree with that either?

LINDA: No.

QUINN: Think for a moment of that poor young man who so nearly, so very nearly married Elise Birling. Could he have loved her, do you suppose? Even for some brief moment in tropical moonlight could he have held her in his arms and found her desirable enough, warm enough to live his life with, to work for, even to sleep with? Could he have suspected intelligence or integrity in that rattling anæmic little mind? Was the moon so strong? Was the night so enchanted?

LINDA: Perhaps she loved him.

QUINN: Do you believe she did? Come now, honestly, do you believe she could?

LINDA [turning away]: No.

QUINN: She wanted to be married, she wanted to be clothed and fed and kept.

LINDA: That's quite natural.

QUINN: But hardly honest, to try to turn his young enchantment of her to such cheap account.

LINDA [rising and speaking with sudden anger]: Nonsense.

QUINN [startled]: I beg your pardon.

LINDA: I'm a business woman, Mr. Quinn.

QUINN [smiling]: And I am sure a very excellent one.

LINDA: I'm sorry for Elise, not because she lost a romantic moonlight lover, but because she lost a house of her own and a maid of her own and a position of her own.

QUINN [quizzically]: Her own?

LINDA: Yes, her own by right of paying for them. I married a man of small means; it's not all jam by a long way. But it was

[492]

worth it, every minute of it, just to get away from Mother and home and family.

QUINN: And did you love your man of small means?

LINDA: No.

QUINN: I see.

LINDA [*vehemently*]: No, you don't. You see something, perhaps, because you are a writer, and it's your job to make little dramas out of people.

QUINN [*meekly*]: I sometimes make little comedies.

LINDA [*ignoring his interruption*]: But what you see needn't be the truth. It needn't be anywhere near the truth.

QUINN: It needn't be, but it occasionally is.

LINDA: You see me as being hard and efficient, don't you?

QUINN: At the moment, yes.

LINDA: Well, you're wrong.

QUINN: At least I knew you were going to say that.

LINDA: I expect you despise me for marrying a man I was not in love with.

QUINN: Yes. For you I think it was the wrong policy.

LINDA: It was nothing of the sort.

QUINN: I'm delighted that it all turned out so well.

LINDA: He died.

QUINN: Good.

LINDA: He died in the war.

QUINN: Better and better.

LINDA: Not at all. It would have been nicer for him to die peacefully at home, in Martinique, where he had lived all his life.

QUINN: One can't have everything.

LINDA: Are you ever sorry for people, or are you too clever?

QUINN: I'm certainly too clever to be deceived by your painstaking detachment.

LINDA: You'd like to make me angry, wouldn't you? So that I might say more than I meant to say? It would be good for the book.

QUINN: To hell with the book!

LINDA: I quite agree.

QUINN: Would you like me to go away?

LINDA: Certainly not. You're occupying my best suite. I should like you to stay for years.

QUINN: I feel deeply touched.

LINDA: That was rude, wasn't it? I apologize.

QUINN: Please don't. I asked for it.

LINDA: There are other reasons why I should like you to stay.

QUINN: What are they?

LINDA: You're funny.

QUINN: Funny!

LINDA: Yes, you make people laugh. The other guests, I mean.

QUINN: Good God!

LINDA: You're no trouble. You never make stupid complaints.

QUINN: There was a bat in my room last night.

LINDA: You're nice to talk to in spite of——

QUINN: In spite of being too damned inquisitive.

LINDA: Exactly.

QUINN [*rising*]: After that, even if I did go away, I couldn't fail to come back.

LINDA: Don't go for a minute—I'm frightened.

QUINN [*gently*]: What are you frightened of?

LINDA: I don't quite know. I really don't quite know. [*There is a spatter of rain on the roof.*] Help me with the blinds, will you?

QUINN: Of course.

They both go out onto the verandah and let down the blinds.

LINDA: That one sticks a bit.

QUINN: I can manage it—there.

LINDA [*violently*]: I hate this bloody rain!

QUINN: Very fraying to the nerves.

LINDA: Does it shock you when I swear? I oughtn't to really. It isn't respectable.

QUINN: Respectability is bloody important.

[*494*]

LINDA [*almost breathlessly*]: I sit here sometimes and swear all by myself. At the mosquitoes, at those silly screeching little birds. I think of words, all the horrible words I've ever heard, and I say them over and over. I curse the heat, and the thickness of the air, and those dull boring people chattering on the verandah. I'm a missionary's daughter, you see, and missionary's children take easily to the bad. I was brought up in this very house when it was a mission. There were no motor launches then, and I used to have to row and row backwards and forwards between here and the mainland until my back ached and my muscles cracked, boatloads of snivelling little half-caste children singing hymns, interminable whining hymns to the Lord. I know them all now; every note of them, every word; they're branded on my memory. Mother used to play the harmonium in the evenings while Father roared and bellowed to God till the sweat ran down his kind foolish face. I was brought up to believe that God made this sea and this earth and this sky, so now I swear at God too! God damn him!

QUINN: What do you want? What do you really need?

LINDA: I don't know—that's just it—I don't know.

QUINN: You might marry again.

LINDA: No, I couldn't—I couldn't do that. [*She looks suddenly frightened.*]

QUINN: Why not?

LINDA: I'm too used to being alone. Too happy with my own independence.

QUINN: Happy?

LINDA: Contented, then; on the whole, very contented; this is just a mood, that's all—it doesn't go very deep—I get them sometimes when the heat is oppressive, moods like this, but they don't last long.

QUINN: Why did you come back here, once you had escaped and been married?

LINDA: There was nowhere else to go. Mother was all alone, Father had been dead for some years. I was working in Lyons as a stenographer when my husband was killed. I had managed to save a little——

QUINN: A missionary's daughter alone in Lyons.

LINDA: It's a very big town, rich and noisy.

QUINN: I know it well.

LINDA: When I got back here I sent Mother home, back to England—she died eight years ago—and I started this place as a hotel, gradually at first, only just a few guests, planters generally, and a few people from the main island who needed somewhere quiet to convalesce after fever. I cooked most of the meals myself. Then it began to pay—more and more people came for week-ends, and I could afford to make improvements. I made the bathing pool and built extra rooms—all that wing out at the back is new. I engaged extra servants——

QUINN: When did Stefan arrive?

LINDA: Stefan? About six, no, seven years ago.

QUINN: He's very efficient.

LINDA: Very.

QUINN: A long time, seven years.

LINDA: He started as outside boy, just odd jobs; then he helped in the kitchen; and then he became a waiter.

QUINN: And now he runs practically everything.

LINDA [*sharply*]: Under my supervision.

QUINN: I intended no slur upon your own efficiency.

LINDA: I think the rain's stopping.

QUINN: Not quite yet. [*He peeps through the blind.*] It's still pretty thick: there'll be another burst before it's through.

LINDA: I hope it will clear before six—I hate people arriving in the rain.

QUINN: He has very strange eyes.

LINDA: Who?

QUINN: Stefan.

LINDA [*lightly*]: He's very strange altogether. Russians frequently are. I don't care for him much, but he does his work well.

QUINN [*meditatively*]: Honest and industrious.

LINDA: His story would be very useful to you. You must get him to tell it.

QUINN: I have.

LINDA: I congratulate you. He seldom speaks much.

QUINN: I have my own secret ways of making people speak.

LINDA [*smiling*]: I've noticed that.

QUINN: As a matter of fact, his tale is too melodramatic for me, too obvious. Stowaway voyages in oil tankers—New York docks—South American nitrate mines—revolutions—escapings from prison. Magazine stuff. I prefer more subtle drama, strange little twists in psychology—small unaccountable happenings in people's minds.

LINDA: I hope your afternoon has been profitable.

QUINN: I can see that you are going to be defensive again, so I shall go.

LINDA [*smiling*]: Come again—the island legends are very interesting.

QUINN: Thank you. I will.

LINDA: Be nice to Hilda James, won't you? She's very eager.

QUINN: I'll do my best.

LINDA: I'm afraid you won't find any strange little twists in her mind.

QUINN: My first step will be to discover whether or not she has a mind at all.

LINDA: Good luck.

MORTIMER QUINN *goes out.*

LINDA *wanders over to the desk, sits down at it, and then gets up again irritably. The pattering of the rain swells into a downpour. She stands quite still in the middle of the room with her back to the window. She is trembling a little, and listening intently.*

STEFAN *pushes one of the blinds aside and climbs silently onto the verandah. His white coat and trousers are soaking wet, and his feet are bare.* LINDA *hears him but she doesn't turn. He comes*

down into the room and stands in front of her, staring at her.
She makes no movement. He slips his hand over her body and
presses her into his arms with his mouth on hers.
    The lights fade.

SCENE III

The scene is the verandah again. It is about six o'clock on the
same day as the preceding scenes. It is no longer raining, and
everything is bathed in strong evening sunlight.

When the curtain rises the stage is empty except for STEFAN,
who is standing with his back to the audience, scanning the sea
through the binocular. GEORGE *and* TED *come in from the right.*

TED: Two rum punches, Stefan.

STEFAN [*putting down the binocular*]: Yes, sir.

GEORGE: Got any potato chips?

STEFAN: Yes, sir.

GEORGE: Good.

STEFAN *goes off.*

TED: Funny about the Russians, isn't it?

GEORGE: Damn funny.

TED: That fellow gives me the creeps.

GEORGE: That's because you're oversensitive, my lad. Just a
bundle of nerves, that's all.

TED: Oh, shut up!

GEORGE: Look at the way you got the jitters when you saw that
shark.

TED: It was a hammerhead.

GEORGE: The woods are full of them.

TED: I wouldn't swim in the open sea round about here whatever you paid me.

GEORGE: You'd probably be all right in the daytime.

TED: D'you think that yarn's true about the man swimming
from here to the main island?

[*498*]

GEORGE: Yes. He never saw so much as a porpoise.

TED: Damn fool.

GEORGE: Mrs. Valaine was good and mad, I believe.

TED: Bad advert for the hotel if he'd got bitten in half.

GEORGE: You bet.

MORTIMER QUINN *comes up the steps.*

QUINN: Hallo!

GEORGE: Want a rum punch?

QUINN: Yes, badly.

STEFAN *enters with two rum punches.*

GEORGE: Bring another one for Mr. Quinn, Stefan.

STEFAN: Yes, sir. [*He goes off again.*]

GEORGE: Here, you have this one.

QUINN: No no, I can wait.

GEORGE: Go on—take it—I'll share Ted's until the other one comes.

QUINN: Thanks.

TED: How was the work?

QUINN: It wasn't.

GEORGE: Rain put you off your stride?

QUINN: Yes, it gave me ideas.

TED: I should have thought that would have been a help.

QUINN: They were unwritable.

GEORGE: I have ideas like that sometimes.

TED: George often gets lecherous in the rainy season. Only this morning he fell in love with a shark.

QUINN: A big one?

GEORGE: I like them big.

QUINN: Did you catch anything?

TED: Two groupers, a few flat-looking things like skate, and a poor little bastard with frills on it.

GEORGE: We put him back, he looked kind of sissy.

QUINN: You mustn't be sexually intolerant.

TED: George would be sexually anything at the drop of a hat.

STEFAN *enters with the other rum punch.*

QUINN: The next round on me, Stefan.

STEFAN: Yes, sir. [*He goes off.*]

TED: I can't bear that man.

QUINN: Why?

GEORGE: He's a Russian. Ted's got a hate on Russians.

TED: Remember that son of a bitch in La Paz?

GEORGE: He wasn't Russian, he was Polish.

TED: He got drunk in the Strangers' Club and started to fight me.

QUINN: What did you do?

TED: Socked him.

GEORGE: And then we weren't allowed into the club any more.

QUINN: Boys will be boys.

GEORGE and TED [*together*]: That's what I always say.

MRS. BIRLING *and* ELISE *come up the steps from the bathing pool.* ELISE *is wearing a bathing costume with a bath robe over it, and pink rubber shoes.*

MRS. BIRLING: Oh, dear, it is hot. I was almost tempted to bathe myself.

ELISE: The water was lovely.

TED: No jellyfish?

ELISE: No—it was beautifully clear, too—you could see right away down to the bottom.

MRS. BIRLING: I must speak to Mrs. Valaine; Elise says there's a splinter in the chute.

QUINN: Still?

GEORGE *and* TED *laugh.*

MRS. BIRLING: It's very dangerous, you might get blood-poisoning or anything.

ELISE *takes off her bathing cap, releasing a great deal of damp hair.*

ELISE: Oh, dear, this cap's no use at all.

MRS. BIRLING: Run and get dressed, dear, the launch will be here in a minute.

ELISE: All right, Mother.

QUINN: Would you like a rum punch, Mrs. Birling, as you haven't bathed?

MRS. BIRLING: No, thank you, Mr. Quinn. Rum always goes straight to my liver.

QUINN: How horrid of it!

MRS. BIRLING: I feel ill for days if I have so much as a sip—go along, Elise.

They both go off upstairs.

GEORGE and TED [*together*]: Which only goes to show!

QUINN: You are both sadly lacking in human sympathy.

GEORGE: Yeah, we're tough, we are.

QUINN: At that I don't believe you're either of you one quarter as tough as Mrs. Birling.

The launch Klaxon is heard.

TED: Oh, God! No peace.

GEORGE: Come and sit down.

QUINN: All right.

They go up to the back and sit down with their feet up on the rail. STEFAN enters from the right with a tray of rum punches. He is followed by LOLA and MAY, who go across the verandah and down the steps. STEFAN gives TED, GEORGE, and QUINN their drinks and waits while QUINN signs a chit for them; then he also goes down the steps.

LINDA comes in from the left. She is wearing a sort of semi-evening dress, very simply made of some cottony material. The three men get up.

TED: Hallo, Mrs. Valaine.

GEORGE: Have you come to receive?

LINDA: Yes.

GEORGE: Have a rum punch?

LINDA: No, thanks.

TED: Come on, just a sip, to give you courage. [*He hands her his glass.*]

LINDA [*smiling*]: Oh, very well. [*She sips a little.*]

QUINN: You look very cool.

LINDA: I've just been swimming.

GEORGE: In the pool? We didn't see you go down.

LINDA: I went off the rocks just beyond my verandah.

TED: Isn't that a bit risky?

LINDA: Not really, in the day time, it's only at night that the big marauding fish come in close.

QUINN: It is dangerous all the same.

LINDA: I never swim far out.

MRS. BIRLING *comes down from the stairs.*

MRS. BIRLING: Elise will be down in a moment.

LINDA: Did she enjoy her bathe?

MRS. BIRLING: Yes, but there was a splinter in the chute; luckily she saw it in time.

TED: In time for what?

LINDA [*quickly*]: I'm so sorry, I'll have it seen to.

GEORGE: Here they all come.

There is a murmur of voices below the verandah. LINDA *goes to the top of the steps.* MRS. HALL-FENTON *appears first. She is a buxom, jolly, rather common woman. She is followed by her two eldest girls,* GLADYS *and* PHYLLIS. SYLVIA, *the youngest, follows with* HILDA JAMES. *All four girls are unremarkable in appearance.* HILDA, *however, is rather more smartly dressed than the other three.* MARTIN WELFORD *comes last. He is a nice sensitive-looking boy. He wears the usual white tropical suit and a Panama hat. They all come onto the verandah, chattering.* MARTIN *hangs back a little.*

MRS. HALL-FENTON: Here we all are, Mrs. Valaine. The car broke down just near the new bridge, and we nearly as anything missed the launch.

GLADYS: Mother was in the most awful state.

MRS. HALL-FENTON: I wasn't at all. I kept calm.

PHYLLIS: Mother, how *can* you!

SYLVIA: A man went to the petrol station on a bicycle and fetched another man. He——

GLADYS: It was one of the sparking plugs.

HILDA: Hallo, Linda.

She kisses her warmly. All the others have shaken hands.

LINDA: Hallo, Hilda.

MRS. HALL-FENTON [*shaking hands with* MRS. BIRLING]: Hallo, Mrs. Birling. Where's Elise? The girls are dying to see her.

MRS. BIRLING: She's changing. She'll be down in a minute.

MRS. HALL-FENTON [*furtively*]: Better?

MRS. BIRLING: Much better, I think; beginning to take more interest in things.

MRS. HALL-FENTON: Building up, that's what she needs, building up.

LINDA: Mr. Welford?

MARTIN: Yes.

LINDA [*shaking hands*]: How do you do.

MARTIN: How do you do.

LINDA: You came on the *Colombie,* didn't you?

MARTIN: Yes.

LINDA: She's a beautiful ship.

ELISE *comes rushing downstairs.*

ELISE: Phyl—Glad—Syl! How lovely!

They all kiss.

HILDA: Hallo, Elise, feeling brighter?

ELISE [*a little stiffly*]: Yes, thank you, Hilda. I hope you're all right.

GLADYS: Isn't that a lovely hat of Hilda's?

PHYLLIS: She got it at Harrison's, a whole new lot came in on Tuesday. Trust Hilda to get there first.

LINDA: Mr. Quinn.

QUINN [*coming to her*]: Yes.

LINDA: This is Mr. Welford.

QUINN: Hallo. Welcome to the colony.

MARTIN [*shaking hands*]: Thanks.

LINDA: Do you mind very much waiting for a few minutes before I show you your room?

MARTIN: Not a bit.

QUINN: Come and have a rum punch.

MARTIN: Thanks awfully.

QUINN *takes him up to the back and introduces him to* TED *and* GEORGE. *Meanwhile* STEFAN *and* LOLA *and* MAY *have passed through with the luggage.* TED *yells for* STEFAN, *who presently comes on and takes their orders and goes off again.*

LINDA: I've given you the suite, Mrs. Hall-Fenton, and you have your usual little room, Hilda.

HILDA [*whispering*]: Did you tell him?

LINDA: Yes. Wait until after dinner to tackle him.

HILDA: All right—lovely.

GLADYS: Mum, have we got time for a bathe before dressing?

MRS. HALL-FENTON: Yes, if you hurry—go on up.

MRS. BIRLING: Be careful of the chute, there's a splinter in it.

LINDA: I'll take you all up—come along.

ELISE: Oh, Mother, I do wish I'd waited for my bathe.

MRS. BIRLING: Never mind, we can go down to the pool and watch.

PHYLLIS: Why not bathe again?

ELISE: Oh, I couldn't, I've just changed and everything.

SYLVIA: Come on—do——

MRS. BIRLING [*firmly*]: No, Elise mustn't bathe again so soon. She stayed in too long as it was. We'll see you at the pool. Come along, dear.

ELISE: Oh, all right.

MRS. HALL-FENTON [*as she goes off with* LINDA]: It's so nice being here again.

GLADYS: Are you going to bathe, Hilda?

HILDA: Of course. Come on—hurry——

They all go chattering upstairs. ELISE *and* MRS. BIRLING *go down the steps.* STEFAN *enters with another round of rum punches. They all take them and "Cheerio" each other.*

TED: These are a speciality of the place.

MARTIN: Damn good.

QUINN: Did you stop long in La Guayra?

MARTIN: Only one night, then I went up to Caracas for three days and came down again and caught the boat.

GEORGE: I know a swell guy in Caracas. Friedman. He's in the Western Union. Did you see him by any chance?

MARTIN: No, I didn't meet anyone really. I was feeling rather ill most of the time.

TED: Fever.

MARTIN: Yes, I had a bad go of it in Brazil.

GEORGE: Are you in coffee or sugar or something?

MARTIN: No, I fly, air survey work. We've been trying to map the Matto Grosso.

TED: Good God! You're not by any chance the chap who got lost, are you?

MARTIN [*smiling*]: Yes, I'm afraid I am.

GEORGE: Jesus, what a scoop for Hilda James! This'll take the front page away from you, Quinn.

QUINN: Perhaps he won't want to talk about it.

MARTIN [*looking at him gratefully*]: I don't much.

TED: That's all right, we won't say a word.

GEORGE: We read about it, of course. About three months ago, wasn't it?

MARTIN: Yes.

TED: Must have been pretty average bloody.

MARTIN: It was.

GEORGE: How many days?

MARTIN: Thirteen.

QUINN: Shut up, you two. You read the story in the papers. Leave him alone.

TED: Oh, sorry.

MARTIN: Oh, I don't mind telling you about it sometime.

GEORGE: Come out fishing with us tomorrow.

MARTIN: Fine. I'd love to.

QUINN: Have you room in your filthy little boat for a crabbed embittered old writer?

[505]

GEORGE: I'll try and use influence with my friend Ted. He pays for the gas.

TED: What about a swim?

QUINN: God! What energy!

GEORGE: All right.

TED [*to* MARTIN]: Do you want to swim?

MARTIN: I haven't unpacked my things yet.

TED: I can lend you some trunks, if you like—you can change in our room.

MARTIN: I don't think I will, thanks all the same. I'll wait until tomorrow.

GEORGE: Come on, then, Ted.

TED: Right—see you later.

GEORGE *and* TED *rush off upstairs.*

QUINN: Have another punch.

MARTIN: Thanks.—This lot's on me.

QUINN: Nonsense, you can do the next.—Stefan——

MARTIN: It's nice here, isn't it?

QUINN: It would be better without quite so many jolly people.

STEFAN *enters.*

QUINN: Two more, please, Stefan.

STEFAN: Yes, sir. [*He goes out.*]

MARTIN: I've read a lot of your books.

QUINN [*smiling*]: Have you?

MARTIN: I think you're a grand writer.

QUINN: I'm glad.

MARTIN: I suppose you're working on something new here?

QUINN: Just making notes, that's all.

MARTIN: Is it nice being a celebrity?

QUINN: You ought to know. You're a celebrity yourself since your escapade in the jungle.

MARTIN: Oh no, that's just one of those things that happen, mere chance. I mean a real celebrity. Do you like it or does it bore you?

[506]

QUINN: I sometimes pretend that it bores me, but really I like it very much.

MARTIN: Have you been here long?

QUINN: About three weeks.

MARTIN: I want to stay a little and rest. They won't let me fly again, you know, for a year. I had blood-poisoning and a lot of fever, and it did something queer to my heart, and my eyes went a bit wrong too. I don't feel like going home just yet.

QUINN: Have you got a family?

MARTIN: A father and a sister. My mother died five years ago.

QUINN: Not married?

MARTIN: Oh no.

QUINN: Do you want to be?

MARTIN: Not a bit. I'm quite happy as I am.

STEFAN *comes in with the drinks.* QUINN *signs for them.* STEFAN *goes out again.*

MARTIN: He's foreign, isn't he?

QUINN: Yes, Russian.

MARTIN: He moves funnily, doesn't he? Like some sort of animal.

QUINN: He is some sort of animal.

MARTIN: Is she nice?

QUINN: Who, Mrs. Valaine?

MARTIN: Yes.

QUINN: Very nice, rather aloof, rather shut up inside herself, but very nice—I think.

MARTIN: You don't seem quite sure.

QUINN: I'm never quite sure.

MARTIN: Will you have another punch?

QUINN: No, thanks. I think I'll go and change.

MARTIN: I shall too when Mrs. Valaine shows me where my room is.

QUINN: She'll be down in a minute.

MARTIN: Don't worry about me, I'll be all right.

QUINN: Perhaps you'd like to dine at my table as it's your first evening here. You might feel rather strange among all these shrill virgins.

MARTIN: It's most awfully nice of you. I'd like to very much.

QUINN: Fine. See you later. [*He goes off upstairs.*]

MARTIN, *left alone, perches himself on the rail and looks at the view.* PHYLLIS, SYLVIA, GLADYS, *and* HILDA *come running on in bath robes.*

PHYLLIS [*to* HILDA]: . . . and when the band stopped, they went on, to the gramophone, until five.

SYLVIA: I was nearly dead, I can tell you.

HILDA: Elise still looks a bit peaky, doesn't she?

GLADYS: I'd be peaky with a mother like that.

PHYLLIS: Oh, I've forgotten my cap.

HILDA: Have mine. I can't dive anyway. I got a bad ear last winter from diving.

PHYLLIS: I hope the chute's working.

They run off down the steps.

STEFAN *comes on and collects the empty glasses. He scrutinizes* MARTIN *covertly as he does so. He goes off as* LINDA *comes on, down the stairs.*

LINDA: Oh, Mr. Welford, I'm so sorry to have kept you waiting.

MARTIN [*jumping down from the rail*]: It doesn't matter a bit. [*He smiles at her.*] It's lovely here.

LINDA: This is a bad time of year, really. A good deal of rain.

MARTIN: I don't mind rain.

LINDA: Who told you about this hotel?

MARTIN: I met some officers from the H.M.S. *Durban.* They were in Rio for a few days. They told me about it.

LINDA: It's quite primitive, I'm afraid, but I hope you'll be comfortable.

MARTIN [*looking at her intently*]: I'm sure I shall.

LINDA [*conscious of his gaze*]: You've been ill, haven't you?

MARTIN: Yes. How did you know?

LINDA: You look a little as if you'd been ill.

MARTIN: Fever does pull one down a lot.

LINDA: You must get well and strong again.

MARTIN: I'm feeling much better already. The voyage did me good.

LINDA [*after a slight pause*]: Well—will you come with me and see your room?

MARTIN: Rather—thanks.

LINDA: This way.

She goes off up the stairs, and he follows her.

CURTAIN

ACT II

SCENE I

The scene is LINDA's *sitting room again. It is late afternoon four days later.*

When the curtain rises LINDA *is lying on the chaise-longue. On the low table by her side are a tea tray and a box of cigarettes. She has finished her tea and is reading a magazine and smoking.* LOLA *enters.*

LINDA: What is it, Lola?

LOLA: The list, ma'am, for the town. Stefan made it out.

LINDA: Let me see it.

LOLA [*giving her list*]: There is no more Worcester sauce.

LINDA: Is it down here?

LOLA: No, ma'am.

LINDA [*irritably*]: Why not? Give me a pencil. There's one on the desk.

LOLA [*fetching pencil*]: Yes, ma'am.

LINDA [*reading through the list*]: What's this?

LOLA [*giving her pencil*]: Eraser, ma'am, for Mr. Quinn. Stefan forgot it last time.

LINDA [*writing*]: Night-lights. By the way, Lola, see that Mrs. Birling has two in her room always. She says she saw a bat last night on her verandah, and her light had gone out.

LOLA: Yes, ma'am.

LINDA: Do you always put water in the saucers?

LOLA: Yes, ma'am.

LINDA: And ask Mr. Burchell and Mr. Fox not to take their face towels down to the pool. The rough ones are quite good enough.

[*510*]

LOLA: Yes, ma'am.

LINDA: All right, Lola. You can leave the list here. Tell Stefan to see me about it tomorrow morning before he leaves.

LOLA: Yes, ma'am.

LINDA: And take the tray, I've finished with it.

LOLA *is just picking up the tray when there is a knock on the door.*

Who is it?

MARTIN [*poking his head through the bead curtains*]: It's me. Are you busy?

LINDA: No. Come in.

MARTIN [*coming into the room*]: Thanks. [*He holds aside the curtains for* LOLA *to go out with the tray.*]

LINDA: Have you had tea?

MARTIN: Yes, thanks.

LINDA: Are you feeling better?

MARTIN: Ever so much better. That's why I came to see you, really, to thank you for being so kind. The bouts don't last very long, but they're beastly while they do. I'm afraid I used up a lot of blankets.

LINDA: That doesn't matter. We have enough and to spare. Fever isn't exactly rare in these parts.

MARTIN: No, I suppose not.

LINDA: Sit down, won't you?

MARTIN: Thanks. [*He sits in a cane armchair.*]

LINDA [*offering him cigarette box*]: Cigarette?

MARTIN: No, I don't think I will just now. My head still feels a bit wobbly.

LINDA: Is everybody out?

MARTIN: Yes, all except Mrs. Birling. She's reading on the verandah. Fox and Burchell and Mortimer Quinn are fishing. All the others are in the pool, I think. He's nice, isn't he?

LINDA: Who, Mr. Quinn?

MARTIN: Yes.

LINDA: Very nice.

[*511*]

MARTIN: I envy him.

LINDA: Do you—why?

MARTIN: It must be wonderful, being a writer. To be able to wander about the world and work whenever you like and wherever you like, without being dependent on anybody but yourself. And not to mind being alone.

LINDA: Do you mind being alone?

MARTIN: I hate it, except when I'm flying, but that's quite different. It's grand being alone then.

LINDA: I've always wanted to fly.

MARTIN: You'd love it.

LINDA: Perhaps I should be sick.

MARTIN: No, you wouldn't. Not in an open plane, with the wind in your face, blowing your cheeks out like balloons.

LINDA: That doesn't sound very nice.

MARTIN: It is though, it's marvellous.

LINDA: Have you ever had any accidents?—I mean apart from your jungle adventure.

MARTIN: No, except one, when I was learning, I fell into a turnip field, but that was nothing. How did you know about the jungle business?

LINDA: I recognized your face the day you arrived. Your photograph was in all the papers, you know.

MARTIN: There was a lot of silly fuss about it.

LINDA: And now you're going home?

MARTIN: Yes.

LINDA: I've never been to England.

MARTIN [surprised]: You are English, though, aren't you?

LINDA: Yes, but I've lived all my life in the Islands. I married a Frenchman and went to France for a year during the war. Apart from that I've been nowhere, seen nothing.

MARTIN: How funny.

LINDA: Funny?

MARTIN: Yes, you don't seem a bit like that, like a person who's stuck in the same place, I mean.

[512]

LINDA: How long have you been an—an aviator?

MARTIN: Since I was eighteen. I'm twenty-five now. That's seven years.

LINDA [*ruminatively*]: Twenty-five.

MARTIN: Did you think I was older?

LINDA [*with a sudden smile*]: No, I didn't.

MARTIN: I've got to waste a whole year, not flying at all.

LINDA: What a shame. But still, you're lucky to be alive, really, aren't you?

MARTIN: Yes, I suppose I am.

LINDA: Did you ever give up hope entirely, all that time you were lost?

MARTIN: Only once, the last day. I was a bit crazy by then, anyway.

LINDA [*suddenly getting up and moving out onto the verandah; she speaks with her back turned*]: It's a horrible feeling being lost, isn't it?

MARTIN [*faintly surprised at her tone*]: Yes—horrible.

LINDA [*turning*]: Why did you crash? What happened?

MARTIN: I didn't crash. I had to make a forced landing because the damn fool mechanic hadn't put in enough petrol. I pancaked onto the trees.

LINDA: Pancaked?

MARTIN: Yes, that means shutting off your engine and dropping, as slowly and gently as you can.

LINDA: I see.

MARTIN: I hardly damaged the plane at all.

LINDA: And then?

MARTIN: Then we climbed out and got down into the jungle.

LINDA: We?

MARTIN: I had a mechanic with me.

LINDA: Oh, I thought you were entirely alone.

MARTIN: I was, after a little while.

LINDA: Why—did he die?

MARTIN: Yes. He went mad and hanged himself with his belt.

[513]

I'd left him in a clearing for a few hours, because I thought we were near the main river where I could get help. But it wasn't the main river at all, and when I got back I found him like that, hanging from a tree. It was quite a low tree, his feet were only a few inches from the ground. That was on the sixth day.

LINDA: And you went on?

MARTIN: Yes, I went on. There wasn't anything else to do.

LINDA: What did you eat?

MARTIN: Roots mostly, and leaves. I used to try to catch animals at night, but I never succeeded.

LINDA: You had no gun or anything?

MARTIN: We started with a revolver, and we took the compass out of the plane too, but we lost them both in the first river we crossed.

LINDA: How did you finally get out?

MARTIN: I got to within about fifty yards of the main river and collapsed—I'd been going for twelve days. I was torn to bits by thorns, and the blood-poisoning had given me a fever. Then suddenly I heard the hooter of a steamer, quite close, and I staggered up and started yelling like mad; then about a quarter of an hour later I heard it again—in the distance. Then I knew I was done for because steamers only go down that river once or twice a month at most. So I just lay down on the ground.

LINDA: And then?

MARTIN: Then halfway through the next day I sort of came to my senses for a bit, and struggled on to the actual bank of the river, and just by a fluke there happened to be a solitary Indian passing in a canoe. If I'd been five minutes later he wouldn't have seen me. But he did, thank God, and he got me down river to San José, where an old Brazilian priest looked after me until I was well enough to be moved to São Paolo.

LINDA: What a dreadful story!

MARTIN: It was pretty awful.

LINDA: You're very young to be so strong.

MARTIN: I'm not particularly strong.

LINDA: I mean strong in spirit.

MARTIN: Oh, I don't know about that.

LINDA: You must be; after all, the mechanic lost courage early, didn't he? He killed himself.

MARTIN: He went out of his mind, poor devil!

LINDA: Did you ever feel that you wanted to kill yourself?

MARTIN: No. I don't think I ever should.

LINDA: I often wonder—— [*She stops.*]

MARTIN: What?

LINDA: I was going to say I often wonder if it isn't braver to kill yourself really, in some circumstances, than to go on living. Then that sounded as though I thought that the mechanic was braver than you, and I don't. I don't at all. I think you must be very brave indeed.

MARTIN: Oh no, I'm not, really I'm not. I'm scared stiff of a whole heap of things.

LINDA: So am I.

MARTIN: You don't look as though you'd be easily frightened by anything.

LINDA [*smiling*]: Don't I?

MARTIN: You seem very calm, and—and still. [*The sound of the accordion is heard in the distance.*] What's that?

LINDA: Stefan. I allow him to play his accordion at certain hours of the day when nobody's trying to sleep or anything. It gives him a great deal of pleasure.

MARTIN: It's not one of my favourite instruments.

LINDA: He has a passion for music, and that's all he can play.

MARTIN [*laughing*]: It's a good long way off, anyhow.

LINDA: He only plays it in his own quarters, down at the very end of the garden. Every now and then he takes it with him when he goes out fishing. I hear it sometimes at night, right out at sea. It sounds rather nice, gay—as though someone were giving a party.

MARTIN: I shouldn't think he'd catch many fish.

[*515*]

LINDA: He does. A great many.

MARTIN: Perhaps the music hypnotizes them onto the hook.

LINDA [*absently*]: Perhaps it does.

MARTIN: He's an odd-looking bloke.

LINDA [*sharply*]: He's a very good head waiter.

MARTIN: Are you angry?

LINDA: Angry! No, of course not. Why should I be angry?

MARTIN: I don't know. I thought your voice sounded a little edgy—[*he rises*] perhaps I'm boring you——

LINDA: You're not boring me in the least.

MARTIN: I think I'd better be getting along now, anyhow.

LINDA [*with an effort*]: Please don't go. It was nice of you to come and talk to me.

MARTIN: I love talking to you.

LINDA [*slightly at a loss*]: Oh.

MARTIN: I was a bit afraid of you at first, when I arrived.

LINDA [*with a half smile*]: I'm sorry.

MARTIN: But I'm not any more.

LINDA: I'm glad.

They both laugh.

MARTIN: Do I seem awfully young and idiotic to you?

LINDA: No, of course you don't. Why should you think that?

MARTIN: I feel somehow as if I wasn't quite making sense. I expect it's the result of the fever.

LINDA [*gently*]: Please sit down again.

MARTIN: All right, if you really don't mind. [*He sits.*]

LINDA [*after a slight pause*]: It's hardly rained today at all, has it?

MARTIN: No, only a small shower this morning.

LINDA: There'll probably be a storm soon, just to make up for it.

MARTIN: Is your husband dead?

LINDA: Yes. Why?

MARTIN: I only wondered.

LINDA: He was killed in nineteen seventeen.

[*516*]

MARTIN: Valaine's a pretty name.

LINDA: This island always used to be known as Shark Point. I changed it when I started the hotel.

MARTIN: What's your other name?

LINDA [*after hesitating a moment*]: Linda.

MARTIN: That's a pretty name, too. Linda Valaine [*he says it over again*]—Linda Valaine.

LINDA: I'm glad you like it.

She walks restlessly onto the verandah. MARTIN *follows her with his eyes.*

MARTIN: It is hot, isn't it? Sticky!

LINDA: Yes.

MARTIN: What's the name of that tree—the scarlet one?

LINDA: There are several names for it: Flamboyant Poinciana —sometimes it's called Flame in the Forest.

MARTIN: I like that best. There are lots of them in Brazil, and some yellow ones too, called "Ipê" or something. [*He rises and comes out onto the verandah.*]

LINDA: Do you ever get homesick?

MARTIN: Sometimes. Not very often.

LINDA: Most English people do. They sit on the verandah and talk very sentimentally about gray skies and fogs and Piccadilly.

MARTIN [*laughing*]: Piccadilly?

LINDA: Yes, they all seem to miss Piccadilly.

MARTIN: I don't see why they should. It's no nicer than Regent Street, really, or the Mall.

LINDA: I suppose I should miss this very much if I ever went away. But I don't expect I ever shall.

MARTIN: The accordion's stopped.

LINDA [*looking out to sea*]: I was right about the storm. Look at those clouds.

MARTIN: They're beautiful, aren't they?

LINDA: Yes, I suppose they are.

MARTIN: It's marvellous when you're flying to go right through a bank like that and come out the other side into clear sky.

[*517*]

LINDA: Then you have to come down again, don't you, after you've seen your clear sky? Down into the thick of it.

MARTIN: Yes, that's not so good.

LINDA [*coming back into the room*]: Would you like a drink?

MARTIN [*following her*]: No, thanks—I don't think I'd better. [*He puts his hand up to his head.*]

LINDA: What's the matter?

MARTIN: Nothing. I feel a bit dizzy, that's all. I expect it's the heat——

He makes a grab at the chair to save himself from falling, but misses it and sprawls onto the floor. LINDA *runs to him and, kneeling down, lifts his head onto her lap.*

LINDA [*putting her hand on his heart; whispering*]: Poor boy —poor little boy——

She lifts him up gently and drags him onto the chaise-longue. Then, having placed a cushion under his head, she goes to a corner cupboard and takes out a bottle of brandy and a glass. She pours out some brandy and brings it over to him. With great tenderness she hoists him up and puts the glass to his lips. He opens his eyes and moves his head a little.

Just drink a little of this, you'll be all right in a moment.

MARTIN [*weakly*]: Thanks—thanks awfully——

He drinks some of the brandy and relaxes again in her arms. She puts the glass down on the table with her free hand and then strokes his forehead very gently.

LINDA: Stay still a minute, stay quite still.

MARTIN: That's lovely.

LINDA: Shh! Don't try to talk.

MARTIN [*very softly*]: Linda Valaine.

LINDA: Shhh!

MARTIN *puts his hand up to hers and pulls it down to his lips. They both remain still for a few seconds.* LINDA *then gently disengages her hand and rises to her feet, leaning him carefully against the cushions.*

MARTIN: Don't leave me.

[*518*]

LINDA [*brusquely*]: Here, finish the brandy. [*She gives him the glass again.*]

MARTIN [*smiling up at her*]: All right.

LINDA: You got up too soon. You should have stayed in bed.

MARTIN: It's not a very comfortable bed. I wish to complain.

LINDA: Don't be silly.

MARTIN: I wish to complain to the management. You're the management, aren't you?—Linda Valaine!

LINDA: You'd better go to your room and lie down. I'll have your dinner sent up to you.

MARTIN: I want to have my dinner on the verandah. I've fallen in love—with Mrs. Birling.

LINDA: Come along now—please come.

MARTIN [*rising rather unsteadily*]: Mrs. Birling's liver is in a very poor state. I think, as the management, you ought to know.

LINDA: Come along. Take my arm——

MARTIN [*simply*]: You are a dear. [*He takes her arm and, leaning on her a little, goes out with her through the bead curtains.*]

The room is empty and silent for a few moments, then there is a sudden gust of wind which rattles the shutters and the blinds. STEFAN *comes swiftly in from the verandah. He stands still in the center of the room with his head up, listening. Then he sniffs twice and makes an odd little grunting noise like an animal. He begins to move about the room, swiftly and silently. He goes into* LINDA's *bedroom and then comes back again. He kneels on the ground by the side of the chaise-longue, and smooths the cushions of it with his hands. Then he sees the empty brandy glass, picks it up, sniffs at it, and puts it down again. Then he slides himself up onto the chaise-longue until he is full length upon it, and buries his face in the cushions. There is another sharp gust of wind, and* LINDA's *bedroom door bangs.* STEFAN *jumps to his feet and disappears over the verandah again as the lights fade.*

POINT VALAINE

SCENE II

The scene is the verandah again. It is about nine o'clock on the following evening. It is raining hard, and all the blinds are down.

Most of the chairs have been moved away from the balustrade and are placed in groups about the stage. LINDA *and* QUINN *occupy two downstage, with their backs half turned to the audience.* MRS. HALL-FENTON *and* MRS. BIRLING *are sitting together on the right. The portable gramophone is playing a dance record.* MARTIN *is at the table sorting over the records.* TED *is dancing with* SYLVIA, GEORGE *with* HILDA JAMES. PHYLLIS *and* GLADYS *are dancing together.*

The music comes to an end.

PHYLLIS: Put on another.

MRS. HALL-FENTON [*rising*]: No, dear—we really must go.

GLADYS: But, Mum, it's still pouring.

SYLVIA: Just one more, Mum.

MRS. HALL-FENTON: We shan't be home before midnight as it is, and you know your father's expecting us.

LINDA [*rising*]: Is your launch ready? Shall I tell Lola to run down and see?

MRS. HALL-FENTON: He'll be there, he's always punctual.

TED [*pulling aside one of the blinds and looking out*]: Yes, he's there—I can see the light.

MRS. HALL-FENTON: Come along, girls.

PHYLLIS: But, Mum, the bags aren't down or anything.

MRS. HALL-FENTON: That won't take a minute.

MAY *enters from the right.*

LINDA: May, take Mrs. Hall-Fenton's luggage down to the landing stage.

MAY: Yes, ma'am. [*She goes off upstairs.*]

MRS. HALL-FENTON: We've had a lovely time, Mrs. Valaine. We

[520]

shall probably be out again in two weeks' time. My husband has
to go up to the plantation.

LINDA: Let me know a day or two before and your rooms will
be ready for you.

ELISE *runs in from the right.*

ELISE: I can't find them anywhere, Mother.

MRS. BIRLING: You must have left them on the edge and they
got knocked over.

GEORGE: What's lost?

ELISE: My iron jelloids.

LINDA: I expect Stefan found them and put them away.

MRS. BIRLING: You really are very careless, Elise.

LINDA: He'll be back soon, and we can ask him.

PHYLLIS: Good-bye, Elise, Mum's dragging us home.

ELISE: Don't forget Wednesday week.

SYLVIA: Of course not.

GLADYS: Come early, about half-past four, we can have tea at
home before we go.

ELISE: All right.

PHYLLIS: You can stay the night if you like, can't she, Mum?
It's an awfully long way to drive back.

MRS. HALL-FENTON: Certainly, if Mrs. Birling will let her.

SYLVIA: Will you, Mrs. Birling?

MRS. BIRLING: Elise is not strong enough yet to stay up late.

GLADYS: But Wednesday week's a long way off, she'll be much
stronger by then. Do say yes.

ELISE: Do let me, Mother.

MRS. BIRLING: I'll think about it.

MAY *comes down with two suitcases and goes down the steps.*

MRS. HALL-FENTON: Come along, there go the bags.

PHYLLIS: Oh, all right. Good-bye, Mr. Welford.

MARTIN: Good-bye.

SYLVIA: Come and see us when you come into town.

GLADYS: Yes, he must, mustn't he, Mother?

MRS. HALL-FENTON: I should be delighted. We're quite easy to find, Mr. Welford. The third house behind the tennis club—you can't possibly miss it.

MARTIN: Thank you very much.

PHYLLIS: Good-bye, Mr. Fox. Good-bye, Mr. Burchell.

GEORGE: Good-bye.

TED: Good-bye.

MRS. HALL-FENTON: Good-bye, Mr. Quinn. It's been so interesting meeting you.

QUINN [*politely*]: How nice of you to say so.

SYLVIA: It's been thrilling, hasn't it, Mum?

MRS. HALL-FENTON: Yes, dear.

PHYLLIS: Good-bye, Mr. Quinn.

QUINN: Good-bye.

GLADYS: Good-bye, Mr. Quinn. It was very naughty of you not to dance.

PHYLLIS: I'm sure he really dances beautifully, aren't you, Mum?

MRS. HALL-FENTON: Yes, dear. Hurry up. Say good-bye to Mrs. Valaine.

PHYLLIS: Good-bye, Mrs. Valaine.

LINDA: Good-bye.

SYLVIA: Good-bye, Mrs. Valaine.

LINDA: Good-bye.

GLADYS: We've had a heavenly time. Good-bye, Mrs. Valaine.

LINDA: I'll come down to the launch.

MRS. HALL-FENTON: No, no, you mustn't do any such thing, you'll get soaked.

LINDA: I have my raincoat here.

PHYLLIS: It's not raining as much as it was.

ELISE: It'll stop soon, I expect. Can I go down too, Mother?

MRS. BIRLING: No, dear. I don't want you to catch a chill. You know what you are.

ELISE: Oh, all right.

MRS. HALL-FENTON: Good-bye, Mr. Quinn. Good-bye, Mr. Burchell. Good-bye, Mr. Fox.

TED: Good-bye.

GEORGE: Good-bye.

QUINN: Good-bye, good-bye, good-bye.

ELISE: The book! Don't forget the book.

MRS. HALL-FENTON: Oh, dear. Quick, girls. Write in the book.

PHYLLIS: Where's the pen?

MARTIN [*at table*]: Here.

PHYLLIS: What's the date?

TED: Seventeenth.

GEORGE: Eighteenth.

QUINN: Twenty-ninth.

They all scramble round the table signing their names in the book. MRS. HALL-FENTON *signs last.*

MRS. HALL-FENTON: There now. Come along.

After a fresh chorus of good-byes, they all go off. LOLA *has previously brought in their raincoats.* LINDA *has gone with them. The rest are left.* ELISE *runs to the top of the steps and waves.* MARTIN *drops into the chair next to* QUINN.

MARTIN: Want a drink?

QUINN: A strong brandy-and-soda.

MARTIN: I'll have the same. Stefan——

QUINN: He isn't here.

MARTIN: Of course not, I keep forgetting.

MAY *comes up the steps.*

QUINN: May—two brandy-and-sodas, please.

MAY: Yes, sir. [*She goes off.*]

TED [*up at the back*]: Where are the cards?

GEORGE: Probably in the bar. I'll get them. [*He runs off.*]

TED [*to* ELISE]: Do you want to play hearts?

ELISE: Yes, I'd love to—may I, Mother?

MRS. BIRLING: Just for a little while.

TED: Will you play, Mrs. Birling?

MRS. BIRLING: No, thank you. I've never had a head for cards. I shall just read my book.

QUINN [*softly to* MARTIN]: I do hope she has a head for books.

[*523*]

MAY *comes in with two brandy-and-sodas.* MARTIN *signs for them.*

TED: Are you coming, Quinn?

QUINN: I'll join in a little later.

TED: Welford?

MARTIN: So will I.

HILDA: Remember your promise, Mr. Quinn.

QUINN: I haven't forgotten.

HILDA: I shan't let you escape.

GEORGE *comes back with the cards and joins* HILDA, TED, *and* ELISE *at the back. They all sit down at a table.* MRS. BIRLING *goes up and sits near them.*

QUINN [*holding up his glass to* MARTIN]: *Salud y amor y pesetas.*

MARTIN: *Gracias. Amor?*

QUINN: *Porque no?* At your age you ought to be thinking of nothing else.

MARTIN: You don't really mean that, do you?

QUINN: I was only just wondering.

MARTIN: Were you? Why?

QUINN: Don't look so stern. It was quite an amiable toast. Health, love, and wealth. What could be fairer than that?

MARTIN: I don't seem to have any of them at the moment.

LINDA *comes up the steps, taking off her raincoat.*

LINDA: They've all gone, and the rain's stopped.

QUINN: Come and talk to us.

LOLA, *who has followed* LINDA *onto the verandah, goes round pulling up the blinds.* LINDA *comes over to* MARTIN *and* QUINN *and sits down.*

MARTIN: Drink?

LINDA: No, thank you.

QUINN: Tired?

LINDA: No, not really. But when Stefan has to go into town it leaves us short-handed.

MARTIN: Dinner seemed to go off all right.

[524]

LINDA: We had to wait hours between courses. Mamma Dangan's helping in the kitchen, and she dropped a whole tray of hot plates.

MARTIN: I thought I heard a crash.

QUINN: What does Stefan do in the town, carouse?

LINDA: No. He does all the shopping for the week, then he catches the eight o'clock train as far as Baila and bicycles on from there to the landing stage. Our launch has gone to fetch him now.

TED [*immersed in their game*]: She's trying to jump the moon.

GEORGE: Someone must stop her.

HILDA: I don't believe you can.

MARTIN: Fox and Burchell nearly got drowned this morning.

LINDA: I know. They ought not to use the *Maria,* she's very old, and the engine's always going wrong.

QUINN: They drifted for two hours. Lucky for them the wind was right, and lucky for me I wasn't with them. I should have been sick as a dog.

TED: There's your Queen of Spades.

ELISE [*excitedly*]: Oh, do be careful, do be careful!

GEORGE: Whose lead?

HILDA: Mine.

LINDA: They'll have to row tomorrow.

QUINN: Just like you, with your mission children.

LINDA: Yes, without the hymns, and Father's harmonium wailing after them across the water.

QUINN: There's always the accordion.

LINDA [*looking at him evenly*]: Yes. I'd forgotten that.

MARTIN [*laughing*]: I wish I knew what you were talking about.

LINDA: It's only that I was telling Mr. Quinn the other day about my childhood here, when this place was a mission. And he remembered. He has a very well-trained memory.

MARTIN: It must all have been very different then.

QUINN: The externals were pretty much the same, I expect.

The same storms and insects and stickiness. It's merely the atmosphere that has changed a bit. [*To* LINDA] The atmosphere has changed a good deal, hasn't it?

LINDA [*coldly*]: Naturally.

TED: She's done it. I knew she would. You could have stopped her, George, by taking that one trick.

GEORGE: With all those hearts in it? Not on your life.

ELISE: Oh, dear! It's my deal now, isn't it?

HILDA: No, it's Mr. Fox's.

TED: Cut for me, somebody.

LOLA *comes in and comes down to* LINDA.

LOLA: Please, ma'am.

LINDA: What is it, Lola?

LOLA: The launch, ma'am.

LINDA: Hasn't it gone? It ought to have gone a half an hour ago.

LOLA: It won't start.

LINDA: Where's Farrell?

LOLA: He's down there now. He told me to tell you.

LINDA: What's wrong with it?

LOLA: I don't know, ma'am.

LINDA: I'll come. [*She gets up.*]

MARTIN [*also rising*]: I'll come too, I'm used to engines.

QUINN: I shall stay here because I hate everything to do with them.

LINDA [*to* MARTIN]: Please don't trouble.

MARTIN: It's no trouble at all. I should like to.

LINDA [*smiling*]: Very well.

QUINN: Bring me another brandy-and-soda, Lola.

LOLA: Yes, sir. [*She goes off.*]

LINDA *and* MARTIN *go off down the steps.*

GEORGE [*as they go*]: Anything wrong?

LINDA [*irritably*]: Only the damned launch.

GEORGE *and* TED *laugh.*

MRS. BIRLING: It always gives me quite a little shock when Mrs. Valaine speaks like that.

QUINN: Pardonable irritation. She's had rather a trying evening.

MRS. BIRLING: Yes, I know, but still——

TED: But it really is a damned launch, Mrs. Birling, though not as bad as the *Maria*. That's God-damned!

MRS. BIRLING: Mr. Burchell, really!

ELISE: He's only teasing you, Mother.

GEORGE: Are we going to play or not?

HILDA: Play this hand without me, I want to talk to Mr. Quinn.

QUINN: Oh, God!

HILDA: Mr. Quinn. You promised.

QUINN: Oh, very well.

LOLA *comes in with his brandy-and-soda. He signs for it.* HILDA *comes over and sits next to him.*

Would you like a drink?

HILDA: Yes, please. A crème de menthe.

QUINN [*resigned*]: One crème de menthe, Lola. [*To* HILDA] Frappé?

HILDA: Yes, please.

QUINN: Frappé.

LOLA: Yes, sir. [*She goes off.*]

HILDA: Now then. [*She produces a small writing block and a pencil.*]

QUINN: Do you like doing this?

HILDA: Yes, I love it.

QUINN: I suppose it must be fun interviewing strange people you've never seen before in your life.

HILDA: Yes, it is.

QUINN: When did you first start writing?

HILDA: About five years ago. I used to do little articles, you know.

QUINN: Yes, I know.

[527]

HILDA: I suppose you've been writing all your life?

QUINN: Tell me, what did your parents say when you broke away and got a job of your own?

HILDA: Oh, they were furious at first—at least, Father was, but he got used to it.

QUINN: I like girls to be independent. I think it's splendid.

HILDA: Oh, I'm so glad.

QUINN: Did you ever think of writing a novel?

HILDA: I started one once, but it didn't get very far. I've written a play, though.

QUINN: A play?

HILDA: Yes, plays are easier than novels, aren't they? I mean you don't have to worry about grammar or anything.

LOLA *comes in with the crème de menthe.*

QUINN: Here's your crème de menthe.

HILDA: Oh, thank you.

QUINN *signs for it, and* LOLA *goes off again.*

QUINN: What's your play about?

HILDA: Oh, it's nothing much really.

QUINN: Don't you think it's good?

HILDA: Oh yes, I think it's good, but I don't suppose you would.

QUINN: Drama or comedy?

HILDA: Oh, sort of drama really—you see it's about this girl who falls in love with a married man——

QUINN: I see.

HILDA: And the wife finds out, and there's a sort of party at Government House, and she gives the whole thing away, and the Governor's absolutely furious and says that the man will have to leave the island and give up his job and everything, and he has an awful scene with the wife and says that she has ruined his career through being so jealous and possessive and all that, and then he goes to find the girl and pour it all out to her, but she's disappeared, and the next morning they find that she's committed suicide!

QUINN: I see that it is a sort of drama, in a way.

HILDA: There are lots of funny bits in it.

QUINN: I'm glad to hear it.

HILDA: After all, you can't have the whole thing on one note, can you? I mean, I always think an audience likes to laugh every now and then.

QUINN: You mustn't pander to that.

HILDA: Yes, but life's awfully funny sometimes, isn't it?

QUINN: Hilariously.

HILDA: Often when the most dreadful things have happened to me, I've suddenly found myself laughing at something that had nothing to do with it at all.

QUINN: That shows lack of concentration but a gallant spirit.

HILDA: Oh, do you really think so?

QUINN: Certainly.

HILDA: It's most awfully sweet of you.

QUINN: Not at all.

LINDA *comes up the steps.*

What news?

LINDA: It seems to have broken down completely. Farrell and Mr. Welford are tinkering at it.

QUINN: That means Stefan won't be able to get back.

LINDA: Not until tomorrow.

QUINN: How annoying.

LINDA: It doesn't really matter. It's often happened before.

QUINN: Where does he sleep? On the beach?

LINDA: No. There's that little clubhouse place by the landing stage. I'd better signal to him. [*She calls*] Lola—May——

TED, GEORGE, *and* ELISE *finish their game and come downstage.*

TED: No luck with the launch?

LINDA: I'm afraid not.

GEORGE: Can't he row across?

LINDA [*looking out*]: He wouldn't attempt it tonight. It's a long pull at the best of times, and the wind's dead against him.

LOLA *enters.*

[529]

TED: We might go and fetch him. It would be rather fun.

LINDA: I wouldn't hear of such a thing. Lola, get me the flashlight.

LOLA: Yes, ma'am.

MARTIN *comes up the steps.*

MARTIN: No good. It won't budge.

LINDA: Thank you so much for taking all that trouble.

GEORGE: Poor old Stefan's out of luck.

LINDA: He can get here first thing in the morning in the quarantine launch. It always calls there.

TED: There's always the *Maria,* that's over there.

GEORGE: And likely to remain there forever.

TED: The man said he could mend it in two days.

GEORGE: That's as good as "forever" as far as Stefan is concerned.

LOLA *comes in with a flashlight.*

LOLA [*giving it to* LINDA]: Here's the light, ma'am.

LINDA: Thank you. [*She goes over to the balustrade and flashes the light three times.*]

QUINN: Perhaps he isn't there yet.

LINDA: He's sure to be.

HILDA [*to* MARTIN]: It's awfully romantic, isn't it? Being on an island and having to flash signals across the sea?

MARTIN: Yes, awfully.

ELISE: There—I thought I saw a light.

QUINN: Does he always have one handy for occasions like this?

LINDA: He'll use his bicycle lamp.

She flashes the light again. Everybody waits, gazing out to sea in silence.

Suddenly a pin-point of light appears on the main island.

TED: That's him.

HILDA: Is it moving?

LINDA: Hand me the glass.

GEORGE *picks up the glass from the rail and gives it to her.*

[*530*]

Take the light and give three short flashes, then two long ones, and then three more short ones. I'll watch.

ELISE: Let me! Oh, do let me!

LINDA: All right.

ELISE [*brandishing the flashlight*]: Say when.

LINDA: Go on. Three short—now wait—now two long—now wait again—now three short. That's right.

MARTIN: Can you see?

LINDA: Yes, there, he's waving the lamp. [*She puts down the glasses and comes downstage.*] That's that.

TED: It's blowing up again.

QUINN: It's always blowing up again.

MRS. BIRLING: Come along, Elise. Bedtime.

ELISE: Oh, Mother, not yet.

MRS. BIRLING: It's after half-past ten.

HILDA: Mr. Quinn kept his promise, Linda.

LINDA: Did he? I'm so glad.

HILDA: He gave me a lovely interview.

TED: What about a drink?

GEORGE: All right.

TED: Welford?

MARTIN: Thanks.

TED: Quinn?

QUINN: No more for me, thanks.

TED: Any good asking you, Mrs. Valaine?

LINDA: No, I must go into the kitchen and arrange about breakfasts.

MRS. BIRLING: Come along, Elise. Good-night, Mrs. Valaine. Good-night, everybody.

LOLA *comes in and takes the drink orders from* TED. MRS. BIRLING *and* ELISE *go off upstairs after saying good-nights to everyone.*

HILDA: Will you talk to me again tomorrow, Mr. Quinn?

QUINN: I'm afraid I shall be working all the morning.

HILDA: Just five minutes.

[531]

QUINN: We'll see.

HILDA: Well, thank you ever so much, anyhow. Good-night.

QUINN: Sleep well.

HILDA: Good-night, everybody. See you all in the morning.

TED: I hope so.

HILDA *goes off laughing.*

MAY *comes in.*

LINDA: You'd better put the blinds down again, May, we don't want everything to get wet.

MAY: Yes, ma'am.

LINDA [*going off to the kitchen*]: Has Mamma Dangan gone home yet? I shall need her in the morning.

MAY: She's still in the kitchen, ma'am.

LINDA *goes off.*

MAY *begins to pull down the blinds.* LOLA *comes in with drinks.* TED *and* GEORGE *come downstage and join* QUINN. MARTIN *stands with his back turned looking over towards the main island until* MAY *lets down the blind; then he comes down and joins the others.*

TED [*to* QUINN]: Are you sure you won't have a drink?

QUINN: No, thanks. I'm going to bed.

TED: Here you are, Welford. [*He gives him drink.*]

MARTIN: Thanks.

GEORGE: Poor old Stefan.

TED: I don't suppose he minds.

GEORGE: That old clubhouse is a bit gloomy, hasn't been used for years.

QUINN: It will probably fit in nicely with his mood.

GEORGE: A few scorpions and vampire bats, and it'd be home from home. Cheerio, everybody.

MARTIN: Cheerio!

QUINN: Well, good-night.

TED: Did you enjoy your interview with La Garçonne?

QUINN: I now have no secrets from her.

TED: There's the sort of girl you ought to marry, Quinn.

[532]

QUINN: I know. I've been thinking very seriously about it.

GEORGE: Imagine the headlines in the *Comet*. "Local girl makes good!" "Local girl makes eminent novelist!"

TED: Now's your chance, Quinn. Her room's quite near yours. Now's your chance to clinch it. You must be pretty lonely thrashing about under that big mosquito net all by yourself.

QUINN [*severely*]: I am willing to exchange banter with you boys. I am willing, even at the expense of a little dignity, to prove to you that the gulf between intellect and mere brawn is not necessarily unbridgeable. I have been at pains, during the last week or so, to make you feel at ease in my company. I have laughed, God help me, at your jokes. But there are some subjects upon which I cannot bring myself to jest. One of them is marriage. Marriage is a beautiful thing. A sacrament.

GEORGE: Nuts, Mr. Quinn!

QUINN: Thank you very much. [*He goes off upstairs.*]

TED [*laughing*]: Good old Quinn.

GEORGE: That's a swell guy.

MARTIN: Yes. He laughs at everything, doesn't he?

GEORGE: Yeah. That's what I like about him.

MARTIN: I expect he's quite right.

TED: At that he'll get caught one day. You mark my words.

MARTIN: Caught?

TED: Some dizzy little blonde will get under his skin.

MARTIN: I wonder?

TED: I've seen it happen time and time again. These cynical chaps without any illusions, they get bowled out quicker than anyone.

GEORGE: If you ask me, I believe he's got a bit of a yen for Mrs. Valaine right now.

MARTIN: Mrs. Valaine!

GEORGE: Yeah, why not? He goes and visits her most afternoons. They talk and have tea and admire the view.

MARTIN: I don't see that that means——

GEORGE: Maybe it does, maybe it doesn't, but she's not a bad

[533]

looker when she's got her glasses off—just the right age for him. Red hair, too——

MARTIN: What's that got to do with it?

GEORGE [*humming*]: "When a red-haired momma gets ants in the pants——"

MARTIN: Oh, shut up!

GEORGE [*surprised*]: What's wrong?

MARTIN: She's nice, Mrs. Valaine. It sounds rather rotten, talking about her like that.

GEORGE: I never said she wasn't nice.

TED: Don't take any notice of George. He's got a mind like a drain.

MARTIN [*forcing a smile*]: All right.

GEORGE: Have another drink?

MARTIN: No, thanks.

GEORGE: Come on, just to show there's no hard feeling.

MARTIN: Just a half, then.

GEORGE: Lola!

TED: The bar's shut, I expect.

GEORGE: I'll go to the kitchen. [*He goes off.*]

TED: He's a funny chap—George. He doesn't mean half he says.

MARTIN: I feel a bit on edge tonight, anyway.

TED: You're right about Mrs. Valaine. She is damned nice.

MARTIN: She was awfully kind to me when I was ill the other day.

TED: I bet she was. No nonsense about her. That's what I like.

MARTIN: You've been here before, haven't you?

TED: Yes, last year. George had an overseeing job in British Guiana and got a couple of weeks' leave, so I wangled ten days and joined up with him. It's a good spot.

MARTIN: Must be a bit monotonous all the year round.

TED: Yes.

MARTIN: I expect she's lonely.

TED [*looking at him quickly*]: Yes, I expect she is.

POINT VALAINE

GEORGE *comes back with three drinks.*

GEORGE: May was just closing down.

TED: Fine.

MARTIN [*taking drink*]: Thanks.

GEORGE: Well, here goes.

MARTIN: Cheerio!

TED [*to* MARTIN]: Good luck!

They all drink.

GEORGE: Well, that's that.

TED: No fishing tomorrow.

MARTIN: Why not?

TED: Poor old *Maria's* having her face lifted.

GEORGE: We can go a bit of a way out in the rowboat.

TED: Thank you for nothing. I wouldn't care to land anything bigger than a prawn in that little tub.

GEORGE: No spirit, that's your trouble. No guts.

TED: We might throw a line off the rocks and just sit and wait.

GEORGE: Why trouble to throw the line? Let's just sit and wait.

TED: Bed for me, anyway.

GEORGE: All right.

TED [*to* MARTIN]: Coming?

MARTIN: No, I don't feel like sleeping yet.

TED: I always allow a half an hour extra. George likes bedtime stories.

GEORGE: The hell I do! Good-night.

MARTIN: Good-night.

TED: See you in the morning.

MARTIN: Fine. Good-night.

TED: Good-night.

TED *and* GEORGE *go off upstairs.*

MARTIN, *left alone, settles himself into his chair and lights a cigarette. A shower starts, swells rather louder and then dies down again.* LINDA *comes in from the kitchen.* MARTIN *jumps up.*

LINDA: Oh, I thought everybody had gone to bed.

MARTIN: So they have, except me.

[535]

LINDA: I see that.

MARTIN: I felt I couldn't sleep just yet.

LINDA: Do you feel all right?

MARTIN: Fine.

LINDA: Good.

MARTIN: That's an awfully pretty dress.

LINDA [*brusquely*]: I'm glad you like it.

MARTIN: It looks so cool.

LINDA: It is.

MARTIN: Have you forgiven me for being so silly yesterday afternoon?

LINDA: Silly?

MARTIN: Yes. Fainting about all over your room.

LINDA: Well, you could hardly help that, could you?

MARTIN: I felt idiotic afterwards.

LINDA: Anyway, I'm glad you're all right again now.

MARTIN: I still feel a little foolish.

LINDA: You've no reason to. Good-night.

MARTIN: Good-night.

LINDA *goes towards her room.*

MARTIN [*desperately*]: I suppose you must go to bed.

LINDA [*turning*]: Yes, I'm tired.

MARTIN: It's been a hard day for you, hasn't it?

LINDA: Very.

MARTIN: I wish it hadn't.

LINDA: How do you mean?

MARTIN: If you weren't so tired, you might have stayed and talked for a little.

LINDA: You ought to be in bed yourself. You need all the sleep you can get, at your age.

MARTIN: What's my age got to do with it?

LINDA: You're young, and you've been ill.

MARTIN: I'm not so terribly young.

LINDA: Aren't you?

MARTIN [*smiling*]: And you're not so terribly old, if it comes to that.

LINDA: Thank you.

MARTIN: Why do you pretend to be?

LINDA: I don't pretend.

MARTIN [*offering her his case*]: Will you have a cigarette?

LINDA: Very well. [*She takes one.*]

MARTIN [*lighting it*]: And then will you sit down for a minute?

LINDA: Very well. [*She sits down.*]

MARTIN: It's most awfully sweet of you. I'm feeling rather miserable.

LINDA: Why?

MARTIN: I don't know, just a mood.

LINDA: You ought to get away from the tropics. You ought to go home.

MARTIN: I know.

LINDA: You need cold winds and fresher air.

MARTIN: That's not enough to go home for.

LINDA: Isn't there anyone you want to see?

MARTIN: Only my father and sister. Father's all right, but we're not exactly companions, and Edith's married. She's going to have a baby soon, I think.

LINDA: No one else?

MARTIN: No. No one else.

LINDA: I should have thought at least that you'd have a fiancée waiting to welcome you.

MARTIN: No. I was engaged once, though.

LINDA: What happened?

MARTIN: We used to quarrel rather, over little things, then I was mad about flying, and she wasn't interested in it at all, and then, just before I went out to Brazil, she broke it off.

LINDA: Did you love her?

MARTIN: I thought I did.

LINDA: Were you unhappy?

MARTIN: Yes, at first, but I got over it after a while.

LINDA: One can get over anything providing one can get away —escape.

MARTIN: Yes, I suppose one can.

LINDA: Were you her lover?

MARTIN [*startled*]: What?

LINDA [*distinctly*]: Were you ever her lover?

MARTIN [*after a slight pause*]: Yes—once.

LINDA [*gently*]: I'm sorry—please forgive me—I didn't mean to be inquisitive.

MARTIN: It wasn't because of that the engagement was broken off, it had nothing to do with it—it just sort of happened; and then, afterwards, I felt rather beastly about it and——

LINDA: Did she? Feel beastly about it, I mean.

MARTIN: No, I don't think she did.

LINDA: You're romantic, aren't you?

MARTIN: Yes, I think I must be.

LINDA: It's dangerous to be romantic.

MARTIN: Dangerous?

LINDA: Yes. It lets you down.

MARTIN: That can't be helped, can it? If you're made like that, you've just got to put up with it. I often feel it would be nice to be like Fox or Burchell—they don't seem to worry at all, they don't seem to want anything——

LINDA: What do you want?

MARTIN: I don't know. That's just it. That's what's so silly.

LINDA: Marriage?

MARTIN: No, not really. I don't think I want to be married.

LINDA: You said the other day that you hated being alone.

MARTIN: Don't let's talk about me any more.

LINDA: Why not?

MARTIN: It's dull.

LINDA: I don't find it so.

MARTIN: That's because you're kind. You are tremendously kind, you know.

LINDA [*getting up suddenly*]: No, I'm not.

MARTIN: Don't go away.

LINDA: I must.

MARTIN: Just to prove that you're not kind?

LINDA: Come and have tea with me tomorrow. We'll talk some more then.

MARTIN [*rising slowly to his feet*]: All right.

LINDA: Go to bed now, like a good boy.

MARTIN [*very quietly*]: I'm not a boy.

LINDA [*lightly*]: I'll try to remember.

MARTIN: You can't go away now, just at this moment.

LINDA: Why not?

MARTIN: It's too important.

LINDA: What do you mean?

MARTIN: You know, you know perfectly well.

LINDA: You're talking nonsense.

MARTIN: Perhaps I am. It hasn't anything to do with words anyhow. It doesn't matter what you say or what I say.

LINDA: Good-night.

MARTIN: Good-night. [*They stand still looking at each other.*] You see I was right, Linda Valaine.

LINDA: Even if you were right, what then?

MARTIN: Please come a little nearer.

LINDA: No.

MARTIN: Please.

LINDA *walks up to him and very gently kisses him. His arms go round her, and they stand there very still for a few moments. The rain is steadily growing louder on the roof.* LINDA *moves a little away from him.*

LINDA [*looking away from him*]: That's all.

MARTIN: No. No, it isn't. It couldn't be.

LINDA: It must be.

MARTIN: Why do you say that?

LINDA: Please go away.

MARTIN: How can I—possibly?

[539]

LINDA [*miserably*]: You don't understand.

MARTIN: What is there to understand? I love you. Isn't that enough?

LINDA: Love?

MARTIN: Yes. There isn't any other word. When you put your hand on my forehead yesterday, I knew it then. I knew that I loved you. It isn't just that I want to go to bed with you, really it isn't. It's much more. Please believe that—it's so necessary that you should believe that.

LINDA [*with an effort*]: Why is it so necessary?

MARTIN: And don't try to be hard any more. I heard it in your voice then. It didn't sound real a bit.

LINDA: How could you love me? You don't know anything about me.

MARTIN: Yes, I do. I know all that I want to know. Facts don't matter anyhow. One knows things inside, deep down.

LINDA [*looking at him*]: Yes—that's true.

MARTIN: I know how you feel about me too.

LINDA: Do you?

MARTIN: Yes. It's part of the whole thing. It's through myself that I know you. I couldn't feel like this about anybody—about anybody in the world—if they didn't feel the same about me. You do love me, don't you?

LINDA [*softly*]: Yes.

MARTIN: Linda—— [*He makes a movement towards her.*]

LINDA [*holding up her hand*]: No, no—please don't.

MARTIN [*stopping*]: All right.

LINDA [*speaking quickly*]: You said I was kind a little while ago, and it sounded, when you said it, a very lovely thing to be.

MARTIN: I think it is.

LINDA: If I let you love me it wouldn't be kind at all, it would be cruel.

MARTIN: Why? Why do you say that?

LINDA: There are too many things between us. Too many things in the way.

[540]

MARTIN: Do you love anybody else?

LINDA [*violently*]: No, no—I don't. I've never loved anybody else—never in my life. And now it's too late—it's too late——

MARTIN: What do you mean? Why is it too late?

LINDA: Fifteen years ago, ten years ago, I might have been able to hold this for a little. Long enough at any rate to have made it worth while. But now it's too late. It's too late, I tell you. It's all right for you, you're young, whatever happens, however deeply you may suffer, you have time ahead of you, time to forget and change and build something new. But I have no time at all——

MARTIN: None of this is what you really mean.

LINDA: It is. I swear it.

MARTIN: You're being kind again. Kind to me. Why?

LINDA: I'm trying to save you.

MARTIN: From what?

LINDA: Humiliation.

MARTIN: What on earth do you mean?

LINDA: The humiliation of realizing afterwards that you have given so much for so little. That's what I want to save you from. With all my heart I want to, but I don't believe I'm strong enough.

MARTIN: I'm not scared. I'll take the risk.

LINDA: It's my risk too.

MARTIN: You don't trust me at all, do you?

LINDA: Remember what I said just now. Promise me that whatever happens you'll remember it.

MARTIN: I promise.

LINDA: If only you'd go away, go upstairs to bed now, loving me as you do, then tomorrow leave, leave the island for good— I should be so deeply grateful.

MARTIN: You know I can't do that.

LINDA: Very well.

MARTIN: I do love you terribly. Honestly I do.

LINDA: I know. That's why I want you to go.

[*541*]

MARTIN: That sounds foolish to me, unreasonable.

LINDA: Yes. I expect it does.

MARTIN: This should be so wonderful, this moment. So thrilling. And yet somehow there's something wrong. I wish I knew what it was. I wish you'd tell me. You're frightened—I can see that—I'm a little frightened too. Perhaps it's the strangeness of the whole thing that's scaring us both, the suddenness of finding how we feel about each other. It's like a sort of dream to me, it has been ever since the first moment when I arrived, when you introduced me to Quinn and the others and I had several rum punches, and then you came back and showed me my room and you made a joke about the mosquito net—do you remember?

LINDA: Yes. I remember.

MARTIN: My heart was thumping, and I didn't know why a bit. I hadn't the least idea. The whole place and everyone in it seemed unreal. You seemed the most unreal of all. You see, I expected Mrs. Valaine to be an old half-caste woman with brass earrings. Then, when I got ill and you came to see how I was and were so sweet, and gentle, then I began to know, I began to realize. It isn't casual, this. It isn't just meeting an attractive woman and wanting to have an affair with her—I swear it isn't. You do believe that, don't you?

LINDA: Yes. I believe it.

MARTIN: It's twisted me up a good deal. I can't even look at you steadily, without trembling, and just now, a few minutes ago, when you came over to me, it was as though the world had come to an end, as though there wasn't anyone anywhere but just you and me.

LINDA: I should have liked that moment to be all. That moment when I kissed you. If you could have gone away then, suddenly, forever, there would never be anything to prevent you loving the memory of me always.

MARTIN: I don't understand. I can't see why you're so sad, so dreadfully troubled about us loving each other. Why shouldn't it be happy? Even if only for a little while, why shouldn't it be happy?

LINDA [*very quietly—almost whispering*]: Even if only for a little while.

MARTIN: Dearest—dear love.

LINDA: Yes.

MARTIN: I want you so.

LINDA: I know.

MARTIN: It's all right, isn't it?

LINDA: Yes. It's all right.

He takes her in his arms and kisses her, gently at first, then with more and more passion. The downpour of rain on the roof reaches a crescendo as the lights fade on the scene.

When the lights come up again it is a few hours later. The rain has stopped, and brilliant moonlight is shining through the chinks in the blinds. The verandah is empty.

. MORTIMER QUINN comes down from the stairs. He is in his pajamas and a dressing gown. He walks about the verandah aimlessly for a moment or two, then, observing the moonlight through the blinds, he goes round pulling them all up. The night outside is brilliant and still except for the ceaseless chirruping of tree frogs. He draws a chair up to the balustrade and, after lighting a cigarette, settles himself comfortably in it with his feet up on the rail. Suddenly he becomes alert and listens intently for a moment. Then, jumping to his feet, he picks up the binocular and scans the sea between the island and the mainland. He puts down the binocular again and looks sharply over towards LINDA's apartments. He snaps his fingers indecisively for a second, then, very quietly and swiftly, he goes off upstairs again.

The stage remains empty for a little while; then, gradually, above the noise of the insects and frogs, the chug-chug of a motor launch is heard.

CURTAIN

[543]

ACT III

SCENE I

It is LINDA's *sitting room. The time is about 4 A.M.*

The moonlight is still strong and is streaming into the room. The verandah blinds are up. The rocks just beyond are silhouetted black against the sea.

When the curtain rises the room is empty. Presently STEFAN *comes stealthily in through the bead curtains. He is carrying his accordion, slung round his shoulders. He stands silently in the centre of the room, gazing at* LINDA's *bedroom door, then, savagely and wildly, he begins to play. There is no melody in his playing. Just a series of crashing discords. He stops dead for a moment or two, then goes on again.*

LINDA *comes out of the bedroom. She is wearing a dressing gown over her nightgown. She switches on the light by the door. She stands staring at him, and he stops playing.*

LINDA [*quietly*]: Stefan! Have you gone mad?

STEFAN *plays a little run on the accordion.*

Please go out of my room.

STEFAN *laughs, and plays another little run.*

Go at once. Do you hear me!

STEFAN *laughs louder, and plays some more chords.*

[*Going up to him*] You're drunk!

STEFAN *shakes his head, and goes on playing.*

[*Her voice rising*] Go away—go away!

STEFAN *walks about the room playing louder and louder. Suddenly he comes up close to her, still playing, and spits full in her face. She wipes her face slowly with the sleeve of her dress-*

[544]

ing gown. Finally he comes to a standstill opposite her, stops playing, and quietly unstraps the accordion from his shoulders. They stand silent, looking at each other for a few moments.

STEFAN: I will stay.

LINDA [*tonelessly*]: Very well.

STEFAN: We will talk, eh?

LINDA: I am very tired.

STEFAN: Poor Linda. Poor tired Linda.

LINDA: Oh God! [*She rubs at her face again with her sleeve.*]

STEFAN: You thought to be very clever, didn't you? To leave me alone over there, with no boat.

LINDA [*in a high matter-of-fact voice, obviously calculated to reach the bedroom*]: The launch broke down, Stefan.

STEFAN: You are lying.

LINDA: You must not speak like that, Stefan. I won't have it.

STEFAN: No, ma'am. No, ma'am. I am sorry, ma'am. Yes, ma'am. I am indeed sorry.

LINDA: I've warned you before about being drunk. The next time it happens I shall dismiss you.

STEFAN [*with a sneer*]: It will never happen again, ma'am. Never, never again.

LINDA [*with a gesture of supplication, imploring him to go*]: Very well, Stefan. Now take that ridiculous accordion away and go to bed.

STEFAN: I think I will stay.

LINDA: Go at once, and you'd better make yourself some strong black coffee in the kitchen on your way.

STEFAN: You are frightened now. I have never seen you frightened before. Perhaps it is because you are so tired.

LINDA: Please go immediately, Stefan.

STEFAN [*patting the chaise-longue*]: Sit down here, like you always do, quiet and still, then you will not be tired any more. [*He takes her by the arm. She shrinks away from him.*]

LINDA: Please don't touch me.

STEFAN [*gripping her wrist*]: Why should I not touch you?

[545]

Why should I not touch you as much as I wish? [*He forces her down onto the chaise-longue and stands over her, still holding her wrist.*]

LINDA [*whispering*]: You're hurting me.

STEFAN: I am sorry.

He suddenly releases her hand and, seizing her in his arms, forces his mouth onto hers. His eyes, all the time, are staring fixedly at the bedroom door. LINDA *struggles for an instant in his arms and then lies still. He throws her back onto the cushions and stands away from her.*

STEFAN [*clearly and loudly*]: Now go back to your lover. Your young baby lover. Hold his body tight and close, as you have held mine so often——

LINDA [*agonized*]: Stop, stop—please—I implore you——

STEFAN: Young love is very thrilling, isn't it? For a woman who is tired! For a woman who is no longer young herself——

LINDA [*whispering frantically*]: Go away—Stefan—go away——

STEFAN [*still louder*]: I have a right to be here.

LINDA [*getting up and coming to him*]: Stefan—Stefan——

STEFAN: All these years. So many hours of so many years I have been here with you. Why should I not be here now?

LINDA *clings to him and tries to put her hand over his mouth. He pushes it away.*

Why do you not have the shutters closed, my Linda dear? It is so quiet and good in here with the shutters closed. Do you remember that night——

LINDA [*urgently*]: I'll do anything you say. I'll never see him again. I swear it—I swear I'll never see him again if only you'll go away now.

STEFAN: Why are you whispering, Linda? Who is there near to hear what we say to each other?

LINDA: Go away now—please, please—be kind—just this once —come back in a little while—ten minutes only—come back in ten minutes and I'll be alone—I swear I will. See, I'm on my knees to you—— [*She slithers down onto her knees at his feet.*]

STEFAN [*pulling her up*]: I remember the first time you wore that pretty dressing gown. It was when I had been away—just like tonight—but then you wore it to welcome me back.

LINDA [*whispering frantically*]: Please, please, Stefan—for God's sake—don't—don't——

STEFAN: He is a lucky little boy. Lucky to find a woman so warm, so tender, who knows so much of love. Be gentle with him at first, my dear—do not show him too much delight—he will only faint again. His poor young heart will stop beating, he will be lost in your arms as he was lost in the jungle. The scent of your hair will give him a fever, a fever too strong for a nice young Englishman. Do take care with him, my Linda. Let him think sweetly of you. Let him feel you a little cold, just at first, a little surprised at his passion. This will be only kind because he is such a nice young lover. He would not understand you as I know you, as I have known you for so long. He would shudder away from you——

LINDA [*the tears are running down her face*]: I see—I see what you're doing.

STEFAN: He would like to feel in his inside that you were lonely, a lonely woman without love, that by giving you his body, his brave, nice young body, he was doing for you a favour. That is how Englishmen like to feel, because it makes for them a romance. He would like to go away from you with a sadness and write back letters to you from his home—not very many, just a few, to show that he was a gentleman, just as he would give me a tip and perhaps shake my hand. Then after a little he would write once more and say good-bye because he was going to be married, and that he would never forget you, and that he hoped very much that you would be happy.

LINDA [*quietly, in a dead voice*]: That is enough now, Stefan.

STEFAN: You are a fool, my Linda.

LINDA: That is enough now, Stefan.

STEFAN [*violently*]: Come here.

LINDA: No.

[547]

STEFAN *drags her into his arms again and kisses her brutally. She stands rigid. Then he shoves her with all his force in the direction of the bedroom. She staggers against the chaise-longue and just manages to save herself from falling.*

STEFAN [*almost shrieking*]: Go back to him! Go back to your little English gentleman. Slip into his arms. Press him onto your breast, with my kisses on your lips and my spittle on your face——

He spits at her again. She moves, and it goes on her dressing gown. She stands still for a moment with her head down; then she sinks onto the chaise-longue.

STEFAN *is standing trembling and watching the bedroom door.* MARTIN *comes out. He is wearing only a shirt and trousers and slippers. He is carrying his coat in his left hand. It trails on the three steps as he comes down them. His face is lifeless, and he moves slowly across the room as though he were walking in his sleep. He goes out without looking once at either* LINDA *or* STEFAN. *The bead curtains jangle into place behind him.*

LINDA *sits dully looking after him.* STEFAN *snatches up the accordion and plays a wild fanfare of chords.* LINDA *gets up very wearily and goes towards the bedroom.* STEFAN *flings down the accordion with a crash and darts after her. He catches her just as she reaches the door.*

STEFAN [*breathlessly, almost grunting*]: Linda—Linda——

LINDA [*looking at him*]: I wish that you were dead.

STEFAN [*clutching her hand*]: No—you must not say that—Linda——

LINDA [*without emotion*]: I wish that you were blind and dead and deep down under the earth. Out of sight forever.

STEFAN [*pressing her hand to his face*]: No, no—Linda——

LINDA: Let go of my hand.

STEFAN *lets go of her hand. She comes down the steps, brushing past him as though he weren't there, and walks over to the corner cupboard. She takes out the brandy bottle and a glass and pours herself out a little. She drinks it thoughtfully, and*

*then puts the bottle back in the cupboard and the glass on the
desk.* STEFAN *watches her miserably. She walks over to the
accordion and taps it with her foot.*

LINDA: Take this away.

STEFAN: I will take it, Linda.

LINDA: Thank you.

STEFAN: I have loved you so much, Linda.

LINDA: Please go away. You have done what you wanted to
do. You can go to bed now.

STEFAN: Linda—please, Linda——

LINDA: What do you want?

STEFAN: You will forgive me. Not now, perhaps you will not
forgive me now—but soon——?

LINDA [*looking at him, wonderingly*]: Forgive you?

STEFAN: I was crazy, Linda—I was crazy with pain that you
did not love me any more. It has been going round in my head
for days.

LINDA: I have never loved you.

STEFAN: You say that because you are so angry.

LINDA: No. It is quite true.

STEFAN: For seven years we have been together.

LINDA: I have never loved you.

STEFAN: You belong to me. We belong to each other.

LINDA: No, Stefan.

STEFAN: What was it, then? This that has been between us
for so long?

LINDA: Something that I needed. Something that I needed, or
thought I needed, enough to sacrifice my pride for. Something
that has humiliated me deeply and forever.

STEFAN: No, no—that is not true.

LINDA: Yes. I can see it clearly now.

STEFAN: This young Englishman. It is he who has made you
think that way.

LINDA: Yes.

STEFAN: Do you love him then so much?

LINDA: Yes.

STEFAN: You are a fool.

LINDA: Yes. I see that too.

STEFAN: He will go away and leave you.

LINDA: He will never look at me again.

STEFAN: If I had not come tonight. He would still have gone away.

LINDA: Yes.

STEFAN: You are too old for him. Too old in love.

LINDA: This is the first time I have ever loved anyone.

STEFAN [*wildly*]: That is not true! That is a lie you are saying!

LINDA: Would you like me to tell you how much I love him? How much he means to me?

STEFAN: No, no—— [*He makes a movement towards her.*]

LINDA: Stay where you are. Stay quiet. You have made enough noise tonight.

STEFAN [*nearly breaking down*]: You will forgive me one day —please say you will forgive me.

LINDA: I only asked for a little while, because that was all I could possibly have. I told him it was only for a little while.

STEFAN [*flaring up again*]: Did you tell him about me? Did you tell him about you and me? The nights we've been to-gether? The love words we've said?

LINDA: No. I was too ashamed.

STEFAN [*pitifully*]: Ashamed! So ashamed?

LINDA: I couldn't have looked into his eyes and even thought of you without my heart turning sick inside me.

STEFAN: I know you cannot mean these things. It is only be-cause you are so angry. I know it is only because you are so angry.

LINDA: I am not angry.

STEFAN: If you are not angry, then you will understand. You will understand a little how I felt. Why I was so bad——

LINDA: How could I have ever let you touch me!

STEFAN [*wretchedly*]: Oh, Linda——

[550]

LINDA: I didn't know. I thought that was all there was.

STEFAN: There is no more, for me.

LINDA [*contemptuously*]: You?

STEFAN: You are all I have. You are all I love in the world.

LINDA: How horrible! How loathsome!

STEFAN: It is true that I love you.

LINDA: As a dog loves a bitch in the gutter.

STEFAN [*wildly*]: Do not say that! Do not say things so wicked!

LINDA: For God's sake, get out!

STEFAN: This Englishman. Is he so noble? So pure in his heart? So much finer than me? When so quickly he runs to your bed——

LINDA: Don't you see? Can't you understand that this is something deep and tender and dear to me, something that you've smashed, destroyed utterly? I love him. Listen carefully, if you can ever hear. I love him. I love him. I love him!

STEFAN: You will never forget him?

LINDA: Never. Until the day I die.

STEFAN: He will be here always, between us?

LINDA: He will be here always.

STEFAN [*appealingly*]: Linda—please, Linda——

LINDA: If I could forget him, I would. I would give everything I have in the world if I could be able to forget him. If he had died it would be easier. If he had loved me for a little and grown tired it would be easier. But now never—never—— [*Her voice breaks.*]

STEFAN [*tenderly*]: Perhaps that is not quite true—perhaps in time—a long time, Linda—it will be better——

LINDA: It was when he fainted that I knew—when I took him in my arms. It was as though the world had come to an end—that's what he said tonight—— Tonight! Is it still tonight?

She starts to wander about the room. STEFAN *watches her silently. She goes on talking, to herself, as though he were not there at all.*

[*551*]

I tried so hard to be honest—to warn him that there was something strange and horrible quite near, all round us, that it could never possibly be as he wanted it—as I wanted it—I wasn't strong enough to keep him away, and I should have been. I should have pretended I didn't care a bit, that it was only just amusing, a sort of silly little flirtation. Then when he went away nothing would have been spoiled. I should have been able to love his love for me, alone, hold it to myself always. But now it's too late—it's too late. He's lying up there in his room cutting me out of his heart, cutting me out of his memory. He's calling himself a fool, a bloody fool. Laughing bitterly at himself for getting mixed up with a cheap middle-aged hotel keeper, who's the mistress of her own head waiter—— [*She stops still for a moment and looks at* STEFAN; *then she laughs harshly.*] Poor Stefan. Asking to be forgiven. [*She pauses for a moment.*] I will see that your wages are paid up until the end of the month, but you had better leave tomorrow.

STEFAN [*warningly*]: Linda——!

LINDA [*her voice rising*]: Go away tomorrow, do you hear? Go back to the mines, to the prisons, to the scum you came from——

STEFAN: I will kill you if you speak like that!

LINDA: Go away and die.

STEFAN: Do not hurt me so. I will kill you if you hurt me so.

LINDA: Go away and lick your wounds like the senseless animal that you are. Get out of my sight. Get out of my sight, I tell you. Go away and die! [*She walks swiftly into the bedroom and shuts the door behind her. There is the sound of the key turning in the lock.*]

STEFAN *gives a loud cry and rushes up to the door. He batters on it with his fists, whimpering and crying. Presently he sinks down onto the top step, weeping hopelessly.*

STEFAN [*whispering brokenly through the door*]: Please, Linda, you will forgive me one day. You are all I have—all I love in the world——

[552]

He drags himself to his feet and comes slowly down the three steps. He comes to the centre of the room and then turns and stands there looking out to sea. He looks once more, despairingly, at LINDA's *door. He takes his coat off and lays it gently on the bottom step. He looks all round the room as though he were trying to memorize every detail of it. He picks up the accordion and lovingly plays a few notes on it; then he puts it down again, giving it a little pat with his hand as he does so. He gives a small shudder as though he were suddenly cold, then, very swiftly, he goes out onto the verandah and climbs over the balustrade. For a moment he can be seen standing on the rock, silhouetted against the sea; then he jumps and disappears from sight.*

The lights fade.

CURTAIN

SCENE II

The scene is the verandah again. It is about eight o'clock in the morning. The blinds are all up, as it is not raining. The breakfast tables are already laid along by the left-hand balustrade.

MORTIMER QUINN *comes down from upstairs, smoking a cigarette. He goes over and perches himself on the rail, looking out over the sea.* LOLA *enters from the kitchen with a tray of cruets. These she places methodically on the different tables.*

QUINN: Good-morning, Lola.
LOLA: Good-morning, sir.
QUINN: Nobody down yet?
LOLA: Mr. Fox and Mr. Burchell, sir. They are in the pool.
QUINN: Did Stefan get back all right?
LOLA: No, sir.

QUINN: What about the Quarantine launch? That should have got him here by half-past seven, shouldn't it?

LOLA: It passed by on the way to Baila. It did not stop.

QUINN: Oh, I see.

LOLA *goes out.*

TED *and* GEORGE *come up the steps in swimming trunks and bath robes.*

TED: Hallo!

GEORGE: Why didn't you come and swim?

QUINN: Too much effort. How was it?

GEORGE: Fine.

TED: We've got news.

QUINN: News?

TED: Strange doings.

QUINN: Good God! What?

GEORGE: The old *Maria's* back.

TED: Nobody knows why she came. Nobody knows how she came. We asked Farrell—he's still tinkering at the big launch. The poor old girl must have done the trip all by herself in the middle of the night.

GEORGE: I always said that dame had spirit.

TED: We left her yesterday, a derelict, over on the other side, having done her damnedest to drown us——

GEORGE: And here she is at anchor, bouncing up and down as though nothing had happened.

QUINN: Very mysterious.

TED: Have you had breakfast?

QUINN: No, I'm just going to.

TED: Come on, George—I'm hungry.

GEORGE: Was it you banging about in the passage last night?

QUINN: Certainly not. I slept like a new-born babe.

GEORGE: Sounds lousy.

TED: We thought we heard——

GEORGE: *I* thought *I* heard—you were snoring like a hog—I thought I heard someone fall down——

QUINN: Why you should imagine I spend my nights falling down in the passage, I can't think.

TED: No offence. No offence. We only thought you might have been drunk again.

QUINN: Go away, both of you.

GEORGE: Come on, Ted, Uncle's a bit grouchy. [*They both run off upstairs.*]

LOLA *comes on again, this time with* QUINN's *coffee and orange juice. She puts it down on his table.*

QUINN: Thank you, Lola. [*He flicks his cigarette over the rail and sits down at the table.*]

LOLA *goes off again.*

MARTIN *comes down from upstairs. He is carrying a suitcase in either hand. He puts them down by the door. His face looks agonized, but he is obviously making every effort not to display any emotion at all.*

QUINN: Hallo!

MARTIN: Hallo!

QUINN: You're not leaving, are you?

MARTIN: Yes.

QUINN: Oh, I'm so sorry. I didn't know.

MARTIN: This place doesn't agree with me, really—it's too hot and sticky—I'm frightened of the fever coming back again—I think I'd be better at home.

QUINN: Cooler winds and fresher air.

MARTIN [*jumping*]: What!

QUINN: What's the matter?

MARTIN: Nothing.

QUINN: Why did you start like that?

MARTIN: I don't know. I feel a bit jumpy this morning. I didn't sleep very well.

QUINN: Come and sit down and have some coffee.

MARTIN: No, thanks, I don't want any.

QUINN: I think you'd better, really. It'll pull you together.

MARTIN: I'm all right.

QUINN: You look far from all right.

MARTIN [*desperately*]: I've got to go. I must go.

QUINN: The launch doesn't leave until nine-thirty, anyhow, and it's broken down. They've probably made some arrangements about getting one over from the mainland, but it certainly won't be here yet, even if they have.

MARTIN [*trying to control himself*]: Oh—oh, I see.

QUINN: So you'd much better come and sit down and relax.

MARTIN: Perhaps I could get a little boat and row or something.

QUINN: It would be very foolish to attempt it in your present condition.

MARTIN [*quivering*]: I'm all right, I tell you.

QUINN [*gently*]: Come on. Stick by me.

He gets up quickly and goes to MARTIN. MARTIN *shrinks away from him.* QUINN *puts his arm round his shoulders and leads him to the table.*

MARTIN [*sinking down at the table*]: Thanks.

QUINN [*pouring him out some coffee*]: Here.

MARTIN: Thanks awfully—I'm sorry to be so stupid—I do feel rather rotten.

QUINN: Do you know if there's a boat sailing today?

MARTIN: No.

QUINN: I'll come over to the main island with you, and we'll find out.

MARTIN: No, no—please don't trouble—I can manage——

QUINN: I have to go anyway. I have to send some cables and buy carbon paper and collect some prints at the Kodak place— I've been putting off going for days—too lazy—this is a very good excuse.

MARTIN: It's very decent of you.

QUINN: If there isn't a boat, we'll make a night of it and stay at the Royal. We'll dine and go to a cinema. [*He sees that* MARTIN *is on the verge of breaking down.*] Here—have a cigarette.

MARTIN [*taking one*]: Thanks.

QUINN: Between you and me I'm getting a bit sick of this place myself. It's rather nerve-racking. The rain and the insects and the feeling of being shut away from everywhere.

MARTIN: Yes—I——

QUINN [*quickly*]: Don't trouble to answer, I'll go on talking. Just concentrate on your coffee and getting yourself well in hand. Stick at this table with me when the others come down. I never speak to anyone at breakfast anyhow, if I can help it. I have a writer's privilege of being slightly disagreeable. I'll keep them away.

MARTIN [*with his head down*]: I'm very grateful.

QUINN: Never mind about that.

MARTIN [*still not looking up*]: You know a lot, don't you?

QUINN: Yes, I know a lot.

MARTIN: You know that it's nothing to do with fever or heat or insects that I'm leaving?

QUINN: Yes, I know that.

MARTIN: I've been a bloody fool.

QUINN: Perhaps you have, a bit, but you'll get over worrying about it in a little while.

MARTIN: Not for a long time.

QUINN: I can't be much of a comfort I'm afraid, although I'd do all I could to make you mind a little less. I could reel off a few philosophical phrases, stinking with wisdom. Being a dealer in words, that sort of thing comes naturally to me, but they wouldn't be any use.

MARTIN [*with an attempt at a smile*]: No, I'm afraid they wouldn't.

QUINN: I could kick myself, though, for not having warned you.

MARTIN: Warned me?

QUINN: I knew how things were.

MARTIN: Does everybody know?

QUINN: I shouldn't think anybody even remotely suspected.

[557]

MARTIN: How did you find out?

QUINN [*smiling*]: Good luck always pursues me in my researches. I happen on strange chancy little clues. Small unconscious gestures, an overcasual intonation, the dead blandness of people's eyes when they have some tawdry secret to conceal. . . . It's all very interesting, if faintly discouraging.

MARTIN [*looking down again*]: Discouraging?

QUINN: Yes. You see I always affect to despise human nature. My rôle in life is so clearly marked. Cynical, detached, unscrupulous, an ironic observer and recorder of other people's passions. It is a nice façade to sit behind, but a trifle bleak. Perhaps I am misunderstood! I often toy with that idea. Perhaps I have suffered a great deal and am really a very lonely, loving spirit.

MARTIN: You're certainly very considerate.

QUINN: When you are as fundamentally selfish as I am, you have room to be considerate.

MARTIN [*trying to smile again*]: I see.

QUINN: What discourages me most is confusion.

MARTIN: Confusion?

QUINN: The dreary capacity of the human race for putting the right labels on the wrong boxes. People go blithely on their little journeys with all the things they really want in the hold. Right down in the bottom of the ship where they can't possibly get at them without a great deal of trouble. So they just don't take the trouble and make do with what they've got in the cabin. That's why most people's minds are dressed wrong for every situation they encounter.

MARTIN: How did you find out?

QUINN: About Stefan and Mrs. Valaine?

MARTIN: Yes.

QUINN: I wander about at night. I have a very unpleasant character.

MARTIN: I see.

QUINN: It's a tragic story, for them both.

[558]

MARTIN: It's horrible.

QUINN: Don't think about it. Wait until you can view it in clearer perspective. You're too close now. Too tied up. Try to put it out of your mind.

MARTIN: If only I could. Why didn't you warn me?

QUINN: Would it have been any use?

MARTIN: I don't know.

QUINN: It didn't seem to be any of my business.

MARTIN: It wouldn't have made such a good story, anyhow, if I'd known——

QUINN [*with a little laugh*]: Splendid! That's much better.

MARTIN: I'm sorry—that was beastly of me.

QUINN: Don't be silly. I'm here for you to kick against. I'm invulnerable, undentable! Kick away all you like. Snap out of your deep romantic despair and be a man, my son. Take the mood from me. Even if it isn't quite true, it will carry you a little way on your journey. Cry later on, when you're alone. We can all cry when we are alone. But you're not alone now. I'm here, full of resource. I'll entertain you, jolly songs and stories —I'll keep your mind clicking until I get you onto that boat if it kills me!

MARTIN [*very quietly*]: I think you're the nicest man I've ever known.

QUINN [*sharply*]: Shut up.

MARTIN [*with sudden anger*]: Why should it be like this? Is everything that looks lovely and true on the surface so vile and rotten underneath?

QUINN: Don't romanticize unduly. Look at the truth. Never mind about her. Never mind about him. Look at the truth in yourself. What was it that was so lovely and true? The natural physical longing inside yourself for an emotional outlet. You are, I should imagine, temperamentally fastidious. Too fastidious to be able to enjoy the unglamorous sexual buccaneering indulged in by most boys of your age. There's nothing so lovely and true in that particular restraint. It's just a biological fact.

Don't kid yourself. Look at facts first, clearly and without illusion, before you dress them and paint them up and set them in romantic highlights. Take stock of the circumstances and the atmosphere that fooled you into feeling so deeply. Strong moonlight. A small island, so easily enchanted if you care to forget the disadvantages. The scents and sounds of a tropical night. A lonely woman richly endowed with all the qualities your senses need. Ripe, perhaps a little over-ripe. Warm and wise in experience. A trap for the young and unwary——

MARTIN: Please don't say any more——

QUINN: Every nerve in your body is aching with unhappiness, I know that perfectly well, you have been shocked and humiliated unbearably. But it has nothing to do with love. Love has different pains, deeper agonies. You have the capacity for loving with all your heart one day. Don't betray that by even remembering this confused, sordid little episode.

MARTIN: It was more than that. I swear it was. It could have been more than that.

QUINN: Never. The time values were wrong. Time is a very important factor. She knew that, I expect, somewhere at the back of her mind—she's not a fool. But she allowed herself to be swept away too easily. She was confused too. She lost her head and snatched too eagerly. Poor thing.

MARTIN: I hate her.

QUINN: Not even that. In quite a little while you'll be able to afford to be sorry for her. Then you'll forget her.

MARTIN: Will it be as easy as that?

QUINN [firmly]: Yes. If you're wise.

MARTIN: I'm not wise.

QUINN: You will be, after this.

MARTIN: I wonder.

QUINN: Next time, be sure of what you want. Go out only for what you know you can get. Don't try to smear your physical desire with luminous paint. It rubs off too quickly, and then the whole thing looks cock-eyed, supremely ridiculous, like a pleasure park in the early morning: orange peel and paper bags and garbage.

MARTIN: I'll do my best.

QUINN [*smiling*]: Second best is frequently better, and far less exhausting.

LOLA *comes in with two plates of eggs and bacon. She brings them to the table.*

QUINN: Mr. Welford is having breakfast at my table this morning.

LOLA: Yes, sir.

QUINN: Bring some fresh coffee, will you?

LOLA: Yes, sir. [*She goes out again as—*]

MRS. BIRLING *and* ELISE *come down from upstairs.* MRS. BIRLING *goes straight to her table and sits down.* ELISE *goes to the top of the step and looks up at the sky.*

MRS. BIRLING: Good-morning.

QUINN: Good-morning.

MRS. BIRLING: Good-morning, Mr. Welford.

MARTIN: Good-morning.

QUINN [*softly to* MARTIN, *with a smile*]: Well, that's over.

ELISE: There isn't a cloud, it's going to be lovely.

MRS. BIRLING: Come and sit down, dear.

ELISE [*coming over to the table*]: I wish I'd got up earlier now and bathed before breakfast.

MRS. BIRLING: You know what happened last time you bathed before breakfast.

ELISE [*petulantly*]: Oh, Mother——

MRS. BIRLING: You went all to pieces for the rest of the day.

LOLA *brings in the* BIRLINGS' *breakfast.* HILDA JAMES *comes in brightly.*

HILDA: Good-morning, everybody.

MRS. BIRLING: Good-morning.

HILDA: I've been up for hours. I went for a walk, right along that path on the way to the caves. How are you, Mr. Quinn?

QUINN: Liverish, thank you. Very liverish.

[561]

MRS. BIRLING: There now. There *is* something liverish about this place.

HILDA [*coming to* QUINN's *table*]: I've changed my mind after talking to you last night.

QUINN: Completely?

HILDA [*whispering*]: I mean about my play.

QUINN: Oh, I see.

HILDA: She's not going to commit suicide at all.

QUINN: Perhaps you're right.

HILDA: She's going to have a scene with him, saying good-bye and everything, and then she's going away, all alone.

QUINN: Poor thing.

HILDA: It's better, isn't it? I mean it's sort of more like real life?

QUINN [*drily*]: Much more.

There is a slight pause. QUINN *devotes himself to his breakfast.*

HILDA: How are you this morning, Mr. Welford?

MARTIN [*with an effort*]: Fine, thank you.

HILDA [*moving away to her own table*]: We must all have a lovely swim later on.

LOLA *enters with her breakfast at the same moment that* GEORGE *and* TED *come down from upstairs. They have dressed in shirts and trousers and smarmed their hair down.*

TED: Good-morning Good-morning Good-morning.

MRS. BIRLING: Good-morning.

GEORGE: Lola. Bring us food. A lot of food.

LOLA: Yes, sir. [*She goes off.*]

TED: Hallo, Welford!

MARTIN: Hallo!

GEORGE: Mr. Quinn, would you be very kind and write in my autograph book?

QUINN: No.

GEORGE: Thank you so much, I haven't got Mussolini either.

TED: He hasn't even got an autograph book.

ELISE [*laughing*]: Oh dear, you are silly, you really are.

[562]

HILDA: Is the launch mended yet?

TED: Farrell's still working on it. He plans to have it ready by August Bank Holiday.

GEORGE: God, that's only two months. I shall be able to have my baby in the old country after all.

They both sit down at their table. MAY *comes in from the kitchen and goes down the steps to the landing stage.* LOLA *comes in with breakfast for* GEORGE *and* TED.

HILDA [*conversationally*]: It was fun last night, wasn't it?

TED: How do you mean?

GEORGE: Did we miss anything?

HILDA: I mean the dancing and everything, like a party.

MRS. BIRLING: I hope Mrs. Hall-Fenton and the girls got home all right.

ELISE: Oh, I'd forgotten. Is Stefan back?

TED: Haven't seen him.

GEORGE: It must have been him that brought back the *Maria.*

TED: I never thought of that.

GEORGE: Well, if it was, where is he?

HILDA: We'll ask Lola.

MRS. BIRLING: Don't eat so quickly, Elise. It'll only give you indigestion.

ELISE: Oh, Mother!

Suddenly from the direction of the landing stage there comes a loud shriek. Everybody jumps.

GEORGE: What the hell's that?

TED [*jumping to his feet*]: Someone's hurt!

There is another loud shriek. At this everybody jumps up. MAY *comes running wildly up the steps, screaming violently. Her face is distorted with terror. She rushes off into the kitchen, still shrieking.* GEORGE *and* TED *dash off down the steps, followed by* HILDA JAMES.

MRS. BIRLING: What on earth is it? What on earth has happened?

ELISE: Come on, Mother.

ELISE *drags* MRS. BIRLING *off down the steps after the others.* QUINN *and* MARTIN *stare at each other.*

MARTIN [*making a movement to go*]: Oh God! You don't think——

QUINN [*sharply*]: Stay where you are. Sit down. [*He pushes him into his chair.*]

LINDA *comes on from the left. Her face is dead white and quite expressionless.*

LINDA: What's the matter? What's happened? [*She goes swiftly towards the steps.*]

QUINN *intercepts her.*

QUINN: Don't go.

LINDA: Let me pass, please.

QUINN [*firmly*]: Don't go. [*He catches her arm.*] Don't go. Whatever it is, it has nothing to do with you. Stay here until I come back.

LINDA: But I must——

QUINN: You must not! It has nothing to do with you. Remember that. It has nothing whatever to do with you. Stay here. [*He goes quickly down the steps.*]

LINDA *stands still, looking after him, then she turns towards* MARTIN. *She stares at him beseechingly for a moment, but he does not look up. She comes slowly down to his table.*

LINDA: Martin.

MARTIN *doesn't answer.*

[*Pitifully*] Martin—please——

She moves slowly away from him again. Her eyes are filled with tears. She stands by the balustrade and leans her head wearily against one of the poles supporting the roof. She has her back to him and is looking out to sea.

[*In a whisper*] Good-bye, Martin.

MARTIN *at last looks up, but she doesn't see him.*

QUINN *comes up the steps. He goes to* LINDA.

QUINN [*gently*]: I think you'd better go back to your room.

LINDA [*tonelessly*]: What is it?

[564]

QUINN: Stefan has been drowned.

LINDA: Drowned! [*She starts to go towards the steps.*]

QUINN *again stops her.*

QUINN: I shouldn't go if I were you. Really I shouldn't. The sharks have torn him to bits. It's pretty horrible.

LINDA [*slowly*]: Oh—I see.

QUINN: Please go to your room, before they all come up.

LINDA: Yes. Perhaps that would be better. Thank you. Thank you very much for being so considerate.

She goes towards the door on the left; then she turns and sees MARTIN's *suitcases. She looks once more at him. He is still sitting at the table with his hand over his eyes.* LINDA's *face suddenly hardens. She speaks in a harsh cold voice.*

LINDA: I must see about engaging a new head waiter. [*She goes out.*]

CURTAIN

"THIS WAS A MAN"

CAST OF CHARACTERS
[In the order of their appearance]

EDWARD CHURT
CAROL CHURT
HARRY CHALLONER
MARGOT BUTLER
BERRY
BOBBIE ROMFORD
ZOE ST. MERRYN
MAJOR EVELYN BATHURST
BLACKWELL

SCENES

ACT I

SCENE I. *Edward Churt's studio in Knightsbridge—2.30* A.M.
SCENE II. *The same. The following afternoon.*

ACT II

SCENE: *Evelyn Bathurst's flat. The same night.*

ACT III

SCENE: *The same as Act I. The following morning.*

ACT I

SCENE I

EDWARD CHURT'S *studio in Knightsbridge is furnished with mingled opulence and good taste—he is a successful modern portrait-painter.*

When the curtain rises it is about 2.30 A.M. There is a faint glow from the fireplace on the left; a table stands more or less C., upon which is a reading lamp illumining a decanter of whisky, some siphons, a plate of biscuits and another of sandwiches, and two or three glasses; there are also a box of cigarettes and matches. The rest of the room is in comparative darkness. There is the sound of a taxi drawing up in the street, then after a suitable pause the noise of the front door being opened. CAROL CHURT *enters, followed by* HARRY CHALLONER. *They are both in evening dress.* CAROL *is lovely and exquisitely gowned; her vivid personality is composed of a minimum of intellect and a maximum of sex.* HARRY *possesses all the earmarks of a social success—he is an excellent ballroom dancer, compared with which his activities in the city are negligible.*

CAROL: Don't make a noise.

HARRY: I wasn't.

CAROL: I didn't say you were—I said don't.

HARRY: All right.

CAROL: Do you want a drink?

HARRY: Yes, please.

CAROL:. Help yourself then—and give me one. [*She takes off her cloak and lights a cigarette.*]

HARRY: Say when.

[*571*]

CAROL: That's enough.

He fills up the glass with soda and hands it to her.

HARRY: Here.

CAROL: Thanks.

HARRY: You are a marvel.

CAROL: Why?

HARRY: You're so steady.

CAROL: I don't see any reason for being anything else.

HARRY: You don't think he'll find out?

CAROL: Of course not.

HARRY: Where does he sleep?

CAROL [*pointing to door, R.*]: In there.

HARRY, *with big drink in his hand, tiptoes over and listens at the door.*

HARRY: I can't hear a sound.

CAROL: He doesn't snore unless he's taken to it lately.

HARRY [*returning*]: Darling, do you love me?

CAROL: What a silly question!

HARRY: It's all been so wonderful.

CAROL [*smiling*]: Has it?

HARRY: Well, hasn't it?

CAROL: Yes, it has rather.

He puts down his drink and takes her in his arms.

Look out— [*She is holding her glass out at arm's length to prevent it upsetting.*]

HARRY: Put it down, darling——

There is a good deal of passion in his voice when he says, "darling."

CAROL: Why?

HARRY: I want to kiss you.

CAROL: Again?

HARRY: Yes, again and again and again—forever. [*He takes her glass and slams it down on the table.*]

CAROL: Shhh! Don't be a fool.

HARRY: I don't care—— [*He kisses her lingeringly.*]

CAROL [*gently disentangling herself*]: I do—it's silly to be reckless.

HARRY: I don't believe you love me as much as you did before.

CAROL: It isn't that at all—you know it isn't.

HARRY: Kiss me then.

CAROL: Very well.

She goes up to him and quietly kisses him on the mouth. They stand there motionless for a moment.

HARRY: I want you—all over again—for the first time.

CAROL [*stroking his face*]: Darling.

HARRY: I'm crazy about you.

CAROL: You must go home to bed now.

HARRY: Will you telephone me?

CAROL: Yes.

HARRY: First thing?

CAROL: Yes.

HARRY: Promise.

CAROL: Promise.

They go out of the door. There is a little whispering in the hall. Then a silence and the sound of the front door closing gently. CAROL *comes back into the studio pensively. She finishes her whisky and soda, takes a biscuit, and flings her cloak over her arm; then she switches off the light and goes slowly off up R. Her door closes. After a slight pause* EDWARD CHURT *rises from the big armchair by the fire in which he has been sitting with his back to the audience, and goes over to the table. He switches on the lamp again and helps himself to a sandwich; he munches it thoughtfully for a moment, then with an air of determination picks up the whole plate, switches off the lamp and—retires to his room.*

CURTAIN

SCENE II

The scene is the same. It is an afternoon a few weeks later about five o'clock.

When the curtain rises, LADY MARGOT BUTLER *is seated downstage in a slightly picturesque attitude. She is a good-looking woman of about thirty-five.* EDWARD *is working on a sketch of her and is hidden from view behind an easel.*

MARGOT: I'm much more comfortable now, Edward.

EDWARD: Yes, I see you are. Would you mind getting uncomfortable again?

MARGOT [*rearranging herself*]: It *is* a shame. Why do you insist on drawing people in such agonizing positions?

EDWARD: It makes them feel they're getting their money's worth. You can rest in a moment and have a cigarette.

MARGOT: Was Violet Netherson pleased with your malicious portrayal of all her worst points?

EDWARD: Delighted. As a matter of fact, it *is* one of the best things I've done.

MARGOT: Yes, but hardly from her point of view. I should never forgive you if you did that to me.

EDWARD: I shall do something much worse if you don't keep still.

MARGOT: What about that cigarette?

EDWARD: Shut up.

MARGOT: All right. [*There is silence for a moment.*] Is that one by the door new?

EDWARD: Yes, it's the Fenwick girl—her mother's convinced that she's a wild woodland type.

MARGOT: St. John's Woodland.

EDWARD: I had a bit of a tussle with her.

MARGOT: I like it.

EDWARD: There now, you can relax. I shan't do any more to-day.

MARGOT *rises quickly and strides about.*

MARGOT: I should loathe to be a professional model.

EDWARD: There are worse fates I believe. Would you like tea or cocktails or anything?

MARGOT: I should like some tea now and a cocktail later on.

EDWARD: Are you going to stay a long time?

MARGOT: I told Bobbie to pick me up.

EDWARD [*ringing bell*]: How is Bobbie?

MARGOT: Splendid. I'm still mad about him.

EDWARD: That's right.

MARGOT: You don't like him, do you?

EDWARD: I hardly know him.

MARGOT: He's such a darling, and a great comfort to me.

EDWARD [*standing back and regarding his sketch*]: I shall only need one more sitting.

MARGOT: I believe you disapprove of me and Bobbie.

EDWARD: Don't be ridiculous. Why should I?

MARGOT: You must *never* disapprove of things, Edward. It's so second rate.

EDWARD: You don't mean that a bit.

MARGOT: Yes, I do.

EDWARD: You secretly disapprove of the whole affair, your-self, really. That's why you always talk about it so much—to sort of brazen it out and put yourself straight with yourself.

MARGOT: Edward, how *can* you! Anyhow, why shouldn't I talk about it. You all know. Everybody knows.

EDWARD: Reticence as a national quality seems to be on the wane.

MARGOT: What a pompous remark!

EDWARD: Perhaps—but true. [*Enter* BERRY.] Tea please, Berry.

BERRY: Very good, sir.

MARGOT: Lemon with mine, please, Berry.

BERRY: Yes, my lady. [*He goes out.*]

MARGOT: You're an awfully difficult person to know properly.

EDWARD: Am I?

MARGOT: You don't give an inch, do you?

EDWARD: Why should I?

MARGOT: Oh, I don't know. Confidences and discussions of everything make life so much more amusing.

EDWARD: Modern society seems to demand intimacy all in a minute. You all lay bare your private affairs to comparative strangers without a qualm.

MARGOT: Oh, Edward, dear, *we're* not strangers.

EDWARD: We met for the first time six months ago.

MARGOT: It seems *ever* so much more.

EDWARD: You'd told me all about Jim and Bobbie and your exact feelings toward each of them before we'd known each other a month.

MARGOT: It's because you're so sympathetic; you invite confidence.

EDWARD: Nonsense.

MARGOT: You're being perfectly horrid to-day. Has anything happened to upset you?

EDWARD: No, I don't think so.

MARGOT: Well I shan't sit for you again unless you're in a better temper.

EDWARD: Don't be cross.

MARGOT: I'm not cross. I'm hurt.

EDWARD: I think perhaps I do feel a little nervy.

MARGOT: There now, I knew it.

BERRY *enters with tea.*

EDWARD: Here's tea, anyhow. When Lord Romford calls, Berry, show him straight in, will you?

BERRY: Yes, sir.

EDWARD: You'd better make some cocktails.

BERRY: Very well, sir. [*He goes out.*]

MARGOT: Do you want lemon or milk?

EDWARD: Neither, thanks. Just plain unvarnished tea.

MARGOT: Is that Katherine Loring? [*Looking at picture.*]

EDWARD: Yes, unfinished.

MARGOT: She always is unfinished. She has a negligible personality, I'm afraid. Here you are. [*She hands him his tea.*]

EDWARD: Thank you.

MARGOT: I hear Zoe's back.

EDWARD: Yes, she rang me up this morning.

MARGOT: Where's she been, exactly?

EDWARD: All over the place.

MARGOT: Who with?

EDWARD: By herself, I believe.

MARGOT: My dear, she must have been with *somebody*. She couldn't have been all alone after all that awful business. She'd have gone mad.

EDWARD: She'll be here soon. You'll be able to ask her about it.

MARGOT: You were engaged to her once, weren't you?

EDWARD: Now then, Margot.

MARGOT: You were. I *know* you were. Carol told me.

EDWARD: Well, as a matter of fact, we weren't actually. We've been friends since we were children and we did discuss marriage at one time, but without great conviction.

MARGOT: I can't understand why she let Kenneth divorce her. Everybody knows——

EDWARD: Zoe wished for her freedom and just went about getting it as quickly as possible.

MARGOT: Well I don't know how she could have faced it. I shouldn't have dared——

EDWARD: You're less independent than she is.

MARGOT: I believe you're going to be horrid again.

BERRY *enters.*

BERRY [*announcing*]: Lord Romford.

BOBBIE ROMFORD *enters. He is a nice-looking, meaningless young man.*

BOBBIE: Excuse my butting in like this, Churt. [*He and* EDWARD *shake hands.*]

[577]

EDWARD: We were expecting you. The cocktails will be here in a moment.

BOBBIE: Hallo, Margot! How's the picture going?

MARGOT: It's nearly finished, but Edward won't let me see it. He's been thoroughly soured up all the afternoon.

EDWARD: Margot has been trying to persuade me to brush my hair with her.

BOBBIE [*puzzled*]: Brush your hair?

EDWARD: Yes, metaphorically speaking.

BOBBIE [*relieved*]: Oh, I see.

EDWARD: Hair-brushing is a symbol of girlish confidences. Even the nicest people do it.

MARGOT: Edward shuts up like a clam the moment I try to discuss anything in the least interesting. Where have you been, Bobbie?

BOBBIE: Playing squash with Evie at the Bath Club.

EDWARD: Why didn't you bring him along?

BOBBIE: He said he was coming on later.

MARGOT: I suppose he won.

BOBBIE: Yes; he always does.

Enter BERRY *with a tray of cocktails.*

EDWARD: Put them down here, Berry. [*He clears a space on the table.*] Do you want any more tea, Margot?

MARGOT: No, thanks.

EDWARD: Take away the remains, then, Berry.

BERRY: Yes, sir. [*He piles the tea things up and takes them out.*]

BOBBIE: I saw your wife in St. James's Street, Churt.

MARGOT [*eagerly*]: Who was she with?

BOBBIE: Harry Challoner.

MARGOT: I love Harry. Don't you, Edward?

EDWARD: Passionately.

MARGOT: I expect they were going to Fanny's. She's got a mah-jong party. She seems to imagine it's a novelty. I ought to be there, really, but I just felt I couldn't bear it—all those hot scented women squabbling over the scores.

[*578*]

BOBBIE: Do you mind if I take a cigarette, Churt?

EDWARD: Of course not. I'm so sorry. [*He hands the box.*] Margot?

MARGOT: Thanks, Edward dear.

BERRY *enters.*

BERRY [*announcing*]: Mrs. St. Merryn.

ZOE ST. MERRYN *enters. She is beautifully dressed and pleasantly unexaggerated.*

ZOE: Edward! [*She takes both his hands.*] I'm terribly excited at seeing you again.

EDWARD: It's grand, isn't it, after a whole year.

ZOE: I've got so much to say I don't know where to start. [*She sees* MARGOT.] Margot, this is lovely. How are you? [*They kiss.*]

MARGOT: You look divine, darling. Do you know Bobbie?

ZOE [*shaking hands with him*]: Bobbie who?

MARGOT: Romford, dear.

ZOE [*with a swift glance at* MARGOT]: Oh, yes, of course. I've heard of you.

MARGOT: *What* have you heard? You must tell me.

ZOE: I can't remember at the moment. Edward, give me a cigarette and a cocktail and tell me all about everything.

EDWARD [*ministering to her*]: Cigarette—cocktail—there.

ZOE: Thank you. Now then——

EDWARD: I don't know where to start any better than you do.

ZOE: How's Carol?

EDWARD: Awfully well.

ZOE: Where is she?

EDWARD: Out. She leads rather a hectic life I'm afraid—matinées, bridge, mah-jong, dancing——

ZOE: You reel off those four harmless occupations as though they were the most ignoble of human frailties.

EDWARD: I didn't mean to, really.

ZOE: They're wonderful *pis allers* for people who don't do things.

EDWARD: I don't believe in *pis allers*.

ZOE: That's not a virtue; it's just part of your creative equipment.

MARGOT: I want to hear all about your travels, Zoe—where you've been and who with.

ZOE [*laughing*]: It's difficult to remember accurately who I was with all the time. You may rest assured that I had an endless succession of lovers, beginning with an elderly mulatto in Honolulu and finishing with a retired matador in Seville.

EDWARD: I hope you're satisfied, Margot.

MARGOT: Don't be so annoying, Zoe. I really am frightfully interested.

ZOE: You always are, darling, in other people's affairs.

MARGOT: Naturally—they all sound so much more entertaining than my own. Did you see Jim anywhere about in Spain?

ZOE: Yes, in Barcelona. He'd just come in from a yachting cruise.

MARGOT [*eagerly*]: *Who* was with him? *Do* tell me!

ZOE: Nobody. I met him coming out of a bathroom at the Ritz.

MARGOT: Did he look more or less unattached?

ZOE: Yes. He seemed quite happy.

EDWARD: Margot's interest in her husband is so maternal, it always makes me feel as though I were in the presence of something sacred!

MARGOT: I'm awfully fond of Jim, really—particularly when he's on a yachting cruise.

ZOE: Are you definitely living apart now?

MARGOT: Oh yes—except for religious festivals like Easter and Christmas; then we forgather and go down to Draycott with the children.

EDWARD [*smiling*]: It seems a comfortable arrangement, doesn't it?

ZOE: Frightfully.

MARGOT [*reflectively*]: We *could* get a divorce, I suppose, but it would make such dreary complications. And then when

[580]

you're free there's the awful danger of starting the whole thing over again with someone else.

ZOE: I haven't noticed it.

MARGOT: You will, I expect, dear—later on. [*She rises.*] I've enjoyed my nice cocktail very much, thank you, Edward. I must go now. Come and lunch on Thursday, Zoe darling. I've only got Rebecca coming. She'll adore seeing you again.

ZOE: All right. One-thirty?

MARGOT: Yes. Come along, Bobbie. Good-by, Edward. Give my love to Carol.

EDWARD: I will. Good-by.

BOBBIE: Good-by.

MARGOT [*at door*]: You've come back from abroad a changed woman, Zoe, if *that's* any comfort to you. [*She and* BOBBIE *go out.*]

ZOE: What a sham Margot is, isn't she?

EDWARD: Not really. Just a type.

ZOE: Yes, but she's a type that couldn't exist unless surrounded by false values.

EDWARD: She's making the best of a bad job.

ZOE: She's letting everything slide—morals, dignity, and discretion. Thank Heaven, I broke away. I might have got like that.

EDWARD: I wonder if breaking away *is* such a very good plan.

ZOE: Of course it is. It's the most regenerating thing in the world.

EDWARD: You're so dashing, Zoe. Have another cigarette?

ZOE [*taking one*]: Thanks. I feel almost panic-stricken, you know.

EDWARD: Why?

ZOE: Coming back anywhere is always such a dreadful anti-climax.

EDWARD: Not such an anti-climax as staying still.

ZOE: To think that all this used to be my life before I let Kenneth divorce me.

EDWARD: It's pretty futile, isn't it?

[*581*]

ZOE: Futile! I return after a year's oblivion, thrilled and excited, longing to see all my old friends, and what do I find? Clacking shallow nonentities doing the same things, saying the same things, thinking the same things. They're stale. They seem to have lost all wit and charm, and restraint—or perhaps they never had any. Oh dear! I've never felt so depressed in my life.

EDWARD: I hope I haven't let you down, too.

ZOE: No, Edward. You're unchanged; a little dim, perhaps.

EDWARD: Dim?

ZOE: Yes. All your vitality seems to have been snuffed out by something. I expect it's success. That's always frightfully undermining.

EDWARD: Yes, I suppose it is.

ZOE: Are you pleased with everything?

EDWARD: Naturally.

ZOE: I'm sorry.

EDWARD: Why? Oughtn't I to be?

ZOE: You oughtn't to pretend.

EDWARD: Pretend?

ZOE: Yes. You never used to—with me, anyhow.

EDWARD: One gets into the habit of accepting things at their surface value and not looking any deeper.

ZOE: It's a bad habit.

EDWARD: I must pretend. Don't you see?

ZOE: No.

EDWARD: I'm successful—prosperous. I've got everything I wanted.

ZOE: You haven't. You've merely got what other people think you wanted.

EDWARD [smiling]: You're wonderfully stimulating, Zoe—like a breath of Brighton air.

ZOE: You look as if you need stimulating, badly.

EDWARD: I do.

ZOE: I'm glad I came back now.

EDWARD: So am I. Devoutly glad.

[582]

ZOE: What's wrong?

EDWARD: Lots of things.

ZOE: Carol?

EDWARD: Yes.

ZOE: I thought so.

EDWARD: You were right from the first. It's been a dreary failure.

ZOE: I apologize. It's so irritating being right.

EDWARD: It doesn't irritate me in the least. With anyone else it would, perhaps. But you're different; you always have been.

ZOE: I know you better than most people.

EDWARD: I know you do.

ZOE: What has she been doing?

EDWARD: The obvious thing.

ZOE: I must say I consider marriage an overrated amusement.

EDWARD: I feel rather lost.

ZOE: Yes, I did, too—over Kenneth. It's a nasty feeling.

EDWARD: It's so difficult to know exactly the right attitude to adopt.

ZOE: Are you in love with her still?

EDWARD: I don't know, really. Not violently like at first—that's died down, naturally—but somehow—things get an awful hold on you, don't they?

ZOE: Yes, fortunately for the sanctity of home life.

EDWARD: But the hold ought to be mutual.

ZOE: Quite.

EDWARD: I have moments of fierce rage, you know; then it evaporates, leaving a dead sort of a calm.

ZOE: How long have you known?

EDWARD: Ages, subconsciously; definitely, only a few weeks.

ZOE: Does she know you know?

EDWARD: She hasn't the faintest suspicion. She's always been marvelously self-assured.

ZOE: She's a lovely creature—governed entirely by sex. That's why she's self-assured.

[583]

EDWARD: Will she always go on like this?

ZOE: I expect so. Anyhow, as long as she remains attractive—probably after. That's the penalty of her type.

EDWARD: It's beastly, isn't it?

ZOE: Yes, but quite inevitable, I'm afraid. You see she's got no intellect to provide ballast.

EDWARD: Poor Carol.

ZOE: I think you're the one to be considered most at the present moment.

EDWARD: Do you think I ought to have a scene with her about it? I shrink from that. It seems to double the humiliation.

ZOE: I honestly don't know what to say. She's been actually unfaithful to you?

EDWARD: Yes.

ZOE: Often?

EDWARD [*wearily*]: I suppose so. Harry Challoner is in possession at present.

ZOE: Oh dear! How typical.

EDWARD: Everything of that sort is made so much easier for people nowadays. I suppose it's an aftermath of the war.

ZOE: It's the obvious result of this "barriers down" phase through which we seem to be passing. Everyone is at close quarters with everyone else. There's no more glamour. Everything's indefinite and blurred except sex, so people are instinctively turning to that with a rather jaded vigor. It's pathetic when you begin to analyze it.

EDWARD: What fools they all are!

ZOE [*half smiling*]: Has being a success made you realize that?

EDWARD: Yes. There wasn't time before.

ZOE: Why don't you do what I did—go away?

EDWARD: It means sacrificing a good deal of work here in London. I've only just got my foot in, really.

ZOE: Divorce?

EDWARD: I don't feel equal to it at the moment—all the vile

publicity, and the lascivious curiosity leveled at Carol and me. It makes me shudder to think of it.

ZOE: For a society portrait-painter you seem unduly sensitive.

EDWARD: If I felt vindictive toward Carol it would be so much easier. But I don't—I merely feel nauseated and frightfully, frightfully bored.

ZOE: The longer you allow it to drift, the worse it will become.

EDWARD: You think I ought to clinch it finally.

ZOE: Yes, I do. Once you've embarked you'll feel better.

EDWARD: No, I shan't.

ZOE: I believe you are still in love with her.

EDWARD: No; but I could be again if everything were all right. Oh, Zoe, I loathe this age and everything to do with it. Men of my sort are the products of over-civilization. All the red-blooded honest-to-God emotions have been squeezed out of us. We're incapable of hating enough or loving enough. When any big moment comes along, good or bad, we hedge round it, arguing, weighing it in the balance of reason and psychology, trying to readjust the values until there's nothing left and nothing achieved. I wish I were primitive enough to thrash Carol and drive her out of my life forever—or strong enough to hold her —but I'm not; I'm just an ass—an intelligent spineless ass! [*He flings himself into a chair and takes a cigarette.*]

ZOE: All the same, being the product of an Age equips you for grappling with it. You've got more chance as you are than, say, Evie Bathurst, for instance.

EDWARD: Evie goes straight for what he wants and gets it.

ZOE: He doesn't demand as much as you.

EDWARD: He's a damned sight happier.

ZOE: I should imagine he misses a good deal.

EDWARD: What does that matter? This situation could never happen to him. He wouldn't let it.

ZOE: You mustn't place too much faith in the strong and silent, Edward. They crumple up quicker than any of us when confronted with something outside their very limited range.

[585]

EDWARD: You don't like Evie, do you?

ZOE: You forget I've been married to one of his species.

EDWARD: Evie's not a cad.

ZOE: How do you know?

EDWARD: He could never behave as foully as Kenneth.

ZOE: Kenneth was never anything but an honorable, clean-living Englishman.

EDWARD: He divorced you.

ZOE: Only because I made him.

EDWARD: Why didn't he let you divorce him?

ZOE: It would have been bad for his military career.

EDWARD: You deliberately put yourself in the wrong.

ZOE: Yes.

EDWARD: And you really think it was worth while?

ZOE: Certainly I do. Our mutual boredom was verging on hatred—there was no hope of getting back, ever. What's the use of going on with a thing that's dead and done for? I decided to break free.

EDWARD: Is one really happier free?

ZOE: Don't be fatuous, Edward darling.

EDWARD: I don't think I have enough initiative to do anything definite like that.

ZOE: You don't need much initiative. All you've got to do is wait for your opportunity, and grab it!

Enter BERRY.

BERRY [*announcing*]: Major Bathurst.

Enter EVELYN BATHURST. *He is tall, handsome, soldierly, and essentially masculine. His gaze is frank and correct.*

BERRY *exits.*

EVELYN: Hullo, Edward! Zoe, I haven't seen you for years. [*They shake hands.*]

ZOE: How are you, Evie?

EVELYN: Splendid! I feel awfully guilty, though. I meant to have written and sympathized over all your beastly divorce business. Will you forgive me?

[586]

ZOE: There's nothing to forgive. It was all a howling success, anyway.

EVELYN: Success! Whew! You must have had the hell of a time!

ZOE: It was unpleasant but illuminating.

EDWARD: Want a cocktail, Evie?

EVELYN: No, thanks.

EDWARD: Cigarette?

EVELYN: Rather—yes. [*He takes one.*]

ZOE: How was India?

EVELYN: I don't know. I haven't been there.

ZOE: I'm so sorry. I thought you had.

EVELYN: No. Morocco was quite warm enough for me.

ZOE: You arrived at an opportune moment. We were just discussing you.

EVELYN: Good God! What for?

ZOE: Edward was wishing he were more like you.

EVELYN: That's uncommonly nice and right of him. Why this sudden burst of inferiority, Edward?

EDWARD: It's been brewing up for a long time.

EVELYN [*laughing*]: Oh, well, we all come to our senses sooner or later.

ZOE: Not always, Evie.

EVELYN: My only quarrel with Edward is he doesn't take enough exercise.

EDWARD: I'm not very good at exercise.

EVELYN: You never make any effort. Why don't you come and play squash with me sometimes?

EDWARD: That's not exercise, it's flagellation.

EVELYN: He's looking a bit off color, don't you think, Zoe?

ZOE: Only comparatively.

EVELYN: Been over-working, I suppose?

EDWARD: No, not really.

ZOE [*rising*]: I must go now, Edward.

EVELYN: I shall take it as a personal affront if you leave the moment I arrive.

ZOE: No, you won't, Evie. Good-by.

EVELYN [*shaking hands*]: Come and have a bit of food sometime.

ZOE: I should love to.

EVELYN: Where are you staying?

ZOE: Claridge's.

EVELYN: Right. I'll call you up.

ZOE: Good-by, Edward.

EDWARD: Come again soon, please.

ZOE: Of course. Telephone me to-morrow morning.

EDWARD: I will.

ZOE: Give my love to Carol.

EVELYN *opens the door for her and she goes out.* EDWARD *stands looking after her thoughtfully.*

EVELYN [*sitting down again*]: Extraordinary woman Zoe.

EDWARD: Why extraordinary?

EVELYN: I don't know. She's so self-assured.

EDWARD [*absently*]: Yes. I think she has every reason to be.

EVELYN: She faced all that divorce business very pluckily. Kenneth seems to have behaved like a pretty average swine.

EDWARD: Yes.

EVELYN: Why on earth did she ever marry him?

EDWARD [*wearily*]: Why does anyone ever marry anyone?

EVELYN: I've never felt the urge very strongly. I suppose I've seen too much of it.

EDWARD: That doesn't make any difference, really.

EVELYN: Women are so damned complicated to live with—specially Zoe's sort.

EDWARD: I don't think Zoe is particularly complicated. She's always appeared to me to be pretty clear headed and direct.

EVELYN: Oh well, you know her better than I do.

EDWARD: You're wonderfully single-minded, aren't you?

EVELYN: Single-minded?

EDWARD: Yes. You live according to formulated codes, and you never try to look either under or over them. I do envy you.

EVELYN: You needn't. I have my ups and downs.

EDWARD: Do you,. really? Ever since we were at school I've always regarded you as being quite invulnerable.

EVELYN [*complacently*]: Don't be a fool, old man.

EDWARD: I suppose it's a remnant of hero worship.

EVELYN: Rot! I'm a bit more balanced than you, that's all.

EDWARD: That wouldn't be very difficult.

EVELYN: I came here to-day with a purpose. I'm a bit worried. I want to talk to you seriously.

EDWARD: What about?

EVELYN: Lots of things.

EDWARD: All right. Go on.

EVELYN: I don't know how to start, quite; it's difficult.

EDWARD: Why difficult?

EVELYN: Well, you're a bit touchy at times, aren't you?

EDWARD: What's the matter, Evie?

EVELYN: Nothing actually yet—at least, I hope not.

EDWARD: I know what you're driving at.

EVELYN: Do you?

EDWARD: Yes.

EVELYN: Are you sure you do?

EDWARD: People have been talking about Carol, I suppose.

EVELYN: Exactly.

EDWARD: Well, you needn't worry.

EVELYN: I shouldn't, ordinarily, but somehow in this case it's different.

EDWARD: No, it isn't; it's exactly the same; it's a situation that occurs over and over again with everybody. That's why it's such a bore.

EVELYN: That's a silly sort of attitude to take up.

EDWARD: No sillier than any other.

EVELYN: Aren't you going to do anything?

EDWARD: O God! [*He turns away*.]

EVELYN: Well, you'll have to sooner or later.

EDWARD: What is there to do?

[589]

EVELYN: Read the riot act.

EDWARD: Do you seriously imagine that that's in any way a final solution?

EVELYN: It ought to bring her to her senses a bit, if you did it with conviction.

EDWARD: That's the trouble. I haven't got a conviction.

EVELYN: Hang it all, man, she is your wife!

EDWARD: I'm not a man of property.

EVELYN: How do you mean?

EDWARD: I mean I can't look on Carol as a sort of American trunk.

EVELYN [*exasperated*]: What *are* you talking about?

EDWARD: She's a human being, not an inanimate object over which I can assert legal rights.

EVELYN: If all husbands adopted that tone, England would be in a nice state.

EDWARD: It *is* in a nice state.

EVELYN: You make me tired sometimes, Edward.

EDWARD: I expect I do, but it can't be helped.

EVELYN: Yes, it can.

EDWARD: How?

EVELYN: Pull yourself together; show a little spirit.

EDWARD: I suppose you think that if I grabbed Carol by the hair of the head and banged her about and hurled abuse at her, she'd fall at my feet in ecstasies of adoration?

EVELYN: I shouldn't be surprised. Anyhow, it probably would do her good.

EDWARD: For an upstanding British soldier you have an astounding sense of the theater.

EVELYN: Oh, you can think me a red-blooded savage if you like, but I'm damned if I'd sit down quietly and let my wife make a fool of me.

EDWARD [*gently*]: You haven't got a wife, Evie. If you had you'd probably be utterly vanquished quicker than anyone.

EVELYN: Not me. I know the game too well.

EDWARD: Only from looking on, though. That makes an enormous difference.

EVELYN: Look here, Edward. Why not be sensible about all this?

EDWARD: I am, really.

EVELYN: Nonsense!

EDWARD: It's no use, Evie. Things will have to take their course.

EVELYN [*contemptuously*]: Line of least resistance, eh?

EDWARD: Yes.

EVELYN: To hell with the line of least resistance.

EDWARD: She can't help herself; she's made like that.

EVELYN: Rubbish!

EDWARD: It isn't rubbish. She's the sort of woman who must attract people all the time. One conquest isn't enough; she must go on and on.

EVELYN: You talk as though she were only just flirting about for the fun of the thing.

EDWARD: Perhaps she is.

EVELYN: What's the use of blinding yourself?

EDWARD: Oh, shut up, Evie!

EVELYN: This is more serious than you think.

EDWARD: No, it isn't.

EVELYN: What do you feel—honestly?

EDWARD: I've told you—bored.

EVELYN: That's not true.

EDWARD: All right.

EVELYN: I know it isn't. We haven't been pals all these years for nothing. You can't deceive me as easily as that.

EDWARD: What do you want me to feel, exactly?

EVELYN: You've got to *do* something.

EDWARD: What?

EVELYN: If you don't, I shall.

EDWARD: Evie, if you mention one word of all this to Carol or anyone in the world, I'll never forgive you.

EVELYN: You needn't worry. I've got a better plan than talking.

EDWARD: What is it?

EVELYN: Leave it to me.

EDWARD: Evie——

EVELYN: She ought to be taught a lesson.

EDWARD: What sort of lesson?

EVELYN: She wants some of the self-assurance knocked out of her.

EDWARD [*smiling*]: Really, Evie!

EVELYN: She needs humiliating.

EDWARD: You're positively vindictive.

EVELYN: Perhaps I am, but it's for your sake.

EDWARD: I'd no idea you disliked Carol so heartily.

EVELYN: It isn't that at all. I don't like or dislike her. She never pays attention to me, anyhow.

EDWARD: To think that there's even a streak of feminine in you!

EVELYN: What do you mean?

EDWARD: Never mind.

EVELYN: I won't stand by and see you let down all along the line.

EDWARD: It's awfully sweet of you, Evie, to be so cross, but you really mustn't be. I'm the one to get cross if necessary.

EVELYN: It is necessary.

EDWARD: You must allow me to be the best judge of that.

EVELYN: Now look here, Edward——

EDWARD: Remember what I said—you're not to interfere. It's my affair, and mine alone.

EVELYN: I know a good deal more about women than you.

EDWARD: Do you, Evie?

EVELYN: I've handled too many of them not to.

EDWARD: How mechanical that sounds. [*He laughs.*]

EVELYN: Oh, you're hopeless.

The door opens and CAROL *comes in. She is, as usual, looking delightful.*

CAROL: Hallo, Evie! [*She shakes hands with him.*] Are there any telephone messages for me, Edward?

EDWARD: No.

CAROL [*taking off her gloves*]: I'm quite exhausted.

EDWARD: Where have you been?

CAROL: Playing mah-jong with Fanny. I won a good deal.

EVELYN: Splendid.

CAROL: How's Margot's picture going?

EDWARD: It's nearly finished.

CAROL: Give me a cigarette, Evie.

EVELYN [*handing her a cigarette*]: You look remarkably fit, Carol.

CAROL [*smiling*]: I am fit, but I'm a tiny bit worried over Edward.

EVELYN: Why, he looks all right to me.

CAROL: You don't know him like I do. I can always tell when he's tired and overworked, can't I, darling?

EDWARD: Yes, I'm sure you can.

CAROL: It's all these people buzzing round him all day. Let's go away, Edward, and have a real holiday—somewhere quiet.

EVELYN: That's a damned good idea.

EDWARD [*smiling*]: I can't—for the next six weeks, anyhow.

CAROL [*with a slight shrug*]: There, you see? It's quite impossible to do anything with him.

EVELYN: Why don't you chuck everything, and just go?

EDWARD: Funnily enough, Zoe suggested that this afternoon.

CAROL: Zoe? I didn't know she was back.

EDWARD: She arrived yesterday.

CAROL: Why didn't you tell me?

EDWARD: I didn't know until this morning. She rang me up.

CAROL: Well, she didn't lose much time anyhow.

EDWARD: I don't see why she should.

CAROL: I suppose she talked and talked and talked as usual.

EDWARD: Yes, we both talked a good bit.

CAROL: What about?

EDWARD: Everything.

CAROL: No wonder you look tired.

[*593*]

EVELYN: She looked awfully well.

CAROL: She always does. She's wonderfully healthy.

EDWARD [*with faint malice*]: She sent you her love.

CAROL [*bored*]: Oh—give her mine when she rings up again.

EDWARD: You'll see her to-night at the Harringtons'.

CAROL: No, I shan't. I'm not going. They're going to have that awful string quartette again. I suffered so acutely last time.

EDWARD: I shall go by myself, then.

CAROL: Never mind. You'll be able to talk to Zoe.

EDWARD: Where are you dining?

CAROL: With the Challoners at the Embassy; then we're going on somewhere.

EDWARD: Do you want the car?

CAROL: No. They're picking me up.

EDWARD: Right. I'll go and dress. Don't go, Evie. We might have a slight aperitif at one of your disreputable clubs before dinner.

CAROL: Are you dining together?

EDWARD: No. I'm going to the Russian Ballet with Richard and Sheila. They've got a box or something. [EDWARD *goes off into his bedroom.*]

EVELYN: You're looking charming, Carol.

CAROL [*raising her eyebrows*]: Thank you.

EVELYN: That's a splendid hat. Is it new?

CAROL: No—incredibly old.

EVELYN: Well, it doesn't look it.

CAROL: I'm glad. [*She goes toward the door.*]

EVELYN: Carol——

CAROL [*turning*]: Yes?

EVELYN: Nothing.

CAROL [*surprised*]: Is there anything the matter?

EVELYN: No—honestly it's nothing.

CAROL: Oh well, I must go and dress, too. See you later on.

EVELYN: I shall be gone when you come down.

CAROL: Really, Evie, you're behaving very strangely.

EVELYN: Why?

CAROL: I don't know. You seem different, somehow.

EVELYN: Won't you stay and talk for a moment? I haven't seen you to speak to for ages.

CAROL: That's your fault.

EVELYN: You're always so engaged.

CAROL: I never seem to have a minute for anything. I *do* wish life wasn't so hectic.

EVELYN: Why do you let it be?

CAROL: I don't. It just happens like that.

EVELYN: I'd resent it a good deal if you were my wife.

CAROL [*smiling*]: Aren't you glad I'm not, Evie?

EVELYN: I don't know.

CAROL [*surprised*]: Well, now! I thought you disliked me thoroughly!

EVELYN: Disliked you?

CAROL: Yes. You always have such a polite preoccupied air with me. It makes me feel terribly frivolous and shallow.

EVELYN: How can you, Carol?

CAROL [*gayly*]: It's true. You're the kind of man who despises women dreadfully—I know you are.

EVELYN: You're quite wrong. I adore them.

CAROL: Well, that's a lovely surprise, isn't it?

EVELYN: I can't get over you imagining that I disliked you.

CAROL: I expect it's because you're so tremendously fond of Edward. One always feels that with one's husband's friends.

EVELYN: I don't see any reason, just because I like Edward, that——

CAROL: Don't you, Evie?

EVELYN: Of course not.

CAROL: Well, I'm very, very glad.

EVELYN: That's settled, then, isn't it?

CAROL: Quite. I shan't be frightened of you any more.

EVELYN: Frightened of me! How ridiculous!

CAROL: It isn't ridiculous; it's quite natural.

EVELYN: I don't see why. I'm perfectly harmless.

CAROL: Are you?

EVELYN: Mild as a kitten.

CAROL: I wonder.

EVELYN: To think you've been building up the most frightful image of me in your mind all this time and I never knew.

CAROL: You can't blame me, really.

EVELYN: Yes, I can. It's awfully suspicious and distrustful of you.

CAROL: It's your own fault, for holding so aloof.

EVELYN: I don't hold aloof a bit.

CAROL: You've never talked anything but commonplaces to me ever since I've known you.

EVELYN: You never gave me the chance.

CAROL: What did you expect me to do?

EVELYN: I don't know. Just be nice.

CAROL: Haven't I been nice? I'm so sorry.

EVELYN: Yes, I suppose you have, really, but I've always felt you thought me rather dull.

CAROL: You have been—up to now.

EVELYN [despondently]: There you are, then!

CAROL [quietly]: I said "up to now."

EVELYN: Men of my sort are all wrong in society. We don't seem to fit in, somehow.

CAROL: Are you glad or sorry?

EVELYN: Well, to be frank, I'm glad, until moments like this crop up.

CAROL: You're awfully funny, you know.

EVELYN: Funny?

CAROL: Yes. You do despise women, after all.

EVELYN: How do you mean?

CAROL: You think we only like men who play up and talk well and dance well.

EVELYN: It's only natural that you should.

CAROL: Oh no, it isn't.

EVELYN: You think there's some hope for me, after all, then?

CAROL: Now you're fishing.

EVELYN: It's cruel of you to snap me up like that.

CAROL: I'm sorry, Evie.

EVELYN: You'd find me a fearful bore after a bit, you know.

CAROL: Why should I?

EVELYN: I take things so damned seriously.

CAROL: That's refreshing! Most of the men I know don't take things seriously enough.

EVELYN: What an extraordinary woman you are!

CAROL: Why extraordinary?

EVELYN: Making me talk like this. I never have before.

CAROL: I shall take that as a compliment, whether you like it or not.

EVELYN: I mean it.

CAROL: Yes, I know you do.

EVELYN: I see now why your life's so hectic and why everyone runs after you so much.

CAROL [smiling]: Why?

EVELYN: You've got the most amazing knack of drawing people out.

CAROL: Not always. Only people I like.

EVELYN: You've made me feel lonely for the first time in my life.

CAROL: How hateful of me!

EVELYN: It's not your fault; it's mine.

CAROL: In what way?

EVELYN: I ought to make more efforts and not be so boorish.

CAROL: You're not in the least boorish.

EVELYN: Yes, I am—utterly wrapped up in my own affairs, then suddenly some one like you comes along and makes me realize all in a minute what a lot I'm missing.

CAROL: You're not missing much, really. It's much better to remain yourself than try to be something you're not.

EVELYN: It's awfully sweet of you to say that.

[597]

CAROL: I mean it honestly. You never can guess how tired I get by having the same sort of things said to me always.

EVELYN: Do you really?

CAROL: Of course.

EVELYN: I wish you weren't dining out to-night.

CAROL: Why?

EVELYN: I'd like better than anything in the world for you to come and dine with me quietly.

CAROL: I'd adore to, Evie, but, you see——

EVELYN: Oh, I know you can't possibly; but it seems hard that the moment I begin to get to know you properly you're whisked out of sight again.

CAROL [*gently*]: There are lots of other nights.

EVELYN: Yes, I suppose there are.

CAROL: I'm certainly not frightened of you any more now—you're an absolute baby.

EVELYN: Crying for the moon?

CAROL: I don't rate myself quite so high as that.

EVELYN: You're just as unattainable.

CAROL: Evie!

EVELYN: I'm sorry. I oughtn't to have said that.

CAROL [*after a slight pause*]: I don't mind.

EVELYN: You are a dear.

CAROL: Am I?

EVELYN: May I ring you up to-morrow morning?

CAROL: Of course.

EVELYN: And perhaps—some time soon—?

CAROL [*with determination*]: I'll dine with you to-night, Evie.

EVELYN: Carol!

CAROL: Yes. I can put off the Challoners. They bore me stiff, anyway. I'd much rather talk to you.

EVELYN: I say, it's most terribly sweet of you to take pity on me like this.

CAROL: Don't be silly. It'll be a mutual benefit. I'm bored and you're bored. Where shall we dine?

EVELYN: Anywhere you choose.

CAROL: The awful thing is I simply daren't go anywhere where I'm likely to be seen.

EVELYN: We could dine at the flat if you like, but it will be fearfully dull.

CAROL: Oh, *let's* do that. And we can creep out somewhere afterward if we feel like it.

EVELYN: Are you sure that's all right?

CAROL: Positive. It will be divine being quiet for once.

EVELYN: Don't say anything to Edward.

CAROL [*quickly*]: Why not?

EVELYN: Well, I got out of dining with him to-night. I wanted to be by myself, you see.

CAROL: Well, you're not going to be now.

EVELYN: I know. Isn't it damnable?

CAROL: Beastly. Will you fetch me?

EVELYN: Yes. What time?

CAROL: Latish—about nine.

EVELYN: Splendid——

Enter EDWARD *in evening dress.*

CAROL: You have been quick.

EDWARD: I've hurried. I know how impatient Evie is. Are you quite determined about the Harringtons, Carol?

CAROL: *Quite!* I simply couldn't bear it.

EDWARD: Oh, all right, then. I'll apologize for you.

CAROL: Do, there's a dear. Good-by, Evie. Come and see me again soon.

EVELYN: Thanks. I will.

EDWARD: Come on. I haven't got much time. Good-night, Carol.

CAROL: Good-night, darling.

EDWARD *and* EVELYN *go off.* CAROL *lights a cigarette and goes to the telephone.*

CAROL [*at telephone*]: Mayfair 7,065 please. . . . Yes. [*A pause*] Hallo! Is that you, Fay. . . . Yes. Can I speak to Harry? Oh yes, rather. I'll hold on. . . . Harry. . . . Yes, it's me. Look

[599]

here, I can't dine to-night, because I can't, I feel too tired. I may not have looked tired this afternoon, but I tell you I am now. . . . Don't be so annoying, Harry. . . . No, it isn't that at all. I'm going to dine in bed. . . . No, don't. I shall probably be asleep. . . . Well, of course, if you're going to talk like that. . . . I'm afraid you're developing into a bore, Harry. I'm *so* sorry! [*She bangs down the receiver.*] Silly fool! [*She picks up her bag and gloves and goes off.*]

CURTAIN

ACT II

The scene is EVELYN BATHURST's *flat. It is a manly apartment, furnished with precision but no imagination. There is a door up left opening into a small hall and thence to the front door. Up right is* EVIE's *bedroom and down left a service door. Between these two is the fireplace, in front of which is a large sofa and a couple of armchairs. The windows occupy the right wall. The table, center, is laid for two.*

When the curtain rises, it is about 9.15 P.M. and BLACKWELL *is putting the finishing touches, which consist of a bowl of roses and a bottle of champagne in an ice bucket. He is regarding his handiwork pensively when there comes the sound of a key in the front door. After a moment* EVELYN *and* CAROL *enter.* EVELYN *is wearing a dinner jacket;* CAROL, *an elaborately simple dinner dress and cloak.*

CAROL: What a nice flat!

EVELYN: I've been here for years.

CAROL: It's all quite typical of you.

EVELYN: How do you know?

CAROL: Well, don't you think it is?

EVELYN: I've never thought about it much.

CAROL: Solid and rather austere.

EVELYN: That sounds beastly.

CAROL: No. I like it.

EVELYN: I'm glad. Let me take your cloak. [*He takes her cloak and lays it over a chair.*] Cocktails please, Blackwell.

BLACKWELL: Yes, sir. [*He goes off.*]

CAROL: I suppose he's been with you as long as the flat?

EVELYN: Longer, really; he was my batman when I was a raw subaltern.

CAROL [*smiling*]: You must have been rather nice as a subaltern.

EVELYN: Oh no, I wasn't. You ask Edward.

CAROL: Edward adores you.

EVELYN: We're very old friends.

CAROL: It's always puzzled me. You're so very different from each other.

EVELYN: Edward's a damn sight cleverer.

CAROL: Now then——

EVELYN: But he is.

CAROL: You seem to have done very well at your job and you're always winning things.

EVELYN: I haven't done anything.

CAROL: Nonsense. [*She wanders round the room, looking at photographs.*] Who's this?

EVELYN: Mary Liddle. I was engaged to her once.

CAROL: Oh, I see.

EVELYN: I suppose you want to know why nothing ever came of it.

CAROL: Of course.

EVELYN: She ran off with someone she hardly knew.

CAROL: What a shame!

EVELYN: I expect I bored her stiff——

CAROL: Were you very much in love with her?

EVELYN: Yes. I think I was.

CAROL: I can't imagine you in love.

EVELYN: It doesn't happen often.

CAROL [*smiling and patting his arm*]: Never mind, Evie.

EVELYN: I don't. It's a relief really.

BLACKWELL *enters with the cocktails; they both take them.*

EVELYN: Dinner please, Blackwell.

BLACKWELL: Very good, sir. [*He goes out.*]

CAROL [*at another photograph*]: Is this your mother?

EVELYN: Yes.

CAROL: You're awfully like her.

EVELYN: It's the nose, I think.

CAROL: And the chin—so firm and unrelenting. I love firm chins.

EVELYN: They're awfully deceptive.

CAROL [*sipping her cocktail*]: Are they, Evie?

EVELYN: Yes. I'm as weak as water, really.

CAROL: You'll have to prove it to me before I believe it.

EVELYN: I'd rather not.

BLACKWELL *enters with caviare.*

EVELYN: Come and sit down.

CAROL [*sitting at table*]: What divine roses!

EVELYN: They're in your honor.

CAROL: Thank you. I hoped they were.

BLACKWELL *helps her to caviare.*

EVELYN [*opening champagne*]: I feel awfully flattered at your being here.

CAROL: Why should you?

EVELYN: I just do.

CAROL: Don't be silly. [*He fills her glass and his own.*] Thanks.

EVELYN: I feel flattered because it's something I never thought possible.

CAROL: Me dining with you?

EVELYN: Yes.

CAROL: Idiot. [*She smiles.*]

EVELYN: I've always seen you as a frightfully dazzling creature —always in demand—always rushing about.

CAROL: Just because you feel flattered yourself, you mustn't begin to flatter me.

EVELYN: Is that flattery?

CAROL: Isn't it?

EVELYN: Well yes, and no.

CAROL: You mean you've never quite approved of me.

EVELYN: I didn't say that.

CAROL: I believe it's true, all the same.

EVELYN: I've wondered a bit what you were really like.

CAROL [*with subtle pathos*]: I don't think I know, myself.

EVELYN: You haven't had much time to think, have you?

CAROL: No—I suppose not.

EVELYN [*sententiously*]: We're all so different underneath.

CAROL [*laughing*]: Oh, Evie!

EVELYN: What?

CAROL: You're awfully serious.

EVELYN: Don't laugh at me.

CAROL: I wasn't.

EVELYN: I don't mind, really; it shows that you're enjoying yourself.

CAROL: I am thoroughly.

EVELYN: I was terrified that you'd be bored.

CAROL: You're fishing again.

EVELYN: I wish you weren't so quick; it embarrasses me. [*He laughs.*]

CAROL: I'll try to be slower. [*She laughs too.*]

EVELYN: I'm the plodding sort, you know—gets there in the end, but takes a long time about it.

CAROL: Nonsense!

EVELYN: The British army doesn't specialize in wit.

CAROL: I won't hear a word against the British army.

EVELYN [*with jocularity*]: Hurrah! [*They both laugh.*]

CAROL: You're like a schoolboy.

EVELYN: I feel one with you.

CAROL: Do I look so terribly old?

EVELYN: You know I didn't mean that.

CAROL: I'll let you off this time, but you mustn't do it again.

BLACKWELL *enters with the soup; he takes away the caviare plates.*

EVELYN: How long is it since you dined quietly like this?

CAROL: Oh, ages.

EVELYN: I thought so.

[*604*]

CAROL: You're looking disapproving again.

BLACKWELL *serves the soup and exits.*

EVELYN: I think I'm envious.

CAROL: Envious?

EVELYN: Yes.

CAROL: No, you're not, really.

EVELYN: Your life would never suit me, I know, but somehow it does sound rather fun, for a change.

CAROL: Let's make a bargain.

EVELYN: I know what you're going to say.

CAROL: Change over for a bit.

EVELYN: Temptress.

CAROL: You come out to a few theaters and parties with me——

EVELYN: I can't dance well enough.

CAROL: I'll soon teach you.

EVELYN: I'd drive you mad.

CAROL: Have you a gramophone here?

EVELYN: Yes.

CAROL: We'll start after dinner.

EVELYN: All right.

CAROL: And whenever I'm tired and sick of everything, I'll come here and dine quietly like this.

EVELYN: Will you, honestly?

CAROL: Of course, if you stick to your side of the compact.

EVELYN: I don't believe you'll have the patience to carry it through.

CAROL: You must despise me.

EVELYN: Despise you? Good Heavens! Why?

CAROL: You're so untrusting.

EVELYN: No, I'm not; but it does look as though I were going to get more out of this than you.

CAROL: Not at all. It's a perfectly fair exchange. You've no idea how utterly weary I get every now and then.

EVELYN: Poor Carol.

CAROL: This is peace, absolute peace, and I'm tremendously grateful to you for it.

They look at each other in silence for a moment. EVELYN'S *expression is faintly nonplused.*

EVELYN: The compact's on.

CAROL: Good! Shake hands.

EVELYN: Right you are.

They shake hands across the table. CAROL *allows hers to remain in his a shade more than is strictly necessary.*

CAROL: Do you want to come to the first night of "Round Pegs" on Thursday?

EVELYN: What on earth's that?

CAROL: A new play by Burton Trask.

EVELYN: Who's he?

CAROL [*laughing*]: Oh, Evie!

EVELYN: Well, how should I know?

CAROL: He's only the most talked of dramatist we've got.

EVELYN: Sorry.

CAROL: He wrote "The Sinful Spinster."

EVELYN: Oh, the play all the fuss was about last year.

CAROL: Yes.

EVELYN: It sounded pretty hot stuff.

CAROL: It wasn't, really, but the woman in it fell in love with a man younger than herself and the Church of England didn't like it.

EVELYN: Oh, I see!

CAROL: You need educating badly.

EVELYN: I'm afraid I do.

BLACKWELL *enters and takes away their soup plates.*

CAROL: Wasn't it funny us talking this afternoon and you asking me to dine all in a minute?

EVELYN: Awfully funny, but very lucky for me.

CAROL: You make me feel shy when you say things like that. It was just as lucky for me.

EVELYN [*with intensity*]: Was it, honestly?

[606]

CAROL [*looking down*]: Of course.

BLACKWELL *enters with partridges and attendant vegetables. He serves them during the ensuing dialogue.*

EVELYN: Edward's looking awfully tired these days.

CAROL [*absently*]: Is he? I haven't noticed it.

EVELYN: Why, you said so yourself this afternoon.

CAROL: So I did. I remember he looked very wan when I came in. By the way, what were you two discussing so intently. I felt as though I were interrupting a Masonic meeting.

EVELYN: Nothing particular.

CAROL: Me, by any chance?

EVELYN: Good Heavens, no!

CAROL: There's no need to be so vehement about it; it wouldn't have mattered if you had been.

EVELYN: Have some more champagne.

CAROL: Thanks—just a little. [*She holds out her glass and he fills it, also his own.*]

EVELYN [*with great boldness*]: Why did you think we were talking about you?

CAROL: You both looked so guilty.

EVELYN: Surely that proves we weren't.

CAROL: Very good, Evie.

EVELYN: You're embarrassing me dreadfully.

CAROL: Am I? Why?

EVELYN: Because we *were* discussing you.

CAROL: Ah!

EVELYN: I see it's useless to try and deceive you for a moment.

CAROL: What were you saying?

EVELYN: Must I tell you?

CAROL: Certainly.

EVELYN: You're terribly unrelenting.

CAROL: Come on—out with it.

EVELYN: I was lecturing Edward.

BLACKWELL *goes out.*

CAROL: Lecturing him?

EVELYN: Yes. I said he was paying too much attention to his work and not enough to you.

CAROL: And do you think that's true?

EVELYN: Yes.

CAROL: It isn't; it's the other way round, really. I neglect Edward. You should have saved your lecture for me.

EVELYN: I'm sure it's his fault, really, he's so damned lackadaisical.

CAROL: It was nice of you, but a little interfering.

EVELYN: I'm sorry. I suppose I deserve to be snubbed.

CAROL: I'm not snubbing you, exactly, but I'm puzzled.

EVELYN: Why puzzled?

CAROL: It seems so strange that you should have taken up the cudgels on my side.

EVELYN: That was how I saw the situation.

CAROL: I never realized there was a situation.

EVELYN: There isn't, but there may be soon.

CAROL: How horrid of you!

EVELYN: I know Edward pretty well, you know.

CAROL: And me hardly at all.

EVELYN: Exactly. That's why I went to him, as I told you this afternoon. I always felt that you disliked me and thought me dull.

CAROL: How absurd!

EVELYN: You did, all the same. You'd have crushed me to the earth if I'd dared mention the subject to you.

CAROL: You must have thought me a prig.

EVELYN: Not in the least. I quite saw your point.

CAROL: And now——?

EVELYN: Now I'm muddled.

CAROL: Have I muddled you, Evie?

EVELYN: Yes, terribly.

CAROL: I'm so glad.

EVELYN: That's malicious of you.

CAROL: Go ahead with your lecture.

EVELYN: Certainly not.

CAROL: Whose fault do you consider this slight drifting apart —Edward's or mine?

EVELYN: Edward's.

CAROL: I told you it was mine.

EVELYN: I don't believe you.

CAROL: Stubborn.

EVELYN: Is it yours?

CAROL: Yes.

EVELYN: Why?

CAROL [*seriously*]: Oh, Evie——

EVELYN: Tell me.

CAROL: It's rather difficult.

EVELYN: I'm awfully sympathetic.

CAROL: I believe you are.

EVELYN: You love him still, don't you?

CAROL: Yes—in a way.

EVELYN: But not so much as you did?

CAROL: Not quite so much.

EVELYN: I suppose that's inevitable in married life, always.

CAROL: I expect it is.

EVELYN: It's sad, though.

CAROL: Not if one isn't sentimental about it.

EVELYN: Are you ever sentimental about anything?

CAROL [*wistfully*]: Do I seem so hard?

EVELYN: A little, I think.

CAROL: I'm not, really.

EVELYN: I'm afraid Edward's unhappy.

CAROL: Not deep down inside.

EVELYN: Are you sure?

CAROL: He may think he is.

EVELYN: Poor Edward.

CAROL: He doesn't love me quite so much, either, you know.

EVELYN: Perhaps he wants to, but you won't let him.

CAROL: Evie, why are we talking like this?

EVELYN: I don't know.

CAROL: I can't bear to pretend about things.

EVELYN: You're quite right; it doesn't pay in the long run.

CAROL: But I don't want you to blame Edward and lecture him for something that's not entirely his fault.

EVELYN: I see.

CAROL: I'm awfully fond of him and I always shall be, but——

EVELYN: But what?

CAROL: Don't let's say any more about it.

EVELYN: All right. You're rather a dear, you know.

CAROL: Am I?

EVELYN: More than I ever suspected!

CAROL: Oh, Evie!

They look at each other for a moment, EVELYN *intently,* CAROL *with a faintly wistful smile.* BLACKWELL *enters to collect the plates and serve the sweet—pêche Melba—which he does during ensuing dialogue.*

EVELYN: You don't like Zoe St. Merryn, do you?

CAROL: Why do you suddenly ask that?

EVELYN: I felt you didn't this afternoon.

CAROL: She's rather obvious, I think.

EVELYN: In what way?

CAROL: She tries to be clever.

EVELYN: I always thought she was clever.

CAROL: Yes, most men do, but very few women.

EVELYN: Why is that?

CAROL: Because they see through her. All that divorce business was a put-up job.

EVELYN: I say, Carol!

CAROL: Don't look so shocked. Of course it was. She's been so brave and defiant over it. Men love that.

EVELYN: Aren't you being a little hard on her?

CAROL: No, not really. I know her type so well.

EVELYN: She's an old friend of Edward's, isn't she?

CAROL: Yes, but that hasn't anything to do with it. She tried to marry him once.

EVELYN: He seems very fond of her.

CAROL: She flatters him terribly. He's an awful baby.

EVELYN: Thank Heaven I haven't got your feminine intuition. It must complicate life dreadfully.

CAROL: It's very useful sometimes.

EVELYN: Do you size everyone up so mercilessly?

CAROL [*laughing*]: Perhaps.

EVELYN: I'm trembling visibly.

CAROL: Nonsense! You're not frightened by anything, really.

EVELYN: You don't know!

BLACKWELL *goes out.*

CAROL: Well, you shouldn't be, anyhow.

EVELYN: That's different.

CAROL: Why did you ask me not to tell Edward I was dining with you?

EVELYN [*nonplused*]: Did I?

CAROL: You know you did.

EVELYN: Perhaps I was afraid he'd think I was interfering again.

CAROL: Did he tell you that, too?

EVELYN: Yes.

CAROL [*smiling*]: Never mind.

EVELYN: I don't. I'm used to Edward.

CAROL: So am I.

EVELYN: But when you tell me I'm interfering, I feel beastly.

CAROL: You are, you know.

EVELYN: There! You've done it again.

CAROL: People like Edward and me should be left to manage our own troubles.

EVELYN: All right. From now on I won't say a word.

CAROL: Cheer up.

EVELYN: I'm a blundering fool, anyhow.

[*611*]

CAROL [*laughing*]: Yes.

EVELYN: And instead of making you like me, I've made you laugh at me.

CAROL: That's not quite true.

EVELYN: I'm afraid it is.

CAROL: You don't know a bit what I'm really like.

EVELYN: No.

CAROL: Do you want to?

EVELYN: Yes.

CAROL: I'm not sure that it's wise.

EVELYN: Why not?

CAROL: You might be shocked.

EVELYN: As bad as that?

CAROL: Yes—as bad as that.

EVELYN: I don't believe it.

CAROL: Good.

EVELYN: You're too sensitive to behave really badly.

CAROL: That's nonsense.

EVELYN: No, it isn't.

CAROL: Sensitiveness hasn't anything to do with it.

EVELYN: Yes, it has.

CAROL: Don't contradict me.

EVELYN [*with truculence*]: Why shouldn't I?

CAROL: Because it infuriates me.

EVELYN [*slowly*]: We're almost quarreling.

CAROL: Yes.

EVELYN: I'm sorry.

CAROL: Antagonism is a bad sign.

EVELYN: What do you mean?

CAROL [*suddenly burying her face in her hands*]: Oh, Evie!

EVELYN [*alarmed*]: What on earth's the matter?

CAROL [*muffled*]: Nothing.

EVELYN: Carol, don't—please—— [*He gets up and comes to her.*]

CAROL: No, no. Sit down. Your man will be in in a moment.

[*612*]

EVELYN: Do tell me what's wrong.

CAROL: Sit down, please.

EVELYN: All right. [*He sits down.*]

CAROL: Give me my bag, will you? It's over there. I want to powder my nose.

EVELYN *rises. When his back is toward her, an expression of extreme satisfaction flits across* CAROL'S *face. By the time he has turned she is once again bravely melancholy.*

EVELYN: Here. [*He gives her her bag.*]

CAROL: Thank you. [*She looks up at him with a weary smile.*]

BLACKWELL *enters and takes away the remains of the sweet.*

EVELYN: Serve the coffee at once, Blackwell; then I shan't want you any more.

BLACKWELL: Very good, sir. [*He goes out.*]

CAROL: I feel better now.

EVELYN: I don't suppose you'll ever want to dine with me again.

CAROL: Don't be silly. Of course I shall.

EVELYN: I seem to have depressed you terribly.

CAROL: No—it's not your fault, really.

EVELYN: I wish I understood you a bit better.

CAROL: I'm glad you don't.

BLACKWELL *enters with coffee and liqueurs, which he places beside* EVELYN.

EVELYN: Thank you, Blackwell. Good night.

BLACKWELL: Good night, sir. [*He goes out.*]

EVELYN: Coffee?

CAROL: Yes, please.

EVELYN [*pouring it out*]: Sugar?

CAROL: One.

EVELYN [*handing it to her*]: There. Cointreau or brandy?

CAROL: Cointreau—just a little.

EVELYN: The brandy's very good.

CAROL: All right. Brandy, then—you're so dominant.

EVELYN: Don't laugh at me any more.

[*613*]

CAROL: I must a little.

EVELYN: Here you are. [*He gives her some brandy and takes some himself.*]

CAROL: Next time I come I'll try to be more amusing.

EVELYN: I don't want you to be amusing if you don't feel like it.

CAROL: You're awfully kind and gentle.

EVELYN: I want you to relax completely.

CAROL: I am relaxing completely.

EVELYN: I feel you need it.

CAROL: No one else has ever taken the trouble to feel that.

EVELYN: They're all too occupied in enjoying themselves.

CAROL: But I don't think they do, really.

EVELYN: That's true, but they wouldn't dare admit it.

CAROL: Put the gramophone on.

EVELYN: Now?

CAROL: Yes, please, or I shall cry again.

EVELYN [*rising*]: What shall we have?

CAROL: Something blaring and noisy.

EVELYN: What a baby you are!

CAROL: Am I? [*He puts on a foxtrot and stands by the machine looking at her. After a pause she speaks.*] I love this tune.

EVELYN: It's not very new, I'm afraid. I must get some more of the latest ones.

CAROL: Are you ready for your lesson?

EVELYN: Lesson?

CAROL: Yes, your dancing lesson.

EVELYN: If you are.

CAROL: Of course I am! Come on. [*She rises.*]

EVELYN: I'll push the table back. [*He does so.*] There.

CAROL: Now then. [*They begin to dance.*]

EVELYN: Is the time all right?

CAROL: A scrap too fast.

EVELYN: Wait a minute. [*He stops for a second and regulates the time.*]

CAROL: That's better. [*They dance again.*]

[*614*]

EVELYN: I'm so sorry. Did I kick you?

CAROL: No.

EVELYN: I warned you, didn't I?

CAROL: Hold me a little tighter.

EVELYN: All right. [*They dance in silence for a moment.*]

CAROL: This is divine.

EVELYN: You're not teaching me a thing.

CAROL: You don't need it.

EVELYN: You're just being polite. I dance like an elephant.

CAROL: Don't be ridiculous. It would be terribly funny if any-one suddenly came in and found us.

EVELYN: There's not the least chance of it. [*They dance in silence for a little.*]

CAROL: Oh!

EVELYN: What is it?

CAROL: We nearly crashed into that chair.

EVELYN: I'm afraid I wasn't concentrating.

CAROL: That's very naughty of you. You must.

EVELYN: All right. [*The record comes to an end.*]

CAROL: Put on another.

EVELYN: Very well.

While he does so, CAROL *looks at herself carefully in the glass over the mantelpiece.*

CAROL: I'm enjoying myself frightfully.

EVELYN: Are you, really?

CAROL: Aren't you?

EVELYN: You know I am. [*He takes her in his arms again.*]

CAROL: You really must hold me a little tighter—it's so much easier to follow.

EVELYN: Like that?

CAROL: Yes—like that. [*They stand still, she surrendering her-self to him, and holding up her face deliberately to be kissed.*]

EVELYN [*softly*]: Carol! [*He kisses her. They stand tightly clasped for a moment; then he firmly disentangles himself and turns off the gramophone.*]

[615]

CAROL [*sinking onto the sofa and passing her hand across her eyes*]: Oh, Evie!

EVELYN [*in a different tone*]: I thought so.

CAROL [*looking up quickly*]: What do you mean?

EVELYN: It's unbelievable. [*He strides about a little.*]

CAROL [*alarmed*]: What on earth are you talking about?

EVELYN: I was right. I knew it.

CAROL [*becoming exasperated*]: Knew what?

EVELYN: I'm not quite such easy game as all that.

CAROL [*rising*]: Evie!

EVELYN: What a little rotter you are.

CAROL [*outraged*]: What!

EVELYN: Yes, you may well look surprised. I, unfortunately, am *not* surprised.

CAROL [*after a pause*]: I'm beginning to understand.

EVELYN: I'm glad.

CAROL: Very clever. I must congratulate Edward.

EVELYN: It's nothing to do with Edward.

CAROL: Liar! [*She goes and takes up her cloak.*]

EVELYN: You're not going yet.

CAROL: On the contrary, I'm going immediately.

EVELYN: Not until I choose.

CAROL: Don't speak to me like that.

EVELYN: I'm going to speak to you as you've never been spoken to before.

CAROL: Pompous ass! [*She flings her cloak over her arm and goes toward the door.*]

EVELYN *stands between her and the door.*

EVELYN: You're going to stay here.

CAROL [*contemptuously*]: Don't be so ridiculous.

EVELYN: I mean it.

CAROL: Are you quite mad?

EVELYN: No, not at all; I'm unflatteringly sane.

CAROL: Do you intend to use force to keep me here?

EVELYN: Yes, if necessary.

[*616*]

CAROL: Evie—what have you been reading? [*She flings down her cloak and returns to the sofa.*]

EVELYN: That's right.

CAROL [*helping herself to a cigarette*]: I always thought you were a fool.

EVELYN: Thank you. I'm sorry I was less of a fool than you hoped.

CAROL: I didn't hope for much, whatever happened.

EVELYN: You'd forgotten I was Edward's best friend.

CAROL: You're very, very sure of yourself.

EVELYN: I can afford to be. I live decently.

CAROL: Rubbish!

EVELYN: And I've got a little honor left.

CAROL: Even after living decently.

EVELYN: You would say a thing like that.

CAROL: I did.

EVELYN: I should like to say one thing——

CAROL: Please do.

EVELYN: If you and I were alone on a desert island I wouldn't touch you.

CAROL: That would be very silly of you.

EVELYN [*rapidly losing his temper*]: Haven't you any modesty or shame anywhere?

CAROL [*smiling*]: Oh dear!

EVELYN: Stop being flippant; it's only a mask to cover your humiliation.

CAROL: How discerning you are!

EVELYN: I know you much better than you think I do.

CAROL: Idiot!

EVELYN: Flinging epithets at me won't help.

CAROL: Fatuous prig.

EVELYN: Shut up.

CAROL [*rising*]: May I go now, please?

EVELYN [*almost shouting*]: No.

CAROL [*sitting down*]: Very well.

EVELYN: I'm Edward's best friend.

CAROL: You've said that before.

EVELYN: And I'm damned if I'm going to stand by and see him cheapened and humiliated by you.

CAROL: You're insufferable.

EVELYN: That's beside the point.

CAROL [*suddenly furious*]: It is *not* beside the point! How dare you behave like this! If you were Edward's Siamese twin you've no right to ask me here and insult me. You surely don't imagine that by talking until you're blue in the face you could ever alter my life one way or another. You've played a filthy second-rate trick on me and you think you did it for Edward's sake, but all the time it was only to prove to yourself how clever you are. You've got to let me go now—at once. Do you hear? If not I'll scream the place down. [*She rises and makes a dash for the door. He intercepts her. She struggles. He grasps her wrist.*] Let me go. Help! Help!

EVELYN: Shut up, you little fool! [*He puts his hand over her mouth and drags her back to the sofa, upon which she collapses, sobbing.*]

CAROL [*almost hysterical, in muffled tones*]: How dare you! Oh, how dare you! It's outrageous! It's——

EVELYN: Do you want some brandy?

CAROL: Don't speak to me.

EVELYN [*with emphasis*]: Do you want some brandy!

CAROL: No.

EVELYN: You'd better have some. Stay where you are. [*He goes over and pours out a glass of brandy and brings it to her.*] Here—sit up.

CAROL: Go away. Don't come near me.

EVELYN: You're hysterical. Drink this and pull yourself together. [*He puts his arm round her to lift her up. She wriggles free of him, sits up quickly by herself, snatches the glass from his hand and flings it into the fireplace.*]

CAROL: I don't want your filthy brandy.

EVELYN: That was childish.

CAROL: Why are you doing this to me? Why? Why? What have I ever done to you?

EVELYN: You're on the verge of ruining the life of one of the best men that ever lived.

CAROL [*tearfully*]: How?

EVELYN: You know perfectly well how.

CAROL: It's no business of yours—what I do—ever.

EVELYN: I've made it my business. What you attempted to-night with me you've accomplished with other men—you've flirted and encouraged them to make love to you, and in many cases you've given yourself to them——

CAROL: Evie!

EVELYN: I don't want you to deny it or affirm it. I *know* it's true, but I don't think Edward does; he loves you too much to believe it possible, and my object in playing on you this second-rate trick, as you call it, is to make you realize what a hideous mess you're making both of his life and your own. [*During this speech* CAROL *is looking at* EVIE *intently. He begins to stride up and down while he talks.*] Edward's too sensitive and reserved to fight for his own rights. I've known for ages that he wasn't happy—that something was weighing on his mind. To-day I asked him plump out and he admitted—— [*He pauses.*]

CAROL: What did he admit?

EVELYN: That he was worried and miserable about you.

CAROL [*calmly*]: And what did you advise him to do?

EVELYN: Give you hell.

CAROL: How crude of you!

EVELYN: Women of your sort require a little crudity occasion-ally.

CAROL: What do you mean "women of my sort"?

EVELYN: Do you want me to tell you?

CAROL: No; I don't want you to say any more at all.

EVELYN: You have the soul of a harlot!

CAROL [*suddenly bursting out laughing*]: Oh, Evie!

EVELYN [*losing control*]: Don't laugh. Don't laugh.

CAROL [*continuing to laugh*]: What do you expect me to do? You're so ridiculous——

EVELYN: I suppose you consider anyone with decent ideals ridiculous?

CAROL [*laughing helplessly*]: Oh dear! Oh dear!

EVELYN [*working himself up more and more*]: You think it funny that I should make an attempt to defend the honor of my best friend, who is too shamed by your utter wantonness to defend himself——

CAROL [*growing hysterical*]: You're mad—quite, quite mad——

EVELYN: You're deliberately ruining his reputation and wrecking his happiness because you never make the slightest effort to control your rotten passions——

CAROL [*rising, trying to control her hysteria*]: How dare you say that—how dare you——

EVELYN: Dare! I'll say it again and again. Rotten passions! All you live for, all you think of—women of your type can't exist without men—men—nothing but men all the time——

CAROL [*frantically*]: Stop! Stop! You shan't say any more. [*She gives him a ringing slap on the face. He stands quite still.*] Cad! cad! unutterable cad! [*She gives him another slap between each word. He remains motionless. They stand facing each other. CAROL puts her hand to her head.*] I think—I think I'm going to be ill.

She falls in a heap at his feet. He carries her back to the sofa. He deposits her there and rushes to get some more brandy. When his back is turned she lifts her head sharply and looks at him, then lets it drop attractively against the side of the sofa. He returns and ministers the brandy. After a slight pause she opens her eyes and sits up and finishes the brandy.

EVELYN: Be careful. Don't spill it on your dress.

CAROL: I'm awfully sorry to be so stupid.

EVELYN: I didn't mean to make you ill.

CAROL [*meekly*]: Please may I go home now?

EVELYN: You'd better wait a moment until you feel stronger. I won't say any more—I promise.

CAROL: My head aches.

EVELYN: Would you like some aspirin? I think I've got some somewhere.

CAROL: No, thanks.

EVELYN: It wasn't out of any personal spite, you know——

CAROL: It doesn't matter—it—— [*She bursts into tears.*]

EVELYN: I say, don't cry—please.

CAROL: I can't help it. [*She cries a little more.*]

EVELYN: Please! Please!

CAROL: Leave me alone. I'll be all right in a minute.

EVELYN: I had no intention of losing my temper. I apologize.

CAROL [*with a fresh burst of tears*]: It's all so—so horrible!

EVELYN: Carol—please, please don't!

CAROL [*sobbing bitterly*]: I'd no idea—anyone could think of me like that.

EVELYN: I was only trying to show you, for Edward's sake——

CAROL: Don't—don't say any more. You promised.

EVELYN: All right, but you see I——

CAROL: I understand why you did it. It's not that I'm crying for. It's—it's—— O God!

EVELYN [*appealingly*]: Carol——

CAROL: I'm crying because I'm so bitterly ashamed——

EVELYN [*gently*]: Carol——

CAROL: I don't want you to despise me utterly——

EVELYN: It's all right. Don't think any more about it.

CAROL: The things you've said to me are right—I have been shallow and cheap; but there's a reason that you don't know.

EVELYN: Reason?

CAROL: You've heard Edward's side of the story and you've mixed yourself up in our lives—more than ever now. It's only fair for you to hear my side, too——

EVELYN: Now look here, Carol. Don't let's say any more about it at all.

[*621*]

CAROL: Do you mean that?

EVELYN: Yes.

CAROL [*rising*]: Very well—I suppose I deserve it. Good night. [*She walks sadly toward the door.*]

EVELYN: Carol——

CAROL [*turning*]: Yes?

EVELYN: I'll hear your side if you want me to, but what's the use of going on any further?

CAROL: Only that unless I explain now I can never look you in the face again.

EVELYN: Carol, don't be so absurd.

CAROL: There are circumstances that justify me more than you realize.

EVELYN: Come back, then, and sit down.

CAROL [*wearily returning*]: I feel so horribly tired. [*She comes back to the sofa and leans against it, looking at him. Her face is pale and she looks extremely sad and quite lovely.*]

EVELYN: Do sit down.

CAROL: No, but I want you to. Sit here where you needn't look at me.

EVELYN: Very well. [*He sits down on the sofa and stares into the fire.*]

CAROL *stands just behind him with her hands resting on his shoulders. Both their faces are half turned to the audience. She speaks very slowly.*

CAROL: You've been pretty brutal to me to-night and some of the hard things you said I deserve, but not all of them. I'm selfish and occasionally cheap and rather vain—and I have been unfaithful to my husband, but not before he had been unfaithful to me——

EVELYN [*starting*]: What!

CAROL [*pressing him down*]: Keep still, please. I'm telling you the truth——

EVELYN: You mean that Edward——

CAROL: I mean exactly what I say. I was completely faithful to

Edward until eighteen months ago, when I discovered that he was having an affair with Zoe St. Merryn——

EVELYN: Good God! [*He moves again, but she holds him firmly.*]

CAROL: That broke me up, rather.

EVELYN: I don't believe it.

CAROL: I can't help that; it's true, all the same.

EVELYN: How did you discover it? What proof have you?

CAROL: I suspected for a little while and said nothing until I could bear it no longer; then I asked Edward and he admitted it——

EVELYN [*twisting round*]: I *must* look at you.

CAROL [*firmly, looking into his eyes*]: He admitted it.

EVELYN: It's incredible.

CAROL: Why? Edward's awfully weak, and Zoe—— [*She laughs sadly.*] Will you turn around again now, please. [EVELYN *does so and buries his face in his hands.*] Don't be upset about it, Evie —it's between Edward and me, really, and nobody knew—until now. I made him swear never to tell a soul, otherwise he'd have told you ages ago—he always tells you everything. I've behaved rather badly since then, I know, but something went dead inside me and—well, it doesn't seem to matter much, does it?

EVELYN [*after a pause*]: May I get up now and get a drink?

CAROL: There's nothing more to say, anyhow.

EVELYN *goes over and pours himself out a drink. He turns suddenly.*

EVELYN: You wouldn't lie to me, would you?

CAROL [*with dignity*]: Even I have a little decency left. [*She turns to go again.*]

EVELYN: Carol!

CAROL [*turning*]: Yes.

EVELYN: What can I say to you?

CAROL: Nothing.

EVELYN: I'm desperately sorry.

CAROL: All right.

EVELYN: I've been an abject, blundering fool. It wasn't my business, anyhow.

CAROL [*with a wan smile*]: Your motives were sound.

EVELYN: Can you forgive me?

CAROL: Yes, of course.

EVELYN: I mean really forgive me?

CAROL [*holding out her hand*]: Completely.

EVELYN: You're very generous. [*He takes it.*]

CAROL: There's one more thing I want to clear up.

EVELYN: What?

CAROL: I came here to-night for one reason only.

EVELYN: Yes?

CAROL: I love you!

EVELYN [*dropping her hand*]: Carol!

CAROL: It's all right—don't be afraid. I'm going now—but I didn't want you to think me too cheap—that's all.

EVELYN: I'm utterly bewildered.

CAROL: It hasn't been very easy for either of us, has it?

EVELYN: You can't mean what you say.

CAROL: You know I do—you've known it all along, subconsciously.

EVELYN: Carol—I'm dreadfully—horribly embarrassed.

CAROL: Poor old Evie.

EVELYN: I don't know what to do.

CAROL: We'll both laugh over to-night one day, won't we?

EVELYN: Will we?

CAROL [*with beautifully forced gayety*]: Yes—you see.

EVELYN: You are an extraordinary woman.

CAROL: Just rather silly, I'm afraid. Good night.

EVELYN: I'm going to see you home.

CAROL: No, please. I'd rather go alone. Please, I mean it, honestly.

EVELYN: But——

CAROL: It's only just round the corner.

EVELYN: I can't let you go alone.

[624]

CAROL [*with gentle firmness*]: You must—please.

EVELYN [*looking down*]: All right.

CAROL: We're friends, aren't we?

EVELYN [*still looking down*]: Yes.

CAROL: In spite of everything?

EVELYN: Yes.

CAROL: Because of everything?

EVELYN: Oh, Carol!

CAROL: Good night, my dear. [*She comes to him and kisses him gently on the mouth. Suddenly he crushes her to him. After a moment she disentangles herself.*] No, no! I didn't mean it, really. I'm not going to be cheap any more. Stand quite still where you are, not looking. I don't want you to move until I've gone. [*She goes out quietly, leaving him standing stockstill.*]

After a moment the front door slams. EVELYN *turns in the direction of the sound.*

EVELYN [*emotionally*]: Carol—O God! [*He goes over to the sofa and flings himself down on it, with his face buried in his hands.*]

CAROL *comes softly in again. Her cloak is over her arm. She gives one look in his direction and then goes noiselessly into his bedroom, closing the door after her.*

CURTAIN

ACT III

The scene is the same as Act I. It is about twelve o'clock in the morning. One night has elapsed since Act II.

When the curtain rises the studio is empty. There is the sound of the front-door bell ringing with some violence. BERRY *enters, R., and crosses over L. He exits and reappears in a moment, ushering in* EVELYN. EVELYN *is looking extremely white and strained.*

BERRY: Can I offer you anything to drink, sir?

EVELYN: No, thanks.

BERRY: The master's sure to be in soon, sir.

EVELYN: All right, thanks.

BERRY: He's only taking a walk in the Park.

EVELYN: I think I will have a drink, after all.

BERRY: Very good, sir. Whisky and soda?

EVELYN: Yes, please.

BERRY *goes out.* EVELYN *proceeds to pace up and down the room a little.* BERRY *returns with a whisky and soda.*

EVELYN: Oh, thanks. [*He takes it.*]

BERRY: Would you like the papers, sir, or have you seen them already?

EVELYN: I've seen them, thanks.

BERRY: Shall I tell Mrs. Churt that you are here, sir?

EVELYN: No—no. Please don't disturb her.

BERRY: Very good, sir. [*He goes out again.*]

EVELYN *once more proceeds to pace up and down with the whisky and soda in his hand. He is obviously extremely agitated. After a moment* CAROL *enters from R. She looks fresh and charming. She gives a slight start on seeing* EVELYN.

CAROL: Evie!

EVELYN [*jumping—he turns*]: I've come to see Edward.

CAROL: What's the matter?

EVELYN: I've come to see Edward.

CAROL [*with faint apprehension*]: I know—you just said so. Aren't you going to say good morning?

EVELYN: Good morning.

CAROL [*going over to him*]: No more than that?

EVELYN: No—no more. [*He turns away.*]

CAROL [*biting her lip*]: I see.

EVELYN: I want to see him alone.

CAROL [*putting her hand on his arm*]: Evie, what's wrong?

EVELYN: You can seriously ask me that?

CAROL: Why are you behaving like this?

EVELYN [*turning away*]: You're hopeless.

CAROL: You're not going to do anything foolish, are you?

EVELYN: I'm going to do the only thing possible.

CAROL [*swinging him round*]: Evie!

EVELYN: Leave me alone.

CAROL: But listen——

EVELYN [*wrenching himself free from her*]: Don't touch me, please.

CAROL [*pleading*]: Evie—please—why are you being so horrid?

EVELYN: I don't want to look at you—or see you again ever!

CAROL: Why—why—what have I done?

EVELYN [*sinking into a chair with his face in his hands*]: Leave me alone. Leave me alone.

CAROL: You don't love me at all, then?

EVELYN: For God's sake stop!

CAROL: You don't—you don't——

EVELYN: Shut up! Shut up!

CAROL: You coward! [*She goes over to the window.*]

EVELYN: Please go away. You'll only make everything much worse.

CAROL: Why have you come here this morning?

[627]

EVELYN: To tell Edward about last night.

CAROL: What will you tell him?

EVELYN: The truth.

CAROL: You're insane.

EVELYN: I was—but I'm not any more.

CAROL [*coming quickly back to him*]: You can't mean this.

EVELYN: I do mean it.

CAROL: But why! Why!! Why!!!

EVELYN: I don't expect you to understand.

CAROL: Evie, listen. Be sensible for a moment.

EVELYN: It's no use going on like that. I've made up my mind.

CAROL: Evie——

EVELYN [*rising*]: Go away! Go away!

CAROL [*following him*]: I love you.

EVELYN: Be quiet.

CAROL: I love you—I love you. Tell what you like—shout it from the housetops. I love you!

EVELYN [*catching hold of her*]: Shut up—you must. Some one will hear.

CAROL: I don't care.

EVELYN: You don't love me—you never did for a moment—it was all a trick.

CAROL [*outraged*]: Evie!

EVELYN: I can see it all now—I can see it all.

CAROL: You're talking nonsense.

EVELYN: For God's sake go away from me.

CAROL [*helplessly*]: I don't know what to do.

EVELYN: Leave me alone. I've got to tell Edward the truth.

CAROL: In Heaven's name, why?

EVELYN: Can't you see why?

CAROL: No. What good will it do?

EVELYN: I've betrayed him.

CAROL: That's no reason for you to betray me as well.

EVELYN: He trusted me—completely.

CAROL: Well, why not let him go on trusting you?

[628]

EVELYN: Because I'm unworthy of it forever.

CAROL: And what about me?

EVELYN: It was your fault.

CAROL: How chivalrous.

EVELYN: You lied to me.

CAROL [*firmly*]: I did *not* lie to you.

EVELYN: You said you came last night because you loved me.

CAROL: So I did!

EVELYN: You came out of curiosity and stayed out of revenge.

CAROL: What a fool you are!

EVELYN: You determined to get even with me.

CAROL: Evie!

EVELYN: It's true—it's true—you know it is.

CAROL: Why have you built up this ridiculous story in your mind?

EVELYN: It's true.

CAROL [*with great firmness*]: It's nothing of the sort, and if you calm yourself and think seriously for a moment, you'll realize the complete absurdity of it. You must be sensible. Do you hear—you *must* be sensible. You're on the verge of wrecking everything out of sheer hysteria.

EVELYN: Everything is wrecked already. I've got nothing left —no honor, no decency——

CAROL [*quietly*]: I gave myself to you last night, Evie——

EVELYN: Don't—don't——

CAROL: I gave myself to you completely and for one reason only —I loved you. I love you now.

EVELYN: Carol, please——

CAROL: If you tell Edward—I shall go away and never see either of you again.

EVELYN: I can't help it. I——

CAROL: You *can* help it. What you're contemplating is utterly without reason. If you're trying to vindicate your honor, you can't seriously achieve it by betraying mine. We've both behaved abominably, I admit. We've both been weak and uncontrolled and given way completely and we shall suffer for it accordingly, you needn't doubt that for a minute. We're in a terrible mess, but we're in it together and together we must remain——

EVELYN: I shall never be able to look Edward in the face again.

CAROL: Will you be able to face him any better after you've told him?

EVELYN: Yes.

CAROL: Why?

EVELYN: Because I shall have done the only decent thing left to me.

CAROL: You'll only succeed in making him suffer as well as yourself and me. Can't you see the uselessness of it?

EVELYN: I can't see him and talk to him with this shame between us.

CAROL: You must—so must I. It's the just penalty for what we've done. You said just now you never wanted to see me again. Well, I promise you you never shall—alone. You at least can go away. I can't—I've got to stay and get through the next few months as best I can——

There comes a ring at the front-door bell.

EVELYN [*pacing the room*]: O God! what am I to do?

CAROL [*quickly*]: Nothing—nothing yet, anyhow. Think sensibly and quietly—everything depends on your keeping calm——

BERRY *enters and crosses over L. and exits.*

EVELYN: Is that Edward?

CAROL: Yes, I expect so. He's always forgetting his key.

EVELYN [*terribly undecided*]: Carol, I——

CAROL: Promise you'll do nothing yet.

EVELYN: I can't—I——

CAROL [*whispering violently*]: Promise me—wait a little—promise me. Will you promise me?

EVELYN [*helplessly*]: Yes.

BERRY *re-enters.*

BERRY [*announcing*]: Mrs. St. Merryn.

[*630*]

ZOE *enters briskly.*

ZOE: Good morning, Carol. I haven't seen you for months. How are you?

CAROL [*as they kiss*]: Splendid. I heard you were back.

ZOE: Hallo, Evie!

EVELYN [*coldly*]: Good morning.

ZOE: I gather that Edward is expected?

CAROL: Yes, he'll be back at any minute.

EVELYN: Good-by. [*He goes out abruptly.*]

ZOE [*surprised*]: That was one of the most sudden exits I've ever seen.

CAROL [*carelessly*]: I think Evie's upset about something.

ZOE: I didn't think he was capable of it.

CAROL [*conventionally*]: Are you glad to be back?

ZOE: Delighted. London's looking so pretty with all the roads up.

CAROL [*absently*]: Are they? I hadn't noticed.

ZOE: I don't see how you could fail to unless you travel exclusively in the underground.

CAROL: Where are you staying?

ZOE: Claridge's.

CAROL: Oh!

ZOE: It's so beautifully austere.

CAROL: What?

ZOE [*patiently*]: I said it was so beautifully austere.

CAROL: Oh yes, it is.

ZOE: You're looking awfully well.

CAROL: I am, frightfully well.

ZOE: Don't you think I'm looking frightfully well?

CAROL: Yes, you certainly are. Traveling obviously agrees with you.

ZOE: It's so comforting to know that we both look so awfully well. Can I have a cigarette?

CAROL: Yes, of course. I'm so sorry. Here—— [*She hands her a box open.*]

zoe: Thank you, dear. There aren't any in this box, but it doesn't matter.

carol: How annoying! Wait a minute. [*She takes another box off a table, left.*] Here——

zoe [*taking one*]: You seem a little distrait this morning, if I may say so.

carol: I've got rather a headache.

zoe: I'm so sorry. You don't look very well.

carol: I think, if you'll forgive me, I'll go and take some aspirin.

zoe: Of course. I should lie down until lunch if I were you.

carol: Perhaps I will. Edward's certain to be in soon.

zoe: I'll be perfectly happy waiting.

carol: You must come and dine one night.

zoe: I'd adore to.

carol: Good-by for the present, dear. [*She kisses her.*]

zoe: Good-by. I'm sorry you're so seedy. I'm afraid you've been overdoing it lately.

carol [*irritatedly*]: Overdoing what?

zoe [*vaguely*]: Oh, everything.

carol: No, I haven't.

zoe: I'm so glad.

carol *goes out.* zoe *wanders round the room, smiling to herself, examining various portraits, etc. After a moment* edward *enters.*

edward: Zoe! How long have you been here?

zoe: Only a few minutes.

edward: I've been out in the Park.

zoe: I didn't know it was still there.

edward: I'm afraid you're finding the old town sadly changed.

zoe: I'm sure it's much more hygienic now.

edward: Have you seen Carol?

zoe: Yes. She's just gone to bed.

edward: Gone to bed?

zoe: She said she had a headache.

EDWARD: How do you think she's looking?

ZOE [laughing]: Awfully well.

EDWARD: What are you laughing at?

ZOE: Carol always makes me laugh.

EDWARD: Why?

ZOE: She's so consistent.

EDWARD: Are you lunching with me?

ZOE: If you like. I've got to go to Sloane Street first and look at Mary Phillip's house. She wants to let it to me.

EDWARD: Pick me up here on the way back.

ZOE: I really came to ask you to dine to-night and go to a play.

EDWARD: I'd love to. What do you want to see?

ZOE: A nice clean play, please, Edward.

EDWARD: Splendid. We shan't have any trouble getting seats.

ZOE: I'm so old-fashioned—I like love stories without the slightest suggestion of sex.

EDWARD: You ought to be a critic.

ZOE: You're an awfully nice person to come back to!

EDWARD [smiling]: Am I?

ZOE: Yes. One picks up the threads exactly where they were dropped.

EDWARD: They were never dropped.

ZOE: Carol's an awful fool.

EDWARD: Why?

ZOE: She could hold you if she wanted to.

EDWARD: Don't be tiresome, Zoe.

ZOE: What are you going to do about it?

EDWARD: About what?

ZOE: Do you really want me to be explicit?

EDWARD: No. I know perfectly well what you mean.

ZOE: You're wasting time.

EDWARD: Not at all. I'm working hard.

ZOE: You said that yesterday and it was no more convincing then than it is now.

EDWARD: It's true.

[633]

ZOE: Perhaps, but rather beside the point.

EDWARD: What is the point?

ZOE: Your happiness.

EDWARD: What beautiful thoughts you have, Zoe.

ZOE: Don't be flippant.

EDWARD: Flippancy alleviates my boredom with the whole subject.

ZOE: Are you sure you're not confusing boredom with lack of moral courage?

EDWARD: Possibly.

ZOE: Well, don't.

EDWARD: I refuse to be dominated, Zoe—even by you!

ZOE [smiling]: That's right, dear.

EDWARD: And don't laugh at me.

ZOE: I always have. I fail to see why I should stop now.

EDWARD: I resent it bitterly.

ZOE: Dear Edward.

EDWARD: What do you expect me to do?

ZOE: Deliver an ultimatum.

EDWARD: That would be stepping out of my character.

ZOE: Nonsense!

EDWARD: I am essentially a weak-minded man.

ZOE: Nothing of the sort—you're a lazy idealist.

EDWARD: That sounds delightful.

ZOE: So it is in theory; in practice it's sterility personified.

EDWARD: You're terribly didactic.

ZOE: I'm trying to rouse you.

EDWARD: Why?

ZOE: Because you're discontented and unhappy.

EDWARD: I never said so.

ZOE: You don't need to—it's written all over you.

EDWARD: You think I'd be happier if I bashed about making scenes and delivering ultimatums?

ZOE: Certainly—you at least might achieve something.

[634]

EDWARD: What, for instance?

ZOE: Freedom!

EDWARD: That's a myth.

ZOE: Oh no, it isn't.

EDWARD: In this case it's impossible.

ZOE: Why?

EDWARD [*turning away*]: Oh, don't let's discuss it any more.

ZOE: You *are* annoying, Edward.

EDWARD: Evie went on like that for hours yesterday.

ZOE: Evie?

EDWARD: Yes. He seemed to advocate violence as being the best method.

ZOE: He would.

EDWARD: He even offered to teach Carol a lesson.

ZOE: What sort of lesson?

EDWARD: He didn't explain.

ZOE: Poor Evie.

EDWARD: You needn't despise him so utterly. He's a good sort.

ZOE: He's the quintessence of masculine complacency.

EDWARD: I'm sure it's a great comfort to him. I wish I was.

ZOE: Evie will get into trouble one of these days. He's too worldly.

EDWARD: If I were free, Zoe, would you marry me?

ZOE: Edward!

EDWARD: I suddenly thought of it.

ZOE [*laughing*]: This is terribly sudden.

EDWARD: Don't be silly.

ZOE: You must give me time to think.

EDWARD: Do shut up and be serious.

ZOE: I have a vague feeling that your proposal is a little previous.

EDWARD: It wasn't a proposal—just an idea.

ZOE: Not exactly an original one. We discussed it all ages ago.

EDWARD: And whose fault was it that it never came off?

ZOE [*promptly*]: Yours.

EDWARD: Zoe, how can you? It was entirely yours.

ZOE: Nonsense! I was dead set on it.

EDWARD: You refused me and rushed off to Africa.

ZOE: You can't call Algiers Africa.

EDWARD: It is, all the same.

ZOE: If you'd loved me enough, you'd have followed me.

EDWARD: I was waiting for you to come back.

ZOE: Let's stop talking about it—it's rather painful.

EDWARD: We weren't in love, really, anyhow.

ZOE: Weren't we?

EDWARD: I don't know.

ZOE: It's all very difficult.

EDWARD: Yes.

ZOE: I think I shall go away again soon.

EDWARD: Oh, Zoe, please don't!

ZOE: It's going to be awkward if I stay.

EDWARD: No, it isn't.

ZOE: We're both on rather dangerous ground.

EDWARD: I don't see why.

ZOE: Yes, you do, perfectly.

EDWARD: I do not.

ZOE: If I stay, we shall probably fall in love properly—we're both at a perilous age.

EDWARD: What if we do?

ZOE: It would be too horrible, with all this Carol business going on and everything.

EDWARD: You're crossing your bridges before you come to them.

ZOE: I shall go, all the same.

EDWARD: That is rank cowardice.

ZOE: No, it isn't; it's sound sense.

EDWARD: It will be beastly for me.

ZOE: Not so beastly as if I stayed, really—in the long run.

EDWARD: What could happen?

[*636*]

ZOE: Oh, the usual thing, I suppose—we should have an affair and spoil everything.

EDWARD: I don't see why.

ZOE: You're being very obstinate this morning.

EDWARD: If I were in love with you at all, it would be in a very nice, restrained way.

ZOE: We should both tire of that very quickly.

EDWARD: Zoe, how can you be so unpleasant?

ZOE: I'm only facing facts.

EDWARD: We've been together a good deal in the past.

ZOE: I know.

EDWARD: And everything was above reproach.

ZOE: Entirely.

EDWARD: Well, why can't we go on like that?

ZOE: Because even if we do, people will say we don't.

EDWARD: What does that matter?

ZOE: It matters a lot. I've had enough squalor in the past few years to last me for life.

EDWARD: Yes, but I don't see——

ZOE: Also I have a strange aversion to coming between man and wife.

EDWARD: Oh, shut up, Zoe.

ZOE: It's true. I suffer from a pre-war conscience.

EDWARD: There's no question of that, really.

ZOE: Don't be silly. Of course there is.

EDWARD: Carol wouldn't care.

ZOE: What difference does that make? Really, Edward, you're being horribly flaccid over the whole thing!

EDWARD: Don't let's argue about it.

ZOE: All right.

EDWARD: But please don't go away again—just yet.

ZOE: I'll think it over, Edward.

EDWARD: You've depressed me terribly.

ZOE: I'm sorry.

EDWARD: It's all such a hopeless muddle.

zoe: It needn't be.

edward: I'd no idea you were so designing.

zoe: What a horrid thing to say!

edward: It's true though, isn't it?

zoe: Absolutely.

edward: Oh, Zoe——

zoe: I must go.

edward: Remember lunch.

zoe: I'll pick you up here.

edward: No, don't—I'll meet you.

zoe: Where?

edward: Berkeley—one o'clock.

zoe: I'm sure to be late.

edward: So am I.

zoe: Good-by, dear. [*She goes up to him and kisses him lightly.*]

edward: Zoe!

zoe: That was part of the design! [*She goes out.*]

edward *walks up and down irritably for a moment, then lights a cigarette and flings himself into an armchair. The telephone rings. He gives an exclamation of annoyance and rises to answer it.*

edward [*at telephone*]: Hallo! . . . Yes—yes . . . Who is it speaking? . . . No, I'm afraid you can't. She isn't very well——

carol *enters in time to catch the last sentence.*

carol: Who is it?

edward: Oh. . . . Hold on, please. . . . Harry Challoner. [*He hands her the telephone curtly and goes over to the window.*]

carol [*at telephone*]: Hallo! . . . Yes, it's me. . . . No—no, I can't. I'm sorry. . . . All right, if you like. . . . I'll be in between six and seven. . . . Yes. . . . Good-by. [*She hangs up the receiver and looks toward* edward *who has his back turned. She is about to go out again, when he turns.*]

edward: Carol.

CAROL: Yes?

EDWARD: I want to talk to you.

CAROL: Is anything the matter?

EDWARD: Yes. Sit down, will you?

CAROL [*sitting*]: If you like.

EDWARD: I want to get things settled.

CAROL: Get things settled?

EDWARD: Yes.

CAROL: What sort of things?

EDWARD: Our exact relationship.

CAROL: What *do* you mean?

EDWARD: Just that.

CAROL: I don't understand.

EDWARD: I think you do.

CAROL [*by now extremely apprehensive*]: I don't, Edward, honestly.

EDWARD: Do you intend to pursue your present course indefinitely?

CAROL: What are you talking about?

EDWARD: Infidelity.

CAROL: Are you insinuating that I——

EDWARD: I'm insinuating nothing. I'm stating that you have been unfaithful to me.

CAROL [*rising*]: Edward!

EDWARD [*firmly*]: Sit down. This is not a scene—it's a process of readjustment. Please let us keep it as brief as possible.

CAROL [*sinking down*]: How can you be so horrible!

EDWARD: Do you deny it?

CAROL: Of course I do.

EDWARD: Carol, let me disillusion you. I'm not bluffing. I *know*. I've known for ages. It's no use wasting time denying and arguing. We must decide what's to be done about it.

CAROL: How can you be so foul!

EDWARD [*wearily*]: Oh, Carol, do stop acting.

CAROL: You're insufferable.

EDWARD: Once and for all will you be sensible?

CAROL: I hate you.

EDWARD: That would be beautifully definite if you weren't so unreliable.

CAROL: Do you want me to hate you?

EDWARD: To be honest with you, I really don't mind.

CAROL [outraged]: Edward!

EDWARD: Don't be a fool, Carol.

CAROL: How dare you! How dare you!

EDWARD: We will face facts, please.

CAROL [rising]: I'm not going to stay here and be insulted.

EDWARD: You're not being insulted—it's I who have been insulted. You've been publicly underrating my intelligence for months.

CAROL: That's what's upsetting you, isn't it?

EDWARD: Certainly it is. I wish you'd sit down.

CAROL: I'm going to my room.

EDWARD: You're only temporarily evading the issues by doing that.

CAROL: What's the object of all this?

EDWARD: The object, as I said before, is to get our relationship satisfactorily defined.

CAROL [with grandeur]: It's satisfactorily defined now as far as I'm concerned.

EDWARD: I would prefer the satisfaction to be mutual.

CAROL: You think you're very clever, don't you?

EDWARD: What a common remark! You'll be sticking your tongue out at me in a minute.

CAROL: I suppose Zoe has been putting you up to this.

EDWARD: Meaning that I have no initiative of my own anyhow?

CAROL: Exactly.

EDWARD: That's charming of you—and fits in beautifully with your behavior during the last year.

CAROL: Are you in love with me still?

EDWARD: Do you expect me to be?

CAROL: Are you?

EDWARD: No, Carol.

CAROL: I see.

EDWARD: All of which is beside the point.

CAROL: No, it isn't. If you loved me you'd never say such things to me.

EDWARD: I admit that it would be more comfortable for you if I just suffered and suffered in silence.

CAROL: You're too unemotional to be capable of any suffering.

EDWARD: Do you imagine you're putting up a good defense for yourself?

CAROL: I'm not attempting to.

EDWARD: That brings us to my ultimatum.

CAROL [*with a forced laugh*]: Ultimatum! Really, Edward!

EDWARD: You've been unfaithful to me three times during the past year—Maurice Verney, Geoffrey Poole, and now Harry Challoner!

CAROL [*blanching slightly*]: Edward!

EDWARD: All three married men, which adds considerably to the general sordidness of the whole business.

CAROL [*losing control*]: I will *not* be spoken to like this!

EDWARD [*with sudden force*]: Be quiet! Do you still deny it?

CAROL [*more dimly*]: No.

EDWARD: That's better.

CAROL [*sullenly*]: I'm sorry.

EDWARD: That's too sudden to be convincing.

CAROL [*breaking up slightly; after a long pause*]: What are you going to do?

EDWARD: Wait until next time.

CAROL: Next time?

EDWARD: Yes.

CAROL: And what then?

EDWARD: I shall divorce you.

CAROL: Edward!

[*641*]

EDWARD: I mean it. Whether the man happens to be married or single will not make the slightest difference.

CAROL [*looking down*]: I see.

EDWARD: Is that quite clear?

CAROL: Quite.

EDWARD: Incidentally, I wish you to give up Harry Challoner entirely. I object to you even being seen with such a second-rate bounder.

CAROL [*looking at him*]: Very well.

EDWARD: We'll both do our best to forget the whole thing. We can get along perfectly well together with a little effort.

CAROL: There's no more, is there?

EDWARD: No, that's all.

CAROL *goes slowly toward the door in silence. Her expression is very thoughtful. When she reaches the door she turns.*

CAROL [*in a different voice*]: Edward.

EDWARD: Yes?

CAROL: Please forgive me.

EDWARD: Forgiveness in this case is surely rather unimportant.

CAROL: Oh, please, please—— [*She bursts into tears and goes toward him.*]

EDWARD: Now then, Carol——

CAROL [*standing in front of him weeping*]: You must forgive me—you must!

EDWARD: All right.

CAROL: I didn't love any of them—I swear I didn't.

EDWARD [*turning away irritably*]: Oh, Carol——

CAROL: You've been utterly indifferent to me for ages.

EDWARD: Naturally.

CAROL: No, but before—I mean before—last year you stopped loving me.

EDWARD: Please don't go on like this.

CAROL: It's true—it's true. I was lonely.

EDWARD: Don't talk such utter nonsense.

CAROL [*working herself up*]: It isn't nonsense—it's you I love

[642]

really all the time. I hate Harry Challoner, really. I've been trying to break with him for ages. I made a vow weeks ago that I'd never be unfaithful to you again—honestly I did, I swear it. I'm sick of everybody. I wanted to ask you to take me away abroad somewhere, but I didn't dare—you had so much work to do—and you were so cold and horrid. Edward—Edward—you've got to love me again—you must. I shall go mad if you don't. Please—Edward darling. [*She flings herself into his arms.*]

EDWARD [*gently disentangling himself*]: There now—it's all right. Do stop. [*He kisses her dutifully.*]

CAROL: I feel so bitterly ashamed.

EDWARD: Stop crying.

CAROL: I swear I'll be good. I swear I will.

EDWARD: That's right. Now control yourself.

CAROL: I'll never see Harry again.

EDWARD: Very well. For Heaven's sake stop crying.

CAROL: I do love you really, you know. That's what makes it so awful.

EDWARD: Pull yourself together.

CAROL [*dabbing her eyes*]: I'll try.

EDWARD: Go and lie down and take something.

CAROL: What shall I take?

EDWARD: Aspirin, I should think.

CAROL: I had some just now.

EDWARD: Have some more.

CAROL: All right. Oh, God! [*She goes out slowly, still half sobbing.*]

EDWARD *heaves a sigh of mingled relief and irritation, he again flings himself into an armchair. Then comes the sound of the front-door bell. He groans.* BERRY *enters from R.*

EDWARD: Whoever it is, Berry, I'm out.

BERRY: Very good, sir. [*He goes out L. After a moment he re-enters.*] I'm very sorry, sir; it's Major Bathurst. The porter downstairs told him you'd just come in; he's called already this morning.

EDWARD: Nobody told me. You'd better show him in.

BERRY: Yes, sir. [*He goes out and returns, announcing*] Major Bathurst.

EVELYN *comes in. He looks more harassed than ever.* BERRY *goes out.*

EDWARD: Hallo, Evie!

EVELYN [*haltingly*]: Edward—I—I've come to say good-by.

EDWARD [*surprised*]: Good-by!

EVELYN: Yes. I came earlier this morning, but you were out.

EDWARD: But where on earth are you going?

EVELYN: Australia.

EDWARD: Why Australia?

EVELYN [*weakly*]: I've always wanted to go to Australia.

EDWARD: What *do* you mean?

EVELYN: I mean I've got to go there on business.

EDWARD: It's very sudden, isn't it?

EVELYN: Yes. I had a wire from my brother.

EDWARD: I didn't know he was in Australia.

EVELYN: He isn't. He's in Cheltenham, but he sent me a wire saying I ought to go out there at once.

EDWARD: What's the matter with you, Evie?

EVELYN: Nothing.

EDWARD: You're not only telling me extremely fatuous lies, but you look like death.

EVELYN: They're not lies. I——

EDWARD: Don't be an ass. Have a drink.

EVELYN: No—I don't want a drink.

EDWARD: What's wrong?

EVELYN: There's nothing wrong.

EDWARD: You'd better tell me, you know.

EVELYN: I want to tell you.

EDWARD: Come on, then.

EVELYN: I've got to tell you.

EDWARD: Out with it.

EVELYN: But I can't.

[*644*]

EDWARD: Surely that's rather silly.

EVELYN: I tried to shoot myself this morning.

EDWARD: You what!!!

EVELYN: Tried to shoot myself.

EDWARD [*alarmed*]: In God's name, why?

EVELYN [*brokenly*]: Oh, Edward!

EDWARD: Evie, what *has* happened?

EVELYN: I'm the filthiest cad in the world.

EDWARD: Don't be ridiculous.

EVELYN: Our friendship is over forever.

EDWARD [*with irritation*]: Do stop all this melodrama, Evie, and tell me what's the matter.

EVELYN: I've betrayed you, utterly.

EDWARD [*in great astonishment*]: Betrayed *me?*

EVELYN [*looking down*]: Yes.

EDWARD: How?

EVELYN [*brokenly*]: Carol!

EDWARD: Carol! Well, what about her?

EVELYN: Carol dined with me last night.

EDWARD: Oh, did she?

EVELYN: And—and—O my God! [*He sinks into a chair by the table and leans his head on his arms.*]

EDWARD [*in amazement*]: You don't seriously mean to tell me——

EVELYN [*in muffled tones*]: Yes.

EDWARD: You and Carol!

EVELYN: Yes.

EDWARD: This is too much! [*He bursts out laughing.*]

EVELYN [*looking up astounded*]: Edward!

EDWARD: I can't bear it. [*He laughs louder.*]

EVELYN [*rising*]: Edward—old man—please——

EDWARD [*helplessly*]: It's unbelievable—incredible. Oh dear! [*He collapses on the window seat.*]

EVELYN [*approaching him*]: Edward—for God's sake——

EDWARD [*weakly*]: Don't come near me. I shall be all right in a minute.

EVELYN [*with growing anger*]: You must be mad.

EDWARD: I certainly feel very strange. [*He goes into fits of laughter again.*]

EVELYN [*outraged*]: Edward—do you realize what I've just told you?

EDWARD [*trying to control himself*]: Yes—perfectly.

EVELYN: And you can laugh!

EDWARD: Will you hand me a cigarette, please?

EVELYN [*irately*]: Look here, Edward——

EDWARD [*with sudden firmness*]: Will you hand me a cigarette, please.

EVELYN: Here. [*He offers him his case.*]

EDWARD: Thanks. [*He takes one.*] Light.

EVELYN: Here. [*He strikes a match.*]

EDWARD: Thanks. I feel better now.

EVELYN: Well! What are you going to do about it?

EDWARD: Ring that bell, will you? By the door.

EVELYN: I can find my own way out.

EDWARD [*firmly*]: You're not going yet. Ring the bell, please.

EVELYN *looks at him and then goes and rings the bell.*

EVELYN: Look here, Edward, I came here this morning because I felt I owed it to our friendship to confess the truth to you——

EDWARD: You're out of your depth, Evie—far, far out of your depth.

EVELYN: I don't know what you mean.

EDWARD: This is reality, not fiction.

BERRY *enters.*

BERRY: You rang, sir?

EDWARD: Will you ask your mistress to come down immediately, please, Berry? It's very important.

BERRY: Yes, sir. [*He goes out.*]

EVELYN [*panic-stricken*]: Edward, this is not fair of you.

EDWARD [*unceremoniously*]: Shut up.

[646]

EVELYN: This is between us.

EDWARD: The three of us, Evie—what's known, I believe, as the eternal triangle.

EVELYN: Let me tell you one thing—what happened was not deliberate.

EDWARD: You prefer to be thought a fool rather than a cad!

EVELYN: Yes, if you like to put it that way.

EDWARD: How typical!

EVELYN: I only asked Carol to dine, in the first place, for your sake.

EDWARD: For my sake?

EVELYN: Yes, I intended to teach her a lesson.

EDWARD: And she ended up by teaching you one.

EVELYN [*utterly shocked*]: Edward!

EDWARD: Men of your sort should stick to athletics and not attempt physiology.

EVELYN: I deserve that.

EDWARD [*agreeably*]: Fully.

CAROL *enters from R. She starts visibly on seeing* EVELYN.

CAROL: What's the matter?

EDWARD: Don't look so surprised, Carol. It's terribly irritating.

CAROL: I don't understand.

EDWARD: I gather that you and Evie——

EVELYN [*wounded by such frankness*]: Edward!

CAROL [*looking at* EVELYN]: You cad!

EDWARD: It was very unpleasant of you, Carol——

CAROL [*appealingly*]: Edward, please——

EDWARD: I should like to know how it all happened.

EVELYN: I told you—I——

EDWARD: Carol, will you explain, please?

CAROL: Certainly not.

EDWARD: Very well. You must allow me to reconstruct it for myself.

EVELYN: Surely this is unnecessary.

EDWARD: That is entirely for me to decide.

CAROL: You're being unbelievably cheap.

EDWARD [*mildly*]: Really, Carol—keep a slight grip on your values.

EVELYN: Say what you like. I don't care.

EDWARD: It wouldn't make the slightest difference if you did.

EVELYN: Damned ungenerous.

EDWARD: Shut up and don't be an ass. You and Carol have brought about this abominable situation. It's up to you to keep quiet and let me straighten it out in my own way.

EVELYN [*turning away*]: Very well.

EDWARD: Thank you. Now then—Evie, you asked Carol to dine with you alone at your flat?

EVELYN: Yes.

EDWARD: Why?

EVELYN: I told you.

EDWARD: In order to teach her a lesson.

CAROL: Oh, this is insufferable.

EDWARD: You're perfectly right, it is. I gather that the first part of the lesson, Evie, necessitated you making love to her. Am I right?

EVELYN [*impatiently*]: Oh yes——

EDWARD: And then what? [*Turning*]

EVELYN: Look here, Edward, I'm damned if I'm going to listen to this any longer——

CAROL: Neither am I!

EDWARD: Tell me the truth, then, Carol. It will simplify matters considerably. Do you love Evie?

CAROL: No.

EDWARD: Then why, if it's not an indelicate question, did you——

CAROL [*violently*]: Because he insulted me and tried to humiliate me and I determined to show him that he wasn't as clever as he thought he was.

EDWARD: Admirable. You, Evie, had the ineffable conceit to pit your meager experience of the world against an extremely attractive and obviously unscrupulous woman. You then give in to her completely despite the fact that she is the wife of your friend; and not content with that, you turn on her afterward, work yourself up into a frenzy of false melodramatic values, rush round here and blurt it out to me doubtless under the delusion that by uncovering the whole shameful business you are vindicating your own honor! Oh, Evie, what a pitiful fool you are!

EVELYN: It's no use blackguarding me any more, is it? What are you going to do about it?

EDWARD: I don't quite know yet.

CAROL: There's nothing to be done.

EDWARD: You're too sure of yourself, Carol—you always have been.

EVELYN: I wish to God I had shot myself.

EDWARD: It's a little late to think of that now.

EVELYN: You're being unnecessarily cruel, Edward.

EDWARD: I'm afraid I'm a bitter disappointment to you both. You see emotionally I'm unmoved. The capacity for feeling very deeply over Carol died a long while ago.

EVELYN: I should have thought that for the sake of our friendship——

EDWARD: That's sheer cant. You've considerably over-estimated our friendship for years. If you care to analyze it honestly you'll discover that we both bore one another stiff and always have. We were at school together—in different forms—since when we've dined together on an average of once a month. We've confided our troubles superficially for the want of something to talk about. We're poles apart mentally and physically; we've built up this so-called great friendship on a basis of false tradition, and the only reason I realized it first is because my brain functions quicker than yours——

EVELYN [*shattered*]: Edward!

EDWARD: And I should like to add—having naturally a more acute sense of sex psychology than you—that the reason you

[*649*]

took such a fatal interest in Carol's morals was not on my account at all, but because she'd snubbed you severely several times and you were probably very much attracted to her.

EVELYN: It's not true. You're disgusting.

EDWARD: Be that as it may, the solution to the whole thing is obvious.

EVELYN: What do you mean?

EDWARD: I'll tell you. Carol, you must go away immediately.

CAROL [*horrified*]: Edward——

EVELYN [*stricken*]: But—I—I——

EDWARD: Wait a moment. Let me explain. Carol, you and I have no longer the slightest justification for living together. If you go away abroad somewhere I will make it perfectly easy for you to divorce me. If you don't agree to this, I shall file a petition against you at once, naming Evie as corespondent. That's the second ultimatum I've delivered this morning and I'm feeling extremely tired. [*He sits down.*]

CAROL: Edward, you can't mean this—you can't.

EDWARD: I do. I mean it more than I've ever meant anything in my life.

CAROL [*bursting into tears of rage*]: I won't stand it. I won't!

EDWARD: You're not being very polite to Evie.

EVELYN: You think you're being damned clever.

EDWARD: That's been hurled at me so often just lately that I'm honestly beginning to believe I am.

CAROL: You utter beast.

EDWARD: Well—what's the decision?

CAROL [*wailing*]: I'll never speak to you again—never—never —never.

EDWARD [*rising*]: Evie?

EVELYN [*gruffly*]: You'd better give us time to think.

EDWARD: What is the time now, anyhow?

EVELYN [*looking at his watch*]: Twenty past one.

EDWARD: My God! I knew I should be late. I'll be at the Berkeley if you want me. [EDWARD *goes out.*]

EVELYN *and* CAROL *look after him and then at each other.*
CAROL *after a pause walks over and sits next to* EVIE.
CAROL: Evie.
EVIE: What?
CAROL [*sweetly*]: There's still time for you to shoot yourself!

CURTAIN